Interdisciplinary perspectives on modern history

Editors
Robert Fogel and Stephan Thernstrom

For bread with butter:
The life-worlds of East Central Europeans
in Johnstown, Pennsylvania, 1890–1940

For bread with butter

The life-worlds of East Central
Europeans in Johnstown,
Pennsylvania, 1890–1940

EWA MORAWSKA

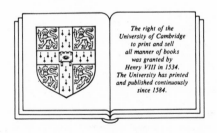

The right of the
University of Cambridge
to print and sell
all manner of books
was granted by
Henry VIII in 1534.
The University has printed
and published continuously
since 1584.

CAMBRIDGE UNIVERSITY PRESS

Cambridge
London   New York   New Rochelle
Melbourne   Sydney

Published by the Press Syndicate of the University of Cambridge
The Pitt Building, Trumpington Street, Cambridge CB2 1RP
32 East 57th Street, New York, NY 10022, USA
10 Stamford Road, Oakleigh, Melbourne 3166, Australia

First published 1985

Printed in the United States of America

Library of Congress Cataloging in Publication Data
Morawska, Ewa T.
For bread with butter.
(Interdisciplinary perspectives on modern history)
Bibliography: p.
Includes index.
1. East European Americans – Pennsylvania – Johnstown
– History.   2. Johnstown (Pa.) – History.   I. Title.
II. Series.
F159.J7M83   1985   974.8'77   85-12781
ISBN 0 521 30633 7

British Library Cataloging-in-Publication applied for.

For Dee and Joe
with great fondness
and gratitude

Contents

Illustrations

ix

Tables

Acknowledgments

This book would not have been written if it were not for the people in Johnstown, Pennsylvania, who took me into their homes, listened to my endless questions, answered them and willingly agreed to repeated visits and repeated questioning, took me around to show me things and places, invited me to their churches and organizations, assisted in deciphering and identifying names, and helped me to make further contacts by "passing me along" through the community. I am indebted to too many individuals to thank each one separately. Let me express my gratitude by mentioning here those who were exceptionally generous with the time they contributed to my project. I am very grateful to the pastors of the East Central European churches in Johnstown: Rev. J. Benedek, Rev. S. Gergel, Rev. J. Golias, Rev. N. Grgurevich, Father Jerome, Rev. G. Johnson, Rev. J. Kraus, the late Rev. W. Kurdzel, Rev. T. Maher, Rev. C. Ossowski, Rev. J. Pier, Rev. W. Sabo, the late Rev. S. Slavik, the late Rev. A. Ulicky, Rev. G. Winning, Rev. G. Yatsko, and Rev. Dr. J. Yurcisin. I would also like to express my sincere gratitude to A. Adamchak, J. Bobovsky, F. Bochenski, J. Brezovec, Mrs. M. Buncic and her daughter Danica, A. Cyburt, his son Walter and daughter Casimira, Mrs. M. Dostal, R. Garbrenya, Mr. and Mrs. P. Holubz, the late Mrs. A. Hozek, M. Hricko, L. Jankowiak, P. Kaminski, Mr. and Mrs. J. Langerholc, Mrs. H. Legat, Mr. and Mrs. A. Mesaros, G. Minno, M. Moncilovich, C. Nagyvathy, E. Neral, the late M. Novak, and Mrs. A. Novak, Mr. and Mrs. M. Novak, J. Ozog, P. Payerchin, Mr. and Mrs. P. Pentz, S. Petruska, H. Sledzanowski, F. Sobditch, Mr. and Mrs. M. Tumbas, Mr. and Mrs. W. Wegrzyn, E. Yesh, and to all the officers of ethnic lodges, clubs, and associations who gave me information and made available their old organizational records.

I would also like to thank heartily the editor, Mr. Richard Mayer, and the whole staff of the *Johnstown Tribune* who graciously offered me a desk in their offices for the long months of my work with the city directories and newspaper microfilms located in the *Tribune's* library. My sincere gratitude is extended to the staff of Cambria County Courthouse in Ebensburg and of the City Hall in Johnstown where I spent many hours researching various records pertaining to the history of Johnstown's East Central Europeans, and to the staff of the Senior Citizens' Center in Johnstown where I conducted many of my interviews. I thank Mrs. M. Oyler from the Greater Johnstown School District, J. Moran and J. Katowchik from the Conemaugh Valley School District, and Rev. Father Bunn from the Johnstown Catholic High School for permission to inspect old school records. Mrs. S. Stevens at Meadowvale School Media Center and Sister Lucia at St. Stephen's Slovak Catholic School assisted me during my research on the educational achievement of East Central European children. J. Coleman and J. Penrod from Bethlehem Steel Company provided information about job structures in the mills, and P. Pebley and facilitated contacts with retired company officials. Michael Yates and Bruce Williams from the University of Pittsburgh at Johnstown deserve special thanks for letting me use their priceless tape collection of oral-history interviews with retired East Central European steelworkers and coal miners in the area.

I would also like to thank the librarians at the UMWA Health and Retirement Fund in Washington, D.C.; the UMWA Health and Retirement Fund in Richland, Pennsylvania; the Berwin-White Coal Company in Windber, Pennsylvania; the Pennsylvania Historical and Museum Commission in Harrisburg; the National Archives in Washington, D.C.; and the Dun & Bradstreet Archives in New York for their kind assistance at various stages of my research.

The following foundations provided generous support during my project: the American Council of Learned Societies, the National Endowment for the Humanities, the Andrew Mellon Foundation, and the Pennsylvania Ethnic Heritage Studies Center at the University of Pittsburgh. At the University of Pittsburgh, the University Center for International Studies and the Research and Development Fund subsidized the typing and retyping of my manuscript, which was done with skill and patience by Nancy Collins, Virginia Enscoe, and Janet Hill.

I would like to thank copyeditor Christie Lerch for her extraordinary patience and professionalism during the arduous editing process. My friends Michael Joyce and Thaddeus Radzialowski worked hard to bring my non-native English into shape and to anglicize my innate Polish baroque style.

I wish to thank Philip Sidel, who assisted in the statistical analysis of data with care and infinite patience, and also Patrick Doreian, Maciej Słomczyński, Paul Allison, Jerry Jacobs, and Philip Morgan for their helpful advice in statistical matters. Katherine Lynch helped with the limited demographic analysis that I conducted.

Several people offered most valuable comments and constructive criticism, both methodological and substantive, as I was writing and rewriting parts of the manuscript: Harold Bershady, Milton Cantor, Renée Fox, Michael Katz, Frank Lechner, John Modell, David Montgomery, Alejandro Portes, Peter Stearns, Stephan Thernstrom, and Charles Tilly. I am most grateful for their kind willingness to contribute their valuable time and perceptive ideas to my endeavor. I am especially indebted to Michael Weber and John Bodnar for providing much-needed help and advice during the long initial stage of my research.

Finally, multiple and very special thanks go to Dee and Joe Dalesandro of Johnstown, who let me become a member of their hospitable home and loving family during four long years I spent on this project. To them this book is dedicated with great fondness and gratitude.

Introduction

In 1905 a young Serb, Nikola B., came to Johnstown, Pennsylvania, in search of work and the money to permit him to better his lot in his home village. Fate and circumstance kept him in Johnstown for most of the next three-quarters of a century until his death a few years ago. His life was typical of the lives of many who came to this city, as he did, from East Central Europe.

He was born in 1889 in Cvijanović, Kordun, as the sixth child in his family. His father owned 5 hectares of land, two cows, three pigs, and two horses, which he took with him each year when he set off with his sons to work on farms in Hungary. In 1902, Nikola's uncle and his cousin departed for America with a group of other men from the village. From Johnstown, where they settled, they sent letters and photographs: "They looked well and I decided to go."

Nikola arrived in Johnstown in April 1905 and moved in with his relatives in a boardinghouse in Woodvale. "I was frightened of everything, different country and different people, and I never saw such big factories. My uncle told me everything, what to do, how to behave, what to say." His uncle and cousin took him to the coal mine at the outskirts of the city that supplied Cambria Company mills. "Soon this hard work began to weigh very heavy on my shoulders. I regretted my coming to America and more and more missed home. All day I sweated in exhausting labor, seeing no sun, only darkness, water up to my ankles, from morning till night."

After two and a half years, Nikola went back to his village. "But there was nothing there for me, same poverty, same hardship as when I left." In 1910, he returned to Johnstown, bringing his younger brother. They worked as "buddies" in the mine: If they stayed there eleven to twelve hours a day, they each made $11 a week. "It was terribly hard work, coal mine, back-breaking, dirty, awful. But I still preferred it here, thought it was better. I saw here some future, and at home there was none."

In 1913, the Cambria Company mines laid off many of their workers. Nikola and his friends set off in search of other em-

1

ployment. They went to Steubenville, Ohio, which had a Serbian colony whose people came from their own region in Kordun, but the two young men did not find anything there; then they moved back to Cambria County and tried several mines in the area. Each new place seemed worse than the preceding one. It was a bad period for Nikola: He had no money, was in debt, and was very depressed.

Then his luck changed. A friend, another Kordunac, got him a good *ples* (place) besides him as a second boiler cleaner in the rolling mill department at the Cambria Company steel mill. For a nine-hour shift, he received $1.90. "I paid my debts, bought things, I repaired myself and stood on my feet. Then, a bolt from the blue, the works stop. I went back to the mine. When the war came, it was good again . . . In 1918, I married a Serbian girl; met her at a dance at St. Nicholas, her father liked me, so we married. Bought her a nice dress in a store, 150 people came to the wedding party. We lived with her parents in Cambria City, paid them rent and shared food expenses. The first son came after a year . . . I worked with my father-in-law and other Serbs in the blast furnace department; we were a gang and moved around together. My father-in-law was in charge, and work was steady."

In 1926, Nikola bought a house on the hills, away from the mill. The house cost $4,000; some of it he had saved, some he borrowed from a next-door neighbor, the rest was to be paid in installments. It had a garden in back, where Mrs. B. grew vegetables and apple trees, and kept a few chickens and geese. "She made almost everything at home, canned tomatoes, and beets, mushrooms, and beans. She also sewed well and sold to the neighbors, $1.50 a dress." At that time, Nikola was on the board of St. Nicholas Church and a vice-president of the Svety Jovan lodge of the Serb National Federation: "People respected me and listened to my opinions."

In 1927, with his brother-in-law he opened a small grocery store in Cambria City. "It took us $1,500 to open, but we could not maintain the business, it was all credit [to people], no money, mostly paper. So I talked to this man, a Rusyn I knew, he worked in the mechanical department at Cambria, and he got me a job there, $34 a week and overtime. I also played at weddings, we had an orchestra and played during the weekends, you could make $3.00 a night. It was not bad then, we had electricity and water in the house, and plenty of food on the table, and we dressed nice, American. I bought a radio and new furniture for the bedroom."

The Depression hit Nikola's family pretty hard. "It was like the first years again. I worked two to three days in two weeks, but we were seven in the family now, it was very tough on all workers here." In 1934, unable to pay the debt on the house, Nikola had to sign it over to Mr. F., a local Slovenian merchant, "because we could not pay for food and groceries. To pay the water bill, I worked at the dam." Five years later, when work at Cambria was steadier, Nikola retrieved his house. His two oldest sons now worked with him in the mills, and there was more money.

"The union came in . . . it was a big thing for us, Roosevelt and all, the whole situation improved, but one always had to be prudent though, as you never knew what may come next . . . Here in America, when things were good, they were better than in the [old] country, but when they turned bad, maybe it was worse . . . It is just that over there they never seemed to get better."

Like Nikola B., thousands of East Central European immigrants and their children struggled in such circumstances in Johnstown to survive, and build a life of dignity and respect. Each life was different yet punctuated by similar twists and turns. This book will be their story.

Concepts and perspectives

This study is about the coping and adaptive strategies used by East Central European peasant-immigrants and their children to solve problems and realize cultural goals and expectations in a restricted and uncertain environment. The process of coping, of "appropriating" any space available under constrained circumstances, generates new purposes and new dilemmas. They are dealt with as people cooperate and invent ways to bring the environment into closer conformity with their purposes.

The number of sociohistorical studies devoted to East Central Europeans and their experience in America has been increasing in recent years.[1] Still, they remain one of the least studied populations among American immigrants. In particular, there is a need for more, and more detailed, accounts of how they perceived America and their position in it; what their expectations were; how they organized their everyday lives in meaningful patterns and strategies in pursuit of their goals; and what they did and did not achieve.

Weaving existing knowledge into my data-analytic framework and interpretations, I attempt to breathe more life into the dull, papier-mâché-like image of East Central Europeans that persists in American social history by showing their backgrounds, both in Europe and in America, as more diversified, their social environment as more complex and multifaceted, and their adaptive options as more underdetermined and open than has often been assumed in ethnic literature.

The structurally induced uncertainty of the existence of immigrant laborers and their families in industrial America in the first decades of this century, along with its implications for their behavior and attitudes, have been convincingly documented by social historians.[2] But the resulting "working-class realism" of the immigrant culture as depicted in these studies seems to me one-dimensional, flat, and tensionless, painted, as it were, with one thick monotonic line, not fully rendering the felt experience of the immigrants. This book brings out the diversity of East Central European life-styles and the tensions and ambiguities generated by coexisting yet often incompatible goals and preferences; the nuances of family economic strategies and the conflicts they engendered; and the internal status divisions and ambivalences involved in utilizing several frames of references and evaluations simultaneously.

This study covers half a century, beginning in East Central Europe at the time of mass peasant migrations and then following those who settled in Johnstown until the outbreak of World War II. In purpose and design it belongs to the genre of historical sociology.

A core element in the works of the sociological masters – Tocqueville, Comte, Spencer, Marx, Durkheim, and Weber – historical sociology has always been part of the "high" sociological tradition. It has been continued over the past half century by the French *Annales* school. In the United States, sociological studies in history have been pursued by individual scholars – sages such as Reinhard Bendix, S. N. Eisenstadt, or Barrington Moore, Jr. Widely known and respected, their studies, however, remained by and large outside of the mainstream of research of both sociology and history. As academic pursuits grew ever more professionalized and specialized in postwar years, these two disciplines likewise became compartmentalized and separate, their relationship commonly depicted in terms of the incompatibilities of "nomothetic" and "idiographic" sciences. Today, the increasing "blurring of genres," as Clifford Geertz put it, of humanistic reflection again has narrowed the gap between history and sociology. With a steadily expanding body of sociologically informed historical work and a growing concern among sociologists with the historical *durée*, historical sociology has been enjoying a renaissance. A series of recent works by Arthur

Stinchcombe, Charles Tilly, Philip Abrams, and Theda Skocpol investigating the relationship between sociology and history demonstrates the theoretical and methodological unity of these two modes of discourse.[3]

Two distinguishable, though in part overlapping approaches inform the work of the "historicals," as Norbert Wiley somewhat ungracefully has termed a growing number of the practitioners of sociological-historical research.[4] One is macrosociological in scope, focusing on large-scale societal formations and processes. It has produced a plethora of excellent studies of a wide variety of problems ranging from social stratification, class formation, and class struggle, the transition to industrialism, and the development of cities and states, to social revolution and the world economic system.[5]

The second perspective represented in historical sociology is more microscopic in emphasis and execution. It calls for the apprehension of the relationship between everyday human actions, on the one hand, and social organization on the other as a continuous development in which fragments of society are seen as historically constructed by people who are in turn constructed by society. In a coinage that seems to be gaining increasing popularity, Anthony Giddens termed this process *structuration* and presented a forceful theoretical appeal for its use in sociology. "Theoretical manifestos" from the affined disciplines, by Fernand Braudel, E. P. Thompson, James Henretta, Clifford Geertz, and Pierre Bourdieu, have advocated a similar approach.[6] It has also been brilliantly realized in sociological-historical practice.[7]

This study falls within the second category of sociological-historical endeavors. Central to its conceptualization is the idea of "structuring" as sustained, dynamic interpenetration of the everyday personal world and the social environment, each constituting and reconstituting the other. This conceptualization conceives of the social environment as limiting and constraining, yet at the same time as enabling and mobilizing the individual in his or her pursuits. Conversely, it sees people and their actions as creative and purposeful agents who manipulate and adjust their social environment. The recriprocity of human action and social environment involves what Giddens terms "the dialectic of power and control."[8] The enabling capacity of the social structure and the corresponding creative capacity of the individuals obviously depend on the degree of the latter's autonomy in society. That of the East Central European peasant-immigrants and their children in Johnstown before World War II was certainly severely restricted. However, as long as they were not totally confined and controlled – that is, as long as they remained agents – they possessed some margin of freedom and choice that they used to "turn their weakness back against the powerful" and to pursue their own purposes.

Analysis of the process of "structuration" requires the apprehension of the concrete, phenomenal world of human actions in which the *becoming* of social reality actually takes place. The focus of this book is on the *Lebenswelten* of the East Central European immigrants and their children. This study takes its place in the tradition of *Geisteswissenschaften*, the social sciences considered to be essentially interpretive, their function to understand the meaning of social reality in people who were taking part in it. A hermeneutically informed sociological-historical study, such as this one aspires to be, reconstructs the phenomenal texture of the life-worlds experienced by the actors. Throughout the study, then, I attempt to interpret the creative coping and adaptive strategies employed by the peasants in Europe at the turn of the century and later as immigrant workers in Johnstown in terms of their own perceptions – that is, through the prism of what Znaniecki termed the "humanistic coefficient," Schutz called the "relevance structures" of everyday lives, and Geertz refers to as "webs of meaning" of social actions.[9] In this endeavor, I am particularly indebted to the guidance and insights of Thomas and Znaniecki, on whose voluminous, brilliant analysis in *The Polish Peasant in Europe and America* I relied extensively.[10]

Such an approach to social history necessitates an analysis that is at the same time microscopic and holistic, embracing the multitude of layers and dimensions of the life-worlds of the people studied. This study, moving across the "thick territory" of the social world of the East Central European families and illuminating, as it were, with a lantern its various parts, has such panoramic quality. Unavoidably it possesses the drawbacks of such an approach. However, I trust it also offers the advantage of furnishing an encompassing depiction of the environment of the people who inhabited it.

Although central, the interpretation of the *Lebenswelten* of the East Central European peasant-immigrants and their children is not the only purpose of the study. An aim of historical sociology is to account for the relationship between people's actions and the social environment as it evolves in their everyday lives. In order to do this, historical sociology attempts to perform two types of work at once and in concert. The first is primarily concerned with the question of "how it was," recreating and narrating the past through factual evidence. The second is basically devoted to discovering its sociological character – "how and why it happened." It is a controlled analysis consisting of a series of arguments that establish significant patternings of social reality.[11]

In the chapters that follow I have tried to accomplish this difficult synthesis of the evidence of the moment with an account of social forces and trends of the longer *durée*. The former constitutes the explicit content and bulk of the book; the latter is more implicit, for the most part built into the narrative that it punctuates as certain arguments are introduced and summarized. In this approach, the study represents what Theda Skocpol has called a *problem-oriented* sociohistorical analysis, seeking not to rework an existing theoretical paradigm or to generate an alternative one but rather "to make sense of historical patterns, using in the process whatever theoretical resources seem useful and valid."[12]

Two major, interconnected themes run through my analysis, both of them related to the general problem of the transition to industrialism. The first one is that of the intermixture of tradition and modernity in the adaptation of peasant-immigrants to American urban industrial society.

Attacked by multiple theoretical and empirical critiques, dichotomous, linear-polar conceptions of tradition and modernity have been discarded. The *becoming* of urban industrial society is now interpreted as an uneven and multifaceted development in which, depending on particular historical circumstances, old and new elements and aggregations, often ill fitting and inconsistent, come to coexist in varying blends and combinations.[13]

At the empirical level, a large body of sociological data testifies to the persistence of solid pockets of traditional patterns and orientations in both the "developing" world and industrialized societies. For the latter of these the United States – its urban communities, its social stratification and political processes, its formal bureaucratic organizations, and its family and career patterns – serves as a test case.[14] For well over a decade, evidence of widespread persistence of preindustrial frameworks in core American institutions in the late nineteenth and twentieth centuries has been accumulating in studies in the so-called new or revisionist American social history, especially in the fields of immigration, urbanism, and labor, which demonstrate how industrial society has positively nurtured traditional attitudes and behavior.[15] Modern society, it is asserted today by commentators on social change, is perfectly capable of accommodating ascriptive bonds and particularist orientations and of incorporating large sectors of traditional economic and social institutions.

The particular concern of this book – the adaptation of peasant-immigrants from rural East Central Europe to American industrial society during the first half of the present century – locates it within the field of ethnic studies. Departing from earlier interpretations that conceived of ethnicity as a set of "given" cultural characteristics and "primordial attachments," recent sociological and sociohistorical scholarship treats it as a dynamic category: a "strategic tool" or "resource" situationally activated and mobilized in the process of interaction between the immigrants and the host system.[16]

This book is intended to exemplify and extend the direction of this newer literature concerning both tradition and modernity, and ethnicity. The analysis that follows attempts to blend these two themes into a more encompassing understanding of the evolution of urban industrial society in the United States. Namely, by showing what the Rudolphs, referring to contemporary Indian society, have aptly called "the modernity of tradition,"[17] this study demonstrates how the ethnic-ascriptive and particularist networks and identities of peasant-immigrants-become-industrial laborers served as the important vehicle of their socioeconomic achievement and of their incorporation into the larger American society.

First I examine the incipient alterations of peasant worldviews in East Central Europe in the last decades of the nineteenth century, as structural changes produced the first cracks in a still prevalent traditionalism. These innovations in the peasants' thinking and behavior consisted of certain elements of gain-instrumental orientation and of their general "mobilization for a better life," which coexisted with traditional outlooks and ideas. Following peasant-immigrants to America, I show how the traditional patterns in their pursuits and attitudes, nurtured by Johnstown's economic and social environment, in fact played an instrumental role in furthering new elements in their orientations that had already surfaced in Europe.

In particular, I look into the role played in the adaptation of peasant-immigrants and their children to industrial society by two characteristics: the persisting familial collectivism and partial fusion or nondifferentiation of kinship/ethnic and work/occupational roles in their economic activities; and the persisting particularist, ethnic-ascriptive foundations of Johnstown's social organization.

The adaptive role and the persistence of the ascriptive networks that members of immigrant groups create and utilize to cope with host environments have been repeatedly noted in ethnic literature.[18] Recent sociohistorical studies, particularly those dealing with people from the rural areas of southern and East Central Europe who came to this country at the turn of the century, have interpreted the immigrants' familial collectivism and their reliance on "fused" kinship and ethnic networks as primarily defensive strategies for survival in the new and adverse industrial environment. These survival strategies, it has been argued, reflected the immigrants' "fundamental concern for [economic] security" and their "limited aspirations [for achievement]."[19] This study argues for a more complex interpretation of the immigrants' orientations and behavior. Their experience as peasants in the impoverished European villages, together with their continuously precarious economic existence as industrial laborers in America, most certainly sustained the immigrants' fundamental concern with security, and it is undoubtedly toward this end that they utilized the ascriptive networks of kinship and ethnicity that they created. At the same time, however, the continuing fusion of kinship/ethnic and work spheres in the lives of immigrant laborers, nurtured by the industrial and normative systems of the host society, also had the effect of solidifying their gain-instrumental attitudes that motivated them to seek to maximize their resources and facilitated their socioeconomic achievement. It was, however, a "particularist achievement," conceived of and pursued differently from a "universalist" one defined and realized as individual advancement based on formal education and skills.

In the classical modernization theory as well as in the assimilation theories of ethnicity, the inclusion of groups and their members into the larger society occurs through the replacement of segmented, particularist loyalties by more embracing, "higher-order" identities and attachments.[20] In a quite different, in fact, an opposite approach, recent sociological studies of "reactive ethnicity" have emphasized the role of intensified ethnic awareness, particularly among groups structurally and culturally disadvantaged, in their "political mobilization for membership" directed against the dominant society.[21]

The experience of peasant-immigrants in Johnstown before World War II lends itself to neither assimilationist nor conflict interpretation but calls for yet a different approach. It is summarized in the title of a recent sociohistorical study of the immigrants in Pittsburgh by John Bodnar, Roger Simon, and Michael Weber: *Lives of Their Own*.[22] Their book deals primarily with the economic pursuits of the immigrants, but its title has broader symbolism. As we shall see in this study, the rigid, segmented class/ethnic divisions of the local society in Johnstown "imposed" on East Central Europeans ascriptive frameworks for identities and actions. At the same time, the immigrants themselves mobilized and sustained their "ethnicity" by forming in the segment that had been assigned to them complex networks of solidarities and associations within which they defined and pursued their goals. They incorporated themselves into the larger American society by a segmental appropriation of sorts: neither "for" nor "against," but, rather, "alongside" the dominant system. This self-incorporation occurred through the crystallization of ethnic awareness and sharpening of the boundaries dividing particular groups, and through the participation in ethnic organizations and daily activities carried on within ethnic communities that extended from neighborhoods to the workplace. This divisive-inclusive process of ethnicization I call "ascriptive inclusion."

Intimately affiliated with the above arguments is the second, concurrent theme that runs through this study: the process of formation of the modern American working class, and "contained" within this process, as it were, the proletarianization of peasant-immigrants and their children. The leitmotiv behind my analysis of the experience of East Central European workers is that the actual "becoming" of these two-in-one processes occurred precisely through the interplay between old and new ways and approaches, as one transformed the other. The social infrastructure and cultural outlook of a large segment of the contemporary American working class came into being and assumed its identity through the adjustments of traditional peasant values and behavioral patterns "tested" in the new environment, and through the ethnicization of bonds and relationships. In advancing these arguments, this study draws from several excellent works by the historians of industrialism and labor, and from sociological studies of social class images and representations.[23] At the same time, it shows the tension and ambivalence involved in the industrial experience of peasant-immigrants and their American-born children, informed by the precariousness and uncertainty of their economic existence and by overlapping, often conflicting cultural orientations and multiple reference frameworks.

Such a minutely documented account of the ambiguous, multi-faceted life-worlds of peasant-immigrant workers contributes, I hope, toward a better, historically grounded understanding of social reality at three levels of generality. The first, in descending order, is the meaning of modernity *tout court*, constituted, as Geertz proposes, by the "dazzling multiformity [of consciousness] . . . and the increasing diversification of individual experience."[24] The second involves the particular experience and worldview of one large segment of American industrial society – the working class – as they were developing, during the first half of this century, into a mosaic of approaches and ideas created and recreated in continuous inter-action between tradition and the challenges and constraints of the new environment. Last, the third level of social reality to which my analysis may contribute better understanding is that of the lives and outlooks of a particular aggregate of people within the American working class: the East Central European peasant-immigrants and their children.

Clifford Geertz's unusual gift for language is as irresistible as is his work itself. Let me, then, borrow a conclusion for the preceding discussion from him:

> Rather than following a rising curve of cumulative findings, cul-tural analysis breaks up into a disconnected yet coherent se-quence of bolder and bolder sorties. Studies do build on other studies [in the sense that] . . . they plunge more deeply into the same things . . . A study is an advance if it is more incisive – whatever that may mean – than those that preceded it; but it less stands on their shoulders, than, challenged and challenging, runs by their side.[25]

Sources and methods

Two problems arise when sociologists or historians set out to dis-cover "how it was" or is and employ a battery of techniques to amass documentation concerning human actions and their meaning. One involves the extent to which such evidence can be thought to rep-resent – or, rather, closely approximate – the social reality of the people studied.

The aptness of a depiction of the surmised reality of a people's experience and values can be "tested" by establishing that, to quote once more from Geertz, "the system of meaningful categories it pos-tulates as guiding them has a detectable effect upon the ongoing flow of social activity. Showing that a cultural paradigm is in fact paradigmatic – that it is an operative force – means showing that it in fact orders behavior."[26] One way of doing this is to meticulously compile historical details to fill in the categories of the "paradigm." Such has been the approach used in this book: to weave a tapestry of a variety of data to reconstruct the "thick territory" of the every-day lives of the people who inhabited it. This brings us to the second problem: the extent to which appropriate evidence is available for study.

In my nearly four years of research on this book, between 1979 and 1982, I tried to compile the most exhaustive documentation possible for an analysis of the pre-emigration backgrounds and the adaptation in Johnstown of the East Central European peasant-immigrants and their American-born children. The study employed three complementary methods of collecting and analyzing the data. The first dealt with the documents pertaining to the situation of peasants in East Central Europe at the turn of the century, and, as they came here, in Johnstown and other centers of heavy East Central European immigration. They included documents from public sources (government and social agencies, schools, newspapers, ethnic parishes, and associations) and private ones (peasant-immigrant letters, diaries, biographies, theater plays, poems, songs, and prayers). In assembling the latter type of documentation, I utilized as much foreign-language source material as possible, because it is less readily available and thus much less familiar to American readers. In addition, studies by turn-of-the-century observers of immigrant communities in American cities, particularly those in Pennsylvania mill and coal towns by Margaret Byington, Peter Roberts, John Fitch, and Emily Balch, also proved to be very enlightening in their emphasis on the diversity of individual and family experiences and pursuits of East Central European immigrants.[27]

The second method was ethnographic fieldwork. During the first two years of the study I practically lived in Johnstown, spending most of my time in the East Central European sections of the town. I visited homes, parishes, and local ethnic organizations and participated in weddings, baptisms, and religious and national celebrations. On these occasions I conducted, in a form of open-ended structured conversations, a total of 217 interviews with first and second generation men and women: with rank-and-file members of East Central European communities; priests; organizational leaders; and businessmen. My initial informants were contacted through local community organizations. Having established initial contacts, I kept expanding them and added more and more people. Twenty-three of them became my key informants, whom I visited and reinterviewed several times over the course of my research, coming back when new questions arose. I also talked to former Bethlehem Steel Company officials and local Johnstown politicians. In addition, I used nearly 200 taped oral-history interviews with immigrant and second generation East Central European workers from Johnstown and vicinity made available to me from the collection of Michael Yates and Bruce Williams at the University of Pittsburgh at Johnstown.

How did I go about this "qualitative" part of my research? What was it that I was seeking in the immigrants' letters, autobiographies and memoirs, their foreign-language newspaper articles, and in my conversations with East Central Europeans in Johnstown? Obviously, I was looking for facts and data about the details of their existence: jobs, lodgings, home life, aspirations, successes, and failures. But also more. I sought to capture in their life-worlds the processes of social transformation that linked the old and the new, the postfeudal village with the industrial city. These were difficult adjustments, realized slowly and unevenly, which saturated the lives of the people with tensions and conflicts and often left them confused and painfully ambivalent. In my reading of documents that they had left behind and in listening to their accounts of the past, I was searching for this experience, trying to grasp its psychological aspects as well as what Robert Merton and Elinor Barber call "sociological ambivalence" – the consequence of living in social situations that pull in different directions.[28]

My own situation, I think, has probably sharpened my eye and ear to some extent. I am myself a foreigner, a recent immigrant in this country. The times are obviously different; with my big-city background and university education I find myself in a very different position from that of illiterate peasant-immigrants from East European villages at the turn of the century. Nobody calls me a "Hunky," and my accent is politely referred to as "nice." Yet, with all these differences and with my unquestionably privileged situation in comparison with that of my fellow East Central Europeans who came a century ago, I think we do share a certain fundamental similarity of experience as emigrants who physically leave one place but forever carry it in their minds and hearts in the other country where they slowly and laboriously put down roots. I think I share, and understand, the profound ambivalence inherent in the decision to settle in new land and the recognition that when it is weighed and reweighed in the scales of the mind, both sides of the balance will be loaded and heavy. I know as they did that the eventual choice unavoidably implies resignation and loss. I understand the multiple perspectives and reference frameworks, sometimes enriching and sometimes tiresome, as things appear simultaneously yellow and green, true and untrue, joyous and sad, with which the immigrants travel through life, evaluate it, and make adjustments.

My effort at "comprehensive interpretation" was admittedly more difficult in the case of the immigrant children, the American-born generation for whom *here*, and not *there*, was the only personally known reality and reference. While reading and listening to their stories, I followed a similar clue: As I placed and described them in their surroundings, I tried to map the tensions and ambiguities built into the structure of their cultural and social situations.

The oral-history method of investigation used in this study is by now neither new nor exceptional. Yet, although it is an established and respected tool in sociohistorical research, it has its potential drawbacks. In particular, I was concerned with possible "sentimentalization" and "reminiscence error" in my informants' accounts of the past. Although my opinion is obviously subjective, I do not think that the natural inclination to "sentimentalize" certain events or parts of their past prevented my informants from delivering a generally balanced picture of their experience. The lives of East Central Europeans in Johnstown before World War II were for the most part overwhelmingly hard, difficult, and insecure, and were perceived as such. If there were any leitmotivs in my informants' life stories, the recurring themes were precisely that: the hard conditions of their existence, and their efforts to cope with and to make the best of them.

I tried to "control" as much as possible for the unavoidable reminiscence error in my informants' account of the past by checking and rechecking the information I received several times. If it pertained to public matters, I verified it against the accounts gathered from other people and with the data I collected from written sources.

Sentimentalization and forgetfulness on the part of the informants are not the only dangers involved in ethnographic fieldwork. The researcher must also stand guard against two more traps of his or her own making. One is that of overrapport, or "so thoroughly merging with the subjects' point of view that one cannot achieve the critical distance necessary for analysis." Another is that of overindebtedness, "so thoroughly feeling a sense of diffuse obligation [to those who make the account possible] that one can no longer assess what one does and does not properly owe his subjects."[29] There is no standard, definitive resolution to these problems. The best protective measure, which I employed as well as I could, seems to be for the researcher to remain constantly and conscientiously aware of these dangers and to check and recheck one's attitudes and interpretations, both in the course of the fieldwork and afterward, when preparing and writing the report.

The third method used in this study was the statistical analysis of data on the occupational shifting, residential mobility, home-ownership, and educational achievement of the East Central Europeans in Johnstown during the first half of this century.

I used the manuscript schedules of the U.S. census for 1900 to identify the city's East Central European residents. As anyone who has used old census schedules knows, they provide a far from perfect source of information.[30] But the floods that recurrently devastated the city destroyed the Bethlehem Steel Company's employment records, a potential source of occupational information, and there was no satisfactory substitute source of aggregate data on the immigrant families and their initial position in Johnstown. As a complementary source, and for verifying names and families, I used immigrant parochial and ethnic organizational records.

From the 1900 manuscript census, then, I took all identifiable Slavic and Magyar names, a total of 4,980. This number included 3,077 immigrants (2,399 men and 678 women) and 1,903 American-born persons (1,304 men and 599 women). Among the group born in America, 1,442 were the second generation – children of the immigrants – and the generational status of the remainder was not specified.[31]

The people recorded in the 1900 census were subsequently traced, for residential, occupational, and homeownership movements, at five-year intervals through Johnstown city directories until 1949 (the analysis was extended to that year in order to cover the peak years of the careers of the second generation). At each directory checkpoint, I used the full 1900 data base for tracing. In this way I traced not only the persisters but also those who left the city and later returned.[32]

Another source of statistical information for my analyses of the economic maneuvers of the East Central European families in Johnstown before World War I was the report of the Dillingham Immigration Commission, which visited the city in 1908–9 to investigate industrial and living conditions. Despite its unpleasant "restrictionist" tone and often forced reasoning, the commission's minute report on the wages, expenditures, housing conditions, and boarders of the East Central European households in Johnstown provides unique data for reconstructing their daily struggle and internal economic differences. I also used tax and real estate records, "mercantile appraiser's" lists from the local newspaper, and Dun & Bradstreet's credit ratings of Slavic and Magyar business enterprises before World War II. The membership rosters and minutes of ethnic organizations for the period from the 1890s to 1940 served as a source of quantitative data for the analysis of internal social differentiation and leadership patterns within the immigrant communities.

Finally, in order to assess the educational performance of the chil-

dren of the second generation, I took name samples from one immigrant parochial elementary school (the records of all others having
been destroyed in the floods) and four public schools located in the
"foreign sections" of town. Since the second generation in this study
were people born shortly before or after 1900, the elementary school
samples were taken for the period 1895–1914. In addition, from the
1915–28 enrollment lists of two junior and senior high schools in
Johnstown I took samples of Slavic- and Magyar-sounding names
of persons born between 1897 and 1914 (this latter extension to allow
for a greater number of students entering secondary training) and
linked them through city directories with their fathers, recording
their occupation and residence.

The last issue to be addressed in this section is the "East Central
Europeans" themselves. The term covers no less than eight groups
from the East Central region of Europe: Slovaks, Magyars (Hungarians), Croatians, Serbs, Slovenes, Poles, Ukrainians (from north
of the Carpathians), and Rusyns (from south of the Carpathians) –
all groups that were present in Johnstown at the turn of the century.
In the title of the book, as in most of the analyses throughout the
study, these groups are treated as one.

Anybody familiar with the divisiveness and complexity of East
Central Europe, the disparate histories of its particular regions, the
cultural cleavages and differences, often petty and superficial yet
deeply felt and surprisingly persistent in collective perceptions,
must be aware that to treat this part of the continent and its peoples
as though they constituted a single entity unavoidably involves
gross oversimplification. These differences did not disappear, and
some of them became accentuated, when the peasant-immigrants
came to America and busied themselves with building their own
ethnic communities, drawing on what they in part discovered and
in part created as their common group heritage of language, customs, and identities.

For the greater peace of my historical-sociological conscience and
to execute more faithfully the interpretive, particularizing approach
that informs this study, I would have much preferred to treat each
of the eight groups and their social and cultural idiosyncrasies separately, with all due attention to detail – but it was not practically
possible. In the first place, the number of East Central Europeans
– immigrants and second generation, men and women – that served
as my data base for quantitative analyses was too small to render
meaningful results for any of the eight subgroups taken alone, and
increasing proportions of the original sample disappeared from the

city at each checkpoint. Second, a systematic comparative analysis of the peasant-immigrants' experience in each of the eight groups, with microscopic examination of their individual and collective life-worlds, was simply not feasible within the scope of one book.

To include only some of the East Central European groups present in Johnstown, so that each could then receive separate treatment throughout the study whereas others would be left out, made much less sense than to take them all and focus on commonalities. And, after all, such generalized treatment is not without important justifications. The socioeconomic conditions in the various areas of East Central Europe at the end of the nineteenth century were fundamentally similar. Such underlying affinities become even more pronounced when one compares the patterns of the development in the western and eastern parts of the continent. All eight of these groups were peasant in origin, and all of them left basically similar situations at home. Peasant-immigrants from eastern Europe and from the Balkans were "pushed out" of their villages at the same time and by similar economic and sociopsychological factors: overpopulation, shortage of land, and increased awareness of the opportunities that existed elsewhere. Those who settled in Johnstown were all brought there by similar mechanisms and confronted the same social and economic conditions. All lived in the same "foreign colonies" and, regardless of nationality, most found similar jobs in the local steel mills and coal mines. All were indiscriminately perceived as "Hunkies" by the native Johnstowners. All, too, developed fundamentally similar economic, social, and cultural responses to the environment in which they acted.

The clearly detectable "dominant profile of sociocultural orientations" among these immigrants did not preclude the simultaneous existence of "substitute or secondary variations" on the same theme specific to particular groups.[33] There were observable peculiarities among the eight groups, some of them evidencing a continuation of old-country relationships transplanted to American soil, and others appearing to have developed locally. Throughout the study, I attempt to mark and comment on as many of these distinctive features as possible.

One other explanation about a group that is not treated in this book is in order. As I began this study in 1979, my intention was to include both Christian and Jewish immigrants from East Central Europe. The idea seemed historically obvious, if rarely implemented by ethnic historians. Both groups had lived side by side in Europe in close economic symbiosis, though socially and culturally distant. They left in the same period, often sharing the journey on trains, in ports, and on ships crossing the ocean. Upon their arrival in Johnstown, Christian and Jewish East Central Europeans again settled in close geographic proximity and reestablished their old-country interdependence: Peasants turned into industrial laborers; Jews peddled their goods among the coal-mining Slavic communities and set up small retail businesses in the "foreign sections" of Johnstown.

As I progressed with my study, however, it soon became apparent that with the rapidly expanding material that I was collecting, which related to an even greater number of subgroups (there were in Johnstown German, Russian, Polish, Lithuanian, and Hungarian Jews), I had, in fact, not one but two books on my hands. I therefore decided to set the "Jewish" project aside and return to it later, after the completion of the "peasant" one. And this is what happened. In my book on the patterns of Jewish adaptation in Johnstown before World War II, which is now in progress, I treat extensively the issue of replication in the American environment of the old-country interrelations between these two groups.

The perennial question of representativity

Before I arrived here from Warsaw in 1979 on a postdoctoral grant in American studies from the American Council of Learned Societies, I carried on extensive correspondence with my colleagues in the United States asking for suggestions as to what place to choose for my research. I was looking for an industrial city with an East Central European population that could be "handled" by a single hard-working researcher whose original intention was to stay only twelve to eighteen months. Pennsylvania was suggested as a promising location: At the beginning of the century it was home to 18 percent of all East Central European immigrants in this country, and nearly 75 percent of them were employed in manufacturing and mining. Johnstown, in the western part of the state – a steel town with a supporting coal industry that had, at the beginning of the century, a population of between fifty and sixty thousand – seemed to meet my needs. Moreover, the location was not atypical of East Central European settlement in the United States. At the time of World War I, about one-half of the foreign-born population from East Central Europe lived in places with fewer than one hundred thousand inhabitants. Also, nearly one-fourth of the total immigrant male labor force from that region was employed in American steel and coal-mining industries.[34]

So Johnstown became the site of my research. As it turned out, having decided to remain in America for good, I spent not one but nearly four years in the city, first living there and then visiting regularly. Let me, however, elaborate a little further on the question of representativity, since important issues remain.

This study is about the situation in Johnstown and the reactions of a people to it. Since it concerns the structuring or intertwining of environment and action, not one but two questions of representativity are involved. The first is: How typical was the situation in Johnstown as I have described it? The second is: How typical were the reactions of its East Central European residents presented here?

In the field of American social history of the nineteenth and twentieth centuries, there are hundreds of monographs dealing with particular cities and towns, not to mention those by economists, geographers, political scientists, and ethnographers. Even those that deal with similar epochs and problems have, quite naturally, different focuses and emphases. Asking differently phrased questions, they collect and expose different sets of data. The more historically specific, contextual, and microscopic the analysis, the less readily comparable are the findings and the more perplexing is the problem of representativity.

The matter, then, is difficult, and I have no definitive answers to either of the two questions. Let me, however, present a few reasonable suggestions. First, for Johnstown itself. To locate it in some comparative perspective, we can use an interesting typology propounded by Hollingsworth and Hollingsworth in their sociological-historical analysis of small- and middle-sized American cities since 1870.[35] By "abstracting" from several hundred urban communities certain underlying structural and cultural properties or dimensions, the Hollingsworths construct three ideal-types of cities: autocratic, oligarchic, and polyarchic. They then classify selected cities under particular categories. Johnstown is not on their list; without much hesitation, however, I classify it as an essentially autocratic type, with certain characteristics of the oligarchic pattern.

The Hollingsworths' autocratic ideal-type city possessed the following features: an undifferentiated economic base and a low level of horizontal socioeconomic differentiation; a pyramid-shaped social structure (i.e., pronounced inequality in the distribution of status and wealth, with a small homogeneous elite and a large lower class); a rigid stratification system with sharp ethnic cleavages, and a corresponding ascription-based normative system; an autocratic and centralized political system with overlapping political and economic elites; a relatively high level of local autonomy; and a traditionalist political culture, marked by low participation, "bossism," and a perception of the political process as based on ascriptive-particularist rather than rationalist-legal criteria. The oligarchic type of city had a somewhat more complex socioeconomic structure, slightly less rigid social divisions, and somewhat less autonomy.

Self-contained amid the hills of western Pennsylvania and dominated by one industry and one powerful employer – the Cambria, later the Bethlehem, Steel Company – with about two-thirds of its male population in manufacturing and mining; nonunionized, ethnically fragmented, and tightly controlled by the established Anglo-Protestant elite, until World War II Johnstown remained fundamentally an autocratic city. When, after the First World War, the city had lost its importance as one of the nation's leading steel-producing centers, it had possibly acquired some traits of the oligarchic type as its autonomy decreased. But the sluggishness of its economic development and the continuing dependence on one industry prevented the heterogenization of Johnstown's horizontal socioeconomic structure and set constraints on the vertical differentiation (mobility) of its population.

As an autocratic type of urban community, Johnstown would have been comparable to such places, as (from the Hollingsworths' list) Irontown, Pennsylvania; Marinette, Wisconsin; Shenandoah, Pennsylvania; Spartanburg, South Carolina; and Wilkinsburg, Pennsylvania. For more specific comparisons, we can add to this list a few more cities in which, at the beginning of the century, iron and steel production accounted for 50 percent or more of the total industrial output: McKeesport, Pennsylvania; Newcastle, Pennsylvania; Youngstown, Ohio; and Joliet, Illinois. The conditions in Johnstown also seem to have been strikingly similar to those described by Bodnar in his study of immigrants in Steeltown, Pennsylvania.[36]

The second issue relating to the representativity of my study concerns the actions of the people that it describes. How typical were their behavior and attitudes, displayed as reaction and challenge to cultural traditions and the surrounding environment?

The development of institutionally complex immigrant communities, and "ethnicization" as the mediating mechanism in the process of collective and individual adaptation of newcomers to American society, have occurred in most cities with sufficiently large and concentrated numbers of immigrants. Such was also the case in Johnstown with East Central Europeans. There, however, the sustained structural and dominant cultural conditions constituted a virtual textbook setting for what Yancey, Ericksen, and Juliani called "emergent ethnicity."[37] It may be suggested, then, that in some aspects the general ethnic processes occurring in American society (or, to be more exact, in its urban industrial regions) in the first half of the century could be observed in Johnstown in purer, more pronounced form.

It has been also reported from several cities that East Central Europeans did not adhere to the standard American set of cultural values that mandate the pursuit of individual success through formal education and occupational advancement. Instead, they pursued through family efforts economic viability, good reputation, and status within their ethnic communities. The cultural goals and the general direction of the actions of the East Central Europeans in Johnstown essentially meet this description. However, the concrete methods and tactics that they used for their purposes were specifically tailored to the particular circumstances in which they lived. The scope of their actual achievements was also specific to the constraining structural conditions of a small autocratic town.

In order to find out more about these specificities and determinants, the Hollingsworths postulate the undertaking of planned, comparative endeavor in urban history. For instance, one might select two or more cities of similar type but in different regions, or each with a distinct local ambience, and compare the performance of the same ethnic group, or better yet, a few different ones in the two cities. Or one might carry out such comparisons in a few urban settings of different types. Some such analyses have been conducted,[38] but the systematic comparative work that would link historical case studies of several urban ethnic communities under one theoretical framework still remains to be done.

This book consists of eight chapters. Chapters 1 and 2 are devoted to the rural backgrounds in East Central Europe at the turn of the century and the conditions leading to mass peasant migrations. Chapters 3 and 5 characterize the dominant structural and cultural "framework" of the peasant-immigrants' actions: Johnstown before World War I, and during the 1920s and 1930s. Chapters 4 and 6 are devoted to an examination of the life-worlds of East Central Europeans during the initial years of their settlement in Johnstown and between the two world wars. Chapter 7 deals with the internal social stratification of the immigrant communities. The concluding chapter, Chapter 8, is about the second generation, the sons and daughters of peasant-immigrants.

1   *Backgrounds*

The image of late nineteenth-century East Central European societies as societies in the process of "transition" and "significant change" has by now almost replaced the old persistent stereotype of "stagnant villages" in the American historiography of immigration and ethnicity. The abolition of serfdom in East Central Europe and the resulting transformations of the rural economy in the last decade of the nineteenth century, particularly mass peasant migrations into the outside world, were closely related to the slow but irreversibly progressive decomposition of traditional peasant society and culture.

Although most historians today stress the transitional character of the socioeconomic system emerging at the turn of the century in rural East Central Europe, there has been relatively little analysis of the cultural and psychological implications of these changes for the people themselves. The discussion is usually limited to a general statement of one of the two following interpretations. Some authors – for instance John Bodnar and Michael Weber, John Cumbler and Caroline Golab – emphasize the primarily defensive, survival-oriented character of the behavior of the East Central European peasantry, which they perceive as having been affected in an almost exclusively negative way by undergoing changes.[1] This view has been predominant in American ethnic historiography during the last decade. However, other scholars, such as Timothy Smith, Josef Barton, and Paula Benkart, relate the gradual transformation of East Central European societies in the decades prior to World War I to the widespread "mobilization for economic and cultural advantage" among the peasantry.[2] This perspective is more closely akin to the underlying premises and interpretative direction of this chapter. However, as I will attempt to demonstrate, the structural transformations in East Central Europe in the last quarter of the nineteenth century made peasant worldviews more complex and ambivalent, and rendered their attitudes more multifaceted than either of the above interpretations assume. The inclusion of the peasant households in the market economy and the rapid proletarianization of increasing segments of East Central European rural societies intro-

22

duced new elements into peasant cultural values and social patterns. Entering piecemeal into the peasant culture, they created new combinations and multiform blends, often ill fitting and inconsistent with older traditional values and approaches.

Given their overall poverty and the limited economic resources of their world, it was certainly true that the ultimate goal of East Central European peasants was security. An observation by Sol Tax in his study of present-day Guatemalan Indians, *Penny Capitalism*,[3] is equally descriptive of the outlooks of East Central European peasants three-quarters of a century earlier. In East Central European villages at the turn of the century, as among the Guatemalan Indians today, even the wealthiest families were not far above the subsistence level:

> They have little margin of safety, and a series of bad times . . . may send them down . . . When a sickness can take in a year what has been accumulated in a dozen or more, and when such catastrophes are ever on the horizon, it is not enough to be just a little ahead . . . The need is to keep as much as possible ahead, for the rainy day.[4]

In such a world, security was without doubt of fundamental importance. However, the opening of rural communities to the larger world and to opportunities for additional income made security, in Tax's words, essentially a *negative want*. Superimposed on it there also appeared in the peasant attitude a positive wish: the desire to improve one's condition and the mobilizing realization that it might be possible to do so. A peasant from Babica, a small village in western Galicia, expressed this new outlook as he watched the train that had passed through his village daily since 1893: "This passing train . . . reminds us of our poverty here, and tells us that somewhere else life is better, that the world is different, big, better."[5]

We shall begin by reviewing the diverse data on the transition processes in the different regions of rural East Central Europe at the turn of the century. Against this background we will examine some of the concrete social and cultural meanings of these transformations for East Central European peasants and their communities. This discussion focuses especially on the particular elements of the emerging peasant *Weltanschauungen* that are significant for understanding the mechanisms of their mass seasonal migrations, travel to America, and the strategies and patterns of their subsequent adaptation in this country. They are grouped here under three general, closely interrelated themes: (1) the peasants' increasing openness to new experience, together with a growing awareness of the diversity of surrounding options – the attitude that S. N. Eisenstadt calls the "world feasible"; (2) the emergent belief in the "manipulability" of the situation: a conviction that it is possible to actively advance one's own goals, rather than being dominated solely by forces created by powerful sources outside one's control; and (3) the incipient instrumentalization of peasants' orientations: the acceptance and partial internalization of quantitative bases for acquiring and distributing rewards, and the resulting belief that the material world is expandable.[6]

Since the fifteenth century East Central Europe had been the major agricultural exporter to the western part of the continent, its economy oriented basically toward the production of foodstuffs and the supplying of external markets. The maintenance of serfdom and of the medieval system of large estates until the nineteenth century petrified semifeudal social relations strikingly different from those developed in western Europe in the course of urbanization and industrialization. As a result, in 1900 the majority of the population in all of East Central Europe was still involved in agriculture, ranging from about 60 percent in Hungary proper, and Congress and "Prussian" Poland, to over 80 percent in Subcarpathian Rus', Transylvania, and Serbia (Table 1.1).

The abolition of serfdom and the alienation of estates and communal lands produced cumulative long-term effects on the rural economy of East Central Europe. On the one hand, it brought about a significant increase in the total acreage owned by the peasantry (an increase of 10 to 25 percent, within twenty-five to thirty years from the implementation of emancipation laws in particular regions). On the other, it intensified the process of internal economic and social stratification of the peasantry. One side of this process was the gradual consolidation of land and the formation of a group of middle peasants, owners of medium-sized holdings. Simultaneously, and at a much faster rate, with more significant consequences, peasant land holdings were systematically fragmented into ever-diminishing pieces as the land was divided and redivided among their progeny. The figures shown in Table 1.1 reflect this process in its already advanced stage at the turn of the century.[7]

The third long-term consequence of the enfranchisement of the East Central European peasantry in the second half of the nineteenth century was the creation of a large mass of rural proletarians. The land reforms of 1848 and 1864 left thousands of peasants as landless as they had been before, and the continuing fragmentation of land holdings within the owning stratum of the peasantry added new members to the ranks of the landless each year.

The proportions of the landless agricultural proletariat and semi-proletariat (rural residents who owned a small plot of land but had to search for outside employment in order to survive) differed by region. In Croatia, Serbia, Slovenia, and Congress Poland, where agriculture still retained a more traditional character, it was relatively low. In Hungary and Greater Poland, more advanced in capitalist transformations, the share of the rural proletariat was higher. All across East Central Europe, however, the numbers of "superfluous" people reached into the millions: about 3 million in Hungary, 1.2 million in Galicia, over 1 million in Congress Poland. In the latter the rural proletariat grew by 550 percent between 1864 and 1901, whereas the country's total population grew by only 175 percent.[8]

Between 1860 and 1910, the average population growth in East Central Europe was over 75 percent.[9] This unprecedented demographic boom, resulting from the decrease in death rates accompanying capitalist transformations, combined with the explosion in births that followed emancipation of the peasantry, greatly fostered the numerical increase of the agrarian proletariat in the whole region.

The enormous rise in the numbers of the landless rural population and of dwarf-holders incapable of maintaining themselves forced peasants out of their villages in search of employment and income. For instance, in Galicia, Subcarpathian Rus', Slovakia, and Greater Poland at the turn of the century, over one-half of the dwarf-holding families regularly earned additional outside income. In some districts of these provinces the proportion reached 70 percent.[10] A study conducted in 1900 in the village of Maszkienice near Brzesko in western Galicia indicated that about 50 percent of the village families could not sustain themselves from the soil alone and were obliged to work elsewhere.[11] Another Galician study conducted in the same period in Zmiąca near Limanowa, which assumed that no peasant family could maintain itself on a farm valued at less than 2,000 kronen ($400, in 1900 dollars), similarly concluded that over 50 percent of the farm owners in the village were "unable to feed their families from the possessed land." Of this number, 26 percent of the farmers derived their principal income from other employment.[12]

Coupled with the prolonged agricultural depression that set in at the beginning of the 1880s and lasted into the 1890s, these demographic and economic transformations in East Central European rural societies put thousands of people on the move. The rapid in-

Table 1.1 *Distribution of gainfully occupied population and peasant landownership in East Central Europe around 1900 (in %)*

Country	In Agriculture	In Industry	Dwarf-holdings and < 2 ha	Small Farms (3–5 ha)	Middle Farms 6–10 ha	Middle Farms 11–20 ha	Large Farms (> 20 ha)	Landless Peasants: Agrarian Proletariat[a]	Semiproletariat
Hungary (Proper)	60.1	17.1	53.7 / 15.2	38.5	45.3 / 35.3	10.0 (11–60 ha)	1.0 (> 60 ha)	39.9	16.0
"Prussian" Poland	57.7[b]	42.3[c]	69.6[d] / 53.8	15.8	30.0 / 25.0	5.0	0.4	> 65.0	
Congress Poland	58.0	17.0	65.0 / 25.0	40.0	35.0 / 33.0	2.0	—	17.0	—
Croatia-Slavonia	78.8	9.0	41.5		57.5		1.0	11.2	8.0
Slovenia	70.1	15.0	54.4 / 33.2	21.2	34.9 / 18.1	16.8	10.7	14.3	13.2
Slovakia	68.0	16.3	76.4 / 52.0 (up to 3 ha)	24.4 (3–6 ha)	23.1 / 16.2 (6–12 ha)	6.9 (12–60 ha)	0.5 (> 60 ha)	32.5	15.1
Galicia	79.8	9.5	83.4 / 49.8	33.6	15.6 / 14.6	1.0	1.0	12.6	37.2
Subcarpathian Rus'	93.6	3.4	77.7 / 54.7	23.0	22.3			22.6	42.3
Serbia	84.0	7.5	53.1 / 19.5 (up to 3 ha)	33.6	41.4 / 27.5 (4–10 ha)	13.9	5.5	10.0	
Transylvania	86.3	7.8	72.0 (up to 3 ha)		28.0 (4–10 ha)		—	29.1	19.4

Note: Ha. = hectares. In all of these countries, small industry predominated, taking up most of the industrial labor force. The categories "agriculture" and "industry" do not add up to 100 percent, owing to the omission of "commerce and trade" ("Prussian" Poland is an exception).

[a] The data on the rural proletariat are compiled from diverse sources, some published before World War II by conservatively inclined economists, some others (more recently) by Marxist historians in East Central Europe, who sometimes inflate the figures on landless agricultural labor in the region by applying very broad definitions of the "proletariat" that include rural artisans, craftsmen, or even small landholders. For Congress Poland I found no data on the agrarian "semiproletariat".

[b] Figures include both Polish and German population. It should be kept in mind, however, that although the Poles predominated on the land, the Germans prevailed in the cities.

[c] With transportation and trade.

[d] The distribution includes only Polish-owned land.

Source: Polish Encyclopaedia, s.v. "Economic Life of Poland" 3.52–3, 55–7, 250, 404; *Gospodarska in Družbena Zgodovina Slovencev* (Ljubljana, 1970), 170–9; Robert Magocsi, *The Shaping of a National Identity: Subcarpathian Rus', 1848–1948* (Cambridge, Mass.: 1978), 16–17; Ladislav Tajtak, "Slovak Emigration and Migration in the Years 1900–1914," *Studia Historica Slovaca* 10 (1978), 46–8; Władysław Grabski, *Materyaływ Sprawie Włościańskiej* (Warsaw, 1907), vol. 1, T.I, pt. 2, 3–7; Istvan Berend and Gyorgi Ranki, *Hungary: A Century of Economic Development* (New York, 1974), 74–8, and *Underdevelopment and Economic Growth: Studies in Hungarian Social and Economic History* (Budapest, 1979), 91–2; Tibor Kolossa, "The Social Structure of the Peasant Class in Austro-Hungary: Statistical Sources and Methods," *East European Quarterly,* (January, 1970), 420–37; Anna Zarnowska, *Klasa Robotnicza Krolestwa Polskiego, 1870–1914* (Warsaw, 1974), 65; Zanna Kormanowa and Irena Pietrzak-Pawłowska, eds., *Historia Polski* (Warsaw, 1963), vol. 3, pt. 1 (1864–1900), 108–9, 193–5, 531–4, 562–7; Ion Aluas, "Industrialization and Migration of the Transylvanian Peasantry at the End of the Nineteenth Century and the Beginning of the Twentieth Century," *East European Quarterly* (January 1970), 504–5; Celina Bobińska and Andrzej Pilch, eds., *Mechanizmy Polskich Migracji Zarobkowych* (Warsaw, 1976), 55, 63, 72; Toussaint Hočevar, *The Structure of the Slovenian Economy, 1848–1963* (New York, 1965), 86–8; Elzbieta Kaczyńska, *Dzieje Robotnikow Przemysłowych w Polsce Pod Zaborami* (Warsaw, 1970); W. P. Kopczak and S. I. Kopczak, *Naseljenje Zakarpatja za 100 Let* (Lvov, 1977), 16–17; Irena Kostrowicka, Zbigniew Landau, and Jerzy Tomaszewski, *Historia Gospodarcza Polski XIX i XX Wieku* (Warsaw, 1978), 175, 237; Witold Nowosz, "Tradycjne Gospodarstwo Chłopskie i Jego Przemiany," *Prace i Materiały Muzeum Archeologii i Etnografii w Łodzi* I (1976), 110; Władysław Rusiński, "The Role of the Peasantry of Poznan (Wielkopolska) in the Formation of the Non-Agricultural Labor Market," *East European Quarterly* (January 1970), 521–2, Istvan Racz, "Emigration from Hungary to the United States," *Magyar Trteneti Tanulmanyok* 10 (1977), 117–56; Ervin Pamlenyi, ed., *Social-Economic Researches on the History of East Central Europe* (Budapest, 1970), 55–65; Igor Karaman, *Privreda i Društvo Hrvatske u 19. Stoljecu* (Zagreb, 1972), 175–86; Vladimir Dedijer, Ivan Božić, Siena Cinković, et al., *History of Yugoslavia* (New York, 1974), 358–65; Michael Petrovich, *A History of Modern Serbia, 1804–1918* (New York, 1976), 2:527; R. W. Seton-Watson, *The Southern Slav Question and the Habsburg Monarchy* (London, 1911), 389; Doreen Warriner, ed., *Contrasts in Emerging Societies: Readings in the Social and Economic History of South-Eastern Europe in the 19th Century* (Bloomington, Ind.: 1965), 307, 328, 354, 360–1; Ivan Kolomiets, *Sotsial'no-Ekonomitcheskie Otnoszenii v Zakarpatie vo Vtoroj Polovine XIX Veka* (Tomsk, 1962), 2 vols, and *Ocherki po Istorii Zakarpat'ia* (Tomsk, 1953); Oscar Jászi, *The Dissolution of the Habsburg Monarchy* (London, 1929), 279; C. A. Macartney, *The Habsburg Empire, 1790–1918* (London, 1968), 704–5; Jan Svetoň, *Obyvatel'stvo Slovenska za Kapitalizmu* (Bratislava, 1958), 66, 73, 76; Istvan Barta, ed., *A History of Hungary* (New York, 1973); B. Il'ko, *Zakarpatske Selo na Pocatku XXst.* (Lvov, 1973), 115–22.

crements of the "economic density" in the rural parts of the region in the last decades of the nineteenth century and the fast demographic growth that could not be readily absorbed locally were the primary contributing factors to the huge and unceasing migratory movements of the peasants, whose paths crisscrossed in all directions: within the provinces of East Central Europe; between them, inside the region; far outside to western Europe; and yet farther still, across the Atlantic.

The colossal dimensions of these migratory movements that had been sweeping through all of East Central Europe were evidenced in reports from virtually all quarters of the region, indicating that at the beginning of the twentieth century no less than one-third of the adult agrarian population of the vast territory covering Hungary proper, Slovakia, all of Poland, the western part of the Ukraine, Subcarpathian Rus', Transylvania, Croatia-Slavonia, northern Serbia, and Slovenia had lived or worked in places different from those of their birth.[13]

Poor and insufficient records preclude accurate assessment of the numerical size of peasant migrations around and outside of East Central Europe in the last decades of the nineteenth century and in the years preceding the outbreak of World War I. Historical demographers, however, offer some gross evaluations of the size of migrations directed outside of the region between 1860–70 and 1914, covering both permanent and seasonal movements. Their estimates show that the combined migrations from all Polish territories affected about 9 million people. Of this number, a total of 3.5 million migrated from the Prussian part (this figure also includes a significant number of Germans); about 3 million from Galicia and approximately 2.5 million from Congress Poland.[14] In Hungary in the same period, an estimated total of about 6 million people migrated from their permanent residences, either in seasonal movements to western Europe or in journeys across the ocean.[15] In only six years, from 1906 to 1911, nearly 3 million people migrated from Austrian territories across the continent at the astonishing rate of almost 500,000 annually.[16]

These estimates do not include the movements within and among particular regions of East Central Europe: between Hungary's several provinces; in and around the three segments of Poland; and among all of these areas. It is estimated, however, that systematic underreporting in the official statistics of continuous migrations between adjacent areas deflated the actual number of seasonal migrants by as much as 60 to 100 percent, and in borderline areas, where crossing was particularly intense, by 200 to 250 percent.[17]

The migratory movements of the rural population in this region in the last decades before World War I can be classified in three major categories: (1) rural (from farm to farm, including both local and long-distance movements); (2) rural-urban (from farms to cities and industries); and (3) transoceanic, to the United States, Canada, Brazil, Argentina, or other parts of the New World.[18]

Into the first category, the earliest chronologically, fall the traditional short- and medium-distance migrations that, during the times of sowing, plowing, harvesting, threshing, rafting, and grazing, regularly moved very large numbers of peasants from county to county or over the mountains to neighboring regions. In one fairly typical village in western Galicia investigated in the summer of 1900, of the total number (107) of young adults born between 1875 and 1880, over 40 percent were temporarily gone. Most of those who had left stayed in relatively close proximity. About one-fifth moved farther away to farms in eastern Galicia, Hungary, and Austria.[19] Intensive migrations between villages, started soon after the abolition of serfdom, also occurred on the southern slopes of the Carpathian mountains in Slovakia and farther down in Hungary and Transylvania.[20] For instance, as calculated from local Transylvanian sources, "between 1870 and 1890, the three sheep-raising villages of Gales, Saćel and Sibiel gained between 20 and 40 percent of their shepherds through migration. Most of the newcomers arrived from villages within a fifteen-kilometer radius."[21]

With the passage of time, annual migrations to farms in more distant provinces became increasingly more common than moving to a nearby manor or hiring oneself out for a season to a better-off farmer in an adjacent village. The crisscrossing migrant traffic within East Central Europe reached huge proportions after the opening of the Prussian border in 1890. From Galicia, and particularly from Congress Poland, thousands of peasants (about 50,000 every year) – *bandosi*, as they were called – migrated into Prussia and hired themselves out for the season as farm laborers. In fact, by 1900 this movement reached what the official sources considered to be "alarming proportions."[22] From western Galicia, the Polish and Rusyn peasants also moved in the opposite direction, to eastern parts of the province: The West Galician census for 1890 reported that there were in the Ukraine over 60,000 residents from western Galicia, and by 1900 their number increased to about 100,000. From Subcarpathia, people traveled to work in Slovakia, Hungary, and Transylvania.[23] Meanwhile, in other parts of the region, the Croatians migrated to the Slovene farmlands; the Serbs moved into Croatia; and every year the Slovene peasants went to work in the Croatian vineyards and to lower Austria to labor on the farms.[24] Thousands of Slovaks also migrated to Austria, leaving their villages in early spring and staying until late autumn. In 1910 alone, about 300,000 people from Hungary were found working in Austria; of those, one-third were Slovaks.[25] In the same year, lower and upper Austria provided employment for nearly 200,000 Galicians, the majority of whom worked on farms.[26] Lowland Hungary also attracted thousands of peasant laborers from Galicia, Slovakia, the Carpathian mountains, Croatia, and Serbia. In 1910 alone, there were in Hungary proper about one-half million people born in Croatia-Slavonia, Slovakia, Poland, and Transylvania, many of whom worked in the fields of Hungarian farmers. Every year "they set off in groups; some went to the same farmer every year whereas others, after arriving [in Hungary], stopped at a nearby tavern where the Hungarian farmers came and hired them . . . They went there for the harvest, starting in late June . . . The poorer folks went on foot [better-off farmers drove in carriages] to help to dig potatoes, work in the vineyards, pick corn, and plant tobacco." They returned home late in the fall.[27]

Far greater numbers of the peasants, however, migrated to Germany as seasonal farmhands. The 1907 German census recorded over 1.5 million from Poznania, Silesia, and eastern and western Prussia as residing in Westphalia, the Rhine provinces, and the Berlin-Brandenburg district. A significant proportion of them were ethnic Germans, many of whom had migrated permanently. But among the more than 30 percent of these "foreigners" who were found employed in agriculture, there were also a large number of Slavic peasant-migrants. In 1910, well over 1 million seasonal foreign workers were reported in Germany. From Galicia alone, the numbers of *Sachsengänger* – Polish and Rusyn agricultural laborers – who made annual migrations to Germany reached 300,000 at the beginning of the century. The numbers for Congress Poland were about 300,000, and for Slovakia about 150,000.[28] The overwhelming majority of these peasant-workers – as many as 90 percent, according to some contemporary estimates – returned home each year and set off again the following spring.[29]

The movements of peasants to cities and industries constituted the second form of migration. The urbanization and industrialization of East Central Europe lagged behind that of the western part of the continent by more than half a century. In the last quarter of the nineteenth century, however, both processes accelerated. The rate of the transformation was not, however, uniform throughout the region: Some parts of East Central Europe developed more rapidly than others. Data concerning the growth of the urban population and of the industrial labor force in particular provinces between 1870–90 and 1910–13 are given in Tables 1.2 and 1.3. Hungary, Congress and "Prussian" Poland, and to some extent also Slovakia and Slovenia were more advanced in capitalist transformation than other parts of the region. More centrally located, they possessed well-developed transportation systems and easier access to the expanding markets of Austria and western Europe, on the one hand, and Russia on the other. During the last third of the nineteenth century, the national income of Hungary steadily increased at an annual rate of over 3 percent – quite an impressive average in this part of the continent. In fact, by the turn of the century the "takeoff" stage of Hungary's capitalist adaptation was practically completed. Next came Congress Poland, where the opening up after 1864 of the vast markets of the Russian Empire to Polish products accelerated the growth of national income to a respectable 2.5 percent annually.[30] The capitalist development of the "Prussian" part of Poland proceeded unevenly in its different provinces. Upper Silesia, with its mining and heavy industry, was leading the way, and Poznania came second, but the urbanization and industrialization processes in other quarters progressed at a much slower rate.[31] Slovakia, with its supply of natural resources and well-established markets, had also been developing steadily. In 1910, nearly one-fifth of all of the industries in Hungary were located on Slovak territory, and they produced a similar proportion of the total Hungarian industrial output.[32] Finally, Slovenia, with its traditionally close economic ties with neighboring Austria, relatively developed agrarian markets, and the expansion of specialized industries, particularly wood, construction, and building was also progressing at a steady rate. A general increase of about 50 percent in the number of industries in Slovenia during the first decade of this century compared with a similar increase in Cisleithan Austria in the same period.[33]

On the other hand, the eastern parts of the Austro-Hungarian Empire and Serbia were less advanced economically. Transylvania's oil industry, its major resource, expanded substantially during the twenty-five years preceding World War I, but urbanization had not been significant, and a large majority of the population still remained in rural areas. The rate of urbanization and industrial development of Subcarpathian Rus', Galicia, Croatia, and Serbia fell significantly behind that of their northern neighbors.[34] These regional differences

Table 1.2. *Growth of urban population in East Central Europe, 1870–1880 to 1910*

Country	Growth of Population in the Cities (N)[a]				Growth of Urban Population (%)	Urban Population as % of Total		
Hungary (Proper)	1870: 1,536,108	1890: 2,195,919	1900: 2,793,776	1910: 3,151,355	1870–1910: 105.0	1890: 9.8	1900: 17.0	1910: 23.0
Slovakia	1870: 259,370	1890: 314,035	1900: 359,460	1910: 406,175	1870–1910: 56.6	1880: 11.0	1900: 12.9	1910: 12.9
Croatia-Slavonia	1869: 114,718	1890: 152,982	1900: 185,720		1869–1900: 61.9	1869: 6.2	1890: 7.0	1900: 7.7
Transylvania	1879: 209,786	1890: 260,302	1900: 314,859	1910: 366,637	1879–1910: 74.8	1879: 9.7	1890: 11.5	1910: 12.7
Slovenia	1869: 280,926			1910: 526,179	1869–1910: 87.3	1869: 20.1	1890: 23.2	1910: 30.1
Congress Poland	1872: 1,058,000	1897: 2,378,000		1909: 3,943,000	1872–1909: 272.7	1875: 16.2	1897: 26.9	1909: 33.0
Galicia	1878: 943,000		1900: 1,320,000	1910: 1,595,000	1878–1910: 69.0	1878: 15.9	1900: 18.0	1910: 19.9
Prussian Poland		1890: 2,671,682	1900: 3,210,981	1910: 3,795,488	1890–1910: 42.2	1900: 31.4		1910: 41.9
Poznania						32.8		35.0
Pomerania						29.2		33.3
Upper Silesia						50.6		57.5

Note: The data in this table and also in Table 1.3 were not compiled from original sources but from available present-day historical studies. Since it was not possible to cross-match the exact comparable information for particular countries, the table contains some unavoidable "gaps." The East Central European authors of the studies that served as the basis for this compilation all warn against treating the nineteenth-century official statistics of Russia, Austria-Hungary, and Prussia other than as mere rough estimates: Registrars of a number of cities did not specify "permanent" and "temporary" residents, and many of them did not include short-term migrants.

[a] Figures in this column are based on calculations including as "urban" places that were so only nominally. In fact, by 1900 there were in Hungary, for instance, only 45 cities with a population over 20,000; in Congress Poland, 40; in Galicia, no more than 15; in Slovakia, 3.

Source: Istvan Berend and Gyorgi Ránki, *Underdevelopment and Economic Growth: Studies in Hungarian Social and Economic History* (Budapest, 1979), 84, 96; and *Hungary: A Century of Economic Development* (New York, 1974), 62–3; Vladimir Dedijer, Ivan Božić, Sima Cirković, et al., *History of Yugoslavia* (New York, 1974), 358–63; Toussaint Hočevar, *The Structure of the Slovenian Economy, 1848–1963* (New York, 1965), 88–9, 45–8; *Gospodarska i Družbena Zgodovina Slovencev* (Lubljana, 1970), 109; Igor Karaman, *Privreda i Društvo Hrvatska w 19. Stoljecu* (Zagreb, 1972), 316–19; Juliana Puskás, *From Hungary to the United States, 1880–1914* (Budapest 1982), 51–3; Ladislas Tajtak, "Slovak Emigration and Migration in the Years 1900–1914," *Studia Historica Slovaca* 10 (1978), 46, 60; Ion Aluas, "Industrialization and Migration of the Transylvanian Peasantry at the End of the Nineteenth and the Beginning of the Twentieth Century," *East European Quarterly* (January, 1970). 502–4; Wojciech Saryusz-Zaleski, *Dzieje Przemystu w B. Galicji, 1804–1929* (Krakow, 1930), 196; Jerzy Topolski, ed., *Dzieje Polski* (Warsaw, 1978), 160–1; Zanna Kormanowa and Irena Pietrzak-Pawłowska, eds., *Historia Polski* (Warsaw, 1963), vol. 3, pt. 1 (1864–1900), 217–21, 406, 641–52; Anna Zarnowska, *Klasa Robotnicza Królestwa Polskiego, 1870–1914* (Warsaw, 1974), 17–20, 33, 48; Władysław Rusiński, "The Role of the Peasantry of Poznan (Wielkopolska) in the Formation of the Non-Agricultural Labor Market," *East European Quarterly* (January 1970) 520–1; Ireneusz Ihnatowicz, Antoni Mączak, and Benedykt Zientara, eds., *Społeczeństvo Polskie od X do XX Wieku* (Warsaw, 1979), 459–60; Caroline Golab, *Immigrant Destinations* (Philadelphia, 1977), 91–4; Jan Svetoh, *Obyvatl'stvo Slovenska za Kapitalizmu* (Bratislava, 1958), 185–7; *Polish Encyclopaedia,* s. v., "Economic Life of Poland," 3:108, 114–15, 263, 377, 418–19, 539; *Preussische Statistik* (22),121, "Die endgültige Ergebnisse der Volszählung und Volksbeschreibung in preussischen Staate vom 1. Dezember 1910" (Berlin, 1913); *Statisticki Godišnjak Kraljevine Hrvatske i Slavonije,* 1905 vol. 1: *Kraljevski Zemaljski Statisticki Ured* (Zagreb, 1913), 4: *Magyarország Története* (Budapest, 1978), vol. 6, pt. 2, pp. 1138–9; vol. 7, pt. 1, pp. 405–7.

Table 1.3. *Growth of industrial labor force in East Central Europe, 1880–1890 to 1910–1913*

Country		(N)			Growth (%)
Hungary (Proper)					
	1880	1890	1900	1910	1880–1910
Total industry	400,000	488,000	718,000	978,000	144.5
Manufacturing	110,000	165,000	320,000	510,000	363.6
Slovakia					
			1898	1913	1898–1913
Total industry			237,000	284,155	19.9
Manufacturing			110,547	152,023	37.5
Croatia-Slavonia					
		1890	1900	1910	1890–1910
Total industry		9,892	18,799	23,604	138.6
Transylvania					
		1890	1900	1910	1890–1910
Total industry (estimate)		86,500	114,633	159,508	84.4
Slovenia					
	1852			1912	1852–1912
Total Industry	29,290			78,563	168.2
Manufacturing	6,633			36,230	446.2
Congress Poland					
		1893	1900	1913	1893–1913
Total industry		400,000	600,000	850,000	112.5
Manufacturing		150,365	202,126	400,000	166.0
Galicia					
			1902	1910	1902–10
Total industry			336,000	438,000	30.4
Manufacturing			73,150	91,500	25.1
All Prussian Poland					
		1895	1907		1895–1907
Total industry		586,217	782,498		33.5
Manufacturing		168,500	450,861		167.6
Poznania					
Total industry		131,000	221,591		69.2
Manufacturing		28,000	109,044		289.5
Pomerania					
Total industry		117,000	204,124		75.5
Manufacturing		31,500	112,094		255.9
Upper Silesia					
Total industry		248,000	256,788		3.5
Manufacturing		109,000	229,186		110.3

Table 1.3. (*cont.*)

Note: For gaps in table, see note to Table 1.2.

Not all industrial statistics for particular countries distinguished between two types of "industrial labor": the one *sensu stricto* employed in manufacturing (and mining), and the category of small artisans and craftsmen. East Central European historians also point to the fact that a not insignificant part of the registered increase in the size of the industrial labor force in particular countries was the result of gradual improvement in statistical data collection toward the end of the nineteenth century and between 1900 and 1910. The figures concerning handicrafts in Congress Poland are only approximate, since the last census before World War I that specified this category was that of 1897.

Source: Same as for Table 1.2.

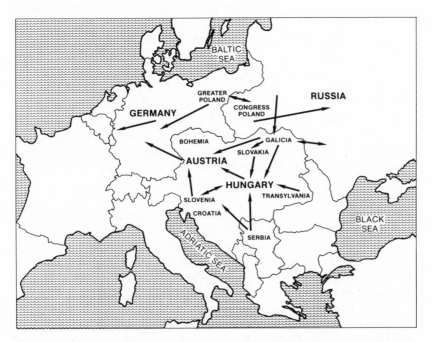

Map A. East Central Europe (about 1900): seasonal migratory movements of peasantry.

in the rate of postfeudal transformations played a role in fashioning the general direction of peasant migrations within the region. The paths of seasonal migrations of East Central European peasants at the turn of the century are shown on Map A.

Although the rates of industrial development were markedly different throughout the region, the basic characteristics of the process were similar. The most pronounced characteristic was the predominance of small-scale, dispersed industries. In fact, the accelerated capitalist growth in East Central Europe in the last quarter of the nineteenth century expressed itself precisely in the expansion of small industry. In Hungary, for instance, which ranked among the most industrially advanced countries in the whole region, in the 1880s over 70 percent of the urban labor force was employed in small craft industries. By 1910, this proportion had decreased to 50 percent.[35] The proportion of workers employed in small enterprises in Slovakia and Congress Poland at the turn of the century was similar.[36] In Galicia, as in the "Prussian" part of Poland and in Croatia-Slavonia, in the first decade of this century small handicraft establishments employing one to ten people still accounted for about 70 percent of all of the industrial labor force.[37] In Subcarpathian Rus', the percentage of workers employed in larger-scale industry – mostly in wood processing – was less than 1 percent.[38]

Although still in its infancy and constrained by a lack of capital and technology, industrial expansion in East Central Europe in the last decades preceding World War I nevertheless provided employment opportunities much needed by the rapidly growing population. At the turn of the century the bulk of the East Central European industrial proletariat were seasonal laborers – the *peasant-workers* who circulated between the countryside and the cities. This fluctuating element was a distinctive characteristic of the region's capitalist development.

It is impossible, again, to assess the exact size of this massive movement between the villages and the expanding industrial centers. A Polish historian estimates the total number of migrants moving into Polish cities in all three partition areas between 1870 and 1914 at approximately 4 million.[39] Inspection of the available employment records of factory workers in various urban centers in the region indicates that, on the average, a proportion variously estimated as one-half to more than two-thirds came from the villages. The latter estimate seems the more accurate one, since the local industrial statistics often left unrecorded large numbers of unskilled seasonal laborers.[40] For instance, during the 1880s, between 60 and 70 percent of the industrial labor force/urban dwellers in the industrial districts of both Warsaw and Lódz and in the Dąbrowa mining region were recruited from among seasonal peasant-migrants. By the outbreak of World War I, only about one-half of the whole industrial labor force in Congress Poland was "autorecruited" – that is, came from the the working-class/urban milieu.[41] The dependence on rural migrants in industrially more advanced Silesia was only 25 percent in 1900, but it had remained the prevailing pattern in the dispersed, small-scale industries of Galicia, Croatia, and Slovenia.[42]

Peasants who came to work in the cities usually spent six to eight months a year there. In the spring and summer, they abandoned their factory jobs and returned home to work in the fields. Thousands of such seasonal industrial laborers crowded into the suburban "industrial villages" that sprang up around the cities, where they maintained their village customs and life-styles. Many an urban center in East Central Europe in the last decades of the previous century grew by incorporating the expanding industrial suburbs inhabited by peasant migrants.[43] The process of urbanization was thus accompanied by a parallel "ruralization" of the cities, to which the peasant-migrant inhabitants added a distinctly rural aura and outlook.

By the turn of the century, the peasant-workers from all over East Central Europe were migrating not only to towns and cities located in the vicinity of their native villages but to more distant urban centers, first within the same province and country and then to other East Central European regions where industry was more advanced and employment prospects better. By 1860, in the Ostrava-Karwin district, over 75 percent of the industrial labor force came originally from within a distance of thirty miles; by 1880, the proportion was less than 40 percent.[44] At the turn of the century, besides the local Slovaks, Germans, and Czechs, over 80,000 workers from Galicia were employed in the mines and at the forges of that district. In 1901, Galicians – Poles and Rusyns (Ukrainians) – constituted about 31 percent of the total number of miners and 39 percent of those employed in the coking plants.[45] Galician villages also routinely sent out masons, bricklayers, and carpenters for seasonal work. A 1911 study of Maszkienice indicated that over 40 percent of all male absentees in that year worked as carpenters and masons, over one-fourth in the Ostrava region and one-fifth within Galicia. In the same year, in the nearby village of Jadowniki, 75 percent of all seasonal migrants were employed as masons and bricklayers; the majority of them found work in nearby cities, but some moved farther away into the industrial centers of Austria.[46] In 1910, the industries in Cisleithania and Austrian Silesia reported nearly 150,000 laborers from Galicia. The majority, about 60 percent, came in a chain migration from the five western counties of Bochnia, Bielsko, Wieliczka, Wadowice, and Zywiec.[47]

Slovaks, Slovenes, and Croatians regularly migrated to Graz, Leoben, and Judenburg, the industrial centers in lowland Austria. Industrial employment in Austria also attracted Hungarians. Between 1860 and 1900 the number of Magyar workers in Austrian cities grew sixfold, from 53,000 to 324,000.[48] Peasant workers from southern parts of Congress Poland and from Galicia also migrated into Silesia, where they worked in the mines. When in 1885 the local German administration ordered the deportation of aliens, about two-thirds of the people removed from the Katowitz district were found to be Galicians.[49] During the same period, migrants from Silesia and Galicia arrived in the industrial centers of Congress Poland. For instance, in the last quarter of the nineteenth century, foreigners constituted from 50 to 70 percent of the total labor force in the mines and forges of the Dąbrowa Basin: Half of them were Silesians; another 40 percent were Rusyns and Poles from Galicia.[50]

Farther south, the factories of Budapest and the industries located in the district of Pest-Pilis in Hungary attracted thousands of peasant-workers from the whole region. In the three decades from 1880 to 1910, nearly 400,000 people migrated to Budapest from all corners of East Central Europe.[51] For instance, in 1910 alone there were over 30,000 Poles and Rusyns from Galicia and probably more than 50,000 Serbs and Croatians in the city of Budapest.[52] During the same period, the census takers found over 90,000 people who were born in Slovakia living in Budapest. The same census report showed more than 150,000 Slovak workers in other cities and towns of Hungary.[53] A great number of these were seasonal migrants:

> In the Liptov Valley [Slovakia] . . . peasants regularly performed additional work. The most common was masonry. The masons left work for Budapest at the beginning of April and returned home in November. At the beginning of the . . . century this work ended in Budapest, and the Liptov masons [began to] migrate mostly to the neighboring districts, to Turec, Orava, Spis, and some went to Kosice and Miskovec. Beside masons and carpenters, there were among the Liptov peasants many loggers who worked at hewing and splitting wood, rafting it for railroad construction to Komarno and . . . even to Budapest.[54]

The migrant peasant-workers also ventured to more remote industrial centers in western Germany. Of the more than 1.5 million workers from eastern parts of Germany reported in 1907 as residents of the Rhineland-Westphalia and Berlin-Brandenburg provinces, nearly 60 percent were employed in industry. For instance, more than two-thirds of the 450,000 Poles recorded in Rhineland-Westphalia in 1912 worked in the mines.[55]

The third form of mass migration of East Central European peasants during the thirty years preceding the First World War was trans-oceanic migration. Between 85 and 95 percent of all East Central Europeans leaving the continent headed to the United States. The social and cultural mechanism of this exodus will be discussed in the following chapter. Let us here conclude the review of the continental migrations of peasants with a brief summary of the American one. In some regions, travel to the United States had by the turn of the century almost completely supplanted movement across East Central Europe and to the western parts of the continent. In others, all three kinds of migration continued until 1914. They fluctuated in size and direction, depending on current economic conditions in Europe and the United States.

According to estimates based on European seaport statistics, in the period between 1870–1 and 1913–14, between 11 and 12 million passengers from East Central Europe crossed the Atlantic.[56] Recent calculations by American as well as eastern European historians indicate that the return rate of Slavs and Magyars was about 35 percent in that period.[57] However, a number of those who returned often traveled again. For instance, a study of re-emigration conducted in a Galician village reported that out of the total number of returnees before World War I, 34.5 percent traveled to America more than once: 20.7 percent went twice, and 13.8 percent went three times.[58] In another village in that region, where overseas emigration started only after 1890, 20 percent were "two-timers."[59] Similar results were reported in a study conducted in the Białystok region in northern Poland, according to which nearly 40 percent of re-emigrants stated that they had crossed the Atlantic more than once.[60]

And so, excluding a few pockets in the most isolated areas, by the turn of the century it was the exception rather than the rule for East Central European peasants to have spent all their lives involved solely in agriculture and staying put in their native villages. With thousands of migrating peasants coming and going every year, passing through towns and villages, the traffic back and forth between the East Central European countryside and America had become a culmination of sorts, the ultimate expression of the already intense and widespread pattern of mobility that characterized the East Central European peasantry in that period.

The migrant peasant-workers were a significant element in the gradual transformation of the old sociocultural system. They were the "diffusion agents" who introduced and spread new trends in village life throughout the whole region. Just as the old economic system was undergoing slow transformation from feudalism to capitalism, the traditional cultural patterns of the peasant societies were changing. The flux of old and new elements began to rearrange themselves into a new cultural configuration.

In the traditional feudal society, peasants were hardly exposed to the money economy, since most of their obligations were paid in kind and labor.[61] The old peasant economy was practically self-sufficient, with almost all products homemade. "In the world of serfdom," noted a Hungarian memorist, grandson of a serf, "there was, truth to tell, no real need for money."[62] After emancipation, however, peasants needed money for "redemption payments, to carry them over a poor harvest, to improve their farms and to buy or rent more land. They needed money, too, for less material reasons such as to pay for a wedding or a funeral, events for which family pride demanded the greatest possible expenditure."[63] And so money – a new kind of value in peasant life – grew in importance as the capitalist economy slowly penetrated the rural communities.

To assist the emancipated peasants in purchasing land and paying mortgages, financial institutions such as agrarian banks, rural cooperatives, credit agencies, and loan associations mushroomed in all provinces of East Central Europe. In the twenty-five years before World War I, their number, in particular regions, grew on the average by 500 percent. Hundreds of thousands of peasants participated, and through this new form of activity they became further enmeshed in the cash nexus.[64]

The agricultural credit and loan associations, however, generally preferred only the most credit-worthy borrowers. Small landholders and landless peasants were often forced to turn for credit to innkeepers, Jewish merchants, the local clergy, or estate owners – moneylenders who charged their customers interest rates much higher than the 6 to 10 percent charged by the peasant banks. The rates charged by private lenders varied greatly from region to region, ranging from 15 to 30 percent in Slovenia, up to 40 percent in Galicia, and 50 percent in Subcarpathian Rus', whereas in Hungary and Transylvania interest of 100 percent was said not to have been uncommon.[65]

The process of contracting for and servicing debt quickly acquainted East European peasants with money operations. As a Hungarian *föispán*, or county administrator, explained in his annual report in 1904, the indebtedness of peasant households was so widespread and chronic that it was necessary to temporarily suspend the collection of taxes in his area because so many indebted families were unable to pay them. In 1911, the average indebtedness of peasant households in the Galician village of Maszkienice was reported as 600 kronen ($120).[66]

But the most spectacular impact of money on the peasants' household economy, and with it on their behavior and attitudes, came with seasonal migrations. In 1900, the Warsaw Statistical Committee published a report indicating that seasonal migrants from Congress Poland to Germany had returned in that year alone with a total sum of nearly 8 million rubles ($4 million; $1 = 2 rubles). In 1901, the sum brought into the country by seasonal workers returning from Germany increased to 9 million rubles and by 1904 it was already 11,425,174 rubles.[67] A study conducted in 1899 in a Galician village revealed that in that one year alone returning seasonal workers, male and female, brought home more than 28,000 kronen ($5,600; $1 = 5 kronen), which exceeded the total net income from the village's local farm production by 20 percent. In 1911, the amount of money that came to the same village from continental migrations more than tripled, reaching 90,000 kronen. The average amount saved by peasant families from their earnings from that year's migration amounted to about 1,000 kronen ($200) per household.[68] Another contemporary investigation of peasant family budgets in seven villages in the Galician county of Ropczyce during the period 1902–7 estimated that the total sum of money earned by the inhabitants from seasonal migrations in these six years was 1,695,651 kronen.[69] Although not all of the villages in the region relied so heavily on income from seasonal migration, certainly most of them had by 1900 become irreversibly tied into the money economy. For thousands of rural households the money earned from seasonal migration could hardly be called an "additional" source of income. Instead it had come to constitute a permanent element in the existence of peasant families.

The economic ethos of peasant societies in East Central Europe admitted not only that wealth was good, but also and increasingly that it was possible, as well as rewarding, to accumulate cash reserves – the more, the better. But although money, in the form of income and wages, had already become the sine qua non ingredient of the majority of rural household economies, the peasants' perceptions and handling of it retained important elements of the earlier, traditional attitude. The peasant, observed Thomas and Znaniecki, felt money to be worth seeking after either so that it could be "treasured up, stashed away in the coffers as an 'investment' of sorts" (a passive, precapitalist form), or else – the midway point toward a modern capitalist attitude – as a "substitute for other kinds of property": first and most important, land, but also for the goods it could eventually buy – articles of personal as well as collective consumption (fine dress, good food and drink, amusement, and music at baptisms and wedding celebrations). However, the authors point out, the money was not seen and valued as a "reproducer," which is its principal function in a capitalist system. In that system, it is sought after not as a concrete object to be possessed for itself, but as a value *ex definitione* meant to expand and to bring profit. The money earned and brought home from the outside was seen by the peasant as distinct from the farm income (the traditional basis of living of the rural household) and often kept separately.[70]

It was toward the former category – the more fluid one – that the quantifying, calculative attitude was developing most quickly. This orientation solidified first among the landless peasants whose livelihood came entirely from sources other than farm and farm-derived income. But nowhere did the old attitudes remain more in force than with regard to land, and to an extent also to land income.

The peasants' entry into the orbit of the monetary system and the presence of cash income and wages as permanent additions to the traditional peasant economy opened up avenues into their minds for new quantitative economic thinking. Property, not liquid assets, had nevertheless remained the primary measure of the socioeconomic position of the family or the individual in the village. The peasant perception of land retained its essentially qualitative character and continued basically unmarred by economic calculation: "In the consciousness of the peasant who pays absurd prices for a piece of land," wrote Thomas and Znaniecki, "there is no equivalence possible for land and any other economic value; they are incommensurable with each other. Land is unique value; and no sum of money can be too large to pay for it."[71]

In the traditional peasant society, work had been perceived as the attribute of human existence. It was a value in and of itself; its mere quality bore little or no relation to its practical function. Peasants did not work to obtain good results; they worked because "Covek mora da radi": Man must work. This Serbian saying had its counterpart in each and every corner of East Central Europe. Under the feudal system the "peasant-serfs did not care whether their compulsory work for the lord was efficient or not." Religion only strengthened the peasants' attitude toward work as an obligatory task: "Man has to work," stated one of the commandments most often repeated from the pulpits in village churches; "it is a curse, but also his duty; the process of working is meritorious, laziness is bad, independent of any results."[72] There was a certain mystical fatalism in the traditional peasants' acceptance of work, with all its monotony and hardship; they viewed it as part of the universal cosmic order of which they were an element. Whatever befell them in their wearisome toiling, be it joy and success or misery and failure, they felt that it was not the result of their own work and effort, or of their negligence, but of luck or of God's help or the devil's plotting. The patient and enduring work of a good Christian might sometimes predispose God favorably toward one – but only if He wished it so. When misfortune struck, however, the peasants started their toilsome plodding again with resigned but unrelenting perseverance.

With the end of serfdom and of the relative isolation of the village, the migration of thousands of peasants across half the continent in search of work and pay altered the old attitude toward work. New ways of looking at and valuing work came to exist alongside the old ones. Thomas and Znaniecki note that peasants who worked as seasonal laborers on farms in Germany or Austria were willing to do as much work as possible and put into it the greatest effort required in order to maximize their earnings but that they refused to behave in the same way on the farms back home. The authors explain this phenomenon by pointing to the difference in the social environment and motivation of the peasant-workers in these two circumstances:

> The peasant who stays at home [and works on an estate] preserves for the time being his old attitude toward work as a "necessary evil" and this attitude, under the influence of traditional ideas . . . produces the nonwillingness to accept piece-work. [On the contrary,] the peasant who goes to Germany is led there by the desire [to maximize his earnings,] and this attitude predominates during the whole period of season work not on account of the conditions themselves, but through the feeling of being in definite new conditions, and produces the desire to earn more by piece-work.[73]

Once the peasants discovered that work could produce money – that it brought practical, quantifiable results – it gradually began to assume a new meaning that entered their thinking alongside the old traditional attitudes. On the one hand, then, they increasingly perceived their work to have functional value, bringing rewards in at least some proportion to the invested effort. First, in their search for income they tried to obtain more money for the same unit of work, but once they realized that they could augment their wages by performing more and harder work, they searched for opportunities to earn the maximal amount of income. On the other hand, however, the peasants' attitude toward work continued also to contain the elements of the old traditional approach: a certain resigned fatalism in accepting the changing fortunes of life and the stress put on the process of work itself, apart from its outcome. Because of this, Thomas and Znaniecki point out, they attached considerable importance to the external conditions of work: the degree of freedom in particular jobs, their facility, companionship – all of this made work more or less desirable, and such considerations played a not unimportant role in the peasants' choice of direction in seasonal migrations.[74]

Simultaneously, with the instrumentalization of their perceptions of work, the peasants' calculative economic thinking grew increasingly more complex. For instance, although the peasant-laborers crisscrossing Europe seem to have generally preferred traditional farm work over industrial employment because of familiarity and custom, that choice was also based on some economic calculation. Research conducted at the beginning of the century in one of the small rural towns of Galicia reported that the local peasant-laborers preferred working on the farms and estates, where they received smaller earnings and none of the "city food" they were so fond of. They knew, however, that work in the factories, though more remunerative, was not steady, whereas on the farm or manor there was some employment for a good part of the year.[75]

Through information and personal experience acquired through seasonal migrations, the agricultural workers and small peasant-landowners became increasingly aware of the value of their labor, and, knowing that they could get at least twice as much pay "out in the world," demanded higher rates at home. In fact, in some regions of East Central Europe such farm labor shortages developed by the end of the century that within the fifteen years between 1890 and 1905 the average daily wages of local farm help increased more than 30 percent, and the rates paid to the seasonal (immigrant) workers even more, by 50 to 100 percent, depending on the province.[76]

Demographic pressure and economic necessity – forces that had inaugurated the peasants' movement out of the villages – were, in the process, strengthening new elements in their thinking and attitudes: the concept of gain, and the motivation to calculate in order to maximize one's possessions.

The labor market became the first area in which this new approach was solidified. From the experience of their own or others' previous migrations, from German and Austrian agents combing the villages, from wandering merchants and pilgrims, the peasants knew very well what kind of earnings they could expect in what places, what kind of work and maintenance: "[Every year] the villagers would talk things over with one another – recalled a Mazurian who at the turn of the century each Spring left with others his village – each inquiring where the conditions were best. They would go back to the same district as the year previous, if the pay there had proved satisfactory."[77]

The prospects for earnings indeed differed quite substantially depending on where one was and what one was doing. On the average, the pay of hired agricultural laborers in East Central Europe was 40 to 50 percent lower than that received by unskilled industrial laborers in the same region. Moreover, the average earnings of industrial workers in East Central Europe were only about half of those paid in western parts of the continent.[78] Data comparing farm and industrial wages paid in selected East Central European countries, Austria, and Germany at the beginning of the twentieth century are given in Table 1.4.

Prospective migrants were well aware of labor market conditions in the areas within their reach. For instance, from a season's work on native farms in Poland, Slovakia, or Hungary, a male laborer would bring home savings of approximately $20 to $25, or even occasionally $30.[79] But after having spent the summer laboring on the fields of a German farmer, he could save as much as $50 to $55. Industrial labor in Austria and Germany was even more rewarding, if one found steady work: It allowed for savings of about $70 or more for the season. But after a long season's labor in one of the major local industries in Ostrava, Dąbrowa, Miszkolc, Diósgyör, Warsaw, Budapest, or Lódz, a man could save no more than $40. In smaller industries, savings were even less impressive – approximately $30.[80] However, it was not only the earnings alone that the prospective migrants considered and evaluated before deciding on where to go for the season. Also important were the kind and amount of food available, whether provided by the employer or purchased on one's own, and the accessibility of other valued items. Returning peasants would thus bring home bread, bacon, gruel, sugar, handicraft tools, and irons. Those coming from Hungary usually sported brightly colored shirts and carried *palenka* (vodka). The homecoming from Germany was even more spectacular. Returning peasants, as pleased with themselves as the village public was impressed with

Table 1.4. *Approximate average wages of farm laborers and industrial workers in selected East Central European countries and Germany at beginning of century (in U.S. dollars)*

Country	Farm Workers[a]		Unskilled Industrial Workers[b]		Skilled Industrial Workers (Men)[b]	Miners
	Men	Women	Men	Women		
Congress Poland	24–37¢/day	17–24¢/day	25–60¢/day, or $124–150/yr.	30–33¢/day	$3.60–4.70/wk, or $201/yr	$1/day, or $145–217/yr
Prussian Poland	Ca. $30–40/200-day season[c]	—	30–60¢/day	20–30¢/day	—	80¢/day (Silesia)
Galicia	20–25¢/day	10–16¢/day	Carpentry, masonry, 40–50¢/day; handicraft, 38–70¢/day; textile work, $138/yr; wood processing, $135/yr	—	—	$7.50–16.00 month, $90–192/yr
Slovakia[d]	24–36¢/day	21–24¢/day	40–50¢/day	15–30¢/day	—	—
Hungary	32–41¢/day	19–25¢/day	50–70¢/day, $2.95–4.00/wk	—	$0.80–1.20/day	$1.60/day
Russia	—	—	$1.44–3.00/wk	—	$2.60–4.10/wk	—
Croatia-Slavonia	27–35¢/day	20¢/day	—	—	—	—
Austria	26–45¢/day	20–26¢/day	Building trades, 60–70¢/day; textile work, $142/yr; wood processing, $130–162/yr; food industry, $117/yr	—	—	—
Germany	50–60¢/day	20–35¢/day	70–80¢/day	—	—	$1.10–1.30/day

Note: In 1900, $1 = 2$ (Russian) rubles, or 2.5 *renski*, or 5 (Austrian) kronen, or 5 (German) marks. Like Tables 1.2 and 1.3, this one also has unavoidable "gaps" where I could not locate the information. The figures here are only approximations: Between 1899 and 1910–11, agricultural wages increased 30 to 40 percent and industrial wages 50 to 100 percent, depending on region and type of industry. In compiling the table I tried to adjust the figures to the "common denominator" of 1900–5.

[a] Rates for agricultural laborers ranged relatively widely depending on the type of task performed and the skills involved. The highest-paid farmhands, the scowlers, received as much as $0.60 to $1.00 daily. Rates provided in the table are for the "average" farmhand. Also, agricultural rates varied by season: They were highest in harvest time, lowest in autumn, with a difference of up to 35 percent.

[b] Wage differentials were quite substantial even within particular countries: E.g., at the beginning of the century the earnings of ironworkers in the Dabrowa district in Congress Poland were five times higher than those in the Staropolskie district in the same country.

[c] Exclusive of payments in kind.

[d] In Slovakia, children hired for farm work were reported to earn 12–17¢/day, and for unskilled industrial work, 10–15¢/day.

Source: Konštantín Čulen, *Dejiny Slovákov v Amerike* (Bratislava, 1942), 1:39; Benjamin Murdzek, *Emigration in Polish Social-Political Thought, 1870–1914* (New York, 1977), 145; Franciszek Bujak, *Maszkienice, Wieś Powiatu Brzeskiego, Stosunki Gospodarcze i Społeczne* (Krakow, 1901), 43–55, and *Maszkienice. Wieś Powiatu Brzeskiego. Rozwój od R.1900 do R.1911* (Krakow, 1914), 65–8, 94–5, 102–5; Jozef Okołowicz, *Wychodźstwo i Osadnictwo Polskie Przed I Wojną Światową* (Warsaw, 1920), 14, 118, 131; Maria Misińska, "Podhale Dawne i Współczesne," *Prace i Materiały Muzeum Archeologicznego i Etnograficznego w Łodzi* 15 (1971), 33–40; Wojciech Saryusz-Zaleski, *Dzieje Przemysłu w B.Galicji, 1804–1919* (Krakow, 1930), 194; Jan Svetoň, "Slovenské Vystahovalectvo v Období Uhorskeho Kapitalizmu," *Ekonomický Časopis* 2 (1956), 190; Jan Lengyel, *Americans from Hungary* (Philadelphia, 1948), 114; Zanna Kormanowa and Irena Pietrzak-Pawłowska, eds., *Historia Polski* (Warsaw, 1963), vol. 3, pt. 1 (1864–1900), 225, 564–6, 643; Emily Balch, *Our Slavic Fellow Citizens* (New York, 1969), 56; Irena Lechowa, "Tradycje Migracyjne w Klonowej," *Prace i Materyały Muzeum Archeologicznego i Etnograficznego w Łodzi* 3 (1961); Julian Marchlewski, *Pisma Wybrane* (Warsaw, 1952), 1:629–31; Jerzy Fierich, *Braniszów Wieś Powiatu Ropczyckiego* (Warsaw, 1929), 68; Elżbieta Kaczyńska, *Społeczeństwo i Gospodarka Północno-Wschodnich Ziem Krolestwa Polskiego w Okresie Rozkwitu Kapitalizmu* (Warsaw, 1974), 109; and *Dzieje Robotników Polskich pod Zaborami* (Warsaw, 1970), 139; Władysław Rusiński, "The Role of the Peasantry of Poznan (Wielkopolska) in the Formation of the Non-Agricultural Labor Market," *East European Quarterly* (January 1970), 521; *Polish Encyclopaedia,* s.v., "Economic Life of Poland," 3:217; Danuta Dobrowolska, *Górnicy Salinarni Wieliczki, 1880–1939* (Wroclaw, 1965), 110; *Reports of the Immigration Commission, Emigration Conditions in Europe,* 61st Congress, 3rd Session, Sen. Doc. 748 (Washington, D.C.: 1911), 270–1, 360–9.

them, wore city suits, coats, watches with chains, rubber gaiters, and brimmed hats.

With the spread of labor migrations and with the increased role of money in these rural communities, the calculative economic orientation also began to influence the management of peasant household budgets. "The crops were abundant," a Polish peasant informed his adult children, "but prices are going up. Bread is 1 copeck a pound dearer, meat costs 15 copecks for a pound of beef, and hogs have got much cheaper, so that it is not worth keeping them because potatoes cost 2 rubles a *korzec* [about 4 bushels] and in autumn they will go up to perhaps 3 rubles."[81]

This market attitude among the East Central European peasants was, however, only partially formed. As Thomas and Znaniecki point out, it was displayed "only within a limited part of [their] economic life and [was] not systematically organized. The quantitative side of economic value, is in [their] eyes only one among its other qualities, brought forward at particular moments, among particular circumstances, with regard to particular people. Each act of buying or selling is a single isolated act, not connected with other actions of the same class."[82] The peasants' economic thinking retained elements of the traditional, nonquantitative approach whereby the social dictates of custom inhibited economic calculation. This traditionalism was stronger and appeared more binding when acted upon in the produce market than in the labor one. And so in their actions involving the farm and the household, the peasants were inclined to "do as the parents did," proceeding in the accepted and familiar way, "so that people would not laugh." For instance, an investigation of peasant family budgets in Galicia at the beginning of the century revealed that "although the making of butter [does] not pay off at all because of a good market for milk, the peasant women constantly bring butter to the market because such is the custom."[83]

Persistence of traditional economic attitudes among East Central European peasants had been additionally fortified and sanctioned by one more factor: the traditional group division of labor in that region. That division was petrified by deeply ingrained cultural stereotypes. Coming to market with their produce – grain, potatoes, buckwheat, fowls, eggs, butter, milk, and cheese – the peasants usually disposed of all or most of it to the Jewish intermediaries who traditionally performed the role of market dealers. The peasants received about two-thirds of the price at which the produce was further distributed in the area by the recipients. Local trade and business in the East Central European countryside had been the domain of the Jews, who were excluded from other pursuits. The peasants, not unlike the nobility, customarily held business to be a Jewish entreprise for which only Jews were really fitted. To be sure, the monetization of the peasant economy at the end of the nineteenth century had permanently installed the peasant in the market as a business partner, but the social environment in which monetization was taking place allowed the old attitudes to continue alongside the newly emergent approaches.

Concurrent with the incipient, piecemeal modifications of the economic attitudes of East Central European peasants that were taking place under the impact of structural transformations of the whole region were alterations in patterns organizing the three concentric social circles in which the peasants moved: the family, the village community, and the outer world.

The traditional peasant household operated as a "fused" family and economic unit in which each member performed an assigned role as producer and consumer.[84] The inclusion, in the last decades of the nineteenth century, of outside wage labor as a permanent element in the rural economy inaugurated the process of partial differentiation of family and economic functions of the peasant household. Household and family continued, however, as the organizing center of peasant economic activities. Thus the new pursuits were, in large part, carried on as a collective family performance.

The main and primary function of a woman in East Central European rural societies was the bearing of children, and next to this her main duty was to perform the household and farm work prescribed by her role.[85] As the employment-seeking migrations became routine in villages across East Central Europe, women, like men, began to hire out their labor for wages. Initially they worked for nearby rich farmers or on the local estates. When the remote seasonal migrations had put the male population on the move, the females, mostly young unmarried girls but also some married women, were quick to follow. It was done, of course, with the approval of the male head of the household, in whose hands lay the ultimate decisions concerning important family matters. The traditional conception of peasant male "dignity" forbade the husband to let his wife and daughter do hired work unless it was absolutely indispensable. But increasingly often, now, he would calculate the potential monetary profits of paid employment of the women of the

Plate 1. Eastern Europe, early twentieth century – the fields. Collection of Mary Mesaros.

Plate 2. Eastern Europe, early twentieth century – the homes. Collection oɪ
Mary Mesaros.

Plate 3. Eastern Europe, early twentieth century – market day. From Bernard Newman, *The Story of Poland* (London: Hutchinson, 1940).

household and decide to use their labor even when it was not necessary for immediate economic survival.

The women usually traveled together in separate groups: mothers, daughters, cousins, and neighbors heading to the places where *babske* (female) work was known to be needed. And so, every year, reminisced a Polish peasant memoirist from Mazuria, "While the grown men went abroad to earn on the river, the women and girls . . . from the smaller farms would cross the Vistula River into the Russian territory to work on the fields . . . They would go on foot, in groups of two or three score, carrying in big kerchiefs their clothes and food with them. They would leave home in the spring and return after the potatoes had been dug in the autumn."[86]

Many women from the villages ventured much farther – to Germany and Denmark, where they spent the long season laboring in the fields. By the turn of the century such seasonal migrations by women had become very common. For instance, in a single year (1899), 14 percent of the total number of seasonal migrants from the Galician village of Maszkienice were young women, most of them sixteen to twenty years of age; twelve years later their proportion increased to 20 percent (and their number tripled). In the nearby village of Bielcza, in 1911 women constituted almost 40 percent of the migrants.[87] In Slovakian villages, the proportion of women among seasonal peasant-workers was about 25 percent.[88] From the local season's farm work the womenfolk would bring home about $20 to $30, and from Germany up to $50. Quite often women also accompanied their fathers, husbands, or brothers who went to the cities to work in the factories. Such seasonal women workers, employed in the textile or cigar factories or in some other branch of light industry in the factories of Ostrava, Dąbrowa, Miszkolc, or Budapest, would average between $30 and $35 for a season.[89] A number also served as maids and servants in nearby cities; they stayed there for most of the year and came home for the harvest.

The children's place in the traditional peasant household was equally well defined. As soon as they finished the first five to six years of their lives, their parents "saw to it that they learned to work hard, or at least to be occupied, for idleness was severely disapproved of. . . . Their fundamental education for life was to learn – well and early – all things their parents knew and did," so that they could earn money and care for themselves.[90] "They would say," wrote a peasant-born memoirist, "where no work is, no one can eat and no one has anything to wear."[91] So the young children began doing things around the house at a very early age: They looked after babies, tended the geese, pigs, and sheep, herded cows, and took the horses to pasture.

When the adults began to migrate in search of employment, their offspring followed. The landless families and the dwarf-holders commonly hired out their thirteen- to fourteen-year-old children to work on nearby manors and collected their daily earnings.[92] Often the youth of both sexes migrated with the women – their mothers or older sisters – and stayed with them all season, laboring in the fields. By the turn of the century, however, groups of young country boys sixteen to seventeen years old covering long distances together became a familiar sight in the region. A study conducted in a Galician village in 1899 and then repeated in 1911 reported a significant increase in seasonal migrations among the youth (predominantly boys) who each year moved far away from their native provinces, because "out in the world" and on their own they could earn five to seven times more than in their native villages and twice as much as the amount they would make going with the women.[93] The parents decided which of the children would go, and they demanded that the season's earnings be turned over to them. Their earnings usually ranged between 40 and 50 percent of the wages earned by the men, or about 70 percent of the wages of the women. A season's work by a youth in Germany sufficed to buy a calf or a pig. Returning from Denmark in 1913, a seventeen-year-old Polish farm boy "saved himself" almost $20, which was to be used toward the purchase of a horse.[94]

The integration of the rural households into the money economy and their increasing dependence on outside employment brought about an expansion of the scope of economic activities of the peasant family collective to include wage contributions of its members. As they began to perceive work and work input increasingly in terms of quantifiable rewards, within the limited opportunities available to them the peasant families also learned to adjust and to an extent plan their economic ventures so as to maximize the total household returns.

The families of the East Central European peasants formed their closest and most immediate social environment. Beyond the family, they identified most closely with their local community: the native village, and what Thomas and Znaniecki called the *okolica* – the surrounding geographic-social area. The social position of a peasant father and his family in the village was carefully evaluated both by the family and by other members of the community. Here, too, the transformations occurring throughout the region during the last decades of the nineteenth century – a rapid proletarianization of the rural population, with simultaneous expansion of the middle peasant stratum, progressive monetization of peasant households, and the social and cultural consequences of mass seasonal migrations – made a significant impact by widening social discrepancies in the villages and intensifying status strivings among the inhabitants.

Although all peasants in the village belonged to one economic class, they occupied different social positions in the rural community. What to outside observers often appeared as one homogeneous and undifferentiated mass was, when viewed more closely and from the inside, revealed as a pyramid of social rank and prestige. A peasant-born writer from Podhale on the northern slopes of the Carpathian mountains noted this double perspective in one of his books describing village life in his region at the beginning of the century:

> To outside observers the peasant mass appears as a solidly homogeneous order differentiated only by type of land. Very little is known about the existence within this mass of hierarchical levels similar to those occurring in the world of dress coats and tuxedos. The peasant society, meanwhile, like the urban one, possesses in its midst its own hereditary or monetary aristocracy, then a numerous class of moderately well off yeomen, and finally – scorned by both – the landless, often homeless and hungry mass toiling away in sweat and misery.[95]

The social pyramid in the local peasant communities was steep, narrow at the top and broad at the bottom. For instance, an investigation conducted in Zmiąca, a large but not untypical Galician village, at the beginning of the century, at a time when seasonal migrations were already intense, showed the following distribution of peasant landholders, ranked (from top to bottom) on a five-point stratification scale: 9 percent (12), rich peasant families that did not personally work their land (valued at over 12,000 kronen, or $2,400) and relying on hired labor; 19.4 percent (26), the group in which all family members worked on the land (valued at 6,000 to 12,000 kronen), but who also regularly hired external labor; 17.9 percent (24), those who maintained themselves sufficiently from their own land (valued at 2,500 to 6,000 kronen), which they alone cultivated; 17.9 percent (24), the group of peasant owners of small-sized holdings (valued at 1,200 kronen), who lived from them but had to take external work; and, finally 35.8 percent (48), the owners of dwarf-sized holdings (valued at about 1,000 kronen), who absolutely could not survive from their land. Still below this category in the village status hierarchy were the cotters – the better-off ones with a tiny lot and one head of livestock, and at the very bottom those who had nothing at all.[96] Another study, conducted in the village of Maszkienice, also in Galicia, in 1911, divided the whole population into five socio-economic categories, the landless peasants included: The top 4.7 percent (11) households were judged to be in "good" economic condition; 12.7 percent (30) in "fair" condition; 27.5 percent (65) were classified as "marginal" (but still able to make ends meet); the condition of 44.5 percent (105) was judged "insufficient," and 10.6 percent (25) were found living in dire "poverty."[97]

Measured in terms of actual wealth, social extremes were certainly much less widely separated in the villages than among the nobility or in the cities. But, small as they were, economic differentials and social ranking in peasant societies were associated with deeply felt status cleavages and status striving. Edward Steiner, an early expert on immigrants from East Central Europe, was certainly wrong when he imagined that peasants in that region took good and sufficient comfort from "bread, potatoes and cabbage to eat and an occasional pull at the vodka bottle."[98] Commenting on the human tendency to strive after and to display status, Tarde called man a "peacock." As poor and needy as they were, East Central European peasants were certainly peacocks. Anthropologists studying the social life of the peasants in Balkan villages at the beginning of the century reported that they were "great boasters," obsessed to "win a place of their own in the world" and showing "ceaseless concern with their . . . importance and reputation."[99] Elsewhere in the region the peasants were no less concerned with their social position, "at each and every step trying to show off greater worth and importance."[100]

Internal stratification in East Central European rural societies naturally reflected the surrounding environment and the prevailing economic conditions. In his *Memoirs*, Wincenty Witos, the self-educated son of a two-acre peasant in Galicia who became the leader of the Polish Peasant Party and later prime minister in the government of independent Poland, summarized succinctly the bases of village social ranking at the beginning of the century:

> The worth of a man was measured by the number of acres, horses, and cows, by the quality of his land, his pastures, and his family background. Also very important were prosperity, honor, and ability. The *gospodarze* (yeomen) always had first and best pews in church, in the tavern, and in the *gmina* (village council). The *zagrodnicy* (petty landowners) tried to keep close to them, the

komornicy (landless) walked on tiptoe, and the *parobki* (farmhands) were total slaves.[101]

Peasants who left their villages and hired themselves out as seasonal laborers on distant farms or in the cities came home with money. It was then used to buy more livestock, build an addition to the barn, put a new roof on the house, show off better clothes, and eat better food – making sure others noticed.

Very religious, peasants over all of East Central Europe scrupulously attended church, the central social institution in the village, and tithed for its upkeep. The influx of ready cash brought from the outside greatly increased opportunities to elevate one's social status by a public display of generosity. Gifts, dues, collections, and money offered for votive masses and patron saint festivities were given to build, remodel, and maintain the village church, its bells, holy figures, and the parsonage. These donations provided occasions to reaffirm and to add to one's family prestige.[102]

This status display by the established *gazdas* (yeomen) and by those who accumulated cash income from seasonal work made others desire it too and feel acutely their own lower position. A *nikogovič* (a "nobody," in Serbian – a peasant from a poor and socially insignificant family) who labored all summer to earn barely enough to pull his family through the harsh winter could, with a dose of fatalistic acquiescence, accept his miserable plight. At the same time, he was deeply and enviously aware of others' better fortunes and might dream of a "successful season" in Austria that would bring him more money. A farmer who saw his neighbor buying an extra cow with the earnings his sons brought home from a season's labor might plan for the following year a similar move by his family.

Ownership of property had been the basis of social stratification in East Central European villages and the primary measure of status, with cash ranking a distant second. The transformations occurring in the region gradually introduced a third element into the peasant prestige system: knowledge and learning of specific sorts. It functioned separately, as a value in itself, and it remained parallel, rather than integrated into the main social ranking system of the village.

Writing on the immigrants' adaptation in America, Timothy Smith has argued that by the turn of the century the "intensified concern for learning" had become an integral part of the sociocultural experience of the East Central European peasants, as a result of the migrations and the awakening desire to have a better life.[103] He makes an important point here, but his emphasis on formal education misses the mark somewhat. True, after the abolition of serfdom schooling was slowly becoming more popular in the villages. Toward the turn of the century there were more peasants – particularly the younger ones – than ever before who read newspapers and agricultural circulars and formed farmers' cooperatives and self-educational societies. Despite these developments, however, popular consensus in the village still considered education acquired by formal schooling to be a pursuit suitable for the nobility, a fancy of the higher orders: "It is all right for the rich man, but not for a poor, stupid peasant." In the virtually unanimous testimony of eyewitnesses – peasant-born memoirists, writers, publicists, and politicians – prolonged schooling and too visible concern with formal education alienated those peasants who possessed it from the rest of the village.[104] For most, the only accepted and comprehensible purpose of schooling for a peasant son at the turn of the century was still the priesthood. Peasant interest in formal education was essentially practice-neutral, and they perceived education primarily as possessing moral rather than pragmatic functions.[105]

Yet the cultural system of East Central European peasants did not lack regard for knowledge and learning of a specific kind. Simple literacy, rather than the number of school grades completed, combined with popular wisdom, life experience, curiosity, and knowledgeability about things of the world were highly respected in all rural societies of the region. Peasants who were able to read from a book or decipher and interpret official documents were held in high regard by village public opinion. "In those days [at the end of the last century], the regard for the printed work was great among peasants," wrote Władysław Orkan, a well-known peasant-born Polish writer, in his autobiographical *Letters from the Countryside*, "since it was not easy to arrive at this secret."[106]

The breaking down of the relative isolation of the East Central European villages, the gradual increase of the general educational level in rural societies, and particularly the mass peasant migrations to the outside world further elevated the value of knowledge and learning as these were understood by the peasants by providing them with an increasingly solid factual base.

In their brilliant discussion of the sociocultural foundations of Polish peasant society at the turn of the century, applicable also to other parts of the region, Thomas and Znaniecki present the three basic variants of village prestige generated by knowledge and learning. Prestige was bestowed on those whom Thomas and Znaniecki call advisers, narrators, and philosophers. *Advisers* were individuals known for their honesty, who had traveled widely and were acquainted with different kinds of people. The second type, the *narrators*, were people knowledgeable about facts and history and widely read. Finally, the third type of wise men were the *philosophers*: self-taught individuals, thinkers and teachers of others. "The social prestige attached to the functions of the adviser, the narrator and the philosopher," conclude Thomas and Znaniecki, "even if mixed at the beginning with a particular kind of condescension . . . is a strong factor in instruction. Reciprocally, when [enlightenment] develops, the prestige of these functions grows."[107]

Increasingly, toward the end of the century, the social world of East Central European peasants extended beyond their immediate family and village community. Traditionally they had maintained relations with the inhabitants of other villages in the surrounding area. Seasonal migrations brought them into new contact with city dwellers, coworkers in factories, and other people in faraway regions where peasants traveled in search of employment and wages.

As *part-societies part-cultures*, to use Kroeber's term, East Central European peasant communities constituted fragments of a hierarchically ordered larger society. Peasants themselves, their families, and their villages were vertically related to social and political orders that surpassed the boundaries of their local world.

It was probably in the vertical dimension of the relationship of the peasants to the outside world that the traditional feudal residue was most spectacular and persistent. Since agriculture remained the principal focus of the East European economy, the estate owners, although formally divested of seignory, maintained their traditionally legitimated, "ideologically hegemonous," superior social position in the overwhelmingly ascriptive social structure that encompassed rural and urbanized areas alike. The centuries-old recognition of feudal privilege and social inequality, sanctioned by religion and cultural custom, remained deeply ingrained in the mentality of East Central European peasants. At the beginning of the twentieth century, these societies were still, in F. M. L. Thompson's coinage, "deference societies."[108]

From their earliest childhood, peasants were confronted, through contacts with the local manor, parish, school, and village officials, with the segregation of things and people into two separate categories: "peasant's" and "gentleman's." From the books that they read in school, from the pulpits at Sunday Mass, from personal dealings with the manor from which came seasonal handouts of food and drink, medical help, and advice in legal matters, peasants learned to accept the "natural" superiority of the upper class, its culture, life-style, and values, as part of God's order on earth.

The peasants' deference toward the representatives of the higher social order had its counterpart in the attitude of the gentry, who thought themselves to be the naturally superior species. The prevailing attitude toward the members of the peasant class, among the East Central European gentry before World War I, was condescending paternalism. Often it was open scorn and contempt.[109] In Hungary, for instance, where the residue of feudal social relations was particularly persistent, the expression *büdös paraszt* (stinking peasant) was often used as a single term. For their part, the peasants, although accepting as the disposition of Providence the existence of the chasm dividing them from the upper class, treated the latter with deep suspicion and mistrust. "There is no equality among the angels in the heavens; there will never be any on earth," went a saying among Galician peasants; "A peasant is always a peasant – a gentleman, a gentleman: Amen." And in Serbia, peasants talked about *pokvarena gospoda* (rotten gentry) and said, "The *gospoda* are devils, and devils are *gospoda*."[110] At the same time, however, the peasants, socialized to accept the superiority of the gentry, used the criterion of "gentility" as a reference framework in evaluating the achievements of those in their own stratum. "He dresses like a *pan* (gentlemen)"; "I eat like the baron"; or "they behave like *gospoda*": Such expressions acknowledged the status-superior symbols, with an admixture of disdain (as in the last one: "[To] behave like *gospoda*" implied that one had assumed lofty airs).

Superimposed on the class domination of the gentry over the peasantry in East Central Europe was a system of ethnic dominance. For the Rusyn, Ukrainian, Slovak, Slovenian, or Serbian peasants, the group that possessed economic and cultural supremacy was one that spoke a different language – whether German, Magyar, Polish, or Turkish – or even confessed a different religion – Roman Catholic, Protestant, or Moslem. As the nineteenth century came to a close, national awakenings occurring throughout the Habsburg Empire were filtering down to the peasant classes, gradually involving more and more peasants in the struggle for civic and cultural autonomy for the subordinated nationality groups. This further increased the distance between the Slovak, Rusyn, Ukrainian, Serbian, and Romanian peasants and the ethnically alien upper stratum.[111] Similar "distancing" superimpositions of class and ethnoreligious factors determined the peasants' attitude toward representatives of government and other political institutions. Although with the creation of the peasant parties toward the end of the century and with the spread throughout East Central European villages of social movements among the peasantry, political activism became more common, their prevailing attitude toward "politics" remained that of submission combined with *désinteressement* and cynicism: "What do I care who is the deputy, let them choose who they will! The peasant can't help there . . . The lord will hold with his kind, so what can be done? Better keep out of it!"[112]

The following chapter will analyze the meaning that the "American option" – the opportunity to extend the paths of seasonal and permanent labor migration across the Atlantic into American cities and factories – had for East Central European peasants. It must be interpreted in the context of the cumulative effects of the enfranchisement of the peasantry and the transformations of the East Central European rural economy. To summarize then: The rapid fragmentation of land holdings and the proletarianization of increasing segments of rural society pushed thousands of peasants out of their villages into the labor market, which led, by the late nineteenth century, to the gradual integration of peasant households into the market economy. These combined processes, in turn, affected traditional peasant culture, gradually introducing into it new elements that functioned alongside the old attitudes and behavioral patterns. Just as the rural societies in East Central Europe at the turn of the century were in a state of transition, the peasant culture, correspondingly, was a mixed bag of traditional and new patterns and values – a patchwork assembly of various bits and pieces in different amounts and combinations.

More than ever before, the villagers began to perceive the world around them as somewhat expandable and to believe that some increment in possessions was feasible. A common proverb expressing traditional peasant thinking, found in several regions of East Central Europe – "Cover your eyes with filth, and eat your bread in content" – meaning that one should avoid expense and risk, making the best of what one has in order to avoid an uncertain future – had lost much of its descriptive power and proscriptive wisdom by the turn of the century.

Seasonal migrations for wage labor had turned into a socially and culturally institutionalized way for the peasants to alter their family standing in the village somewhat, according to the values that defined accomplishment in their rural culture: land, livestock, farm buildings, and other material possessions. Whether they stayed on the land, worked nearby, or decided to move farther in search of better prospects promised by more remote regions, the East Central European peasants in the late nineteenth century were confronted with the *presence of choice*. Within the narrow limits of the economic opportunities accessible to rural migrants, and within the restricting bounds of the still very traditional peasant culture, there had now opened up some room for purposeful action, selected and executed according to individual and family needs, goals, and preferences, and designed to meet the social requirements of the village community.

2   *To America*

The "American option" – the opportunity to extend the paths of seasonal and permanent labor migrations across the Atlantic into American cities and factories – appeared in East Central Europe at the time of the mobilization of the peasantry in the last decades of the nineteenth century. Their movements did not necessarily follow a sequential pattern that increasingly took them farther and farther away from home and tradition: first seasonal migrations within the region and the breakdown of village isolation, then movement to western Europe and changes in attitudes, and finally a trip to America. All these trends coincided in time; they occurred simultaneously and mutually reinforced one another. However, for the sake of clarity, the peasants' decision to cross the Atlantic will be treated here as a culmination, of sorts, of all of the "preceding" processes.

Those who were leaving their villages to go to America were not simply "pushed out" from the countryside by adverse economic forces and demographic pressure. The underlying premise of this chapter is that peasants who decided to cross the Atlantic were simultaneously motivated by a basic survival orientation and a "negative" flight from misery and declining status, *and* by the image of, and the desire for, accomplishment as measured by the prevailing standards of rural society – the "positive" thrust.

The individual preferences, motives, and decisions of large numbers of people involved in a mass phenomenon are notoriously difficult to chronicle and document. Even though certainly there is no lack of historical evidence – peasant biographies, memoirs, novels, and letters; official local reports; and contemporary community studies that may provide us with clues and data – at some points my interpretations are admittedly speculative. The emigration movement involved several million people. Although they chose the same action of leaving Europe, their motives and attitudes were often as different as their individual positions in life and the local conditions from which they started. Moreover, the decision of any one individual was the result of a number of complex calculations and a variety of complementary motives. However, I think it is possible, with the due caution one must exercise in dealing with this inherent human diversity, to attempt a general interpretive framework that illuminates the attraction of overseas migration.

To argue that the decisions of East Central European peasants to go to America contained the motive and vision of accomplishment does not negate the determining role played in their actions by external social and economic forces. The distinction between two kinds of motives proposed by Alfred Schutz seems particularly useful here. He distinguishes, on the one hand, the "in-order-to" motives referring to the imagined future state of affairs or the goal to be brought about by the action that is undertaken. In-order-to motives may be interpreted as the mental readiness or the expectations of the actor who thinks, as it were, in the future perfect tense. On the other hand, there exists another type of motive that Schutz proposes calling the "because" motives, referring to the background conditions surrounding the individual that have influenced his or her actions. A murderer committed the act *because* he or she grew up in an environment of such and such kind but this person murdered *in order to* obtain money.[1]

It is the latter type of motivation that seems not to have received sufficient attention in present-day American ethnic historiography, which for the most part has focused on the "because" conditions of the East Central European emigration.[2] Therefore, while fully acknowledging the presence and impact of the because determinants – the "push" factors that made peasants leave their villages in search of jobs and money – we will concentrate here on the interpretation of the in-order-to motives that brought them to America.

As we have seen, for millions of these peasants migration for work was a necessity. The growing number of dwarf-holdings insufficient to provide for their owners and the fast expansion of the agricultural proletariat led those affected to venture outside their localities to places that promised employment and income. For millions of peasant households, by the turn of the century seasonal migrations had become a permanent element of their economic existence and the income from it a permanent component of family budgets.

Given all this, however, a peasant's decision about where to go, how many sons to take along, and whether or not to let his wife and daughters go too, depended on his and his family's particular needs and "life-style" preferences (defined, of course, within the cultural framework prevailing in the peasant society). Many landless peasant and owners of dwarf-sized holdings left the villages and worked through the season merely so that they could survive the winter. Others wanted to survive it a little better – with somewhat better food, and in warmer clothing. Still others moved in whole family units with the intention of earning enough money to buy a cow (costing, at the turn of the century, about $24 to $30 in Congress Poland and Galicia, $16 to $24 in Hungary), a pig ($12 to $22), or a pair of oxen ($50 to $100) that they could later lease for plowing. Some peasants set off to save for a piece of land. At the beginning of the century a hectare could be purchased for $200 to $500, the prices varying significantly with the region and the quality of soil (the range covers the average price increase between 1902–3 and 1911–12). Some other, newly married ones, sought funds to use in constructing a house and farm buildings (the average cost of the latter varied between $100 and $180, depending again on the size and the region). A father of grown-up daughters set off with his sons for the season in order to get enough money for the dowries to marry them off. A customary dowry for a girl from a respectable, well-off peasant family did not fall far below $400; landless peasants or dwarf-holders gave their daughters approximately $25 to $50. Another common goal of sons who were in line to inherit land was to accumulate enough capital to buy out their siblings: The average amount per farm varied from $500 (for larger farms over 15 hectares) to $25 to $30 (dwarf-holdings). Others migrated to earn money to pay their debts, which commonly exceeded $100 per household. A number of Slavic peasants used seasonal migrations in Europe, particularly to Hungary, as a means of acquiring cash to pay for their journey to America for themselves and their families.[3]

Those for whom seasonal work on nearby estates or in a nearby industrial district did not appear sufficiently lucrative or whose goals required more money could go and seek better fortunes in the neighboring countries or in more distant lands, on farms or factories in western Europe. In 1911, a comparative study of ten Galician villages found their inhabitants following several different paths of seasonal migrations within Galicia and in Austria, Denmark, and Germany. The proportions of migrants from these ten villages who found employment within Galicia ranged from 84 to 7 percent; the proportion who worked in Austria ranged from 38 to 1 percent; in Germany, 49 to 4 percent; and in Denmark, 17 percent to none.[4]

But of all places that were available, it was America that offered the greatest promise and that on the whole attracted the greatest number of emigrants. During the first years of our century, the proportion of the recorded continental and overseas emigration from Austria-Hungary was on the average 25 percent and 75 percent, respectively. In 1908, owing to a severe economic depression in the United States, the proportion was 60 percent and 40 percent, only to be reversed again after the recovery of American industry.[5] Of all places where peasants from East Central Europe could and did go, only America had a "Great Legend."

As shown by official statistics, regions with strong demographic and economic pressures were the ones most affected by overseas emigration. This fundamental and evident relationship, reflecting the internal imbalances in the region created by developing capitalism, did not, however, operate in a mechanical way, but was conditioned by various interacting factors of a social and psychological nature, often elusive or simply impossible to assess in a quantitative manner. The centers of most intensive emigration to America in East Central Europe conspicuously differed in regard to their rates of birth, numbers of landless peasants, taxation, agricultural and industrial development, and ethnic composition. For instance, in the Kassa district (county of Abauj-Torna) in Hungary, the village of Bárcza was reported as having the highest tax rate and unfavorable economic conditions but the lowest percentage of emigration to America. Two other villages in the same district had better economic conditions and were exempted from municipal and school taxes, but their emigration rate was higher than in Bárcza.[6] Similar findings were reported from Congress Poland: For instance, areas of the northeastern Białystok region and of Polesie – the areas where demographic and economic conditions were certainly favorable for emigration – almost entirely failed to produce any significant numbers of migrants to America.[7] This was also true of certain parts of eastern Galicia, such as the two large counties of Halicz and Buczacz and the Stanisławowo vojvodship.[8] Clearly, there was not a direct but only a mediated correlation between emigration to America and the economic characteristics of particular provinces. Some of the poorer districts and the ones with a greater number of landless peasants sent out fewer emigrants across the ocean to America than did more affluent areas and those with a smaller proportion of the agrarian proletariat.

Without systematic inquiry into the local conditions prevailing in particular communities in East Central Europe, it is not possible to assess the impact, patterns, and mechanisms of these mediating factors that affected the intensity and direction of peasant migratory movements. We can at least point out their general character. Key elements were the social acceptance of seasonal movements and the incorporation into village custom and local opinion of particular paths of migration as viable and of proven efficiency, as well as the establishment of social networks linking prospective migrants with target areas outside the homeland that were already known to – or settled by – those who had gone before. Poverty, overpopulation, and segmentation of landholdings provided large numbers of people with increasingly strong incentives to emigrate from those rural areas in which the search to gain a livelihood outside the native territory had become an accepted and socially supported form of behavior.[9] For instance, large areas of Poznania, Silesia, and the border areas between "Prussian" and "Russian" Poland, instead of generating mass emigration to America, until the outbreak of World War I sent thousands of peasant-workers every season to the same places in the western parts of Germany, because the prevailing opinion throughout the villages in this region was that this was "the thing to do" and because in following these paths one could rely on preestablished networks of information and assistance.[10] Among the Polish seasonal workers in Denmark, 85 percent came from Galicia, from districts where this particular route had become a socially approved and supported behavior. It sometimes even happened that migratory customs cut one village in half: In Podgaje (Galicia), the "left side" of the village migrated to Elisabeth, New Jersey, and the "right side" went to Detroit.[11]

But even for peasant men and women in the areas where overseas emigration had become a socially accepted endeavor, in order for them to consider leaving for America and actually going there, the hope of gaining a better livelihood through this endeavor must have penetrated deeply into their minds. "The talk is all about America," wrote a Croatian from Lika-Krbava at the beginning of the century, and it was the same in many corners of East Central Europe.[12] The American success story spread through the region. Louis Adamić recalled,

> I experienced a thrill every time a man returned from the United States. Four or five years before he had quietly left for America, a poor peasant clad in homespun, with a bundle on his back. Now, an *Amerikanac*, he usually sported a blue serge suit, buttoned shoes with india rubber heels, a derby, a celluloid collar and a long necktie made even louder by a dazzling horse-shoe pin, while his two suitcases of imitation leather bulged with gifts from America for his relatives and friends in the community. Thus, the ambition to go to the United States was kindled in boys by men who had been there.[13]

Such and similar images appear time and again in peasants' reminiscences:

> America became the subject of endless and feverish conversations and longings, and going there appeared to incarnate happiness simply beyond words. When, after a few years spent in America, Walenty Podlasek returned to Wierzchosławice [a village in Galicia], such processions of people visited him every day that he was forced to hide so that they could not torment him with their questions.[14]

It was, as the popular song went, "the incredible land," where within two weeks people made as much money as a peasant would earn working on a farm for the whole season from June until October. At the turn of the century, an industrial laborer in Hungary (e.g., in Budapest, Szeged, or Kecskemet) made approximately $3.50 a week. Of this, he spent on the average $2.00 a week, which left him with monthly savings of about $6.00.[15] In America, as peasants at home learned through letters and from returning emigrants, a single man could save at least $15 a month, and a hardworking young woman could save up to $10. The economic calculation was obvious: It meant, in Austrian kronen, the unheard-of ability to afford a full hectare of land out of a single year's savings, or to earn the price of four cows in six months or of a large new brick farm building in nine. "For these minds," noted a contemporary observer, himself of peasant origin, "accustomed to the poor local wages [and living conditions], it was like a fantasy, like a dream pay!"[16]

The principal creators of the opinions about America were the *Amerikanci* themselves – those who sent letters home (not seldom exaggerating their good fortune in order to appear more successful) and, even more important, those who returned home.[17] With the results seen about the village and the vicinity in the households of returnees, the "demonstration effect" – the tendency of people to raise their aspirations when they come into contact, particularly among their peers, with a standard of living higher than that to which they have been accustomed – began working most forcefully.[18]

However humble and insignificant an immigrant had been in America – a miserable, uncivilized "Hunky" – if he acquired some means he appeared the incarnation of success to people in his own village. A contemporary diarist noted this phenomenon in his native Galician village: "When . . . after a few years in America Walenty Podlasek returned [and] with the dollars he brought with him purchased a dozen or so hectares and started to build one house in

Wierzchosławice and one in Tarnów, the people went wild from envy and desire."[19]

Indeed, the enormous amount of money that had come into the possession of peasant households as the result of American migrations – plainly visible to all as it was turned into land, cattle, brick houses, barns, better food and dress – only augmented the ambitions of those who had not yet gone themselves, and fortified their belief that America was the peasant Eldorado. Thus, during the six years from 1900 to 1906, the total amount sent by money orders alone to Russia and Austria-Hungary was as much as $69,041,227. Of this sum, approximately one-third was sent to Hungary, one-third to Austria, and one-third to Russia.[20]

The figures for a few localities may help to better explain what "America" actually meant for the peasant villages. For instance, in 1899, the postal district of Kassa in the county of Abauj-Torna (Hungary) and another in Pozanoy reported that over $400,000 was received in money orders from the United States, with the "average" emigrant from each area sending home $210 a year. In 1903 alone, Hungarian emigrants from the county of Veszprém sent back home no less than $621,846. In the county of Gömör-Kishont the post office received $595,507 during 1900 and 1901, whereas Szabolcs County received $142,292.[21] In 1901, 7,090 Croatian emigrants from one Zagreb county sent home $291,869. The county of Lika-Krbava in Croatia received, in 1902 alone, about $560,860, or about $130 from each emigrant. In one year, 1906, the village of Centinje in Cernogora received $30,000 – "more money than passed through the hands of its postmaster in twenty preceding years." In the period between 1902 and 1907, the amount of money sent from America to seven Galician villages was $449,130. One of them, Broniszów, received during this time $120 per household annually. According to a report of the postmaster of the village of Enrod in the county of Bekes in Hungary, each emigrant sent home $554 between 1904 and 1906. Before 1910, two Slovak villages, But'ka and Zdiar in the Zemplín region, each received from America between $14,000 and $16,000 annually, or about $200 per emigrant.[22]

Besides money orders sent from America through banks and post offices, a great many U.S. dollars were also coming to the villages in the form of cash enclosed in letters or, more especially, brought by the returning emigrants. A contemporary Croatian economist estimated that during the period between 1900 and 1912, in addition to money sent by money order, nearly $40 million reached the country by way of returning emigrants and in letters. The emigrants returning to Maszkienice in Galicia prior to World War I brought or sent home a total of $850 per capita, with the amount varying significantly from $180 to $2,000. The average length of time spent in America was four years. According to a local study in Transylvania, the average capital brought home by peasants returning from America at the beginning of the century was $400 to $600. During the same period, emigrants returning to Galicia after having spent two to three years in America carried an average of $400 to $800, whereas those who stayed longer often brought up to $2,000.[23]

In sum, considering the fact that after a prolonged agrarian crisis that ended in 1895, during almost two decades preceding World War I the economic conditions in Europe, both in the West and in the East, were steadily improving,[24] and, given the presence of other "minor" options through seasonal migrations within the European continent, we may conjecture that for a peasant, already irreversibly caught in the web of the market economy, the decision to leave for America came ultimately as the result of a choice rather than of immediate economic necessity. Further, for a large number of emigrants, this decision contained an in-order-to motive to significantly alter their ordinary course of existence.

These conjectures are not original and have been formulated before. Recently the economic historian Jeffrey Williamson, after having performed a series of statistical tests on a model of predicted emigration from Europe to the United States in the period 1870 to 1910, concluded that

> Even when the analysis is expanded to include Central and South-eastern Europe, push factors still are estimated to be negative. Labor market conditions in Europe as a whole were improving sufficiently in the late nineteenth century to enhance the ability of sending nations to retain potential [overseas] migrants. They still came to America in massive numbers.[25]

Half a century earlier Thomas and Znaniecki provided an elaboration of the same idea in *The Polish Peasant*:

> It is true that as a consequence of the general economic status [in East Central Europe], the standard of wages was lower than in Western Europe, much lower than in the United States, and in the case of agricultural laborers barely above the starvation limit; but aside from industrial crises there was no lack of work which would compel the workmen to emigrate from fear of starving. Emigration [to America] was thus not the necessary result of economic conditions. The latter merely gave a justification to the individual for choosing emigration as the . . . accessible way of

satisfying new needs, or improving his situation, or, less frequently, of keeping himself or his family on their customary level that certain new factors threatened to lower.[26]

According to Thomas and Znaniecki, the motives behind the peasants' decision to leave for America differed in important ways from those of seasonal migrants who stayed on the continent:

> It is obvious that the values which the emigrant wants to obtain [in America] are much more important than those which he expects from season work in Germany . . . By going to season work the migrant (or his family) hopes to satisfy some particular needs which have arisen in his ordinary course of life . . . He considers emigration as a substitute for hired work at home, with a somewhat better living and the possibility of laying a small sum aside . . . Whereas by crossing the ocean he expects to change radically his ordinary course of life . . . to return a different man, to obtain – by earning much and spending little – the economic foundation on which to build a new and superior career.[27]

The "negative want": to gain a minimal level of economic security against the consequences of further subdivision of family land, bad harvests, debts, and other misfortunes of which there were always plenty in rural life, was obviously a constant element in the peasants' thinking and formed a solid motivational layer at the foundation of their actions. Above and beyond this, however, the "American option" created the opportunity to extend, as it were, the peasants' horizon of the achievable to also include a vision of more constructive, "surplus" accomplishments. The peasants' memoirs, their letters to friends and relatives, even songs circulating in the villages at the turn of the century, echo the same story over and over again: "Whoever had in mind a goal that couldn't be fulfilled by life-long work at home," wrote a contemporary peasant memoirist, "began deliberating at night about going overseas."[28] Or another diary: "I lived with this single thought: to earn money and to return home and to buy a farm even better than my father's." And from another: "Like all of us, I wanted to earn a lot of money, to make my life easy. [I told my wife,] 'Here we'll never grow rich!' And everybody around was talking about America." And from a personal relation by a returned immigrant: "I thought this: [I will go to America], work a few years, save money, will return [to Europe] . . . and will marry into a good *gospodarstwo* [farm], and I will be a *kmiec* [yeoman]."[29]

Writing at the turn of the century on the conditions fostering emigration from Galicia, Zofia Daszyńska-Golińska pointed to the rapidly growing dissatisfaction with the prevailing conditions of life among the peasants and to rising expectations that were not satisfied at home.[30] Hungarian *föispánok* filed strikingly similar reports from their counties on causes of overseas emigration, indicating a widespread "desire for making one's fortune," resulting from "the steady increase in the expectations of the people." From Veszprém County the administrator wrote that although local wages were steadily increasing in his and the surrounding area, "I can say that we have more problems with the lack of workers than [with the] lack of wage earning potentials [because peasants leaving for America are driven there] by the hope for quick enrichment, the desire for a better life."[31]

The overwhelming majority of peasants going to America did not intend to leave their native villages for good. The absence was to be temporary: "They planned to use the opportunity to make money . . . A financially independent existence [at home] or at least the improvement of their economic lot was the desire of most emigrants [that] they hoped to realize . . . after a few years' work in America."[32] The "better life" – the success that the prospective migrants saw in their dreams – was not some vague and imprecise notion, but, on the contrary, a practical one, defined according to the criteria of well-being, and prestige prevailing in the peasant society. As was noted already, these involved the amount of land owned or added by purchase, the number of cows in the field, the size and quality of farm buildings and the dowries given to daughters, the kind of weddings and christening celebrations, the dress displayed on Sundays in church, and finally the amount of money actually or purportedly possessed.

Who was going, then, and what might have been the "imagined future" for different groups of emigrants? Between 70 and 80 percent of all emigrants from East Central Europe who migrated to America in the period between 1880 and 1914 came from the rural areas. Various contemporary sources – peasant memoirs, biographies, novels, letters, monographic studies of the villages conducted and written at the beginning of the century – all point to the increasingly heterogeneous social character of rural emigration.

Chronologically speaking, the first ones to leave for America were the peripheral members of village communities, often transitional people: servants and laborers, small rural craftsmen, only marginally bound by local group pressures and controls.[33]

Starting in the 1880s among the small craftsmen and agricultural laborers, the movement soon swept up small- and medium-sized landholders too. Here is the recollection of a Galician peasant: "[At the beginning] better-off farmers . . . considered emigration as the path of advancement suitable for the landless and ill becoming the social status of a *kmieć*. God forbid . . . that a son of a *kmieć* go and become an industrial laborer. The attitude toward emigration among yeomen had changed, however, when re-emigrants started to bring more and more money."[34] And a similar observation by the *föispán* of Borsod County in Hungary reported in 1904 that those who were leaving were not only the landless "farm laborers, the domestic servants who are working in and for the large estates for many years, [but] too, the small farmers, the cotters who own their own homes."[35]

After 1900, during the period of the most intensive emigration to America from East Central Europe and until the outbreak of World War I, the average proportion of landless peasants among the emigrants to America ranged from over one-half, among the Magyars, Rusyns, Croatians, and Poles, to one-third among the Serbs. At the same time, the proportion of landowning peasants among the overseas travelers saw a steady increase, ranging, at the close of the first decade of this century, from one-tenth to nearly one-half, depending on the region. Whereas among all of the Magyar emigrants to the United States between 1900 and 1914 on the average only about 10 percent were small independent farmers, the figure for the Slovaks was 19 percent, 24 percent for the Rusyns, 28 percent for the Slovenes, 29 percent for the Poles, 33 percent for the Croatians, and 46 percent for the Serbs.[36]

As used in contemporary reports and statistics, the category of "landless" peasants did not constitute a homogeneous group, although in most studies dealing with emigration it has been treated as such. It consisted of three major substrata, with fluctuating membership and overlapping boundaries. To the first substratum belonged members of families with small- or even medium-sized holdings who shared the same household waiting to be allotted a piece of their own or to be given funds to purchase land on the outside. They usually possessed their own livestock and small plots for growing potatoes. They hired themselves out to work on the farms of richer peasants or on the local estate, or else migrated to nearby factories as seasonal laborers. In this group the identification with the landowning peasantry and its norms and values was particularly strong. The second group consisted of day laborers, peasants from dwarf-holding families or from the landless cotter households who could not hope to ever get from their parents or siblings enough money to purchase land. This group was more diversified than the first one, and its members sought various employment, whether as manorial workers or as industrial laborers. Its ties to the land were somewhat weaker than in the former category but strong enough to make a significant number from among those agricultural laborers also want to reenter the respected stratum of farmers. The last, third group was made up of manorial workers and servants. It was a specific category, in that its members did not belong to the village community and did not share its traditional concerns. In this group the desire to purchase land was substantially weaker than in the former two categories; with the money they earned, manorial laborers preferred to borrow at high interest or spend on themselves rather than to invest in land. In this group the desire to enter the ranks of the landowning peasantry was already substantially weakened.[37]

Since we lack detailed local community studies for the different regions of East Central Europe, it is not possible to ascertain the proportion of people from each of these particular groups who emigrated to America. However, the numbers were significant in all three, with peasants from the last category probably the most mobile, most intensely migrating across the region, through Europe, and across the Atlantic.

A little more information, although still insufficient, is available with regard to overseas migration by the landowning *kmeti* – also a heterogeneous grouping. For instance, in 1913, among 79 permanent emigrants to America from Zmiąca, a village in western Galicia, there were the following proportions of peasants from different social categories: 21.5 percent from those with dwarf-sized holdings, 30.4 percent from those with small-sized ones, 22.8 percent from the group with medium-sized holdings, and 25.3 percent from those with "large" holdings (over 10 hectares).[38] Another study of three Galician villages reported a similar situation: The most intense emigration before World War I was by peasants with small- and medium-sized holdings, the least intensive by those with the dwarf and "large" ones.[39] A similar tendency was reported among emigrants in other areas of East Central Europe.[40]

What was the "inner vision," or the imagined future, behind – to use once more the Schutzian concept – the "voluntative fiat," the "Let's go!" decision of peasant-emigrants, that was to "transform the inner fancying into performance or action gearing into the outer

world"?[41] In planning a future action to which they attach particular
importance but whose outcome is uncertain, people usually have
in mind some sort of minimum–maximum desiderata: a vision of
the least state of accomplishment, and – at the other end of the
continuum of wishes – should things turn out well, the most desirable achievement, timidly hidden in the depths of their consciousness and not revealed to anyone or only to the closest kin.

The goals of the peasant-emigrants can be interpreted in the same
way. Thus, at the "minimum" end of the continuum of wishes was
Sol Tax's "negative want": to accumulate sufficient resources to
make one's position in the village secure and safe from decline. At
the "positive" end of the continuum there was a vision of a more
substantial economic elevation, relative, of course, to the family's
present standing among its neighbors. In between these extremes,
there was a range of middle-accomplishment goals, encompassing
more or less daring visions of economic betterment and social success.

How, then, can the different groups of peasants emigrating from
East Central Europe at the turn of the century be fitted into this
interpretive framework? The guesses, obviously, will be speculative,
but the exercise may be worth trying. We may, then, surmise that
the prevailing in-order-to motive of emigrants in the first landless
category – the young members of small landowning households,
those who did not yet possess a plot of their own – was the acquisition of a piece of land and a house in the village or vicinity, so
that their nominal membership in the landowning group of families
would become factual. On the "minimum" side, the goal was to
amass sufficient capital to join the ranks of the small farmers as a
landowner and thus to avert actual loss of position. This alone required "big money" but could have been, and, as the evidence
shows, was in fact accomplished by thousands of peasants by means
of migration. For instance, as calculated for sample villages in the
counties of Szatmar, Szabolcs, Abauj-Torna, and Zemplén in
Hungary, the typical size of landholding purchased by emigrants
returning from America before World War I were pieces of 1.2 to
3.0 hectares.[42] Farther on the "continuum of wishes" – and this was
what a number of the prospective emigrants, excited by seeing the
achievements of the successful returnees and by the American legend, had their hopes pinned on – was a vision in which they pictured themselves as owners of more land than the minimum necessary to prevent economic decline. A few returnees in each of the
Hungarian villages in the four investigated counties – those emi-

grants who had stayed in America over ten years – purchased large pieces of land of about 10 hectares. Such people served as the reference point for the "maximum" dreams of the leavers. Further yet along the scale, the latter perhaps saw themselves as the possessors of one or two new brick houses, just like those of Walenty Podlasek from Wierzchosławice, and possibly also as owners of extra capital put away in the coffer and of several city suits or a gold watch or two.

The continuum of wishes from the (minimum) "negative want" to the (maximum) "positive achievement" also operated in the second group of landless emigrants, the day laborers from cotters' families. It is possible, however, that the range of the emigrants' wishes was in this case narrower, covering, so to speak, only the space between the minimum and the middle of the spectrum. Compared with the temporarily landless sons and daughters of the landowning families from the first group, the emigrant peasants in this category – poorer and ranking lower in the village socioeconomic hierarchy – could have cherished before their inner eyes a vision of a small piece of land with a house rather than, say, a 5- and 10-hectare farm. Or, put differently, it is possible that this category of emigrant contained, compared with the first group, a greater number of people whose "in-order-to" motives placed them somewhat closer to the "minimum" end of the continuum of wishes.

As for the last, and large, group of landless emigrants – manorial workers and servants – one may hypothesize with good reason that it was this category that had the greatest numbers of permanent leavers, people who were leaving their villages without the intention of ever returning and who were driven to the American cities by the in-order-to motive of making a better life for themselves there.[43]

The minimum–maximum continuum of wishes also operated in the category of landowning peasant-emigrants. The higher their actual economic position, the more elevated the "minimum" point on the spectrum. It is quite possible, as with the landless strata, that for the emigrants who were dwarf-holders, the range of wishes was narrower than that of the better-off ones, or else that a number of people whose goals had been closer to the minimum end of the spectrum was greater in this group than among emigrants from the higher peasant ranks. Again, however, given the existence of the minor options of saving money through seasonal migrations in Europe, for many of them it was the in-order-to motive to elevate their economic position that made them leave for America. For smallholders, their primary goal was to raise their position from the lower to the middle stratum, and possibly – in their wildest dreams – even to the highest ranks. If, finally, it were the well-to-do yeomen from the middle stratum who were leaving for America, the maximum in-order-to motive could have been to add to family possessions and join the wealthiest and most respected group in the village. If not granted this place by birth, they could now envision themselves entering it with money brought from America.

But even when the journey across the Atlantic had become an accepted cultural idea and social practice in East Central European villages, the decision to take the risk required in an individual a certain mobilization and an activist orientation toward life. Thomas and Znaniecki maintain that a general psychological predisposition of the individual was the important codetermining factor in the actual decision to leave for America:

> Whether a low economic status which an individual has in his country as compared with the status he may reach in another country will induce him to emigrate or not, depends . . . on his predisposition. If his prevalent attitude is the desire for economic advance, he will go unless interfered with by other influences; if it is fear of the unknown, he will not go unless other influences combine with the economic influence.[44]

It is obviously impossible to specify the proportions of those who displayed these different "predispositions" among the emigrants and among peasants who had remained at home, and the argument here does not depend on such evidence. But it is indeed probable, if not empirically provable, that those who went, determined to alter their lives, were the more daring ones.

But even those whose desire to go and try their luck was relatively stronger than other sentiments such as fear of the unknown or attachment to home, family, and friends that pulled in the opposite direction did not make their decisions free of uncertainty and doubt. The same presence of choice that opened up new avenues and opportunities for them engendered ambivalence and an awareness of the negative sides and possible traps of either action. A Polish immigrant, son of a small farmer in Galicia, writes in his memoir:

> I was receiving letters from my sister, my uncle, and aunts from America; they also sent their pictures. They were dressed so nicely that I could not understand how simple workers could afford such things. For a long time I was deliberating about America – what a strange country it is. A photograph shows that they are well fed, and in addition they send money to their relatives . . . After prolonged deliberation I decided to risk my savings for a ticket

to America, if only to see it with my own eyes and try my luck
there. Were I to fail, I thought, I was planning to return to Poland.[45]

And from the diary of another emigrant:

I was constantly looking for a way out of my unpleasant situation.
A young man has several different thoughts at once. I put aside
all my other desires when the thought came to me of going out
into the world, [but] I was undergoing a terrible internal struggle
. . . We came to the railroad station . . . At the thought of leaving
my parents' home, I felt strange and unhappy.[46]

3 Johnstown and the immigrant communities before World War I

The *Lebenswelten* of the East Central European peasant-immigrants who came to live in American towns and cities – their perceptions of existing and desired opportunities, and their actual behavior; their selections of goals, value orientations, and comparative reference frameworks; their achievements and failures – had been molded by three parallel and interacting influences. They were the experience of peasant existence in Europe; the external economic and social conditions in the localities where they settled in America; and the networks and ambience of the particular immigrant communities of which they became members and which they themselves actively created.

Chapters 1 and 2 depicted the sociocultural experience that the peasant emigrants brought with them from Europe. This chapter delineates the economic and social environment that immigrants to Johnstown, Pennsylvania, encountered at the beginning of the century. It also sketches the contours and the emerging networks of the communities in which they recreated their lives. (The socio-economic conditions in the city between the two world wars will be discussed in Chapter 5, after the presentation of the immigrants' initial adaptation in Johnstown. However, for the sake of convenience, the tables presented in Chapter 3 to illustrate the growth of Johnstown's population, industry, and labor force, its ethnic composition, and its housing and residential patterns cover the whole period from 1890 until 1940.)

To many Americans, Johnstown – a medium-sized city in the hills of western Pennsylvania – has been known as the Flood City. For more than a century, with exasperating regularity one flood after another has inundated the town. The floods of 1889, 1936, and 1977 were particularly disastrous, killing hundreds of people and devasting many of Johnstown's neighborhoods. Since the late 1880s, Johnstown has also, and equally accurately, been called "Pittsburgh in miniature" – smoky, busy, noisy – a town of ironworkers and miners.

During the last decades of the nineteenth century, Johnstown de-

79

Plate 4. Western Pennsylvania. Collection of Johnstown Flood Museum.

Plate 5. Johnstown, turn of the century. Collection of Johnstown Flood Museum.

Cambria plant

Gautier plant

Franklin plant

Plate 6. Cambria Iron Works, turn of the century. Collection of Johnstown
Flood Museum.

veloped into a notable example of what the Hollingsworths, in a recently proposed historical typology of medium-sized American cities, call the *autocratic* town.[1] It possessed all the basic characteristics of this particular type: an undifferentiated economic base and a low level of horizontal differentiation; a pyramid-shaped social structure with a small elite and a large lower class; a semicaste social organization with sharp ethnic cleavages and a corresponding ascription-based normative system; and an autocratic political system with overlapping political and economic elites.

The systematic growth of the city dates from the founding in 1852 by George S. King of the Cambria Iron Works, the predecessor of the Bethlehem Steel Company. For the first one hundred years, Cambria was the major impetus for, and the main determinant of, Johnstown's development. In 1870, the first Bessemer foundry was completed, and within one year it was rolling approximately 1,500 tons of rails per week. Cambria had also purchased about 50,000 acres of rich mineral land in the hills surrounding Johnstown, from which 50,000 tons of coal were extracted each year. With efficient rail communications east and west, Johnstown was quickly being transformed from a small village into a booming manufacturing city. In 1872, Cambria mills turned out about 90,000 gross tons of iron and steel rails; in 1873 the output reached 103,743. In 1877, the company formed a partnership with the proprietors of Gautier Mills of Jersey City, New Jersey, and the Gautier Steel Company was organized to build and operate wire and merchant steel mills in Johnstown.[2]

In 1898, when it leased its properties to the newly chartered Cambria Steel Company, the Cambria Iron Company boasted a capital of $24 million and assets of approximately $20 million. The reorganization was accompanied by further expansion. An additional steel plant, as well as by-product coke ovens, were constructed. In 1900, the erection of four new blast furnaces was initiated; in this one year alone the net earnings of the company increased by 300 percent.[3] From 1901 to 1903, the Cambria Steel Company grew by 155 percent, and its annual output of steel increased from 467,000 to 1,193,000 tons.[4] By the time of the outbreak of war in Europe, Cambria, now an industrial mammoth, owned eight other enterprises in Johnstown and had a major share in nine large companies across the country.[5] In 1916, it became a subsidiary of the Midvale Steel and Ordnance Company.[6]

Besides Cambria, other manufacturing enterprises were also located in Johnstown, but none of them was in the least comparable in size and influence. Of these, the largest was the Johnson Steel Rail Company, established in 1883. It was approximately one-fifth the size of the Cambria Iron Works. In 1901 the Johnson Steel Rail Company, whose factory was known in town as the "Lorain Plant," became a subsidiary of the United States Steel Company.[7]

The third largest manufacturing plant in Johnstown was the National Radiator Corporation, founded in 1894. Much smaller in scale were three brick and clay enterprises, whose products were virtually absorbed in toto by Cambria: Hiram Swank & Sons (established in 1856); A. J. Haws & Sons (started in 1859); and M. L. Williams (opened in 1899). In addition to these, there were in the city some ten more small industrial companies that manufactured metal products. They all depended upon the local coal, pig iron, and steel ingots produced by the steel mills, and most of them served the local market exclusively. Finally, a total of forty-seven small coal mines operated in the Johnstown quadrangle, all serving industries in the nearby area, primarily Cambria Steel Company and the Lorain Plant of U.S. Steel.[8]

The demographic expansion of Johnstown progressed concurrently with the city's industrial development. (The growth of the population of the city of Johnstown and the surrounding boroughs between 1840 and 1940 is presented in Table 3.1.) Barely reaching 1,000 in 1840, the population of Johnstown more than quadrupled in the next two decades and doubled again by 1880. Between 1890 and 1910, the period of the Cambria Company's spectacular expansion, the population of Johnstown grew by 150 percent. The influx of new people overflowed the boundaries of the original Johnstown Borough, and every few years new, contiguous boroughs were added to the city. In addition, several administratively independent, unincorporated villages sprang up at its edges. The makeup of "Greater Johnstown" closely reflected its topographic conditions, mounting and descending through slopes and valleys. From its downtown center, the city extended several miles into the three surrounding valleys – Conemaugh Valley, Stony Creek Valley, and Little Conemaugh – and formed what Johnstown has been ever since: an agglomeration of loosely connected boroughs separated from each other by hills and creeks.

With industrial operations rapidly expanding and its population growing every decade, Johnstown was becoming more of a steel town in outlook and character. It became a city dominated by a single manufacturing enterprise that in one way or another was responsible for the employment of thousands of people within a ten-mile

Table 3.1. *Population of Johnstown, 1840–1940*

	Population (N)			Gain (N)		Gain (%)	
Year	Johnstown City	Adjacent Boroughs[a]	Total	City of Johnstown	Johnstown and Boroughs	City of Johnstown	Johnstown and Boroughs
1840	949		949				
1850	1,269		1,269	320		33.7	
1860	4,185	ca. 2,000	ca. 6,185	2,916	4,916	229.8	387.4
1870	6,028	6,510	12,538	1,843	6,353	44.0	102.7
1880	8,380	7,520	15,900	2,352	3,362	39.0	26.8
1890	21,805	8,502	30,307	13,425	14,407	160.2	90.6
1900	35,936	7,868	43,804	14,131	13,497	64.8	44.5
1910	55,482	14,813	70,295	19,546	26,491	54.4	60.5
1920	67,327	21,662	88,989	11,845	18,694	21.5	26.6
1930	66,993	27,230	94,223	−334	5,234	−0.5	5.9
1940	66,668	28,477	95,145[b]	−325	922	−0.5	1.0

[a] In 1890, several originally separate boroughs (Prospect, Cambria City, Millville, Woodvale Conemaugh, Coopersdale, Morrellville), which formed around Johnstown after 1850, con solidated into Johnstown City; the latter was granted a third-class city charter. Others Franklin, East Conemaugh, Lower Yoder, Brownstown–retained their formal separateness In the last decade of the nineteenth century new boroughs sprang up: Daisytown, Dale Ferndale, Rosedale, Lorain, Southmont, Westmont, and Upper Yoder. Some of them were subsequently annexed by Johnstown; others shifted and changed their boundaries several times during the first decades of this century but remained separate.

[b] This total is lower than that of "Johnstown Metropolitan District," established in 194 (population 151,781), which also included five other townships more removed from the cit proper.

Source: *Ninth Census of the United States: 1870*, vol. 1: *Statistics of the Population*, 246; *Compendiur of the Ninth Census: 1870*, 311; *Tenth Census of the United States: 1880*, *Statistics of the Population* 308–9; *Compendium of the Tenth Census: 1880*, 267; *Eleventh Census of the United States: 1890 Report of the Population*, pt. 1, p. 292; *Compendium of the Eleventh Census: 1890*, 342–3; *Twelft. Census of the United States: 1900*, *Abstract of the Twelfth Census*, 101; *Population*, pt. 1, pp. 334 5; *Thirteenth Census of the United States: 1910*, *Population*, vol. 3, pp. 567–9; *Abstract of th Thirteenth Census of the United States with Supplement for Pennsylvania*, 579–80; *Fourteenth Censu of the United States: 1920*, vol. 1, *Population*, *Number and Distribution of Inhabitants*, 285–9 vol. 3, *Population, Characteristics by States*, 893–94; *Fifteenth Census of the United States: 193C Population*, vol. 3, *Report by States*, pt. 2, pp. 670, 722–3; *Sixteenth Census of the United State: 1940*, *Population*, vol. 1, *Number of Inhabitants*, 915, vol. 2, *Characteristics of the Population*, p 66, 197–8.

radius. In effect the Cambria Company controlled the city, its environs, and the lives of the people who lived and worked there. The company's operations stretched across the city, extending in a continuous strip along the little Conemaugh and Conemaugh rivers. Close to the center of town was the Gautier Department, which produced mill bars. To the west stood the Rosedale coke plant, and farther to the northwest was the giant Cambria plant, with blast furnaces and rolling mills. To the northeast was the wheel plant, and far to the north was the wire department. To the south was the huge Franklin plant, with blast furnaces, coke ovens, a large ore yard, and coke and limestone dumps.

As its operations grew, so did Cambria's labor force. Although it had no more than a few hundred workers in 1855, in less than a decade the roster of the Cambria Iron Company's employees reached 1,500. By 1870, Cambria already employed about 4,000 men, and in the 1880s the average number of the company's employees ranged between 5,000 and 6,000, including those employed in the mills, shops, mines, and other satellite establishments. By 1900, the number of workers employed in Johnstown steel and mining industries increased by an additional one-third, and it grew by nearly 100 percent between 1900 and 1914.[9]

In 1910, over 70 percent of all male manual workers in the city drew wages from Cambria. The remainder of Johnstown's labor force, those employed in smaller manufacturing enterprises as well as the city's white-collar workers, were also indirectly dependent on the company for a livelihood. Table 3.2 presents the occupational distribution of Johnstown's male and female work forces between 1900 and 1940 (average employment figures). It shows the predominantly industrial blue-collar character of the city, with 75 to 80 percent of the (male) labor force in manual occupations. Characteristically for steel towns, Johnstown was a "man's place." Even with a certain expansion of the service sector at the beginning of the century, Johnstown offered but very limited opportunities for women's employment.[10] In 1900, only 10.5 percent of the total number of adult women were gainfully employed; by 1910, this proportion increased to 18 percent and remained stable at that level. Mercantile activities in Johnstown had essentially been confined to businesses involved in the feeding and clothing of the employees of the Cambria Company and its subsidiaries. As a corollary to Johnstown's industrial and demographic expansion, business and trade in the city grew, increasing two and a half times in the twenty-five years from the Great Flood of 1889 to the outbreak of World War I. The prosperity of local businesses varied in direct proportion to the fortunes of local steel and coal enterprises.[11]

With over 70 percent of the total male blue-collar force in Johnstown employed at Cambria mills and coal mines and virtually all the rest dependent on the company for a living, Cambria held an unmatched power in the city from the 1880s onward. Its influence penetrated far beyond the economic sphere into social, political, and

Table 3.2. *Occupational distribution in Johnstown, 1900–1940*

Employment Categories	1900 (N)	1900 (%)	1910 (N)	1910 (%)	1920 (N)	1920 (%)	1930 (N)	1930 (%)	1940[b] (N)	1940[b] (%)
Men	13,005[a]		21,329		21,614		19,368		17,108	
Blue-collar jobs	10,359	79.7	17,155	80.4	16,733	77.5	14,425	74.5	12,179	71.2
Manufacturing and mining	7,642	58.8	14,968	70.2	14,016	64.8	12,120	62.6	10,518	61.5
Other manual occupations	2,717	20.9	2,187	10.2	2,717	12.7	2,305	11.9	1,661	9.7
White-collar jobs	2,646	20.3	4,174	19.6	4,881	22.5	4,943	25.5	4,929	28.8
Women[c]	1,633		2,939		4,340		4,710		4,912	
Blue-collar jobs	1,028	63.0	1,500	51.0	1,536	35.4	1,519	32.3	1,612	32.8
Manufacturing	288	17.6	364	12.4	502	11.6	372	7.9	700	14.3
Domestic and personal service	740	45.4	1,136	38.6	1,034	23.8	1,147	24.4	912	18.5
White-collar jobs	605	37.0	1,439	49.0	2,804	64.6	3,191	67.7	3,300	67.2

Note: N represents average number employed. Percentages are based on N. Figures for unincorporated boroughs are excluded.

[a] The census listed, for 1900, 12,249 employed men, considerably undercounting the miners; I added them, estimating from current notations published in the *Johnstown Tribune*.

[b] The figure for 1940 excludes those employed on public emergency works (1,610) and those seeking employment (3,117). The proportions of women gainfully employed, among all women 15 years of age and over, were as follows: 1900, 10.5 percent; 1910, 18.0 percent; 1920, 20.7 percent; 1930, 20.7 percent; 1940, 18.9 percent (plus an additional 5 percent seeking employment).

[c] The proportions of women gainfully employed, among all women 15 years of age and over, were as follows: 1900, 10.5 percent; 1910, 18.0 percent; 1920, 20.8 percent; 1930, 20.7 percent; 1940, 18.9 percent (plus an additional 5 percent seeking employment).

Source: Twelfth Census of the United States: 1900, Special Reports: Occupations, 448–50; *Thirteenth Census of the United States: 1910,* vol. 4: *Population, Occupation Statistics,* 238–42; *Fourteenth Census of the United States: 1920,* vol. 4: *Population, Occupations,* 276–80; *Fifteenth Census of the United States: 1930,* vol. 4: *Population, Occupations by States,* 1395–7; *Sixteenth Census of the United States: 1940, Population,* vol. 2: *Characteristics of the Population,* pt. 6, pp. 189, 287.

cultural realms. The city's major newspaper, the *Johnstown Tribune*, served as a loyal publicity agent for the company and traditionally supported its policies. Cambria managers routinely held high public offices in Johnstown and took a leading part in the social and cultural life of the community. During the 1870s, Cambria's general manager, Daniel Morrell, was president of the two major banks in the city of Johnstown as well as of the Somerset Railroad and the two major city utilities, Johnstown Gas Company and Johnstown Water Manufacturers. Other managers of the Cambria Company also simultaneously held leading positions in various local enterprises, thus forming a tightly knit sociopolitical elite in the city (Table 3.3).[12]

The company's successful suppression of repeated strikes by local miners and mill workers between 1866 and 1874 and its effective crushing of the unions in Johnstown provided the most spectacular test of its influence and power.[13] From its inception, Cambria firmly refused to employ anybody who was a self-proclaimed or even a suspected member or sympathizer of a labor organization. The strike threats by miners and wire drawers in 1877, 1883, and 1885 were met with immediate reprisals, and organizing attempts on the part of Cambria's rail straighteners, stonemasons, bricklayers, and gas fitters during the 1880s were likewise swiftly annihilated by the company.[14] And so, under the iron hand of Cambria Iron Company, trade unionism had disappeared entirely from Johnstown by 1890. It surfaced again, briefly and unsuccessfully, during the steel strikes of 1919 and 1937, and it was not until 1941 that the independent steelworkers' organization became permanently established in the city.

Absolutely refusing to permit any form of organized workers' protest and union activism on its premises, Cambria took upon itself the promotion and supervision of the welfare of Johnstown's residents, its employees and dependents. To the company's paternalism the city owed its night schools for boys (the first one established in 1857), the Opera House (1864), the public library and the Cambria Library Association (1878–92), the English class school, and the Cambria Scientific Institute that provided technical instruction and lectures for the mill workers (1881). The company also sponsored the Art Institute for Women, the Cambria Club Hotel (1882), and the Cambria Mills Relief, later replaced by the Mutual Benefit Association for Cambria employees and their families.[15]

Not surprisingly, considering its conscious efforts to exert maximal control over the labor force, Cambria was also the major rental agency in Johnstown. In the 1890s it owned about eight hundred

Table 3.3. *Interlocking directorates in Johnstown, 1880s*

Name of Director	WMC	CIC	CMBA	FNB	JSB	JMC	JWC	JWAC	CLA	NCTU
Daniel J. Morrell	X	X		X	X		X	X	X	
George Webb		X			X				X	
John Fulton		X	X						X	
Alex. Hamilton		X	X							
James Fronheiser		X	X							
James Cooper		X			X					
Cyrus Elder		X	X		X				X	
Pearson Fisher		X			X					
James McMillen	X				X		X	X		
Frank McMullen	X				X		X	X		X
John Lowman					X		X	X		
C. S. Ellis					X					
Howard J. Roberts					X		X			
H. A. Boggs		X								
William S. Robinson		X				X				
James Eldridge						X	X			
James Williams						X	X	X		
Alexander Kennedy	X		X							X
James O'Callaghan	X		X							
George Raush			X			X				
John C. Devine			X							X

Note: The following abbreviations are used in this table: WMC, Wood, Morrell & Co.; CIC, Cambria Iron Co.; CMBA, Cambria Mutual Benefit Association; FNB, First National Bank; JSB, Johnstown Savings Bank; JMC, Johnstown Manufacturing Co.; JWC, Johnstown Water Co.; JWAC, Johnstown Water & Gas Co.; CLA, Cambria Library Association; NCTU, National Christian Temperance Union.
Source: John William Bennet, Iron Workers in Woods Run and Johnstown: The Union Era, 1865–1895, Ph.D. thesis, University of Pittsburgh, 1977, 157.

Table 3.4. *Number of families and dwellings in Johnstown proper, with homeownership rates, 1900–1950*

Numbers and Proportions	1900	1910	1920	1930	1940	1950
Number of families	6,889	10,665	13,858	15,042	16,323	16,155
Number of dwellings	6,687	9,790	12,444	13,367	16,473	17,475
Number of families owning homes	2,526	3,641	5,038	6,026	5,654	7,371
Proportion owning homes (%)	36.7	34.1	36.4	40.1	34.6	45.6

Source: Abstract of the Twelfth Census of the United States: 1900, 131–4; Thirteenth Census of the United States: 1910, vol. 1, Population, 1363–4; vol. 3, Population, 587; Fourteenth Census of the United States: 1920, vol. 2, Population, 1298; Fifteenth Census of the United States: 1930, Population, vol. 6, "Families," 1148; Sixteenth Census of the United States: 1940, Housing, Pennsylvania, 43–4; Population, vol. 4, p. 227; Seventeenth Census of the United States; 1950, Housing, vol. 1, General Characteristics, pt. 5, pp. 38–22.

houses in different, more and less prestigious sections of the city, renting them to employees at prices somewhat lower than the regular rates in the city.[16] Cambria also offered to its long-standing employees a program whereby houses could be purchased at reasonable prices for money borrowed from the company and later repaid in small installments over an extended period of time. This policy, directed predominantly at Johnstown's skilled laborers, was designed to attract workers to Cambria mills and to tie them more permanently to the city. In fact, as early as the 1870s a significant proportion of Cambria's skilled workforce – approximately one-third – owned the houses in which they lived.[17]

Until the turn of the century there was no significant shortage of houses in Johnstown. But the rapid demographic expansion of the city after 1900, particularly in the poorer sections of town inhabited by unskilled laborers, generated a rather severe shortage of low-priced housing in Johnstown proper. The shortage increased with the passage of time, despite the repeated projects, ordinances, and studies of home-building problems initiated by Cambria management and city officials. Table 3.4 illustrates changes in homeownership rates in the city of Johnstown between 1900 and 1950. The data show an increasing discrepancy between the number of families residing in the city and the number of dwellings available in the first three decades of the century. They also indicate a relatively stable, unchanging homeownership rate from 1900 through the 1930s. Frustrated by the housing shortage in the city proper, however, homeownership aspirations of Johnstown inhabitants were in part satisfied by the availability of open land in the adjacent boroughs and townships of Greater Johnstown.

One further measure applied by the company to control its labor force was its hiring policy. New men were brought into the mills and coal mines through informal kinship networks; they were the sons, brothers, and cousins of workers already employed. The Cambria mills and mines were known in the area as "fathers-and-sons" employers, and since the inception of Cambria's operations a significant proportion of the work force was routinely procured by way of chain family employment, first from the surrounding counties, then from the outside.

With the rapid growth of local steel production, recourse to the employment of foreign labor became a necessity. During the 1880s the ethnic composition of the city's population and of the Cambria work force did not differ substantially from the pattern prevailing in the state of Pennsylvania and in the eastern region of the United States generally. In 1880, the share of foreign-born inhabitants in Johnstown, with the adjacent boroughs, was 40 percent. The corresponding proportion among the workers of the Cambria Company was 50 percent. At that time, the majority of foreign-born inhabitants of the city were German, Irish, and Welsh.[18]

Like other steel manufacturers throughout the country, in the last decade of the nineteenth century and during the early years of the present one, along with further expansion and modernization of production, Cambria underwent a process of restructuring of its work force. When the new technology substantially diminished the skill requirements involved in manufacturing steel, the traditional skilled work, such as that of puddlers, rollers, or heaters, was downgraded and in significant proportion eliminated. Instead, common labor became the major force in the plants, needed to keep up the continuous operation of Bessemer mills, open-hearth and blast furnaces.[19] At the beginning of the century, the *Johnstown Democrat* commented on this change in the composition of the work force in the local mills: "Formerly most of the employees were skilled men. But so great has been the substitution of ponderous machinery for skilled hand work that [over] 60 percent of employees [at Cambria] are now unskilled."[20] (For the American steel and iron industry as a whole, this proportion was 50 percent in 1910.[21]) The estimated

The immigrant communities before World War I 91

Table 3.5. *Estimated distribution of skill in Johnstown's steel industry 1890–1940 (in %)*

Employment Categories	1885–90	1900	1910	1920	1930	1940
Laborers	50	60–5	68	60	56	35
Semiskilled workers (specified and unspecified tasks)	50	35–40	18	20	24	40
Skilled workers			14	20	20	25

Note: The category of "laborer" used in the 1900–30 census classifications is not strictly comparable with that used from 1940 on. Most likely, the older censuses included in this category a number of low-level semiskilled workers. See Margo Conk, *The U.S. Census and Labor Force Change: 1870–1940* (Ann Arbor, Mich.: 1980). The estimates for 1940 exclude steelworkers employed on public emergency works and seeking employment.
Source: John A. Fitch, *The Steel Workers* (New York, 1969 [1910]), 351–3; Isaac Hourwich, *Immigration and Labor* (New York, 1922), 394–413; Nathan D. Shappee, "A History of Johnstown and the Great Flood of 1889: A Study of Disaster and Rehabilitation," *Johnstown Tribune*, November 1, 1940, 5–7; U.S. Bureau of the Census, *Manufactures, 1914,* 1:1281; Raymond E. Murphy, "The Geography of Johnstown, Pennsylvania: An Industrial Center," *Pennsylvania State College Bulletin* 13 (1934), 20–30; also current notations on employment in the local steel industry in *Johnstown Tribune* and *Johnstown Democrat,* 1900–1904; *Thirteenth Census of the United States: 1910,* vol. 4: *Population, Occupation Statistics,* 238–42; *Fourteenth Census of the United States: 1920,* vol. 4: *Population, Occupations,* 276–80; *Fifteenth Census of the United States: 1930,* vol. 4: *Population, Occupation by States,* 1395–7; *Sixteenth Census of the United States: 1940,* vol. 2: *Characteristics of the Population,* pt. 6, pp. 189, 257.

distribution of the work force according to skill in the steel industry in Johnstown between 1890 and 1940 is shown in Table 3.5.

The increased demand for common labor in American iron and steel manufacturing, a side effect of the expansion of the industry, coincided with the influx of East Central and southern European peasant immigrants to the country. Faced by an insufficient supply of native-born American and western European workers needed for its open hearth and blast furnace operations and for its coal mines, the Cambria management, *nolens volens,* welcomed the East Central European immigrants by the turn of the century.

The first immigrants from East Central Europe – no more than a handful of families – had appeared in the city as early as the 1870s as contract laborers procured by the Cambria Iron Company from

New York.[22] Regardless of nationality, they were all called "Hungarians." During the 1889 flood, about 85 people with Slavic and Magyar names were identified among the 2,000 victims. In 1891, the Johnstown city directory listed 75 East Central European names, but clearly only the heads of households and their adult male progeny were enumerated; boarders, as well as women and children, were left out.[23] The actual size of the East Central European population in Johnstown at that time was probably between 400 and 500. In 1895 the Johnstown city directory listed 825 men and 35 women with recognizably Slavic and Magyar names as inhabitants of the city proper and of its adjacent boroughs. Actually the number of East Central European immigrants in the area was probably higher – possibly around 1,500, counting unlisted wives and children of the newcomers and unregistered boarders.

From 1900 on, Johnstown was already a big enough city for the U.S. Census to provide data as to the ethnic distribution of its population. The numbers of East Central Europeans in Johnstown provided by these early censuses should be treated only as estimates: First, the censuses did not differentiate among "Austrians" and "Hungarians" subsuming under these general categories Slovenes, Croatians, Galician Poles and Ukrainians, as well as Slovacs and Rusyns. Second, they lumped together a number of Slavs and Jews under the label "Russian." Third, they did not specify the ethnic composition of the surrounding boroughs and townships in which many new immigrants settled.[24]

According to the 1900 census, there were in Johnstown over 5,000 people of East Central European background. According to the census specifications, over 3,000 of this number were foreign-born Slavs and Magyars, and about 2,000 were born in this country. To this number of East Central Europeans in the city of Johnstown, we should add approximately 1,000 to 1,500 of those who settled in the surrounding boroughs and townships.

During the next decade the influx of Slavs and Magyars into Johnstown continued to increase, a trend that persisted until the outbreak of the war in Europe. The number of East Central Europeans in Johnstown proper more than tripled between 1890 and 1900, and then doubled during the first decade of our century. Despite the increase in the East Central European immigration into the city, however, the core of Johnstown's population remained, as in the earlier period, solidly native-born. The data in Table 3.6 show the approximate proportions of East Central Europeans in the city and vicinity, together with the proportions of native-born Americans and northwestern Europeans from 1890 until 1940.

Most of the East Central European residents of the city were recent arrivals. According to the Immigration Commission investigating Johnstown in 1908–9, over two-thirds of the local iron and steel workers of western European stock at the time of the study had already been in America for more than twenty years. Conversely, the same proportion of East Central European laborers had settled in America less than five years before the investigation.[25] As in most American cities, the immigrants arriving in Johnstown at the turn of the century were also predominantly male. Of the total number of 3,077 Slavic and Magyar immigrants recorded in the city by the 1900 census, only 22 percent were female.[26]

The first East Central Europeans arriving in the city were directed by the Cambria Company management into sections close to the mills traditionally inhabited by foreigners: Cambria City and Minersville. Already in 1870, while Johnstown proper had only 20 percent foreign-born inhabitants, mostly Irish and German, the proportion of immigrants in these neighborhoods was about 40 percent. By 1880, the residential concentration of foreign-born inhabitants of the city became even more pronounced: In Johnstown proper, 40 percent of the inhabitants were immigrants, whereas in Cambria City the proportion was 85 percent, in Minersville 50 percent, and in two other immigrant colonies on the other side of town near another plant – Prospect and Conemaugh – respectively 80 and 70 percent.[27] The Slavs and Magyars who come to Johnstown at the turn of the century "inherited" these territories. First they inhabited the detached, dilapidated company tenements along the edges of Cambria City and Minersville, known in Johnstown as "Rotten Row." It stretched "beyond the works and [is] surrounded by huge piles of refuse from the furnace . . . The houses [are] banked above ground and some of them are built upon rough stone foundations, which give them the appearance of having cellars . . . Outside privies built upon vaults, and prominently exposed to the view of the passerby, are located near the houses. The drainage is surface, there being no escape for slops and other waste matter."[28]

The peasant-immigrants who, after 1890, began arriving in Johnstown in greater numbers followed the "pioneers," taking up more and more of the adjacent territory around the mills as their numbers grew. Of the total number of 860 people with recognizably Slavic and Magyar names listed in the 1895 Johnstown city directory, about

Table 3.6. *Ethnic distribution of Johnstown population, 1890–1940*

Census Category	1890	1900	1910	1920	1930	1940[a]
Total Population	21,805[b]	35,936	55,482	67,327	66,993	66,668
White						
Native of native parentage	11,092 (51.0)	18,675 (52.0)	26,237 (47.3)	34,207 (50.8)	34,687 (51.7)	39,103 (58.7)
Native of foreign parentage	5,978 (27.4)	9,629 (26.8)	13,467 (24.3)	19,307 (28.7)	21,060 (31.4)	18,610 (27.9)
Foreign-born	4,482 (20.6)	7,318 (20.4)	15,316 (27.6)	12,142 (18.0)	9,478 (14.2)	7,290 (10.9)
Foreign-stock whites[c]						
Northern and Western Europeans						
Foreign-born		3,509	5,132	3,806	2,074	1,504
Native-born	} 900–1,500	6,308	9,267	7,976	7,439	—
East Central Europeans						
Foreign-born		3,207[d]	8,117	6,491	5,727	4,345
Native-born		2,073	3,714	9,661	10,959	—
East Central European foreign stock, adjacent townships and boroughs[e]		1,000–1,500	5,000	5,000	3,000–4,000	3,000

Note: Figures in parentheses represent percentages.

ª In the 1940 census, "The population [was] divided into two fundamental nativity groups: native and foreign-born. . . The native population [was] not here subdivided according to the nativity of parents as was done in the previous census" (*Sixteenth Census of the United States: 1940,* vol. 2, *Population,* pt. 6, 44).

ᵇ The number of black residents in Johnstown in the period 1900–40 were as follows: 1890–253 (1.0%); 1900–314 (0.8%); 1910–462 (0.8%); 1920–1,671 (2.5%); 1930–1,768 (2.7%); 1940–1,665 (2.5%).

ᶜ The Italians, Greeks, Syrians, and Mexicans, each group small in numbers, are omitted from "foreign stock whites" in table; their numbers for each decade can be arrived at by subtracting the figures for the northern and western European and the East Central European foreign-born populations from the total number of foreign-born in the city (the same calculation can be made for the "native-born American of foreign parentage" category).

ᵈ The proportions of foreign-born East Central Europeans among the total foreign-born population in the city in the period 1900–40 were as follows: 1900–43.8 percent; 1910–53.0 percent; 1920–53.5 percent; 1930–60.4 percent; 1940–59.6 percent.

ᵉ The figures in this row are estimates. For 1900 and 1910 they are based on the manuscript census enumeration; for later decades, I took the numbers of foreign-born East Central Europeans from the population censuses, whenever given, and estimated the proportions of their American-born children for each of the surrounding townships and boroughs according to the general ethnic compositon as indicated in independent local sources.

Source: Eleventh Census of the United States: 1890, Report of the Population, pt. 1, 551, 728; Twelfth Census of the United States: 1900, Population, pt. 1, 676, 796–9, 878–9; Thirteenth Census of the United States: 1910, Population, vol. 1 p. 180; Abstract of the Thirteenth Census with Supplement for Pennsylvania, 628, 578; Fourteenth Census of the United States: 1920, Population, vol. 2, pp. 954–7 and vol. 3, pp. 866–76; State Compendium for Pennsylvania: 1920, 74–5; Fifteenth Census of the United States: 1930, Population, vol. 3, pt. 2, Report by States, 798; Population, Special Report on Foreign-born Families by Country of Birth of Head, 151; Sixteenth Census of the United States: 1940, Population, vol. 2: Characteristics of the Population, pt. 6, pp. 68, 253–6.

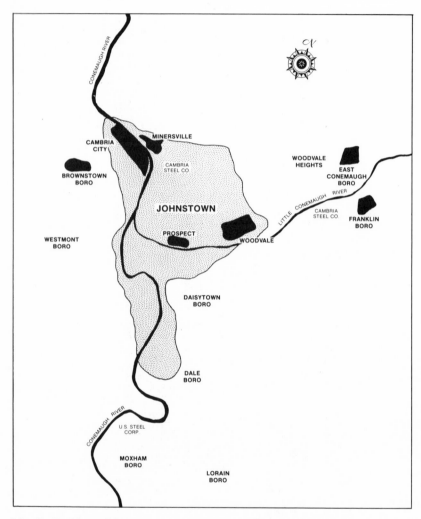

Map B. Residential locations of East Central European immigrants in Johnstown and vicinity, early 1900s.

90 percent resided in the Cambria City–Minersville area.[29] By the beginning of the century the three wards, 14, 15, and 16, that comprised Cambria City and Minersville, together with a few "islands" in the lower sections of the adjacent boroughs of Brownstown and Lower Yoder, originally inhabited almost exclusively by the Irish and German mill workers, became known in the city as the "foreign colony," synonymous with the "Hungarian section." In the same

Table 3.7. *Concentration of East Central Europeans in different sections of Johnstown, 1900–1940 (in %)*

Section of Johnstown	1900	1910	1920	1930	1940
Cambria City and Minersville (primary settlement)	79	70	56	} 49	} 44
Woodvale-Prospect and East Conemaugh–Franklin boroughs (primary settlement)	15	18	16		
Morrellville (secondary settlement)	} 6	} 12	18 }	} 51	} 56
Moxham and surroundings (secondary settlement)			10 }		

Note: The data are for all East Central Europeans from the 1900 census (persisters and returnees of both sexes, immigrants and second generation), who were identified in the city directories in the years indicated.
Source: East Central European population from manuscript schedules of 1900 census, traced in Johnstown city directories for 1910, 1920, 1930, and 1940.

period other small colonies of East Central Europeans were established in the Prospect-Woodvale and Franklin–East Conemaugh areas (see Map B). No fewer than 94 percent of the Slavic and Magyar families recorded in the 1900 census were concentrated in these "foreign colonies."[30] The concentration of East Central Europeans in different sections of Johnstown in the period 1900 to 1940 is shown in Table 3.7.

Mostly male and young, the Slavic and Magyar settlers in the city were taken in by the local industry as much-needed common laborers for open-hearth and blast furnaces; in the brickyards; at railroad works; and in the coal mines. For them, as for the older inhabitants of the city, the Cambria Steel Company had been the major employer: In the first decade of this century, a full 80 percent of all of the male peasant-immigrants residing in Johnstown worked as laborers at Cambria mills, and another 15 percent were employed in the local coal mines and in the brickyards.[31] The Slavs and Magyars, whose proportion among Cambria's work force in 1890 did not exceed 10 to 15 percent, by World War I constituted between 50 and 60 percent of the local miners and brickyard workers and 30 to 40 percent of Johnstown's steel and iron workers.[32]

In order to reveal more fully the position of the East Central European immigrants in the city's occupational structure, we can compare the rate of their actual occupational mobility between 1900 and 1920 with the rate that should have obtained were they to have reached, in 1920, occupational parity with the employed male population in Johnstown generally. (The patterns of immigrants' occupational movements in the first phase of their stay in the city will be discussed in detail in the following chapter.)

Tables 3.8 and 3.9 present two sets of matrices: one for the transition between blue- and white-collar occupations, and one for the transition between unskilled/unspecified semiskilled, and specified semiskilled/skilled occupations within the mills. (The joint treatment of unskilled and unspecified semiskilled occupations is forced by the gross categories used in the Johnstown city directories from which the information on the immigrants' employment was obtained. Specified semiskilled and skilled occupations are combined because of the small number of immigrants in these categories.) In both cases, a model of equivalent destination structures was applied to the observed transition matrices. The observed matrices are based on the calculations for immigrant persisters – men present in Johnstown at both checkpoints in 1900 and 1920.

The matrices on the left side of the tables show the observed percentage distributions of the immigrant-generation East Central European males in blue-collar and white-collar occupations and in the two categories of jobs in the mills. The matrices on the right side of the tables indicate the outcome of adjustments to the criterion of equivalent destination structures. In both comparisons, for the immigrants to have matched Johnstown's occupational distribution as of 1920, their overall rate of mobility should have been double that actually observed: not 10 percent but 21 percent in the blue-collar to white-collar transition, and 23 percent instead of 11 percent in the mills. More significantly, in order to have reached occupational parity with the employed male population in Johnstown in 1920, the foreign-born Slavs and Magyars should have displayed a considerably greater upward mobility rate: 20 percent, rather than 8 percent, in moving between blue- and white-collar occupations, and 21 percent, instead of 7 percent, in advancing within the mills.

An inability to speak English and a lack of industrial skills among the immigrants who had but recently arrived from European villages were obvious determinants of their persistence at the bottom of the city's occupational ladder. The tradition of chain-group and family hiring, openly supported by the Cambria management and sus-

Table 3.8. *Intragenerational occupational mobility of foreign-born East Central European male persisters in Johnstown in blue-collar and white-collar occupations, 1900–1920 (in %)*

Observed Matrix

	1920		
	Blue-collar	White-collar	Total
1900			
Blue-collar	89 (outflow 92)	8 (outflow 8)	97
White-collar	2 (outflow 67)	1 (outflow 33)	3
Total	91	9	100

Observed Mobility

Total mobility	10
% up	8
% down	2
Immobile	90

Adjusted Matrix

	1920		
	Blue-collar	White-collar	Total
1900			
Blue-collar	77 (outflow 79)	20 (outflow 21)	97
White-collar	1 (outflow 40)	2 (outflow 60)	3
Total	78	22	100

Adjusted Mobility

Total mobility	21
% up	20
% down	1
Immobile	79

Source: East Central European foreign-born male population from manuscript schedules of 1900 census, traced in Johnstown city directory for 1920; *Fourteenth Census of the United States: 1920:* vol. 4, *Population, Occupations,* 276–80.

Table 3.9. *Intragenerational occupational mobility of foreign-born East Central European male persisters in Johnstown in manual occupations in the steel industry, 1900–1920 (in %)*

	Observed Matrix			Adjusted Matrix		
	1920			1920		
1900	U and USS[a]	SS and S	Total	U and USS	SS and S	Total
U and USS	88 (outflow 93)	7 (outflow 7)	95	74 (outflow 78)	21 (outflow 22)	95
SS and S	4 (outflow 80)	1 (outflow 20)	5	2 (outflow 40)	3 (outflow 60)	5
Total	92	8	100	76	24	100

	Observed Mobility	Adjusted Mobility
Total Mobility	11	23
% up	7	21
% down	4	2
Immobile	89	77

[a] U = unskilled; USS = unspecified semiskilled; SS = specified semiskilled; S = skilled.
Source: East Central European foreign-born male population from manuscript schedules of 1900 census, traced in Johnstown city directory for 1920; *Fourteenth Census of the United States: 1920:* vol. 4, *Population, Occupations,* 276–80.

tained in the practice of the immigrants themselves, from the start channeled the East Central European workers into the lowest occupational stratum in the local mills. Over and above these factors, the needs of the steel industry and the company's open nativism in job assignments and promotions further greatly limited the immigrants' occupational chances.

The concept of "cultural division of labor" used by social scientists for the analysis of class/ethnic inequities in contemporary societies[33] applies well to the situation in Johnstown at the beginning of this century. There were in the Cambria mills two "occupational circuits" based on ethnic divisions. The first, with higher wages and better working conditions in more prestigious finishing departments, employed predominantly native-born American and western European workers. The second, largely unskilled, with unhealthy and dangerous jobs in open-hearth, blast furnace, and railroad departments, and in the foundries and coal mines, employed the immigrants.

The Cambria management regarded the presence of Slavs and Magyars in Johnstown as a necessary evil: "Racism was very distinct then," admitted a retired superintendent of Cambria: "We all called them Huns, Dagos, and Polacks."[34] The company's traditional policy of informal chain hiring, and the work process itself in the mills and coal mines that bound the immigrants together in homogeneous nativity groupings, deepened castelike divisions between the "Hungarians" and the rest of the work force. Natural divisiveness among the immigrants who spoke different tongues and sought each other's familiar company were deliberately utilized by the Cambria management in its efforts to strengthen control over the work force.

The Immigration Commission reported a distinct tendency in the mills toward segregation according to race, particularly in the unskilled occupations "such as general labor, cleaning up, rough construction labor, etc. [where] gangs of laborers are employed. In these gangs a single race very frequently predominates," a concentration openly encouraged by the bosses.[35] Nearly seventy-five years later, a retired general foreman of Cambria's mechanical department reconfirmed this past policy of the company: "We purposefully constructed the labor gangs according to nationality [as it was easier for everyone and, besides, to mix them together would require bosses who knew several languages]."[36] At the shop level, the bosses "kept foreigners in their place," shifting them and moving them about the plant according to their wishes. As one of the immigrants recalled, he was arbitrarily "shifted about by his foreman in order to make it easier for his [American] favorite. In summer [he] was used as a hookman. Being excessively hot and heavy work, it is not desired in summer, although the pay is good. In winter, however, it is different. Hence in winter [he] would be replaced by an American, a favorite of the foreman or the roller."[37]

In the first phase of job restructuring in the American steel industry, the old steel-making skills were devalued. In the second phase, in order to secure high productivity by providing the laborers with work incentives and a sense of occupational advancement, new job ladders were created involving a range of more or less mechanized tasks differing in pay and status.[38] A similar process also occurred at Cambria in Johnstown, where, during the first and second decade of this century, a number of new jobs that increasingly blurred the once-clear distinction between the skilled and unskilled labor were developed.

However, the demands of the steel industry, and the ethnic-ascriptive hiring and promotional policies of the company, confined the great majority of East Central European workers to the lower "occupational circuit" in the mills. First, despite the restructuring of jobs, Cambria continued to need large quantities of unskilled labor. Second, although the number of more mechanized tasks in the mills was growing, the supply of available skilled jobs and semi-skilled ones with specified tasks such as operating hoists, cranes, or switches had remained limited. By the beginning of the second decade of this century it oscillated around 2,500. At that time, the local steel industry employed on the average between 12,000 and 13,000 workers. Since the East Central European laborers constituted about 40 percent of the total work force, the supply of the more acceptable native-born American and western European candidates was more than sufficient to fill these positions.[39]

And in fact, the preference in promotions "for good jobs in the mills" was openly given to "the Americans, Welsh, then Germans, [and] Irish [who] were greatly preferred": Both the former superintendent at Cambria and his peer, who had been general foreman of one of the plants, admitted this was the company's regular policy.[40] The Immigration Commission investigating employment relations in Johnstown industries at the beginning of the century made identical observations: "[With some exceptions], the Southern and Eastern European races have gone into the skilled occupations only where there were not enough Americans, English, Welsh, Germans, Irish and Swedes to supply the demand for that sort of labor."[41]

In Johnstown there were no institutions – clubs, halls, societies – that could provide different immigrant groups in the city with opportunities for social and cultural integration.[42] In fact, the foreigners – Magyars, Slavs, and Italians – were openly discouraged from attending the places frequented by Americans and older-stock ethnics, even those with whom they shared a similar class position: "The Hunky is not welcome in the 'better' saloons and movies. [On his side] he never thought of visiting a 'better' club."[43] The prevalent sentiment toward the "Hunkies" in Johnstown, shared by the wealthy Protestant businessmen, the company owners, and the "buckwheats" (native-born Americans from the surrounding countryside), as well as by the Scottish, Welsh, German, and Irish laborers, was disdain and scornful superiority.[44]

Crime and industrial accidents had remained the major occasions of the East Central Europeans' otherwise infrequent appearance in the local news throughout the whole period from their early settlement in the city until the outbreak of World War I. By 1910, when the "foreign sections" were already crowded with thousands of immigrants, the East Central Europeans were mentioned in the local media in one additional, more "constructive" context: as builders of several churches in their neighborhoods and as faithful and devout Christians. The religious occasions and festivities celebrated in numerous "Slavish" churches in Cambria City and later also the sports games played by immigrant teams made more or less regular, if greatly abbreviated, news in the *Tribune*. Notes about these events, however, were always placed separately from those concerning the church life and the religious activities of the American segment of the population, as if the East Central Europeans, though part now of the city's *paysage*, belonged, after all, to an alien species.[45]

These, then, were the economic, social, and cultural conditions that the immigrants encountered in Johnstown at the beginning of the century. They clearly had been conducive to what Yancey, Ericksen, and Juliani called "emergent ethnicity."[46] With one powerful employer deliberately using ethnic-divisive residential as well as hiring and promotion policies; with the group-divisive character of the work process in the mills and coal mines; with the absence of unions and therefore of class-based integrative social institutions, ethnic rather than class-based solidarity, institutions, and ties traditionally constituted in Johnstown the primary group binding force. Without unifying, class-based social networks, the immigrant workers, otherwise naturally inclined to seek the company of their own, had become even more absorbed in their own beneficial societies, parishes, clubs, and associations, which split and divided the city's working class into separate units.

The social world created in Johnstown by East Central Europeans was as self-absorbed and separate as that of "Americans."* Concentrated residentially and occupationally, with sharp group boundaries separating the "foreigners" from the rest of the city's inhabitants and sustained by the autocratic ethnic-ascriptive system prevailing in Johnstown, in the two decades from the mid-1890s until the outbreak of World War I the immigrants created vibrant minicommunities within which they maneuvered in pursuit of the goals that had brought them to America.

We will now briefly outline this parallel "internal framework" created by the immigrants: the inside network of relations that they had created themselves while seeking to adapt to the new environment and that they used in purposeful actions toward the realization of their goals.

With more and more new immigrants coming into the city and many of those who had come earlier leaving for other places or going back to Europe, the East Central European population in Johnstown at the turn of the century was in a state of flux. "An accurate estimate of the number of Hungarians in the city at any given time is impossible," stated a contemporary investigator, since they "constantly change from one place to another . . . Only about 60 percent of the [total] foreign population [in Johnstown] is permanently located; the balance constitutes a restless and floating element drifting between American industrial centers and their foreign homes."[47]

Analyses of the immigrants' persistence and residential mobility at the beginning of the century usually consider out-migration as

---

* Throughout this book I use the terms *Americans* and *American world* because these concepts make sense for the interpretation of the experience and perceptions of the new immigrants – concentrated in "foreign colonies" and in national labor gangs, and separated from the rest of the local Johnstown society by castelike social and cultural divisions between the "foreigners," on the one hand, and native-born Americans and western Europeans on the other. But obviously the "American world" was itself internally fragmented along religious and ethnic lines, forming a constellation of overlapping residential, occupational, and private-informal networks. Some of these were penetrated at their edges – in the workplace or in religious life – by new immigrants from particular groups. Basically, however, the East Central Europeans perceived the social system in Johnstown as divided into two general categories: their own, that is the "foreigners," and a generalized out-group – "Americans" (see the discussion of the immigrants' images of the dominant system in Chap. 7).

terminal, excluding from further tracing those who had once left the city. In fact, however, many of those who left later returned. Therefore, in tracing the immigrants originally recorded in the 1900 census through Johnstown's city directories, I also recorded the returnees, each time taking as my comparative base the full 1900 census list of East Central European residents of the city. Of the total number of 2,399 East Central European male immigrants recorded as present in Johnstown in 1900, 22 percent (517) left and returned to the city at least once before 1940.[48] Although tracing the returnees does broaden somewhat our still skimpy knowledge about the mobility patterns of the immigrant workers, it remains a very imperfect measure. My returnees were people recorded as present in Johnstown city directories only at a few arbitrarily selected checkpoints. In reality, a number of them probably returned and left many more times in between.

Persistence in Johnstown of the East Central European male immigrants in the period 1900 to 1940, corrected for mortality, is shown in Table A.1 in the Appendix. During the initial five years after 1900, 4.9 percent of the originally recorded immigrant population should have disappeared, owing to mortality; between 1900 and 1910 this loss should have been 9.2 percent; between 1900 and 1920, 23.6 percent; between 1900 and 1930, 40.0 percent; and by 1940 as many as 61.2 percent of the original East Central European population in 1900 should already have died. Corrected for mortality, the rate of persistence for the immigrants after the initial ten years from 1900 was 39 percent; in 1920, 31 percent.

Although the new immigrants constantly moved in and out of the foreign colonies, those who stayed on displayed an increasing rate of persistence. Between 1900 and 1905, 57 percent of those who had resided in Johnstown at the time of the 1900 census remained in the city; of those who persisted until 1905, 69 percent were present in 1910; and of those present in 1910, as many as 77 percent were still in town by 1920.

It was this group that at the beginning of the century constituted the skeleton, as it were, of the developing immigrant communities. Those who stayed in the city, however, were also highly mobile within its limits, moving within or among the foreign colonies in Johnstown. Between 1900 and 1905, over 66 percent of the East Central Europeans recorded by the 1900 census had changed their address; between 1900 and 1910, over 70 percent had done so.[49]

The high transiency of the East Central European population arriving in Johnstown during the first decade of the new century and the "island-hopping" of the persisters among the city's foreign colonies did not prevent the formation and growth of permanent immigrant communities with complex networks of churches, cemeteries, schools, saloons, business enterprises, clubs, dance halls, and national associations.[50] The network of immigrant institutions – the most dense in Cambria City and Minersville, the core colony – was replicated in a lesser degree in the smaller ones in Woodvale-Prospect, and Franklin–East Conemaugh boroughs. The *hoppers* – the immigrants who moved back and forth among different sections – often initiated in a new place the organizations already formed in the neighborhoods they had just left or else held dual membership in parallel institutions.

The arriving crowd represented eight nationality groups: Slovaks, Magyars, Poles, Croatians, Serbs, Slovenes, Rusyns (the inhabitants of the then Hungarian Transcarpathia, the southern slopes of the Carpathian mountains), and Ukrainians (from Austrian Galicia, on the northern side of the Carpathians).[51] The oldest settlers in the city were Slovaks, followed by a handful of Poles from the Prussian partition and a small group of Magyars. The Serbs, Croatians, Rusyns, and Ukrainians were the most recent arrivals.[52] (Persistence rates in Johnstown for particular nationality groups between 1900 and 1940 are shown in Table A.2 in the Appendix.)

Whether they were "old settlers" who had arrived during the 1880s or "greenhorns" who came after 1900, as elsewhere in American cities the immigrants were migrating to Johnstown in a chain pattern in groupings from adjacent villages in Europe. The local church records indicate that most of the Magyars came to Johnstown from villages in the counties Abauj-Torna and Ung; the majority of Rusyns from the counties Gemer and Ung; the Slovenes from the Rakek-Mokronog area in Krain. The Croatians were from Jaśka and Karlovač; the Poles from the Bochnia-Limanowa and Krosno-Rzeszów counties in Galicia, and from around Mława and Lomża in Congress Poland, as well as from the region of Gostyń in the Prussian part of the country. The Serbs came from the Kordun area in the Croatian territory; the Ukrainians from the counties of Lesko and Sanok, with a smaller group of Lemkians from around Lvov, who later came to call themselves "Russians." The Slovaks, the largest group of all and therefore more dispersed in origin, came from the counties of Spiš, Sariš, Zemplín, and Liptov.[53]

Within the narrow range of residential locations open to them in Johnstown, and probably partly out of nostalgia, the immigrants tended to choose areas that most closely resembled the familiar old-

country *paysage*. So, for instance, the Slovaks from the highest mountain regions of Spiš tended to settle up on the hills, in the boroughs
of Lower Yoder and Brownstown; the Magyars, on the other hand,
chose rather to live in the "lowland" region of Cambria City. The
Poles from the hilly Limanowa region in Galicia, as well as the
Ukrainians from Lesko and the Rusyns from the other side of
the Carpathians, settled either in the hilly parts of Minersville or on
the slopes in East Conemaugh. The "lowland" Congress Poles,
however, like the Magyars, preferred the flat land in Cambria City.[54]

As soon as the immigrants began settling in Johnstown in larger
numbers, mutual-help societies mushroomed in the foreign colonies. Their number increased from a modest eight, in 1899, to sixty
by 1917.[55] "Seed" associations usually preceded by a few years the
founding of churches. The pattern was similar to that described in
most American cities with large immigrant colonies: A group of pioneers got together, formed a committee, organized collection of
funds, arranged for a contract, and hired a pastor to come. Then a
church was erected. New societies were established. New, bigger
churches were projected, funded, and brought into being. In the
1880s, the Slavs and the Magyars residing in the "Rotten Row" tenements in Cambria City attended St. Mary's Immaculate Conception
German Catholic Church. When, in 1891, the Slovak church St. Stephen's was consecrated, all but a handful switched to the new parish.[56] After that, in quick succession, one after another all East Central European groups present in the city erected their own churches,
so that by 1910 there were already 12 of them.[57] In each of the parishes the immigrants organized religious societies for men, women,
and children, and soon afterward parochial schools were established. By 1910 there were 4 of them: Slovak (the largest one); Polish;
Rusyn; and Croatian. Other groups had their children attend Sunday school for religious and language instruction.

As in hundreds of other American cities in which the immigrants
settled in greater numbers, the East Central European saloons, groceries, butcher shops, furniture and clothing stores, foreign exchange, and steamship agencies opened up in the "foreign colonies"
as soon as there was enough clientele to be fed, clothed, and catered
to. The "Mercantile Appraisal" printed in the *Tribune* for the year
1900 mentioned over 30 East Central European businesses located
in "foreign colonies," 11 of them Christian and 20-odd Jewish. By
1915, there were in the immigrant sections 90 Christian and about
100 Jewish business enterprises conducted by East Central Europeans.[58] In that year a Slovenian Savings and Loan Bank was es-

tablished to extend loans to the immigrants for first mortgages on real estate, and credit to those who were either in business or needed money to open one.[59] Immigrant businesses advertised in the foreign-language newspapers published in town at the beginning of the century: the Croatian *Radnička Novina*, the Slovak *Krajan*, the Hungarian *Hirado*, and the Rusyn *Cerkovnaja Nauka*.[60] In addition, business announcements were also printed in local jubilee albums and special programs of East Central European parishes and associations. All these were sold in the churches and in a bookstore operated in Cambria City by a Pole from Galicia, who served as a newspaper agent for the local immigrant communities.[61]

While the contours of the immigrant geographic and national subcommunities were becoming increasingly crystallized, these groupings continued to penetrate each other to a significant degree, not only through physical migrations of the "hoppers" but also through the overlapping of group institutions and leadership, as well as through multiple participation of the immigrants in different social-national circles. For instance, the immigrants inhabiting sections of town where there was no church of their nationality group attended parishes in Cambria City and followed their social and cultural events (which often required a walk of one to one and one-half hours). The geographic and cultural affinities, transplanted from Europe, constituted another factor in the initial fuzziness of the group borders.[62] Although the immigrants also brought with them some old-country regional conflicts and animosities, these did not generally prevent intergroup mingling. During the first decade of the present century, St. Mary's Greek Catholic Church, for example, served Slovak, Rusyn, and Magyar-speaking immigrants from Gemer, Ung, and Spiš counties in Hungary, with one Mass in "Slavish" and one in the Hungarian language said every Sunday.[63] In another "foreign colony," the Rusyns and Slovaks also shared the Greek Catholic church and the "Rusyn-Slovak Hall." The Greek Catholic Union's branches had Rusyn as a well as Slovak members, and the local Rusyn newspaper, *Cerkovnaja Nauka*, was evidently read by Rusyns, Slovaks, and Magyars alike, as indicated by the publication there of letters, notes, and announcements.[64] The Croatians and Slovenes, both groups Catholic, attended the same church – founded, *nota bene*, by a Serbian immigrant – and shared the communal facilities. The same people sat on the boards of two Magyar churches, the Catholic and the Reformed, and the two groups also shared the same organizational and political leaders who served as the officers in both the Catholic and the Reformed societies.[65] The

Rusyns and Ukrainians (Lemkians) circulated at will between the Orthodox and the Greek Catholic churches, often with families split between two parishes, or attending one for part of the year only to join another after an argument with the pastor, or simply following friends.[66] The Galicians – Poles and Ukrainians from the area between Krosno-Przemyśl and Lvov – also shared common organizational leaders. For instance, the Carpathian (Rusyn) Educational Club and the local branch of the Polish National Alliance had for a few years the same president, a Pole who was a store owner in the neighborhood.[67]

With the foundation of East Central European churches, most immigrants abandoned the older German parish, but some retained their membership in it while at the same time joining their own national churches and associations. For instance, Stefan E., Jan L., and John N., the founders of the Slovak Jednota branch No. 23, continued their membership in German St. Mary's, and they baptized their children there. The family supported both St. Mary's and the Slovak St. Stephen's, and the children belonged to the Slovak Sokol. About 10 more Slovak immigrants were members of the local German-American Alliance.[68] These immigrants were called by their countrymen the "German Slovaks," who "thought themselves something better": They knew German (having learned it in Europe) and often used it at home. They also had good relations with German mill workers at Cambria that helped them to get better jobs. Contacts with Germans, mostly of a religious nature, were also maintained by a small group of Lutheran Slovaks in town.[69] Among the Magyars there was a similar small group of immigrants who stayed with the German parish and joined the German (or Austrian) societies but who had also held membership in their own national associations.[70]

At the beginning of the century, Johnstown's Serbs and Croatians enjoyed close relations unusual for these two groups, ordinarily divided by a traditional animosity. The Serbs and Croatians who settled in Johnstown came from the same region in Europe. They had a common pioneer, a dynamic Serb who at the turn of the century "conducted a correspondence with relatives and friends in Europe extolling the virtues of the United States . . . During the period of waiting for [more] Serbians to immigrate into Johnstown [his] energies were devoted to working with the Croatian element in forming the St. Rochus Croatian Catholic church."[71] He served as the president of Serbian as well as Croatian societies and sat on the boards of both churches.[72]

It was in the course of various and expanding group activities such as organizing the churches and the societies, collecting money, calling and conducting meetings, campaigning for new members to the national lodges, participating in religious events and social celebrations, comparing the church bells of one's parish with those of the neighbors, one's own baseball team with that of the competition, and – last but not least – hearing one's own language spoken among many others that from an original confusion of identities, the peasant-immigrants in Johnstown, as in other American cities, slowly and gradually came to feel their ethnic group separateness.[73] This sense of belonging with one's own regional group first, and second with the "foreigners" – the "Hunkies" or the "Slavish," as opposed to the "Americans" – was further reinforced in the ordinary day-to-day life of the East Central European communities. Hard and dreary as it had been, it was at the same time dense and absorbing for those who experienced it, just like the everyday experience in the old-country village: dull and dormant for an outside observer, but for the participants full of significance and meaning. If not focused on church holidays, weddings, funerals, and organizational meetings, public opinion of the foreign colonies in Johnstown was absorbed with news about the frequent street and barroom fights, bankruptcies, petty thefts, minor burglaries, coming and going of relatives, letters from Europe, desertions by wives or husbands, romances, and other gossip concerning the daily affairs of the people. "A foreigner whose name resembles that of a breakfast food because it sounds like Pettijack or something similar" – the *Johnstown Tribune* tried hard to entertain its readers – "guilty of stealing a hat and coat from his cousin, Rady R . . . was taken to Ebensburg [Courthouse]." Or: "Marko B. . . . freed on bail of $2,000. Court issues Writ of Habeas Corpus and slayer of Rada O. . . . is at liberty . . . The case has aroused a vast amount of interest in Cambria City." Or else: "Undertaker Andy G., of Cambria City, debonarily driving out Second Avenue with the body of John S. who was electrocuted in a coalmine yesterday. Failed to notice the approach of one of the big Main Line cars."[74] Time and again the foreign colonies were shaken by the news of the fellow immigrant businessmen's bankruptcies, embezzlements, or larcenies and witnessed the defendants taken to court, attended on such occasions by delegations of East Central Europeans either involved in the case or simply curious.[75] Meanwhile, *Cerkovnaja Nauka* printed desperate appeals of deserted husbands looking for wives who had disappeared: "My wife . . . ran away from me this year, on the 1st of May. Her name is Juliana K., dark, tall . . . She took with her a two year old little boy . . . She speaks some English and good Rusyn and Slovak . . . She left three more children with her husband and beggary, as she took $1,000. The man she ran away with is Vasil C. . . . I will pay for information."[76] Still others were looking for brides, some of them announcing their wishes in *Cerkovnaja Nauka*: "Mike M. . . . 22 years of age, Greek-Catholic religion . . . in the old country has 7,000 *vert* of land, here saved $800. Has steady job and good pay, being a bartender in a Hotel. He is looking for a 18–20 year old girl, must be Greek-Catholic or Roman-Catholic. Does not expect money, but must be good housewife and with a faithful heart."[77]

This was the world in and through which the peasants-immigrants were striving to realize the goals that brought them to America. The "outside" Johnstown had meaning for them as a source of employment and income, whether at the Cambria Company's mills and coal mines, which needed unskilled labor, or in the American homes that used foreign servants and maids. At the same time the immigrants were absorbed in an engrossing life of their own in "foreign colonies" with quickly thickening networks of personal relations and ethnic institutions. The following chapters show how they utilized the space available to them in order to bring about the desired results.

4 The beginnings: strategies of adaptation

Within the limits of their constrained environment and available opportunities, Johnstown peasant-immigrants domesticated the space open to them and imaginatively realized as best they could the values they considered desirable. In this process, some of their old, preindustrial ways proved effective and were reinforced. At the same time, the new environment and its challenges strengthened attitudes and behavior born out of those processes that were transforming the East Central European countryside at the turn of the century.

In particular, the traditional reliance on the family collective and the continuing interpenetration of kin/ethnic and work/occupational spheres in the lives of the immigrants served two simultaneous purposes. On the one hand, it organized the defensive, survival tactics of the immigrant households designed to cope with a harsh and often adverse environment. On the other, it also facilitated their "particularist achievement" as the intensified gain-instrumental orientations of the immigrants were realized through purposeful reliance on partial fusion between kinship/ethnic and work/occupational roles. In defining their goals and evaluating results, peasant-immigrants utilized superimposed multiple-reference frameworks of the old country and their local American communities.

Soon after having arrived in this country, thousands of immigrants saw America for what it actually was. A promise, perhaps, but one to be redeemed at the price of terribly hard work, dismal living conditions, recurrent insecurity, and deteriorating health – a price much steeper than they had imagined in Europe. "Ameryka dla byka, Europa dla chłopa" – "America for the oxen, Europe for the men," went a popular saying among immigrants, implying that only those with unusual stamina and strength could meet the challenge of work demands in America, whereas men of average physique should stay in Europe. Their experience in this country was fundamentally ambivalent, and their perceptions of it correspondingly equivocal. In 1895, a Polish-American newspaper published a poem about America in which each stanza ended with the same refrain: "Avoid excessive praise;/Do not criticize too much;/Wherever roses grow,/You will also find thorns."[1]

The ambivalence and heart-rending uncertainty that accompanied the immigrants when they made their decision to cross the ocean to try their luck in America became further sharpened in this country by feelings of bewilderment and nostalgia, and by disillusionment with the reality of the "Promised Land" as compared with the dreams they had harbored in Europe. To a number of East Central Europeans, the arrival in Johnstown was bitterly disappointing. The town was soiled and the air filled with soot and fumes from the furnace chimneys. "My disappointment was unspeakable," recalls an eighty-four-year-old Galician, "when after a twelve-day journey I saw the city of Johnstown: squalid and ugly, with those congested shabby houses, blackened with soot from the factory chimneys – this was the America I saw."[2] In such surroundings, the lush greenery of the European villages appeared even greener and the fields more aromatic. Throughout western Pennsylvania, Magyar immigrants sang:

> Könnyeinket szénpor issza
> Kacagásunk füstbe fúl
> Kis falunkba vágyunk vissza
> ahol minden füszál értett magyarul

> [The local powder absorbs our tears
> Our laughter is drowned in smoke
> We yearn to return to our little village
> Where every blade of grass we know.][3]

Despite these disillusionments, however, the immigrants who had already taken a significant step in an attempt to shape their own fate by leaving the village and crossing the ocean were stubborn and determined to confront the new situation: "I came to Johnstown, so dirty, awful," recalls a Polish woman who joined her brother in 1906 at the age of sixteen, "but I was already here, so whether it pleased me or not, I had to go at it, and make the best of it."[4]

The industrial environment in which the immigrants found themselves petrified some elements of the traditional peasant culture and supported some new ones. In the decades preceding World War I, Johnstown was steadily expanding: the operations at Cambria were growing, and labor was in demand. But the unstable conditions in the steel and coal-mining industries, the ups and downs and ups again, were not conducive to a dissipation of the underlying fatalism of peasant-immigrant attitudes. Recurrently in America, the hopes that only yesterday seemed justified and close to realization had to be limited or even abandoned today, to be resurrected tomorrow. In the old country, however, although the world there had also begun to expand, there was even less hope. Paradoxically, it might have been precisely this "fluctuating reality" in America that had kept the immigrants active and mobilized. Here, good fortune followed bad. Back home, the future was bleaker: Prospects for a better life in the village were monotonously bad. To find a better fate, one had to leave it.

In America, the opportunities open to the immigrants, limited as they were to what was available on the unskilled job market in the mills and coal mines, nevertheless fostered, if incompletely and partially, further solidification of the new elements in their *Weltanschauungen* that appeared in peasant orientations by the end of the nineteenth century.

Rather than the passivity and sense of resignation that Oscar Lewis saw as inherent in the "culture of poverty,"[5] the American conditions fortified in the peasant-immigrant workers a blend of attitudes that were apparently inconsistent yet were experienced simultaneously. These were a deep anxiety for tomorrow coupled with an underlying readiness to accept adversity, inextricably bound with an intensified effort to maximize the desired goals. The wish to survive, not to "go under," was solidly embedded in the minds of the immigrants. This was a "negative want," not unlike that experienced by peasants in Europe who strove to maintain their subsistence. The other simultaneously experienced attitude was manifested in actions that had as their in-order-to motive the accomplishment of what was most achievable under the circumstances. Faced with adversity, the immigrants "retreated" into their fatalism, which made them accept repeated failures as a natural part of existence but also made them keep stubbornly, patiently at what they had set out to accomplish. Having experienced success, they expanded their goals just a little, setting their hopes somewhat farther within the range of the accessible.

The prevailing industrial conditions in which the immigrants operated were by no means conducive to swift transformation of economic attitudes that would dictate a rationally planned behavior in pursuit of ever-expanding profit. In fact, the American industrial system, at least that part of it in which the immigrants acted at the beginning of the century, did not allow much long-range economic planning whereby the exact rewards could be predicted from dili-

gent and efficient performance. In the eyes of the classic modernization theorists, the factory was to be, ideally, the "source and motor
of modernization of individual attitudes and behavior" by its promotion of order, routine, performance, competence, and rationality.[6] Instead, the impact of the American factory on the peasant-
workers was much more complex and equivocal. Many essential
characteristics of work relations in contemporary American factories
that directly affected immigrant laborers were the opposite of what
is called for by a model of rational organization: irregular employment, personalized ways of recruitment and promotion, ubiquitous
"bossism," and, not least, the sheer physical exhaustion of workers.[7]

But the incipient alterations in peasants' economic thinking that
had already occurred in Europe progressed farther in the new environment. The immigrants' everyday participation in the industrial
world irreversibly tied monetary rewards to work, making for its
further instrumentalization. Increasingly they now perceived work
primarily as a quantifiable means, to be calculated and used for
realization of preferred goals. With traditional elements still linger-
ing in the peasant-immigrants' economic thinking, the gradual
transformation of their attitudes toward work and financial gain
nevertheless entered a new phase in America. In the earliest stage
of the postfeudal transition, East Central European peasants were
known to prefer less work to more pay. Later, when they began to
migrate en masse across the continent in search of seasonal employment, they tended to choose places where they would obtain
more money for the same input of labor and would routinely quit
one job, breaking contracts, to get another in order to get more pay
for the identical amount of activity. In America, in order to maximize
their monetary gains, many immigrants deliberately searched for
opportunities to perform jobs with longer hours and in harder conditions, if only they promised increased remuneration.[8] "We are
lucky," peasants wrote home, "because there is very much work
now and may it last twelve hours a day." Gradually, as they became
permanent members of the industrial working class, the immigrants'
work ethos was enriched by an element of a "proletarian" attitude
of defiance toward the bosses and the exploitative factory system.
This development will be discussed in Chapters 6 and 7, which deal
with the second phase of the immigrants' adaptation in Johnstown.

Deep-rooted peasant materialism and practicality found a particularly fertile soil in America, since the immigrants' strivings for a

better existence – to be achieved back home upon their return or else in this country as they eventually settled – were centered on material things possessed, enjoyed, and displayed in public as symbols of social standing.[9] Perceiving some opportunities toward this end within the limited space in which they could maneuver, the immigrants proceeded to act instrumentally in an attempt to accomplish the desired goals. In a pattern more typical of the traditional form of economic thinking, these goals were encompassed within a fixed range on the minimum–maximum desiderata, defined, first, by the old-country peasant culture, then, increasingly with the passage of time, by the standards prevalent in the immigrant community. The range was fixed, in the sense that it encompassed only particular goals, to attain which the immigrants used all of the combined effort of the family collective: a cow, a dowry, a few additional acres, in Europe; or good food, decent dress, nice furniture, a house, in America. But within the range of goals cherished by immigrants, what they actually were striving for at a given time was potentially expandable. It depended on an accumulated surplus of income and family as well as individual preferences: One could eat more richly, dress more nicely, give more generously to the church so as to have one's name read from the pulpit or even have a plaque with the family name affixed to the pews, move from a shabby one-room apartment in Cambria City's "tenement rows" at the edge of the foreign colony to a nicer one in its center, or even to a house.

Most of the East Central European immigrants who came to America at the turn of the century had originally been sojourners, that is, they had no intention of remaining in this country for good.[10] As the years passed, and amid prolonged uncertainty and indecision, the plans of a great many of them to return home gradually weakened and eventually evaporated. For analytic purposes and for greater clarity of argument, we will distinguish here between two kinds of "achievement behavior" displayed by the peasant-immigrants during the first decades of their stay in this country.

In one pattern, the achievement behavior was generated by the image of accomplishment projected homeward, with emigration perceived as the path toward the alteration of socioeconomic position in the native village and conceived of according to the peasant criteria of well-being and social respect. In this pattern, the immediate goal of the immigrants was to work hard and incessantly, "in-order-to" save money and send it home. The parallel achievement behavior, often displayed simultaneously with the former, and then gradually taking precedence among those who extended their stay and eventually remained in this country, was to strive for the rewards to be enjoyed in the new American context: the optimum possible combination of wages and working conditions, food, dress, housing, and prestige among fellow immigrants in the foreign colony. With the passage of time this pattern was to become incorporated into American working-class culture.

Steady work, the primary concern of East Central Europeans in America, has been interpreted by ethnic historians as the mere function of their survival–security orientation.[11] We need, I think, a more complex interpretation of the immigrants' action. Their concern for steady employment was not only a response to a precarious economic existence. Above and beyond this, the joint and steady work effort of the household collective was the best possible means of creating some surplus capital that could be saved up and later invested in goods or consumption. Mere survival, as I will show, was possible, if obviously unpleasant, on the basis of fluctuating irregular employment of the head of the household. Steady or even steadier work opened up opportunities to practice, in Sol Tax's apt phrase, "penny capitalism" in peasant-immigrant households. Small savings, accumulating slowly and with exasperating setbacks, meant for the immigrants a better, more affluent existence either back in the old country or in the foreign colony in America.[12]

In pursuit of their goals, the immigrants applied a collective family effort and relied on the sustained fusion of kinship/ethnic and work/occupational roles.[13] Seasonal labor migrations of peasants in Europe had inaugurated some differentiation between kin and work spheres, but the collective family character of this endeavor sustained the interpenetration. As they became industrial laborers in Johnstown's mills and coal mines, the kinship roles were now taken into the factory and reestablished there as the basis of work organization. The roles of the "father," "son," "older brother," "cousin," "godfather," or "boarder" merged with occupational ones.

Immigrant children knew the Cambria mills and coal mines well long before they became employees themselves. They walked to and from work every day with their relatives or brought their lunches to them at midday, often staying with the men while they ate. Soon they took up gainful employment side by side with their fathers, older siblings, or cousins, who trained them in that part of labor with which they were not yet familiar. The same pattern extended to *kums* (buddies) from the immigrant colonies: men who lived on the same block, often village acquaintances now boarding together, who worked together all day long in the same labor gangs in the mills or as "buddies" in the coal mines. The new workers, recently arrived from Europe, performed the job under the instruction of more experienced immigrant fellow laborers.

Based on ascriptive-particularist criteria, the company's hiring policy was complemented by the initiative coming from the foreign colonies themselves. Typically the recent arrivals were accompanied to the employment office or shop floor by a "veteran" laborer – kin, kum, or fellow boarder. Often they also carried a letter of recommendation from one of the pastors in the immigrant sections, who mediated between the company and their parishioners in providing jobs for newcomers and those who were idle. "Rev. K., [a Serbian pastor], had close contacts with Cambria, and he could get anybody a job." And a similar recollection from a Pole: "Our priest had some connections in Cambria. If only one of his people needed a job or maybe a greenhorn came seeking employment, it was enough for Father to write a little note, and [a] job was waiting there for the asking, from the priest." In exchange for the provision of labor, the company regularly deducted a sum of money from Polish workers' paychecks for the upkeep of St. Casimir's Church.[14]

If it were not through the priest, the immigrants arranged for employment through relatives, friends from the village, the local sosejda (society), or fellow boarders. The easy availability of what John Bodnar has called "horizontal entries" into the unskilled labor market, and the openness and fluidity of the immigrant communities, facilitated this process.

There were multiple reasons for the immigrants' frequent moves inside the Cambria Company and inside and out of town during the years following their arrival in Johnstown. Without doubt, a large number of these movements were involuntary, caused by fluctuations in the local steel and coal industries. Even when business conditions were generally good, the iron and steel industry in Pennsylvania before World War I worked on the average about 290 days in a year. Since most of Cambria's unskilled laborers worked six days a week, full employment would be 317 days a year. As it was, they were idle for at least a month, and often closer to two. In practice, they experienced a succession of short-duration slumps and full-time work periods. In the local coal mines, work was less steady, with an average of two and a half to three idle months per mine. In times of more severe economic depressions, such as the one in 1907–8, idleness lasted much longer and affected most Cambria departments as well as the company's coal mines.[15]

Fluctuations in employment, with periods during the year when there was no work to do, were familiar to peasant-immigrants who in Europe were, *nolens volens*, accustomed to the seasonal character of agricultural labor. But in America, no work meant no savings – the primary goal of the immigrants – or, even more depressing, the prospect of surviving on store credit and supplements from friends and neighbors. The immigrants often reacted to slackened work in their department or in a coal mine by moving. Whenever, as happened recurrently, particular units of Cambria were shut down temporarily, "the unskilled labor [were] usually assigned to other duties."[16] If there were no transfer and the slump was expected to last for some time, the immigrants fell back on their private and community networks in order to secure some other employment. With the huge Cambria mills, almost fifty small coal mines, and several lumberyards in the Johnstown district, there was nearly always some work to be found.

But involuntary movements forced by irregular production constituted only one form of the immigrants' spatial mobility. At the beginning of the century the Cambria Company reported close to a 100-percent annual labor turnover, which covered temporary layoffs due to slackened production, as well as a substantial proportion of voluntary quitting by men whose family situation or individual needs and preferences prompted them to search actively for different employment.[17] Certainly a good number of the immigrants stuck to their jobs, whatever they were, and did not move for many years, determined to "play it safe." However, evidence from various sources – immigrant diaries, letters, and biographies, foreign-language newspaper articles and oral histories does not support the generalization that for immigrants "once a job was secured, it was not easily abandoned" and that their goal was "simply to get a job, any job," to which they subsequently clung regardless of its nature.[18] According to contemporary estimates of labor turnover in American industries before World War I, among the unskilled workers voluntarily leaving their jobs, the average proportion of those who quit because they were "dissatisfied with the current working conditions" was two-thirds, whereas the remaining one-third moved in search of "better prospects." The latter proportion, however, significantly increased in times of industrial prosperity.[19]

Within the limited scope of the job opportunities available to peasant-immigrants in Johnstown, there still remained some room for choice and purposeful action, depending upon their family needs and individual preferences. Work that to an observer remote from the lowest, unskilled level of labor seemed undifferentiated and monotonously identical appeared to those who performed it as offering some real options. The immigrants perceived them, and acted accordingly. The foreign-language newspapers – Rusyn, Hungarian, Slovak, and Croatian – often lamented "wild competition" among the immigrants in the factories; the immigrants themselves often mentioned it in their diaries. Reminiscing about his first years in this country, a Slovenian noted a pronounced competitiveness among immigrants: "First of all, for any kind of work, then for better work, then for better-paid work."[20]

As they worked, the immigrants accumulated knowledge about different placements and labor conditions within the mills, as well as in nearby areas. After they got their first jobs, East Central European laborers continued to rely on the interpenetration of their kinship/ethnic and occupational roles to learn about and seek better job opportunities. Their "occupational achievement" had a particularist character. In order to place oneself in a desirable position, most important were what network sociologists call "social resources": both "strong" and "weak" ties[21] with persons advantageously located or well connected from among both close and distant relatives and members of the ethnic community. Whom one knew was much more important for wages and wage prospects than a (rudimentary) knowledge of English and a certain number of years on the job.

"[In various departments] in the mills," reported the Immigration Commission from Johnstown in 1909, "a single race very frequently predominates on account of the importance of a certain laborer among his fellows who shapes the personnel of the gang in various ways and is instrumental in securing positions for friends of his own race."[22] The same commission found a certain number of Magyar and Slovak immigrants employed in skilled positions at Cambria. But their skills alone were not enough to get them there. They had been early settlers and had already established connections, mostly with Germans, whose societies they sometimes joined. This informal sponsorship by a group higher up in the mill pecking order facilitated more advantageous placement. And indeed, according to the commission, the annual earnings of the foreign-born Magyar workers were 16 percent higher than those of all the remaining East Central European groups; for the Slovaks the difference was 9 percent in their favor.[23] Others relied on their own group. The Croatians concentrated in the brickyards, traveling in groups through the area in search of better employment. When, in 1911, a good contract was offered in Ligonier, a nearby town, by a man whose favor they had won on previous occasions, a group of Croatians left Cambria mills, then working full-time, and moved there. Later they returned.[24] Similarly, the Ukrainians, employed predominantly in railroad construction in 1914 picked up and left as a group, leaving behind their jobs after having received information from a well-placed *kum* in Altoona about "good work" to be had there.[25]

Among the jobs available to immigrants, there were clearly better and worse ones, depending on at least two kinds of considerations: the basic wage and wage increase prospects, and the character of the work itself. Although there were different reasons why the immigrants quit one job and searched for a better one, they all involved complex calculations of anticipated gains and losses, depending on their family situation and individual preferences.

Money was of course of primary consideration, because there was so little of it, and getting it was the immigrants' primary goal: the very purpose for their coming to America. And so, for instance, at the beginning of the century the peasant-immigrants in Johnstown knew very well that a laborer without skills and a command of English could get from as little as $1.20 to as much as $1.45 a day, depending on the department and the type of work. At the railroad, a teamster driving a single horse was getting $10.00 a week, and the driver of a two-horse team received $12.00. Work trainers at the railroad received between $1.35 and $1.75 a day, whereas section hands' pay ranged from $1.50 to $1.80. The highest wages were in the mines. As everywhere else, some jobs were better and some were worse. A common laborer working underground received approximately $2.40 a day, whereas the loaders, paid by the ton, earned between $2.00 and $3.00, and pit men made from $2.30 to $2.40 for working twelve hours.

The Immigration Commission found that most East Central European laborers at Cambria's open-hearth division and in the railroad department earned less than $10.00 a week. In the Bessemer mills, car shops, and foundries about 40 percent of the East Central Europeans earned less than $10.00 a week, and approximately one-fourth of them earned $13.00 to $18.00 a week. In the billet mills, one-fourth of the Slavic and Magyar workers earned over $18.00 a week.[26] All this made a considerable difference in the immigrants' calculations: "At that time [a few] more dollars a week made a whole world of difference," concluded an eighty-four-year-old Pole after he had described what immigrants in Johnstown considered as better and worse jobs before World War I.[27] And from another immigrant, a recollection of his first years in America in the 1890s: "My very first job was in a coopery . . . with a pay of fifty cents apiece, so for the first day I made fifty cents, that is half a dollar, whereas for food alone I have to pay two dollars a week and what with board. So I decided to look for another job [and found one]; at first I made fourteen and a half cents an hour and put [in] twelve, sometimes fourteen hours per day, and [then] I got a half-cent raise, that is fifteen cents an hour . . . [sometime later] I decided to go to Philadelphia . . . , but conditions there turned out not so favorable, so I returned . . . and found a job in the same [place], but a better one, twenty cents an hour."[28]

Besides the immediate financial considerations, there were also other reasons behind the maneuvers of immigrant job shifters. First, there were jobs that were more or less independent, a quality the peasants rated highly. "My uncle, I remember," recalls Anthony C., "he preferred working in the mine, because, he thought, it was more independent. He was his own boss. In the mills one had to do what others told you, do this, do that, he did not like it."[29] Even though pick and shovel work in the mines paid more money, others preferred the mills, because it was a cleaner and less dangerous environment and public opinion in the foreign colonies considered mining as "lowly and dirty work," all day in darkness, in water up to one's ankles. Another consideration that kept the immigrants away from the mines – something not unimportant for the young men, who greatly outnumbered the women – was that a coal miner often had trouble finding a wife, since "young girls did not want to go *na majne* [to the mine], as they knew it was a very difficult life."[30]

Futher, there were jobs in the mills where conditions were better – cleaner, with more fresh air – and this was appreciated by peasant-immigrants accustomed to working outside in the fields. "Laborer in a car or repair shop, or in the mechanical department, this was better jobs than blast furnace or open-hearth where you suffocated from heat."[31] On the other hand, an important consideration to those who tried to minimize the risk of irregular employment at all costs was the fluctuations of the work: in the rolling mills and steel works departments they were usually more intense than in blast furnace production, where the reaction to seasonal slumps was generally delayed. It often happened that before the decrease had reached these departments, work picked up again.[32]

There was, then, among the peasant-immigrants in Johnstown at the beginning of the century a significant number who shifted and moved around and utilized their kinship and ethnic connections in an active search for some better prospects, which they defined according to their needs and preferences, calculated in terms of finances and other considerations. In explaining why the membership of the local Polish National Alliance lodge, approximately 300 in 1907–8, had dwindled by one-third by the end of World War I, Walter W. noted: "The decision to quit [a job and go to another town] was an outcome between the job offer [as related by friends] and one's needs. If you wanted money, you went after the biggest pay; if other things, too – working conditions, the company of friends – then you decided on the whole."[33]

For immigrants with wives and children, the current pressures of the family situation, rather than a desire to maximize financial gains, were frequently the reason for quitting one job and getting another. It was a sort of involuntary decision with voluntary elements. Often, for instance, it was the need to decrease family expenditures after a new member was added to the household or after a working one had temporarily lost a job, coupled with the impossibility or undesirability of using other means to reconstruct the family budget. "We moved around a lot, my parents going after the cheap living," explained a Slovak miner whose family changed places seven times before settling for good in Johnstown after World War I.[34] Recurrently during their early years in America, the "negative want" of family survival and minimal security stood behind the job-shifting decision of peasant-immigrant families who settled permanently in Johnstown. However, when in their "fluctuating" existence things picked up and some opportunities appeared on the horizon, the same action of quitting one job and taking another acquired a "positive" meaning as an approximation of the second type of "achievement behavior." Anna C., whose recollection was echoed in other immigrants' accounts of their first years in this country, noted: "After moving around this area, my parents came to [the borough of] Franklin because they learned Cambria was selling some houses there for $1,000, and they wanted to own one, since they were tired of living in small rented apartments. By that time they knew they were going to stay in America."[35]

It has been argued by students of the adaptation of immigrant families in industrial America at the beginning of the century that it was "impossible to subsist on a man's earnings alone" and that "what immigrant families earned at best sufficed for the barest survival."[36] Let us reexamine more closely the economic strategies that the immigrants used in pursuing their goals.

Among the East Central European women recorded in Johnstown by the 1900 census, 73 percent were married immigrants who lived with their husbands, and 27 percent were unmarried women who stayed with relatives or boarded with fellow immigrants from the home country. For the single women, the source of income was housework, cooking, or working in the cigar factory in Cambria City or in the match factory in nearby Windber. If they could read and write, young immigrant women could work as clerks or cashiers in the neighborhood stores. Young women working as housemaids and servants received $2.00 to $3.00 a week with board. In the local cigar and match factories, a young foreign woman could make as much as $4.00 to $5.00 a week. In a store, if she was not working for a relative who paid her nothing, earnings were also about $4.00 to $5.00 a week. According to an estimate made by the local newspaper in 1913, a single working American woman needed an absolute minimum of $10.00 a month to support herself ($2.50 for rent, $5.00 for food, $1.50 for clothes, $0.75 for church and other purposes, $0.25 for insurance).[37] A young immigrant woman, spending no more than $2.00 for a "cot with the family" in the foreign colony and about $3.00 for food plus the maximum of $1.00 for clothing, $0.25 for insurance, and $0.25 for church, needed even less.[38] A thrifty East Central European housemaid could, then, have saved $50.00 to $90.00 a year – unless, of course, which occasionally happened, she found a particularly generous home. The cigar and match factories, if they worked steadily for at least ten months a year, allowed their young women employees willing to reduce spending to the bare minimum to save $90.00 to $130.00 annually.

The average monthly expenditures of single East Central European men in Johnstown at the beginning of the century ranged between $17.00 and $19.00 (including room and board, approximately $12.00; a drinking bill, usually approximately $2.00 to $3.00; insurance [optional], $0.50; church dues and donations, if paid dutifully whenever asked, approximately $2.00; recreation, and clothing purchased in the immigrant "variety stores," about $1.00 to $1.50). The actual monthly wage of unskilled laborers in Johnstown before World War I averaged between $25.00 and $30.00, after we have subtracted about a 15-percent loss due to unemployment, if there was no automatic or voluntary transfer, or to sickness not covered by insurance benefits. A single mill worker who on Sundays attended church, dated, and dressed a little could therefore put away, unless he spent most of his money on drinking, $8.00 to $13.00 a month. In prosperous times, a number of immigrants, determined to maximize their gains at the price of living in the most unpleasant conditions with no recreation, or those who held better-paid jobs, could save even more, $20.00 to $25.00 a month. Allowing for individual differences in jobs and life-styles, single East Central European men in Johnstown could on the average have saved about $100.00 to $200.00 annually.[39] And indeed, the Immigration Commission found Johnstown immigrants to have sent home to Europe during 1907 alone the staggering sum of over $350,000.00.[40]

Although they strongly resented the pace and character of industrial labor and cursed its lack of security, those who came here "in-order-to" save the maximal amount of money to be sent home perceived their work as the instrument for the realization of goals cherished in the old country. Like Szabo Janoś, an emigrant from Baranya County in Hungary, they "kept on working and thinking . . . Every ten minutes he had made a nickel. What could he buy with that? Lots. [Then he made] a dollar and that was a landmark . . . And if you have been a farmhand in Baranya County, a dollar is not merely a piece of money, it is also power, prestige, command over the universe."[41]

With his inner eyes, Szabo Janoś saw himself returning to his native village dressed in a city suit and flashing a "golden" watch, in a high celluloid collar and a ribbon-trimmed "gentleman's" hat, with suitcases of gifts and a round sum of dollars to be converted into Hungarian forints and subsequently invested in a few acres of land, a pair of good cows, and an addition to the house. The village would obviously notice and evaluate his acquisitions, and the appropriate social position would be assigned to him. At the very least, he would be an "Amerikanac," a worldly traveler with endless and exaggerated stories to tell while treating others to several drinks in a nearby tavern.

As time passed and the prospects of going back to Europe had become rather remote, the goal desired by the immigrant families ever more firmly established in Johnstown was increasingly the accomplishment of the best possible life in America, rather than a vision of success in the village. This achievement was now measured in terms of dress and food consumed at home in the foreign colony, the optimal possible combination of pay and working conditions, savings in the bank to be used to purchase a house some day, respect among fellow immigrants, a future for the children – better and materially more comfortable than that which would have awaited them had they stayed in Europe.

Whether or not an immigrant family in Johnstown before World War I could survive exclusively on the breadwinner's earnings depended first and foremost on the amount of money he brought home every fortnight. And this, as we have seen, varied among Cambria's unskilled employees. Among the household heads of the families of East Central European mill workers investigated by the Immigration Commission, the majority – 59 percent – reported annual earnings of less than $400; 28 percent had earned between $400 and $600; and 13 percent had earned over $600.[42]

Before World War I it was possible for an immigrant family in Johnstown to subsist on a monthly income of $29.00 to $35.00: $6.00 for rent (the minimal rent for a two-room apartment in the dilapidated "tenement rows" owned by Cambria); $2.00 to $2.50 for light, heat, and household operation; $12.00 to $15.00 for food; $1.50 to $2.00 for the man's drinking bill; $1.00 to $3.00 for the church (the regular dues and the minimal special donations for the construction of church buildings); $1.00 for the parochial school ($0.50 for each of the first two children, all others free); $1.00 for insurance; $4.00 for clothing and furniture. One could also spend more and live better. A house in the foreign colony rented for $12.00; food could be made richer and more varied by an outlay of an extra $5.00 a month, which purchased tastier, that is, fatter, pieces of veal, pork legs, and beef cutlets. One could spend more on better, more "American" clothing, more on recreation such as drinking or picnics, or make more generous donations to the church.[43]

According to the Immigration Commission, the average (actual) monthly earnings of East Central European workers in Johnstown were $31.50 in the lowest wage bracket, $41.50 in the middle one, and over $50.00 in the upper bracket. However, according to the commission's report, about 20 percent of the immigrant families subsisted on an annual income below $300.00.[44] For this group, existence was a continuous, exasperating struggle for survival and nothing more, with sparse food obtained mostly on credit, endless debts, and unpaid rent.

The remaining families in the lowest income category, if they did not have other sources of income, through sacrifice and resignation could have fitted their basic expenditures within the limits of about $350.00 earned annually by the husband. Such income, not supplemented, certainly did not secure protection against unemployment longer than usual seasonal work stoppages or against an extended sickness not covered by insurance from the immigrant societies. Nor did it provide for the necessity of extra spending: for the church building, a cousin's christening, a steamship ticket for a nephew who wanted to come to Johnstown, or for a new cow for the family in Europe. In any case, savings were totally impossible.

In this group, then, reaching for additional income was, as it were, the "necessary choice" if the immigrants indeed wanted to live any better than they had in the old country. Kracha, Thomas Bell's hero in *Out of This Furnace*, used to say: "What was the use of coming to America if not to live better than we lived in the old country?"[45] In order to "survive," they did not need America. Life in the European villages, with seasonal trips after work to the cities or the German farmers, had been just that. After they had come to America, the peasant-immigrants' unrealistic visions of easily available riches dissipated very quickly. But they persistently pursued the in-order-to motive toward the achievement of maximum possible gain by "appropriating" the available opportunities.

A typical steel town, Johnstown provided only very limited opportunities for employment for women outside the home, and that almost exclusively for those who were unmarried. Keeping boarders was therefore the dominant secondary source of income for the East Central European families – the financial contribution of women as household members. More than half (51.3 percent) of all East Central European households recorded by the 1900 census in Johnstown kept boarders.[46]

Keeping boarders did not just mean additional income but also more overcrowding, less privacy, more drinking and fighting, and an exhausting seventeen hours a day of work for the wife who had to cook, clean, scrub, wash, iron, carry water, and do the shopping. A decision as to whether or not to take boarders depended, then, on combined considerations involving the life stage of a family, its financial needs, preferences, and social obligations. Table 4.1, modeled after the pattern used by Tamara Hareven and John Modell in their study of native-born working-class families in nineteenth-century American cities,[47] presents the proportions of East Central European immigrant households in Johnstown keeping boarders in 1900, arranged according to family life stage and number of years spent by the household head in the United States. It shows that it was generally the younger and more recently arrived immigrant households that kept boarders, in order to establish themselves in the new country (59 percent among those with less than two years in America, and 54 percent among childless families). However, among families that had been in America longer and were in later life stages, this practice was also common (39 percent among those with over eleven years in America, and 48 percent among households whose head was forty-five years old or more).

The latter finding was also reported by other studies of economic

Table 4.1. *East Central European immigrant households in Johnstown with boarders in 1900, by life stage and number of years spent in U.S. (in %)*

No. of Years in U.S.	Proportion of Households with Boarders[a]	Percentage with Boarders, by Life Stage						Row Total (N)
		Childless	Young Bearing	Middle Bearing	Middle Stopped Bearing	Older Bearing	Older Stopped Bearing	
		54.0	45.5	49.9	43.5	38.9	52.9	
0–2	58.6	5.3 (17)	0.6 (2)	5.6 (18)	0.6 (2)	0.3 (1)	0.3 (1)	41
3–5	55.0	3.4 (11)	0.9 (3)	7.4 (24)	1.6 (5)	—	0.3 (1)	44
6–10	56.0	7.1 (23)	1.6 (5)	24.7 (80)	6.5 (21)	0.9 (3)	2.8 (9)	141
11 and over	38.6	3.1 (10)	—	21.2 (68)	2.8 (9)	0.9 (3)	2.1 (7)	97
Column Total (N)		61	10	190	37	7	18	323

Note: The life-stage categories are based upon the age of the youngest child of the head of the household ("bearing," when a child younger than five years is present) and the age of the male household head ("young" is under twenty-five years, "middle" is twenty-five to forty-four, "older" is forty-five or older). The "Young Not Bearing" category, containing only three cases, was excluded from the table. "Years in U.S." is the number of years spent in this country by the male head of the household.

The proportion of boarder-keeping families differed among nationality groups (although their size was too small to allow for generalizations). Rusyns, Ukrainians, and Serbs scored the highest (60–70 percent), and Slovenes, Magyars and Slovaks the lowest (40–50 percent). The groups whose members – heads as well as boarders – had the shortest average stay in America, had the highest percentage of boarder-keeping families.

[a] Proportion of households with boarders is calculated as of the total number in each subcategory of "Life Stage" and "Years in U.S.": Childless (N = 113); Young Bearing (N = 22); Middle Bearing (N = 381); Middle Stopped Bearing (N = 85); Older Bearing (N = 18); Older Stopped Bearing (N = 34); 0–2 Years in U.S. (N = 70); 3–5 Years (N = 80); 6–10 Years (N = 252); 11 years and over (N = 251). Cell percentages are calculated from the grand total (N = 323).

Source: East Central European population from manuscript schedules of 1900 census.

strategies of working-class families in American cities at the beginning of the century. They suggest that a slow process of capital accumulation, leading, in later life stages of working-class families, to the eventual purchase of a home, required from them the mobilization of all available resources to pay off the mortgage.[48] My 1900 Johnstown data indicate, however, that in that year no more than 25 percent of the East Central European homeowners kept boarders and that it was the renters who mostly accounted for this widespread practice.[49]

The extent to which the immigrant families used boarders as a source of supplementary income varied significantly with the earnings brought in by the head of the household. The Immigration Commission reported that 59 percent of the households in Johnstown's foreign colonies augmented their incomes from sources besides the breadwinner's earnings. Of the investigated families, only 29 percent drew their entire income from husbands' earnings in the mills and coal mines. Another 47 percent relied on the combined income from husbands' earnings and boarders, whereas the remaining 24 percent lived on money coming from the contributions of children and other sources.[50]

Among the boarder-keeping East Central European households investigated by the Immigration Commission, the families in the lowest income bracket (husbands' earnings below $400 annually) constituted over two-thirds of the total. The middle-income families (husbands' earnings $400 to $600) accounted for one-fourth, and the remaining were "upper stratum" immigrant households with husbands earning over $600 a year.[51]

One-third of the families in the lowest income category did not keep boarders. It is possible that there were among them a number of those in the 20-percent group whose actual income fell below $300 and who therefore lived in such misery that they could not even "afford" boarders, lacking both the means and energy to keep them. In the group of middle-income families, the decision to take in boarders was somewhat more a matter of economic choice and the desire to maximize savings than the result of dire necessity. Still, one-half of the East Central European households in this category drew additional income from boarders. In the last group of families – the financial "aristocracy" among the immigrant steelworkers – where the husband brought home over $600, about one-third of the households reported supplementary earnings from boarders. Emma Duke, who investigated infant mortality in Johnstown's immigrant neighborhoods in 1915, reported similar findings: Over 40 percent of the foreign-born families in which the husbands' annual earnings were $500 to $600, and 30 percent of those with husbands' earnings over $600, relied on additional income generally obtained from boarders.[52]

The typical income added to the budget of an immigrant family before World War I by a wife who kept boarders was about $20 to $25 a month – between two-thirds and three-fourths of the standard earnings brought home by the husband from the mill or the mine. My 1900 data, as well as the report of the Immigration Commission, indicate that the most common number of boarders in East European households in Johnstown was five to six. Each of them paid approximately $12 a month for room and board: the food purchased by the housekeeper amounted to between $7 and $8; the rest constituted her "profit."[53] But a number of immigrant women at the beginning of the century had more than five boarders. My 1900 data show 30 percent of such households among the boarder-keeping families; 10 percent kept ten boarders or more, and one woman interviewed reported that her mother had kept fifty boarders in a three-story house with four bedrooms.[54] Ten boarders meant an additional income of about $40 to $50 a month; fifteen, about $60 to $75.

In order to secure bare survival at the minimum level of subsistence, it would have been enough for most boarder-keeping families with the lowest income brought in by the husband to keep seven or eight boarders during no more than six months of the year. Thus, the sum of $150 to $200 would have sufficed to shelter the immigrant family against temporary sickness, during which the immigrant insurance societies paid two-thirds of a daily wage rate of a common laborer. For the rest of the year, desperately overworked immigrant women could have rested a little and limited their services to the members of their own household. But they did not – first and foremost because of the profound fear of the vagaries of fate, a feeling that was a fundamental part of the peasant existence in Europe and that the immigrants' industrial experience in America by no means eradicated. There was always a possibility that one would fall to the dismal bottom category, the 20 percent of bare survivors incessantly struggling to make ends meet. Above and beyond this, however, they continued to take in boarders because they were stubborn and driven by the desire to make the best possible life for themselves and their families, better than in the old country and better than the minimum survival in the "Rotten Row" at the edge of the foreign colony. They wanted to escape or avoid the situation in which they would have no money left over for coping with unpaid credit from the local stores, no meat on the table, no decent dress for Sunday Mass, no means to make a donation like everybody else for the church building or to send a holiday check to the village.

The contributions of children constituted a third source of supplementary income for the families. "The thing was to have children. They all worked and so helped the household economy."[55] The average number of children in the immigrant households in Johnstown before World War I was 6.5; Croatian families had the most children (6.9) and Magyar families the least (5.6).[56] In peasant society, from the age of five or six a child was considered a worker and expected to contribute to the household. The dire economic circumstances of peasant existence and the corresponding cultural ethos condemning all idleness made the attitude of parents toward their children that of strict and demanding employers toward employees. This attitude was sustained by the conditions that the immigrants found in America.

"She loathed idleness": An American-born Slovene remembers her mother as always occupied and expecting the same from the children; "To her, laziness was just sitting, or sitting around and rocking listening to music unless the hands were busy . . . 'Can't understand! Just can't understand,' she'd say, 'how anyone can just sit around on porch steps.'"[57] And so, for instance, every afternoon one could see small immigrant children lining up in front of a warehouse in Cambria City waiting for the horse wagon with stale bread, which they bought for twenty-five cents a sack as feed for poultry. In the morning they toured the neighborhood selling eggs, butter, milk, and parsley from little family gardens. Others, mostly boys, stood at street corners as Sunday shoeshiners, waiting for men who might be going downtown for a walk or a dance with a girl. If patient and lucky, they could sometimes make as much as $1 a day.[58]

In many households, gainful employment of children was necessary for the family to survive. The Immigration Commission reported that in Johnstown 3.5 percent of the East Central European households completely relied on the income brought in by the children. Widows of men killed in industrial accidents; abandoned wives with underage offspring; those with sick parents, drinking parents, or fathers who did not make the minimum subsistence wage – all such families survived on their children's earnings.[59] For others, taking the children in on a job in the mills or a coal mine as early as possible was a decision prompted by the cultural norms and role expectations of the peasant-immigrant community as much as by the deliberate calculation of economic gains to come from supplementary income that could be put to use in the realization of the desired goals. "What with two *pejdas* (pays) brought home, it was more than one, the father's," remembered Anthony C., who started work in the mine at the age of thirteen and a half: "About [finishing] education, it was out of the question, because who would give these dollars for some higher learning?"[60]

In the peasant tradition, reinforced in the parochial schools in America, the immigrants valued learning for moral and spiritual rather than practical reasons.[61] Continues Anthony C., "Besides, our parents, as ardent Catholics, were mostly concerned that their children grow up in the same way, so they built magnificent churches and rectories for their priests and erected [parochial] schools. It was deeply believed that in [public] schools the youth lose their religion and their faith weakens . . . And the priest first cared that the debts on the church be paid as soon as possible."[62] With the children expected to join their parents in work at home or in the mills and to contribute to the collective effort to sustain and possibly also to improve the family's standing as soon as they became adolescents, in the perceptions of the immigrants extended formal schooling was seen as nonrational, unpractical behavior. Children themselves shared the views of their parents. A Chicago survey revealed in 1913 that out of 500 Slavic children 412 (82.4 percent) declared they would prefer employment in the factory over continuing education, even if they were not forced to work by economic factors.[63]

The educational behavior of Slavs and Magyars in Johnstown was similar to that displayed by immigrants in other American cities. Of the total number of immigrant children between the ages of six and fourteen in Cambria County, about three-fourths attended school. In Johnstown, over 70 percent of the East Central European children attended parochial schools; the remainder enrolled in the public school system.[64] Inspection of the enrollment and attendance records from the largest parochial school in Johnstown's "foreign colony," St. Stephen's Slovak Catholic School, indicates that before World War I most children left after the sixth grade; beyond this level, only about 20 percent of the students continued, on the average.[65] Most often, it was a relative or a priest from the parish who signed the papers stating that a thirteen-year-old was "of age" and fit to join his adult relatives in the mills or coal mines. According to the Immigration Commission, about 10 percent of Johnstown's East Central European families drew supplementary income from children's earnings.[66] In fact, the proportion was quite substantially higher, since the parents naturally concealed the fact of having forged the papers of their underage offspring.[67] By their fifteenth birthdays, nearly all children held regular jobs. Among these young workers, there were more males than females, because the latter were more needed at home, and less outside work was readily available.

Similar to adult wage rates, the earning opportunities at Cambria for adolescent boys differed by department: from $0.65 daily in the brickyards and rolling mills, $0.80 in the machine and carpentry shops and for the masons, $0.90 for railroad repairs, to as much as $1.00 in the steel foundries and boiler shops. In the coal mines, a fourteen-year-old boy would make from as little as $0.09 an hour as a doorman to $0.25 an hour driving a pair of mules for five to six hours a day. Underage girls made from $0.20 (plus board) a day as housemaids to $0.50 a day as cooks, or even $0.60 to $0.70 a day in the local cigar factory.[68] What they earned, the young people turned in to their mother, the banker in the peasant-immigrant families, who usually gave them a weekly allowance of between $0.01 and $0.20 to spend on fruit, sweets, picnics, or dances.

The average monthly contributions of the male youth ranged, then, between $10.00 and $30.00 whereas for girls it was between $4.00 and $17.00. With two young offspring at work, an immigrant family gained between a minimum of about $10.00 and a maximum of more than $40.00 a month, which equalled between one-third to more than a full extra subsistence income required for survival. The income turned in by the offspring could either be saved in toto with the purpose of accumulating a reserve against the ever-present possibility of longer than usual unemployment or it could be partially spent on the immediate needs of the family, on rent, new clothing or furniture, a wedding gift for a neighbor, or for a special church donation. Or it could be sent to relatives in the old country as a present for Christmas or maybe to purchase an additional cow. Probably most often, however, the children's earnings were used as a contribution toward the slow and painstaking accumulation of the capital needed by immigrant families for their first mortgage payment on a house. "My father," says Anthony C., already working at the age of thirteen, "could not send me to schools because . . . his greatest dream was to buy his own house, and when he [finally] realized this, it was already time for me to live my own life."[69]

The important fourth element in the Johnstown immigrants' budgets was the fruit of their plots and gardens and other domestic produce consumed by the household as well as sold on the outside. In yet another manifestation of the continuing fusion of work and family spheres directly transplanted from the old country, virtually all of my Johnstown informants admitted that their households relied on this subsistence farming of sorts.

Before World War I, the hills surrounding the "foreign" sections of Johnstown were all farmland, crisscrossed by one- to two-acre plots that the immigrants leased from farmers (very often for free) and on which they erected little shacks where they kept chickens, pigs, or even a cow or two. The animals were tended to and the soil cultivated for beets, cabbage, turnips, potatoes, onions, parsley, and other produce. Chickens and geese were also kept in the foreign colonies inside the city; at night they stayed under the staircases or in the backyards, and during the day they walked among the houses.[70]

All this gave the area inhabited by the immigrants a distinctly semirural appearance. The immigrants were, in fact, "worker-farmers" of sorts – a continuation, as it were, of the process of the formation of a specific category of "peasant-workers" that began emerging in East Central Europe at the turn of the century. In Johnstown, the proportions had now become reversed: The immigrants became industrial workers first and plot-farmers second, but the latter occupation served to preserve many of the essentials of the peasant way of life, not at all incompatible with the urban industrial environment of a small town.[71] In a humoresque played to a Polish audience in Johnstown in 1916, the leading character sang: "To live on *Pork Gryfik* or on *Dupont* [Polonized names of American streets] and to live in a Galician village makes no real difference. Our countrymen here heap the same piles of manure [from the animals], press cabbage in the barrels with their bare feet, and believe in the old magic."[72]

The continuation of subsistence plot-farming, fostered by economic hardship and the insecurity of their industrial existence and facilitated by the geographic conditions of a small town, petrified traditional patterns in peasant-immigrant behavior and attitudes. Although money and wages had already become the dominant modes of exchange in trading in goods and labor, payments in kind were still widely used by immigrant households as a supportive "secondary circuit." When money was lacking or when it was needed for other purposes, the immigrants offered their dues to the church, the parochial school, and the pastor in chicken, milk, butter, eggs, and fruit from their little gardens. Payments in kind were also used in exchange for other consumption products "purchased" in neighborhood stores and for professional services rendered to immigrants in foreign colonies.

The major burden of farming and tending to the garden and animals fell on the shoulders of the women. In addition, these factotums of the immigrant households also made bread, butter, cheese, and noodles; canned food for the winter in hundreds of jars; pickled and marinated; and sewed, mended and wove, in order to minimize the cost of existence. My estimate of the average reduction in the amount of money spent before World War I by an immigrant family achieved by the reduction of food expenditure made possible by women's work is $5 to $6 a month, assuming that the only items purchased from the store were meat, flour, salt, sugar, lard, coffee, and tea. With the exception of the first two, these were items also found on the shopping list of the peasant households in Europe at the turn of the century. It was this $5 to $6 a month saved on cheese, bread, milk, eggs, and vegetables (all produced a home) that made it possible for the immigrant family in Johnstown to limit its food expenditures to a minimum of about $12 to $15 a month and thus to trim the total monthly budget to a bottom figure of $29.[73] Altogether, in the households with boarders, the monthly contributions of women practically equalled those brought in by the husbands from the mills and mines.

Thus far we have examined the opportunities available to Johnstown's immigrants, along with their economic strategies, in the initial years of settlement in the city. We will now look at their accomplishments as they themselves defined and evaluated them, using superimposed comparative frameworks of the old country and the surrounding immigrant community. The conclusion of this chapter will present data on homeownership and occupational shifting among East Central Europeans in Johnstown before World War I and show the incipient social differentiation of the immigrant communities.

Like their desire for steady work, the striving by the immigrants for material objects to be possessed and consumed has been interpreted in ethnic historiography as an expression of their basic "survival orientation." Their attitude was, again, more complex than that. On the one hand, the accumulation of as many possessions as possible for as long as they were available served as a safety net against a bad turn of fate, which, as they well knew, was sure to come. On the other hand, and simultaneously, the immigrants perceived and evaluated their material accomplishments in the double-comparative framework of the old-country village and their local community in Johnstown's foreign colony. In this perspective, these accomplishments were seen as achievements.

Money, the "city" food and clothing available in America, the prospects, however remote at the start, of renting at first and then possessing a house with electricity, running water, a bathroom, "city" furniture, and a large backyard appeared to the immigrants as a tangible improvement over their situation in Europe. In his diary a Slovenian Socialist otherwise very critical of American conditions reflected this double perspective that qualified the immigrants' American experience: "Although my standard of living . . . was at its lowest compared with American standards, it was splendid compared with that in the old country."[74] One finds such comments repeated over and over again in immigrant letters and memoirs. An old Polish immigrant who spent his whole life in Johnstown's immigrant section recalls, "We had very little, but there was more of this bread here than there, and something on this bread, too." And again, "It was terribly hard work [at Cambria], and we lived poorly . . . But we ate good, broth with meat, . . . while at home [in Europe] only borshcht and potatoes, borshcht and potatoes."[75]

Accustomed to a subsistence diet consisting of the monotonous rotation of cabbage, bread, and noodles, the peasant-immigrants measured and experienced their accomplishments in America by the amount and quality of food on their tables. A minimum program of the underprivileged – the "American Dream" for the poor – but these were the categories in which the immigrants genuinely experienced improvement in their life situations.[76] Achievement was also measured by the dress the immigrants could afford, wear, and display in the photographs sent home to the village: "Now I am telling you dear *kum* . . . that I was going to send you our photograph for Christmas . . . so that you could see how we look in this new country. It seems to me dear *kum* that if you'd see my wife and your sister in town, you wouldn't dare to approach her with greetings."[77]

Like the sojourners, the immigrants who settled permanently in America still translated their earnings into the old-country currency, as well as calculating them in dollars. Thus they evaluated their accomplishments against the opportunities of the home village as well as against the earnings of others in the immigrant community. "For a forty-eight-hour week, after a week I received $12 and right away translated it into kronen; it was 60 kronen a week," an im-

migrant wrote in his diary. And from another immigrant memoir:
"When I would get my *pejda* (pay) . . . I thought myself a rich man
because in two weeks here I made more than in the old country in
one year."[78]

Important among the criteria used by the immigrants to measure
their accomplishments in America was the "gentility" of the new
style of living. At first they measured it directly against an old-country standard; however, over time it was altered to fit the context of
the "foreign colony." Thus, a common comparison made by the
immigrants in evaluating their situation was between themselves
and the "nobleman": *pan* or *baron*. "Don't worry about me, 'cause
I live here like a *pan* (gentleman)," wrote an immigrant to his family
in Galicia. And another one: "I am a great *pan* here. I make a ruble
here faster than six *groshen* there." And another: "In America . . .
a pound of the fattest meat costs $.03 and $.04, the leaner the more
expensive, a pound of sausage $.03. I am a *pan* here."[79] Money,
"city" food, American dress, and recreation, and a sense of "world-
liness" – getting to know other places beyond one's native village
– were for the peasant-immigrants the symbols of accomplishment,
an achievement of more elevated social position, closer to that of
the gentry. Although with the passage of time the status values of
the old country became remote and blurred, in the minds of the
foreign-born generation they remained an important point of reference as they evaluated their position in this country. Increasingly,
though, it was the local immigrant community in Johnstown that
served as the immediate comparative framework in which they defined and then "expanded" their goals and actions, as well as the
context within which they evaluated their successes and failures.

Along with the development of the East Central European communities in Johnstown during the decades preceding World War I,
there had appeared incipient signs of their internal social differentiation. The immigrants themselves early perceived this "un-
evenhandedness" of America and noted the differences in accomplishments among their fellow countrymen, all of whom came to
this country in the similar position of peasant-foreigners seeking
jobs. "America is not the same for everyone," an immigrant advised
his cousins in Europe who intended to join him: "For one person,
it is better, for another, worse. I am here almost two years, and I
have only saved $150, [plus] I sent 50 rubles to the homeland; and
one person who came with me from the district of Rypin [saved]
almost 500 rubles."[80]

Plate 7. Johnstown's "foreign colony," beginning of the century.

Plate 8. Slavic children in a "foreign colony," beginning of the century.

Plate 9. St. Nicholas Serbian Orthodox Church, 1906.

Plate 10. Immigrants in Johnstown at the beginning of the century – everyday appearance. Collection of Ann Novak and Anthony Cyburt.

Plate 11. Immigrants in Johnstown dressed up for photographs to be sent to the village or hung on the walls at home in the foreign colony, beginning of the century. Collection of Ann Novak.

Plate 12. Money orders sent home to Europe by the immigrants in Johnstown, beginning of the century. Collection of Walter Wegrzyn.

As the Immigration Commission reported, the total income from all sources combined received by East Central European families in Johnstown was significantly larger than that brought home from the mill or coal mine by the breadwinner alone. All in all, it amounted on the average to $573 annually – certainly a very modest amount, yet about $200 higher than the average income of the East Central European men employed at Cambria. This increment, however, was unequally distributed. One-fifth (20 percent) of the immigrant households surveyed declared a total income of less than $300. These were the "rock bottom survivors," struggling in constant poverty. The second group, approximately 30 percent, was composed of families with a total annual income of between $300 and $500. We can call them "survivors" who existed on just about or a little more than was then needed in Johnstown for an immigrant family to carry on but without systematic savings. The remainder enjoyed an existence a bit more affluent by the prevailing immigrant standards, with 23 percent living on a total income of $500 to $750, and 27 percent on a combined income of over $750.[81]

The same Immigration Commission found an impressive sum of $200,000 deposited by the immigrants in the "foreign banks" of Johnstown during 1907, preceding the economic depression.[82] This sum was most probably composed of hundreds of tiny deposits from immigrant laborers, also including "survivors" who could have put away an occasional handful of dollars to be withdrawn very quickly and used for pressing needs.

It was the families with a total income of over $500 a year that could have afforded somewhat more systematic savings. This group consisted, first, of a small minority of those who had established themselves in local businesses or in the better-skilled jobs in the mills. In 1900, 94.3 percent of the East Central European male immigrants in Johnstown recorded by the census were ordinary laborers, with 3.6 percent reporting better-skilled jobs at Cambria and 2.1 percent employed in ethnic enterprises. By 1915, among the persisters these proportions were 83 percent, 7.5 percent, and 9.5 percent, respectively.[83] The group of families with incomes of over $500 also included immigrant common laborers who managed to entrench themselves in the better-paying unskilled positions at Cambria or whose wives were determined to go on keeping boarders to accumulate money or to pay off the mortgage on the purchased home.

The tastes and life-style preferences of immigrant families also played a role in determining how much of the surplus money would go into the bank to be kept on deposit, how much, if any, would be sent over to Europe, and how much would be used for immediate consumption. The Immigration Commission reported, for instance, significant differences in the amount of savings among the peasant-immigrant households in the small coal-mining communities surrounding Johnstown. With the number of family members held constant and with equal length of employment, they ranged from as little as $7 to $44 a month.[84] In Johnstown itself, occasional bankruptcies of immigrant bankers in the "foreign colonies" usually prompted the local newspapers to publish information about the deposits. For instance, a hearing in the case of one Mihal M., in 1913, revealed that the sums entrusted to him by "foreign residents" ranged from $50 to $165, in the form of deposits usually made every few months.[85]

These differences resulted not only from discrepancies in earnings. There were families in which men drank much more than usually done in the community and those where owing to the particular piety of the wife more contributions were paid to the church. There were households where better meat – pork chops, veal cutlets, choice pieces of lamb – so rare on the peasant tables in Europe, was eaten every day, even for breakfast, the visible symbols of the family's well-being, envied by others. And there were homes where meat was limited to the cheapest cuts and scraps good only for boiling in soup and in which the meals were based predominantly, as in the old country, on cereals and starches. There were families ambitious to own "nice," and expensive, American-looking furniture, and those where the family lived with a few old pieces.

For some immigrants, such as Magyars (according to public opinion in Johnstown's foreign colonies), dress played a more particular role as an outward sign of accomplishment. Others, such as the Serbs, who were said to care first and foremost for abundant food on the table, paid less attention to dress.

Ethnic and labor historians who advocate the "survival" thesis have interpreted the purchase of homes by the immigrant workers as a response to their fundamental concern for security, expressing a "negative want" rather than a "drive for achievement."[86] Recently, Daniel Luria has argued, more specifically, that in the precarious conditions of working-class existence, homeownership actually operated against this important need, since it tied up what little capital the immigrants possessed and inhibited their spatial mobility in search of employment.[87] Indeed, there were disadvantages to possessing a house; my Johnstown interviews indicate that a number of families preferred, for some time at least, to accumulate capital rather than purchase a home. Eventually, however, they all wanted to own one. This strong desire, like that for steady work and for material goods, was an amalgam of two motives at once: that of security, and also of achievement.

It has been implicitly assumed in recent ethnic historiography that these two orientations are discontinuous and in fact opposite, and that the investigated groups should be described as possessing either one or the other. It may indeed be true, if the "achievement" is understood to mean educational and occupational advancement, Anglo-Protestant style. In the immigrant communities, however, the purchase of a house did mean elevating one's family from among the mass of have-nots to a more prestigious social category of owner (see Chapter 7 on internal social stratification). Along with the underlying need for security, the drive to own a home therefore also contained an important element of achievement motivation and symbolism. For the immigrants who remembered their life in Europe well, homeownership meant a further small step on an uneven, slow, and difficult road toward a slightly better, more comfortable existence. "He wanted to live well," Thomas Bell writes of his Slovak hero Kracha in Braddock, Pennsylvania, "[to] live in a nice house, away from the mill . . . and [that in the future] . . . his boys wouldn't have to work with shovel and wheelbarrow like their father."[88]

Inspection of real estate transactions recorded in Cambria County Courthouse between 1890 and 1915 reveals impressive activity on the part of the East Central Europeans, even though the amount of money involved often did not exceed $500.[89] A comparison of the number of real estate transfers among the immigrants recorded during that period with that of the loans and mortgages officially entered indicates that in a great number of cases the money needed for purchase had been obtained "on the note" – from private hands or else through immigrant bankers who did not report it to the courthouse.

Relatives, friends, insurance lodges, local businessmen, even the priest might provide a prospective buyer with the required sum. "Father M. [a Slovak], he let many people borrow from him and did not ask any interest." "My parents had some money put away but not enough, so my mother's sister gave them the rest. She had just then received the death benefit for her husband who was killed in the mills, and she did not need it right away," recalled Mrs. Helen L., who still lives in the house her parents bought in 1912.[90] Loans of $50 to $400 could be taken from ethnic societies to be repaid at 3 to 4 percent interest. The immigrant banks also advanced money on real estate. In 1915, the newly organized Slovenian Savings and Loans Cooperative gave out the first three mortgage loans of $800 each.[91]

The information compiled from the mortgage books in the Cambria County Courthouse for the period 1890 to 1915 shows that the average mortgage obtained by Slavic and Magyar home purchasers from private persons as well as from financial institutions was higher: $1,396.[92] (Probably the reason for the higher figure is that the immigrants who went to the courthouse to record their transactions, rather than concluding them at home, were the more affluent ones, not seldom owners of multiple properties engaged in real estate operations for profit.) A sample of 50 immigrant mortgage loans recorded in the courthouse between 1890 and 1915 shows that the average period needed by purchasers to satisfy their creditors was six years, the length of time varying from one year (12 cases) to twenty (1 case).[93]

Thus, the 1900 census takers recorded in Johnstown 108 homeowners among the East Central Europeans; in 1915, according to the tax assessments for that year there were about 700. Proportionately, the number of immigrant homeowners among all East Central European immigrants originally recorded by the 1900 census who persisted in town until 1915 increased more than fourfold, from 4.5 to 19 percent.[94]

Those few among the immigrants who already possessed a house in 1900 were better established in the city than the majority. In terms of age, they did not differ much from the immigrant family heads who rented or boarded; the mean age for the two groups was thirty-five and thirty-three, respectively. But the home-owners had resided in Johnstown longer. The average length of stay among the 1900 immigrant homeowners was 12.7 years, whereas that of the renting or boarding heads of families was 7.9.[95] It appears, however, that after 1900, with the increased influx of Slavic and Magyar immigrants into the city and with the expansion of the "foreign colonies," the length of time required for the purchase of a home gradually shortened. Of about 200 of the immigrant homeowners in Johnstown listed in the tax assessment records for 1905, more than one-half were new arrivals – that is, people who had not been recorded as present in town in the 1900 city census; in 1910, of approximately 400 immigrant homeowners, over two-thirds had arrived in Johnstown after 1900.[96]

Age, occupational position and continuity of residence significantly

Table 4.2. *Proportion of homeowners among East Central European male immigrants (persisters and returnees) and in different age and occupational groups, 1905–1915 (in %)*

	1905		1910		1915	
Persistence[a]						
Persisters (heads of households)	—		14.8	(112)[b]	19.0	(100)
Returnees	—		3.7	(3)	6.0	(13)
Age (persisters only)						
26–35[c]	—		7.0	(13)	4.2	(3)
36–45	—		13.0	(54)	11.0	(21)
46 and over	—		28.1	(43)	22.2	(76)
Occupation (persisters only)						
Ordinary laborers	6.0	(70)	13.1	(93)	17.6	(82)
Skilled workers	33.3	(18)	48.0	(10)	36.8	(8)
Employed in business and services	34.8	(8)	33.7	(9)	40.1	(10)
Residents of City of Johnstown			34.1			

Note: In 1910 and 1915, only a few immigrants among those present in town in 1900 were recorded in the city directories as "boarders" (3 percent and 4 percent, respectively). Those who appeared as "renters" or "owners" were coded as "household heads." The number of homeowners among female-headed households was too small for tabulation. Also, because of the small number of homeowning households, not much by way of meaningful comparisons can be said about differences among particular nationality groups. Table A.3 in the Appendix shows homeownership rates for immigrants in particular nationality groups for the period 1900–40.
[a] "Returnees" are those who had been recorded in the 1900 Johnstown census, then disappeared – i.e., were not listed in the city directory – at the next checkpoint(s), and reappeared again before or in 1915. Note that since 1905 was my first checkpoint after 1900, there were no "returnees" in 1905.
[b] Figures in parentheses represent *N*.
[c] The age group "25 and younger" was too small numerically to render meaningful results.
Source: East Central European male immigrant population from manuscript schedules of 1900 census, traced in Johnstown city directories for 1905, 1910, 1915. See also Table 3.4, this volume.

affected the homeownership status of the immigrants. Table 4.2 shows the proportions of homeowners among persisters and returnees, in various age groups and occupational categories. Expectedly, the proportion of homeowners was higher among the persisters, among older immigrants, and among those in the higher occupational categories (Table A.3 in the Appendix provides data on home-ownership rates among different nationality groups).

Although their number was steadily increasing, the homeowners constituted a small minority among the Slavs and Magyars in Johnstown, and therefore property ownership alone was sufficient to distinguish a family from the mass of renters and boarders. Within the group of homeowners, however, there had been "better" – more affluent – and "ordinary" ones. Between 1900 and 1915 the median value of homes owned by the immigrants in Johnstown increased from $561, in 1900, to $1,450 in 1915.[97] In 1915, however, there were among the homeowners 27 percent whose property was evaluated at over $2,000 and, at the other extreme, 36 percent of those in the bottom bracket who owned hovels valued at less than $1,000 (see Table A.4 in the Appendix).

Inspection of tax assessments of property values provides more detailed information as to the internal differentiation within the immigrant communities in the first two decades of the century. As Table 4.3 shows, clearly by 1915 there were in the foreign colonies in Johnstown homeowners and homeowners. About 80 percent of the homeowners who held manual jobs at the lowest skill level owned property valued at less than $2,000. On the other hand, the homes of about 60 percent of the skilled mill workers and immigrant businessmen were valued at over $3,000. Among 48 East Central European businessmen homeowners recorded in the 1915 tax assessment lists, 11 owned houses valued at over $10,000. Of this number, 5 were multiple property owners who rented to their fellow countrymen in the foreign colonies, and 6 possessed prosperous businesses serving the immigrants. Ten other entrepreneurs had their homes evaluated at $4,000 to $10,000. Their houses, too, were in the foreign colonies. The purpose of this location, instead of a "nicer" one in the hills, was profit to be made from an immigrant clientele.

To the immigrants, America was not only kinder to some than others; it was also fickle, which made things at once better and worse: bad in winter, better during the spring and summer, and maybe worse in the fall. But unlike back home in the village, here there was hope that the situation would improve again. It was a deceitful feeling, a hope often frustrated, but nevertheless present. The immigrants in Johnstown experienced this "fluctuating reality," as had others in different American cities. It affected their lives tan-

Table 4.3. *Tax valuations of immigrant homes, by homeowner's sex and occupation, 1910, 1915 (in %)*

Value of Home	Men			Women
	Ordinary Laborers[a]	Skilled Workers[b]	Store Owners and other Businessmen[c]	Widows, Boardinghouse Keepers[d]
$100–299				
1910	25.5	12.5	15.3	21.8
1915	5.4	0	0	0
$300–499				
1910	19.6	0	4.2	13.0
1915	7.4	0	0	5.9
$500–999				
1910	40.0	87.5	18.0	43.5
1915	27.5	14.3	10.3	11.8
$1,000–1,999				
1910	13.2	0	37.5	17.4
1915	40.4	28.6	10.3	17.8
$2,000–2,999				
1910	1.7	0	1.4	4.3
1915	12.9	0	16.6	11.8
$3,000–3,999				
1910	0	0	23.6	0
1915	3.4	35.7	18.7	29.4
$4,000 and over				
1910	0	0	0	0
1915	3.0	21.4	44.1	23.3

Note: Invalid and retired homeowners were omitted from the table.
[a] N for 1910 = 235; N for 1915 = 498.
[b] N for 1910 = 8; N for 1915 = 14.
[c] N for 1910 = 36; N for 1915 = 48.
[d] N for 1910 = 23; N for 1915 = 17.
Source: Cambria County Commissioner's Office, Ebensburg, Pa., "Precepts of the Assessors: Annual Enumeration of All Persons, Properties and Things Subject to Taxation," 1910, 1915.

gibly. Homeownership patterns and the occupational movements of the immigrants will illustrate this experience.

We begin with shifts in homeownership between 1905 and 1915. They are shown in Table A.5 in the Appendix. The data confirm the relationship between continuity of residence in the city and homeownership. Among the immigrants who were not present in Johnstown in 1905 and 1910 but who reappeared by 1915, the proportion of homeowners was about 6 percent; among the persisters it was 20 percent. These findings do not necessarily confirm the hypothesis of some ethnic historians that the "movers" were failures and the "stayers" successes.[98] Rather they suggest that the movers, or more properly the returnees (since the fate of permanent leavers remains unknown) had been slower in establishing themselves. The same table also shows that nearly 60 percent of the total number of immigrant homeowners in 1915 had only recently acquired their homes: They were either residents who, in 1910, had rented, or else they were returnees. For a significant number of immigrants, however, their newly acquired homeownership status was an impermanent accomplishment: By 1915, about one-third of the 1910 owners from among the 1900 sample had lost their property.

In recent years the number of so-called social mobility historical studies has declined as criticism of this type of analysis has grown. The most frequently voiced complaints point to neglect of the structural ramifications of mobility processes; historically untenable assumptions about the meaning and importance attached to occupational advancement by the subjects of mobility analyses; unjustified projection of contemporary occupational categories and social ordering onto historical data; and, finally, to a one-sided focus on upward occupational movement and neglect of frequent occurrences of "skidding."[99]

Both the structural and cultural contexts of the immigrants' social mobility have received specific attention in this study: industrial growth and opportunities in Johnstown, the immigrants' value system and their understanding of "success," and the internal "social ordering" of the immigrant communities (discussed in more detail in Chapter 7). Against this background we can now analyze the occupational movements of Slavs and Magyars during the initial phase of their stay in the city.

A classical mobility tabulation shows that between 1900 and 1915 the proportion of laborers of the lowest skill among immigrant persisters in Johnstown decreased by about 10 percent, from 94 to 83 percent. In an important sense this misrepresents the actual experience of a significant number of East Central European workers. In order to get a better picture of their "fluctuating" occupational careers, I reconstructed the individual "career chains" of all men who, between 1900 and 1915, had been recorded at least once at my five-year checkpoints as holding an occupational position higher than ordinary laborer. Both my sources and method have shortcomings. The manuscript schedules of the 1900 census, as well as the early

Johnstown city directories, employed a crude description of lower occupational categories. In particular, they routinely failed to differentiate between common laborers and general operatives with unspecified tasks, the significant distinction for the immigrant workers in terms of both their economic calculations and their perceptions of occupational achievement. The Cambria Company's employment records were destroyed by the floods, and this precluded a finer, culturally more meaningful analysis of the occupational shifting of immigrants and their children. Throughout this book, I therefore use *nolens volens*, three occupational categories: ordinary laborers – that is, unskilled and "unspecified" semiskilled workers, and (pick) miners; skilled workers; and "white-collar workers" occupying various positions in ethnic businesses and services. (Among East Central Europeans traced from the 1900 census through city directories – the population that served as the basis for most of my tabulations – only a score of people, all of them second generation, at some point occupied white-collar positions outside of the foreign colonies.) In the reconstruction of the immigrants' and second generation's career chains, in order to obtain as complete a depiction of their occupational shifting as possible, I also used an additional category of "specified" semiskilled workers.

The second shortcoming has to do with my arbitrary selection of checkpoints. I traced the immigrants' movements at five-year intervals – a rather sparse checking span. We should assume that in between them the occupational shifting obviously continued, among those who persisted in Johnstown as well as among those who temporarily left. It must also have taken place among the immigrants who at none of my five checkpoints were recorded as holding jobs about the unskilled level and were therefore arbitrarily coded as immobile. In short, the results, in all likelihood, underestimate the actual occupational shifting of the immigrants at the beginning of the century.

The individual career chains of the immigrants between 1900 and 1915 are shown in Table A.6 in the Appendix. For that period of time, I counted among the total number of 751 immigrants, from the men listed in the 1900 census who were still present in 1915, including both persisters and returnees, 532, or 71 percent, who at none of the four checkpoints in (1900, 1905, 1910, and 1915) were recorded as holding an occupational position higher than that of an ordinary laborer. The remaining 29 percent (219) were mobile, shifting up from the lowest-level occupational category. Once attained, however, such better positions were very often lost. For over two-thirds of the "achievers," their occupational elevation was a one-time accomplishment. The proportion of immigrants who were found to hold positions higher than the lowest ones at all four checkpoints between 1900 and 1915 was only 5 percent; those holding such positions at three or four checkpoints amounted to 15 percent.

The most frequent shifts were those involving direct or mediated transfers between ordinary manual labor and immigrant businesses and services, accounting for nearly one-half of the total number of moves. The remaining two types of movements, between the lowest-level manual jobs and the skilled and specified semiskilled occupations, each accounted for approximately one-quarter of the transfers.

Immigrant occupational shifting involved "ascents" and "descents." Among the total number of moves, 57 percent were cases of occupational elevations recorded at one of my checkpoints after 1900 and still held in 1915 (ascents), whereas a high 43 percent showed elevated positions held at some earlier checkpoints and lost by 1915 (descents). The proportional share of ascents was highest: 68 percent, versus 32 percent descents, for transfers between the lowest manual positions and immigrant businesses and services. The respective percentages for the movements between the lowest manual and skilled occupations was 56 percent and 44 percent.

By 1915, the numerical size of the particular nationality groups that comprised the original 1900 sample was unfortunately too small to warrant elaborate comparisons. In the groups that had settled earlier in the city, the "German" Poles and Magyars, the proportion of those who had risen above the lowest occupational positions at least once between 1900 and 1915 was about 50 percent – considerably larger than the 29-percent average for the whole East Central European male immigrant population. These groups had established "connection networks" at Cambria with better-placed German mill workers, which could have helped them acquire more elevated occupational positions. In the remaining groups, the proportion of the "achievers" ranged between 13 percent (Serbs, most of whom had arrived in Johnstown shortly before or in 1900 and who concentrated in coal mines where the opportunities for advancement were minimal) and 34 percent (Slovaks).

Without the Cambria Company records, there was no more detailed information available about the patterns and intensity of the immigrants' moving between particular departments, from less to more prestigious shops and back to the labor gangs. It was possible, however, to look a little more closely into the turnover in immigrant businesses by inspecting the "mercantile appraiser's" lists published in the *Tribune* for the selected years between 1900 and 1915. Table A.7 in the Appendix presents this data, collected for all entrepreneurs in the city with recognizably Slavic and Magyar names.

Regardless of the time span between checkpoints, more than one-half of the immigrant businesses disappeared from one checkpoint to the next (the descent rate of 32 percent for occupational transfers between immigrant businesses and the lowest positions quoted earlier was for a more established group of 1900 persisters). But those who had left the entrepreneurial group were promptly replaced by an even greater number of others who tried their luck; an average of nearly 60 percent of all of the immigrant businesses recorded at my six checkpoints between 1900 and 1915 were new entries, people who at the earlier date were either manual laborers at Cambria mills or absent from Johnstown.

Before World War I, opening a business in the foreign colony did not require significant capital investment. "At the beginning of the century, one could start a tiny store in Cambria City with $200 to $250": Anthony C.'s brother opened a store with not much more than this, using the money he had saved from his earnings as a miner.[100] In 1900, the "pecuniary strength" of 70 percent (9) of the immigrant businesses for which Dun & Bradstreet gave credit ratings was estimated at less than $500; by 1918, 50 percent (51) of the immigrant businessmen surveyed had enterprises valued at less than $500 (at the other extreme, 10 percent [10] had a "pecuniary strength" rated at over $5,000).[101] Not difficult to acquire, the status of businessman in the foreign colony was easy to lose. "It was easy to start" – Frank G.'s father had tried and failed several times – "but difficult to maintain. First, there was then tough competition; second, there were always problems with credit, since people did not pay cash, only on the book. On the other hand, in those days these immigrant businessmen, they did not want to make a fortune, just a decent living."[102]

A number of immigrants circulated between the mill and the store, often working in both – a pattern sufficiently common to put into question the standard interpretation found in historical mobility studies, whereby each case of the attainment of a white-collar position, even if it was recorded only once in the whole period under investigation, is classified as "upward mobility," whereas a return to manual work is treated as "skidding."[103] Andrew M., for instance, who in the 1920s eventually became a well-established businessman in the Slovak community, continuously moved for about ten years between a hotel, where he worked first as a clerk, then as the owner; a mine where he dug coal; a saloon where he was a bartender; and the old country, where he was a farmer.[104] The father of Walter W. had a similar career: Within a few years he first mined coal, then quit for several months to work as a teller at the Slovak bank in the city, dug coal again while playing music at immigrant weddings every Saturday and Sunday, and finally opened the business in which he became established.[105] Michael M.'s father worked in the mills for two years, went back to Serbia, returned, opened a small meat market in 1909 (like many peasant-immigrants he had learned butchering in the village), then transferred it to his brother because he was "bored," became a rigger and traveled around the country, and finally returned to Johnstown where he eventually bought a saloon and settled down, putting his extended family to work for him.[106] In this context, the loss by immigrants of a white-collar (business or clerical) position in the foreign colony and the resumption of manual work should more properly be termed occupational "shifting" – the term denoting movement on a horizontal or slightly inclined plane – rather than "skidding" down the vertical line.

The latter notion could perhaps more accurately be applied to big and scandalous bankruptcies, involving thousands of dollars, that occasionally occurred among the established East Central European businessmen in Johnstown. Usually indifferent to what went on in the immigrant sections of town, the *Johnstown Tribune* extensively reported on such events: "Bankrupt Cambria City man's liabilities are $23,000, assets only $4,000," reported the newspaper in 1908; "at least 100 Slavs and Croatians who say they entrusted money to John L., to be forwarded to relatives in Europe report the money never arrived at its destination. Many have lost all their savings!" And four months later, a spectacular bankruptcy, involving a well-known and highly respected leader of one of the immigrant groups is described: "A big delegation from the foreign colony in Cambria City," reported the *Tribune*, "gathered in and about . . . court this morning for the purpose of hearing what Bolo C., the Chestnut Street banker who himself is charged with embezzlement, had to say in the case in which he accuses Peter Z., his former manager, with misappropriating funds aggregating $25,000." The affair ended with the accused suffering a fatal stroke of apoplexy in the courtroom. The liability of his bankrupt estate amounted to $119,000; the estimated assets were $60,000.[107]

To conclude, then, this lengthy discussion: The conditions in which the East Central Europeans strove to realize their goals during the initial years of their stay in America were highly unstable, and the immigrants were keenly aware of the odds against them. As their situation "fluctuated" from better to worse and back again, they lived through times of disappointment and resignation and times of a little promise and hope. The latter, although deceptive, was a feeling new to the peasants. However limited and deprived their condition was in this country, as compared to what they had known at home, the immigrants perceived it as offering more promising grounds for sustained efforts to achieve a better life.

Between 1900 and 1915 the majority of the Slavic and Magyar immigrants in Johnstown had remained where they started: working as common laborers and living as renters. However, by collective family effort and by the purposeful use of ascriptive-particularist networks in their economic maneuvers, they stubbornly calculated and strove to accumulate some surplus capital to be used or invested according to the needs of the household. Despite exasperating setbacks in the saving process resulting from recurrent unemployment, unexpected sickness, and industrial accidents, peasant-immigrants had for the first time in their everyday lives a prospect of generating a surplus of valuables.

In Europe, for most peasants accumulation above the subsistence level was inconceivable unless they migrated every year for an extended period of time, leaving their families behind. As the immigrants settled in Johnstown, which gradually became their home, they found out that although the price was very steep, America did offer a higher standard of living and the possibility of accumulating savings. Between 1900 and 1915, at least 30 percent of the men succeeded, if only once, in achieving an elevated occupational position. Most of them shifted back to common manual labor, but their climb after more money and cleaner and lighter jobs, even if only temporarily successful, proved that such a move was accomplishable, that it was possible – also a new notion for peasants one or two generations removed from feudal serfdom. For most, owning a home still remained a remote dream in 1915. But by that time one of five immigrants among those present in town in 1900 already possessed one. A systematic increase in the number of homeowners was visible to all in the foreign colonies. Although many of the home purchasers subsequently lost their property, they often regained it with time, and many others bought houses every year.

The peasant-immigrants were only too familiar with failure and bad luck in their European existence, and certainly America did not spare them the experience of both. But the accomplishment of a higher standard of living, better food and dress, and some savings was genuinely experienced by the immigrants as something new and worth striving for with hard work by the whole family. The "fluctuating reality" in America was very deeply frustrating, but at the same time it bred and sustained hope that things now bad would turn better again and further mobilized the immigrants to make repeated efforts to acquire the assets needed to achieve the desired goals.

Once they had settled in Johnstown, the immigrants quickly abandoned the unrealistic dreams they had harbored in Europe about this country. Their lives here were hard and insecure and their attitude toward America strongly ambivalent. But, as compared with the alternative they had known in Europe, they perceived this country as a *lesser evil*: "America is not perfect, true, but elsewhere these failings are even more numerous and more pronounced," concluded an editorial in the Polish-language newspaper *Zgoda* in 1910.[108] "My parents," recalled a second-generation Slovenian from Johnstown, "they saw all the bad things in this country, they were not blind, but . . . they still preferred it here than to go back to Europe."[109] In their letters home, the immigrants repeatedly expressed this balanced, ambivalent judgment: "Nowhere there is heaven, everywhere misery, in America no good, but still better than in the [old] country," wrote an immigrant from Chicago to his mother in Europe.[110] The same attitude echoed in the words of Kracha, the Slovak hero of Thomas Bell's *Out of This Furnace*: "Braddock is no paradise, I'll admit, but have you forgotten how we had to live in the old country?"[111]

5 Johnstown and the immigrant communities between the wars

The adaptation of the East Central Europeans in Johnstown continued during the interwar period. The city, in its economic structure, its social and political life, and its dominant cultural aura, had retained its basic autocratic features from the earlier period, and the main conditions that had led to "emergent ethnicity" in the preceding decades were also present.

Within this framework, we can trace the process of further development of the immigrant communities. This process was, at the same time, sustained by Johnstown's sociopolitical organization and "activated" by the immigrants themselves. Crystallization of internal group associations and solidarities within particular communities performed a twofold function. It sharpened ethnic boundaries, providing a symbolic and organizational framework within which the immigrants defined and pursued their interests. Simultaneously, it was through the enhancement of ethnic awareness and through daily participation in ethnic communities that they incorporated themselves into the local Johnstown society. This divisive-inclusive process of ethnicization I call "ascriptive inclusion."

We shall begin with an overview of the main trends in Johnstown's economic and demographic development following World War I, and of its continuing dependence on the city's major employer, the Cambria Steel Company. A spectacular expansion of Cambria and a rapid increase of Johnstown's population constituted two major factors in the development of the city during the half century from the 1870s through World War I. With the termination of the war in Europe, the trend of accelerated growth in the American steel industry had exhausted itself. Although after the recovery from the 1921 depression the growth of automobile and aviation production furnished the steel industry with increasing orders, it never regained the rate of expansion of the earlier period.

As it became easier and cheaper to use the rich ores of the Great Lakes region instead of lower-grade ores available in western Pennsylvania, Johnstown's industrial advantage was reduced. Furthermore, increasing competition in transportation put Johnstown at a disadvantage: The city's rough and difficult terrain and somewhat isolated location had diminished its role as a supplier to remote markets. As shifting markets gradually tipped the scales in favor of other regions, the Johnstown area began to decline in importance as a major mining and industrial center.

This process was accompanied by a slowdown in the rate of demographic growth of the city: Whereas between 1880 and 1910 the population of Greater Johnstown increased by 342 percent, during the decade between 1910 and 1920 the rate was 26.6 percent, and between 1920 and 1940 it was only 7 percent. At the same time, with the improvement in local transportation and communication systems, and with the increasing dispersal of commerce and services, the population was gradually moving away from the city core and into the surrounding boroughs. Between 1920 and 1940 the population of the boroughs and townships immediately adjacent to Johnstown grew by 31.5 percent, from 21,662 to 28,447 (see Table 3.1).

The size of the total labor force in Johnstown shrank by 7 percent between 1920 and 1930 and by another 8 percent between 1930 and 1940 (see Table 3.2). The continuing heavy dependence of Johnstown on steel and coal and the slowdown in the rate of industrial growth after World War I were not conducive to the diversification of the occupational structure of the city. As a result of further mechanization in the mills and mines, the number of semiskilled jobs increased. But in its general character, during the interwar decades Johnstown remained a distinctly blue-collar city.

No less than three-fourths of its male labor force continued to be employed in manual occupations, and about two-thirds of all gainfully employed men worked in metal manufacturing and in mining (see Table 3.2). Of this, Cambria Steel Company – superseded in 1923 by the Bethlehem Steel Company, which purchased Cambria's properties in the city – employed approximately 70 to 75 percent, and an additional 10 percent worked in the local U.S. Steel Company plant.

As in the rest of the country, the languid growth of the steel industry in Johnstown after World War I was accompanied by rapid fluctuations of demand and consequent fluctuations in production levels. The frequent shifts in the volume of steel production caused the size of the work force employed in manufacturing in Johnstown to alternately expand and contract. During the 1920s, the local steel industry utilized, on the average, about 75 percent of its potential labor capacity of 15,000 to 16,000 men; the two leading steel companies in the city had, therefore, on their average payroll, about 11,000 to 12,000 workers.[1] The economic depression of the 1930s drastically decreased this number. In the summer of 1931 the proportion of unemployed workers in Johnstown and vicinity was over 20 percent, and in 1934 it reached 30 percent.[2]

The size and growth of the city's minority white-collar strata directly depended on the prosperity of the local mills and coal mines. The slowdown in industrial expansion after World War I also stabilized the growth of this segment of the occupational structure of the city. Between 1920 and 1940, the total size of the white-collar strata in Johnstown increased by 7 percent, from 7,685 to 8,229 (see Table 3.2).

As in the earlier period, Johnstown, a typical steel town, provided limited opportunities for employment for women. During the two decades preceding World War II, approximately one-fifth of the adult women in the city were gainfully employed, with the numbers of women employed outside the home rising by 13 percent between 1920 and 1940, from 4,340 to 4,912. Approximately two-thirds of them held white-collar jobs. With the sluggish rate of industrial growth in the city, however, the increase in the supply of clerical and sales jobs, traditionally feminine, was limited.

Continuing after the war as the largest producer and the major employer in Johnstown, Cambria/Bethlehem Company also retained its leading position in the city's public life, as well as firm control over the labor force. In the fall of 1919, Johnstown mill workers went on strike, demanding better working conditions and, most of all, recognition of their union. In response to this, the company, with the active help of a 257-member Citizens' Committee composed of city officials, businessmen and community leaders, and assisted by the *Johnstown Tribune*, launched a vigorous carrot-and-stick campaign to induce its labor force to come back to the mills. The strike ended after two months, without the workers' achieving their major purpose. The independent union was not recognized. Instead, the workers gained a 14-percent wage increase and overtime wages of 150 percent of base pay. The company also introduced an Employee Representation Plan to serve as a substitute for the union.[3] With this effective suppression of the union movement, the Johnstown mills were to remain "captive" for two decades to come.

Besides the Employee Representation Plan, Bethlehem introduced other policies designed to soothe and control its labor force: a pension plan for retired workers; a large-scale "safety drive" program in all mill departments; construction of housing projects in the working-class sections of town to ease the undiminished housing shortage; rental to company employees of plots for vegetable gardens on the hills surrounding the city; and substantial enlargement of the old company store to provide the mill workers with moderately priced merchandise and limited credit in times of slackened production.[4]

In the summer months of 1937, the Johnstown mills became the scene of another labor protest, part of a wider strike action organized by the CIO and involving the bloc of companies known as "Little Steel" (Republic, Inland, Youngstown, and Bethlehem), all of which refused their workers the right to join an independent labor organization. Like its predecessor, the brief strike in 1937 ended in failure, effectively suppressed by Bethlehem management, which was again supported, as in 1919, by the *Johnstown Tribune* and by a Citizens' Committee of similar composition to the first. In the spring of 1939, as a result of a court order obtained by the National Labor Relations Board, the Little Steel companies were forced to dissolve their company unions. Shortly after, a Steel Workers' Organizing Committee (SWOC) office was set up in the city, but the union was not officially recognized by the Bethlehem Steel Company until 1941.[5]

The ethnic composition of Johnstown's population during the 1920s and 1930s remained essentially unchanged except for a slight increase in the number of black residents and the arrival of a few score Mexicans. A small community of blacks, which before World War I numbered less than 500 people (0.8 percent of the city's population), was joined by over 1,000 more, most of them "imported" by Cambria during the steel strike of 1919 and placed in company houses. During the 1920s and 1930s the number of blacks in Johnstown was between 1,600 and 1,700; they constituted 2.5 percent of the city's population (Table 3.6, note b). In 1919 the company also brought in a small group of Mexican workers from Chicago.

The native-born Americans of native parentage made up, as before, one-half of the city's population, and the East Central European foreign-stock residents – both immigrants and the second generation – comprised one-fourth. The former constituted approximately 60 percent of all foreign-born residents, and the latter comprised one-half of the natives of foreign-born parentage.

During the interwar period the East Central European Johnstowners participated in the general population movement out of the downtown core of the city into the more elevated sections of town and to the adjacent boroughs. Despite the increased residential relocation of Slavs and Magyars from the original foreign colonies into the areas of secondary settlement, however, their geographic concentration had been maintained through World War II. In 1920, about 70 percent of the East Central Europeans who had persisted in town since 1900 still lived in the old foreign colonies. By 1940, over 40 percent of the Slavs and Magyars who were already present in Johnstown at the time of the 1900 census were still living in the old areas of primary settlement, whereas most of the remainder had moved into areas of secondary immigrant settlement (see Table 3.7).

As they gradually moved out of the primary foreign colonies near the mills into new areas, East Central Europeans tended to occupy there blocks close to each other, forming tight ethnic clusters (see Map C; Tables A.8 and A.9 in the Appendix show intracity residential movements of immigrants in the between-war period). And so, for instance, in the nineteenth ward of Morrellville they settled in the area below Strayer Street, whereas streets above this line were mostly inhabited by native-born Americans and representatives of older, western European stock. Similarly, in the adjacent eighteenth ward, the boundary seems to have run along I Street, with a rapidly diminishing number of East Central European residents as one moved beyond this line to the westward.[6] In Moxham, a section that Slavs and Magyars began moving into during and after World War I, this pattern of block concentration was even more pronounced. Not only did they move into particular streets – Forrest, Russel, Linden, and Woodland Avenues – but on these streets they concentrated in particular blocks, separated from the native-born Americans and the western Europeans alike.

Residential segmentation of Johnstown along ethnic lines was replicated in the workplace, in the public-political realm, as well as in the social and cultural life of the city.

In Chapter 3, the occupational disadvantage of the East Central Europeans in Johnstown was illustrated by showing how much their occupational distribution "lagged behind" that of the city as a whole. Let us repeat the same demonstration for the interwar period.

Tables 5.1 and 5.2 show the actual and expected occupational performance of the foreign-born East Central European men in the period 1915–30. Tables 5.3 and 5.4 show the actual and expected performance of the second generation between 1920 and 1949/50.

As the tables show, for the East Central European men to have reached occupational parity with the employed male population of the city as a whole, their rates of upward occupational mobility

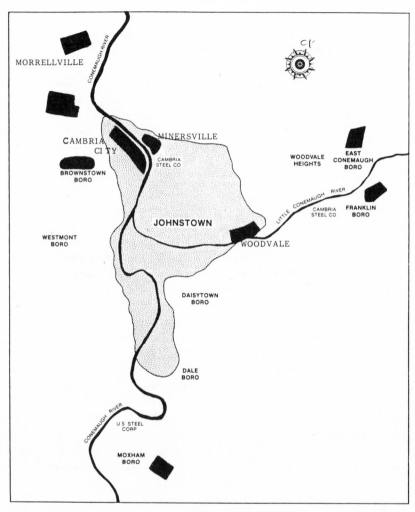

Map C. Residential locations of East Central Europeans in Johnstown, between the wars.

should have been considerably greater than those actually observed. For example, in the period 1915–30, 19 instead of 11 percent of the immigrants should have moved from blue- to white-collar occupations, and 20 instead of 10 percent from less- to better-skilled jobs in the mills. In comparison with the earlier phase, however, the immigrants' disadvantage had slightly diminished. In the preceding period, the catching up necessary for the foreign-born Slavs and

Table 5.1. Intragenerational occupational mobility of foreign-born East Central European male persisters in Johnstown in blue-collar and white-collar occupations, 1915–1930 (in %)

1915	Observed Matrix 1930			Adjusted Matrix 1930		
	Blue-collar	White-collar	Total	Blue-collar	White-collar	Total
Blue-collar	76 (outflow 87)	11 (outflow 13)	87	68 (outflow 78)	19 (outflow 22)	87
White-collar	8 (outflow 62)	5 (outflow 38)	13	7 (outflow 54)	6 (outflow 46)	13
Total	84	16	100	75	25	100

	Observed Mobility	Adjusted Mobility
Total mobility	19	26
% up	11	19
% down	8	7
Immobile	81	74

Note: Table spans only 1915–30, since by 1940 my original 1900 sample was too small for comparisons.
Source: Fifteenth Census of the United States: 1930, vol. 4: Population, Occupations by States, 1395–7; U.S. Department of Labor and Industry, "How Many Are Jobless in Pennsylvania?," Special Bulletin (July 1931), 5–15; East Central European foreign-born male population from manuscript schedules of 1900 census, traced in the Johnstown city directories for 1915 and 1930.

Table 5.2. *Intragenerational occupational mobility of foreign-born East Central European male persisters in Johnstown in manual occupations in the steel industry, 1915–1930 (in %)*

1915	Observed Matrix 1930			Adjusted Matrix[a] 1930		
	U and USS[b]	SS and S	Total	U and USS	SS and S	Total
U and USS	85 (outflow 89)	10 (outflow 11)	95	75 (outflow 79)	20 (outflow 21)	95
SS and S	4 (outflow 80)	1 (outflow 20)	5	4 (outflow 80)	1 (outflow 20)	5
Total	89	11	100	79	21	100

	Observed Mobility	*Adjusted Mobility*
Total mobility	14	24
% up	10	20
% down	4	4
Immobile	86	76

Note: Table spans only 1915–30, since by 1940 my original 1900 sample was too small for comparisons.
[a] Data based on distribution of men actually employed in the local mills in 1930.
[b] U = unskilled; USS = unspecified semiskilled; SS = specified semiskilled; S = skilled.
Source: Same as in Table 5.1.

Table 5.3. *Intragenerational occupational mobility of second generation East Central European male persisters in Johnstown in blue-collar and white-collar occupations, 1920–1949/50 (in %)*

1920	Observed Matrix 1949–50			Adjusted Matrix 1949–50		
	Blue-collar	White-collar	Total	Blue-collar	White-collar	Total
Blue-collar	76 (outflow 86)	12 (outflow 14)	88	66 (outflow 75)	22 (outflow 25)	88
White-collar	9 (outflow 75)	3 (outflow 25)	12	8 (outflow 66)	4 (outflow 34)	12
Total	85	15	100	74	26	100

	Observed Mobility	Adjusted Mobility
Total mobility	21	30
% up	12	22
% down	9	8
Immobile	79	70

Source: Seventeenth Census of the United States: 1950, Population, vol. 2, *Characteristics of the Population,* pt. 38, pp. 39–132; East Central European native-born male population from manuscript schedule of 1900 census, traced in Johnstown city directories for 1920 and 1949.

Table 5.4. *Intragenerational occupational mobility of second generation East Central European male persisters in Johnstown in manual occupations in the steel industry, 1920–1949/50 (in %)*

1920	Observed Matrix 1949–50			Adjusted Matrix 1949–50		
	U and USS[a]	SS and S	Total	U and USS	SS and S	Total
U and USS	65 (outflow 79)	17 (outflow 21)	82	50 (outflow 60)	31 (outflow 40)	81
SS and S	14 (outflow 77)	4 (outflow 23)	18	10 (outflow 53)	9 (outflow 47)	19
Total	79	21	100	60	40	100

	Observed Mobility	Adjusted Mobility
Total mobility	31	41
% up	17	31
% down	14	10
Immobile	69	59

[a] U = unskilled; USS = unspecified semiskilled; SS = specified semiskilled; S = skilled.
Source: Seventeenth Census of the United States: 1950, Population, vol. 2, *Characteristics of the Population,* pt. 38, pp. 39–132; East Central European native-born male population from manuscript schedule of 1900 census, traced in Johnstown city directories for 1920 and 1949.

Magyars in order for them to have matched the occupational distribution of the employed male population of Johnstown as a whole would have required upward mobility rates in the two respective transitions 2.5 and 3.0 times greater than those actually observed. Between 1915 and 1930, these figures were 1.7 and 2.0, respectively.

As for the occupational performance of the second generation between 1920 and 1949–50, the mobility rate needed for them to have achieved occupational parity with the other employed men in Johnstown in 1949–50 was 22 instead of 12 percent in the blue- to white-collar transition, and 31 instead of 17 in advancing to higher-skilled jobs within the mills. The catching up necessary for the immigrant sons to have matched the occupational distribution of the employed male population in Johnstown as of 1949–50 would have required, in both transitions, upward mobility rates 1.8 times greater than those actually observed. (The patterns of occupational movements of both the immigrants and the second generation during the interwar period will be discussed in Chapters 6 through 8).

The "cultural division of labor" that characterized the job market in Johnstown in the earlier phase had continued in the interwar period. During the two decades following World War I, the company maintained the ethnic divisions inside the mills. The Cambria and Gautier divisions of Bethlehem Steel, known in the city as "status plants," employed mostly skilled workers such as blacksmiths, carpenters, machinists, and rollers, and most of the men who held these jobs were either American or western European. Similarly, a job at U.S. Steel's Lorain Plant was considered a prestigious one, and this plant had a predominantly American and western European work force. On the other hand, the giant Franklin division of Bethlehem, with its open-hearth furnaces and coke ovens – known as the "foreign plant" – employed large numbers of East Central Europeans.[7]

The nativist sentiments that prevailed among the Bethlehem management and plant supervisors reduced the chances of promotion for the Slavic and Magyar workers. With the languid growth of the steel industry after World War I, the supply of better positions had remained limited. Further mechanization of steel production and of the work process in the mines created a number of semiskilled jobs with more and less specified tasks. Although the East Central European workers now had easier access to lower-level semiskilled jobs, the skilled jobs had, by and large, remained out of their reach. "Industry needed different mechanical jobs," Louis M., who had been a superintendent at Cambria during the 1920s told me, "so the foreign element was taken in and given various [semiskilled] jobs more often than their fathers, the immigrants . . . But not too many were taken to the skilled trades, and this was because of racism at that time."[8] And from Charles H., who in that period served as general foreman in Bethlehem's prestigious mechanical department:

> Second generation, sons of the Slavish immigrants, their chances for advancement were better, most of them learned on the job, but a lot of those second generation, even those born here, for us Americans were like immigrants; they stayed at home with their parents until twenty-four or twenty-five and spoke old-country language [recalls a case of a "young, able foreigner" whom he knew long and well and whose father had also worked for him, whose promotion the management resisted] . . . When they had a list of names for promotions: White, McKinnley, Baumgarten, Borowski, and so on, they tended to scratch out the "Hunky" ones."[9]

The number of native-born American workers and those of Western European origin was, as in the earlier period, amply sufficient to fill the better positions in the mills. The proportion of southern and eastern European foreign-stock workers in Johnstown metal manufacturing plants during the 1920s was about 35 to 40 percent of the average total work force employed, or about 4,000 to 4,500. The remaining 7,000 to 7,500 were native-born Americans and men of Welsh, Scottish, German, and Irish background.[10] During the 1920s, the number of better positions in the Johnstown mills – the highly skilled jobs and those of cranemen, hoistmen, switchmen, as opposed to the category of "unspecified general operatives" – was around or somewhat over 3,000.[11] There were, then, on the whole, many more potential aspirants for these jobs from among groups "more suitable" than the East Central Europeans.

Whatever meager opportunities for occupational mobility existed in the Johnstown mills in the period of industrial stabilization that followed World War I were effectively controlled by the ethnic-ascriptive policies of the Bethlehem Company. Similar criteria obtained in the political life of the city. The "foreigners" continued to be conspicuously absent from municipal politics. During the 1920s, they were represented in Johnstown's public offices by one assessor, one alderman, and five policemen; a decade later, by one (the same) assessor, one member of the school board, four justices of the peace, four aldermen – all from the immigrant sections of town – and fourteen men on the Johnstown police force and in the fire department.[12]

The adjacent borough of Franklin, where the East Central Europeans constituted the majority of residents, had by the late 1930s a "Slavish" burgess, and one-half of the members of the Franklin Fire Department were Slavic. But in neighboring East Conemaugh borough, where native-born Americans were more numerous and kept a tight hold on public offices, there was, before World War II, only one Slavic councilman and three policemen. In addition, Slavs constituted 8 percent of the membership of the East Conemaugh Fire Company.[13]

The ethnic-ascriptive labor and political practices in Johnstown were underlined by the nativist attitudes prevailing in the dominant local society. Its antiforeign sentiments took the form of intensified American nationalism during and after World War I that was manifested in various Americanization programs targeted at Johnstown's foreign-born population and actively sponsored by the Bethlehem Company and municipal, welfare, and public agencies. The YMCA English and citizenship classes, organized in several foreign colonies in the city, were designed to teach the participants "the history of America, the land of opportunity; its constitution and citizenship, hygiene and cleanliness."[14] The welfare and safety programs carried out in the local mills since 1917 explicitly stressed "American themes." The English night classes sponsored by the company in the shops denounced the "foreign ties" of the immigrants. In leaflets printed in several languages and posted in the immigrant sections of town, the *Tribune* publicized "Instructions for Those Who Desire to Be Naturalized." The explanation of "What It Means to Be an American Citizen" read as follows:

> (1) You must first of all realize that you have cast off all relationship with your foreign country to which you were formerly attached . . . (2) The intelligent, naturalized citizen realizes at once that he and his family are immeasurably benefited when they adopt American customs and American ideals . . . (3) The English language should be spoken and read in the home. The one aim of the household should be to become assimilated as rapidly as possible.[15]

Despite a variety of Americanization programs offered in Johnstown, the native community seemed to carry them out only halfheartedly, without conviction that the endeavor would succeed. With the continuing residential segregation of the East Central Europeans, the lack of developed class and supra-ethnic institutional networks to serve as social integrative bases, and with the persistent nativism in the dominant local society, the division between the new immigrants and the "Americans" continued to segment the city into separate sociocultural worlds. The same young men from Slavic and Magyar homes who, as American soliders fighting in Europe during World War I, had been praised by the *Johnstown Tribune* as "our Johnstown boys" and lauded for heroism in the struggle "in defense of their country" (the United States) were again labeled "foreigners" after they returned to the city. Interestingly, during the 1920s and 1930s the only context in which the local newspapers still referred to the East Central European inhabitants of the city as "our Johnstowners" was on the sports page (the second-generation Slavs and Magyars not only played on company teams but also – and predominantly – on their own ethnic teams sponsored by immigrant organizations, clubs, schools, and parishes). It was enough, however, to turn a page in the newspaper to find familiar and much more common references to "foreigners." In the job advertisements section throughout the 1920s one read announcements seeking a "foreign girl for general housework" or "strong foreign men for the construction projects" – quite obviously referring to the American-born children of immigrants.

It was in such contexts that the immigrants "incorporated themselves" into the local Johnstown society. Its distancing attitude toward East Central Europeans had its counterpart in the behavior and sentiments of the latter. For the most part, they were preoccupied with themselves. Just as the "Americans" in Johnstown during the 1920s and 1930s had on the whole remained remote and indifferent toward the "foreigners," most East Central Europeans remained, by and large, unconcerned with the pursuits of the native community.

The language courses offered in the immigrant sections of town and in the mills taught their participants a somewhat better "industrial English," but they did not make them "cast off all relations with foreign homelands," as advocated by the Americanization leaflets posted in foreign colonies. The East Central Europeans clung to their own. Their naturalization rate remained low long after they had realized that they were going to stay in America for good. According to the 1920 census, about 75 percent of the Slavs and Magyars residing in the city had arrived in this country before 1914, but at the beginning of the 1920s no more than one-third of them were naturalized, and by 1930 this proportion rose by only 10 percent (an additional reason, by the way, for their absence from municipal politics).[16] Throughout the interwar period, the intermarriage rate between the East Central Europeans and native-born Americans and persons of western European stock did not exceed 5 to 10 percent. Such bonds were obviously not considered socially appropriate by the latter, and they were equally frowned upon and discouraged by public opinion in the immigrant communities.[17]

Distanced from and distancing themselves, during the decades following the First World War the East Central Europeans in Johnstown, like immigrants in other American cities with large immigrant colonies, were becoming increasingly involved in their ethnic communities and increasingly aware of their ethnic group separateness. They were making Johnstown "their home" and America "their country," not, however, through the "adoption of American ideals" and "rapid assimilation" advocated by the *Tribune* but through the ethnicization of consciousness, life-styles, and activities and through daily participation in an engrossing ethnic communal life. This self-incorporation occurred by a segmental appropriation of sorts that evolved neither "for" nor "against" the dominant local society but, rather, developed alongside of or in spite of it by appropriating what was available and fusing into ethnic patterns the old-country traditions and "American" ways and attitudes.

In the decades following World War I, the immigrants added new groups and associations to the already established networks of parishes, clubs, and organizations. Between 1915 and 1940, they founded 86 new organizations, 12 new parishes, and 2 new parochial schools. Together with the already existing institutions, this made a total of about 140 organizations, 13 churches, and 6 parochial schools. During the 1920s three foreign-language newspapers also appeared in town: the Hungarian *Hirado*, the Rusyn *Chranitel*, and the Polish *Postęp*.[18]

The expanding institutional networks in the immigrant communities reflected two simultaneous tendencies occurring in each of the ethnic groups. On the one hand there was increasing solidification and expansion of ethnic group boundaries and an intensified awareness among the members of their collective identities. On the other we see the growing internal complexity and differentiation – territorial, religious, and social – of the immigrant communities.

Living in close proximity in the immigrant sections of town, East Central Europeans from different nationality groups continued to attend each others' picnics and the balls and public events that took place year-round in the ethnic halls. The younger generation met in ethnic sports teams that accepted also members of other nationalities. Still, in the 1930s, the ethnic homogeneity in those clubs was, on the average, a high 70 to 75 percent.[19] Also, as the announcements by East Central Europeans in the *Johnstown Tribune* indicate, social gatherings in private, more intimate circles – weddings, birthdays, anniversaries, baptisms – were ethnically homogeneous affairs in the interwar period. The guests at assemblies in Serbian homes were predominantly Serbs; at Slovak parties they were Slovak; at Polish ones, Polish; and so on.[20] The rate of intermarriage among different East Central European groups in Johnstown was also low. For 9 ethnic parishes checked, the average rate of intermarriage in the interwar period was about 10 percent, with the rate for Ukrainians and Serbs close to zero, whereas the Slovenes from the new St. Therese's parish in a mixed East Central European neighborhood had a rate of 15 percent. The Slovak St. Francis, also in a mixed neighborhood in an area of secondary immigrant settlement, had a rate of only 8 percent.[21]

During the 1920s and 1930s the East Central European population in the city formed at least four different territorial groupings: Cambria City – Minersville; East Conemaugh – Franklin; Moxham; and Morrellville. Within these territorial divisions, each of the nationality groups formed several distinguishable social circles, even though they crisscrossed and overlapped inside the ethnic boundaries. At the same time, members of these diversified subgroups and circles within the immigrant communities had become strongly conscious during that period of their common ethnicity. This bond, uniting the nationality groups across the internal divisions, was expressed in the shared language with which they communicated and in collective celebrations of the particular groups' national pasts and traditions. Such festive occasions as Pulaski Day, President Masaryk's visit to Johnstown, the Kossuth Anniversary, or the Day of St. Sava invariably attracted large crowds of participants from all parts of the city and its surroundings and from the various circles and quarreling factions in particular groups. The tendency toward increased collective awareness and demarcation of the originally fluid ethnic group boundaries was expressed in the formation of umbrella federations representing the members of several organizations in the local community with membership often crossing the local boundaries and reaching into a larger geographic area. Thus in the 1930s in Johnstown 9 such umbrella organizations existed: 4 Citizen's Clubs and 5 *Centralas*, or associations of various ethnic societies of a particular group.[22]

The second tendency – toward growing internal complexity – was expressed by the multiplication and increasing diversification of institutions within each group. On the one hand, the gradual territorial relocation of the East Central Europeans from the original foreign colonies and their concentration in new areas led to the formation of new parishes and organizations. Thus 3 new Slovak churches, 2 Slovenian parishes, and 1 Polish one, additional branches of already existing associations, and new groups and societies were founded. On the other hand, splinter groups were also formed as a result of internal strife and disputes. From the beginning of the century, the East Central European parishes in Johnstown, as in other American cities, were the scene of recurrent conflicts between the pastors and the parishioners and among the latter themselves. These conflicts strengthened the collective identities of the members of the involved communities, since it was the internal matters that positioned and defined particular nationalities in the foreign colonies and sharpened group ethnic boundaries. In some instances, the intense internal disputes led to secessions. In 1918, about 50 Poles, dissatisfied with what they perceived as the insufficiently "national" character of St. Casimir's Roman Catholic parish, left it and formed a Polish National Catholic church. In 1927 a group of 40 Ukrainian dissenters withdrew from St. John the Baptist Ukrainian Byzantine Catholic parish and founded a separate, Orthodox one as an expression of "true" Ukrainian identity. In 1937, a similar split occurred in the Rusyn Greek Catholic parish, and a Carpatho-Russian Orthodox Greek Catholic church was formed. About the same time, as a result of sharp differences of opinion on matters concerning old-country allegiances, a group of Serbs from St. Nicholas parish founded a separate church, St. Petka's.[23]

Internal competition and disagreements over personalities and issues in the immigrant communities also led to the formation of new secular organizations. In the Polish group, from the beginning of the century the Polish Roman Catholic Union competed with the Polish National Alliance. With the solidification of the old lodges and the proliferation of new ones, their disputes, reflected in the local newspaper *Postęp*, became so intense at times that they were even echoed in the Buffalo Polish daily *Dziennik dla Wszystkich*.[24] The Slovene Socialists in Johnstown, although numerically small (the group never exceeded 30-odd people) were active enough to incite the wrath of more clerically oriented groups in the city.[25] The different branches of the Slovak Jednota, the Rusyn Greek Catholic Union, the Ukrainian National Association, and the Serb National Federation competed for members and influence with each other and with the smaller, independent ethnic societies that mushroomed after World War I.

Finally, the multiplication of ethnic organizations in Johnstown during the 1920s and 1930s expressed the internal diversification of interests, status, and life-styles within the immigrant communities. For instance, just as the foundation in Morrellville of the Slovak St. Francis church in 1922 expressed, in addition to considerations of geographic convenience, the social advancement of those who had managed to move out of the primary foreign colony in Cambria City, so did the multiple groups and organizations that subsequently emerged around the parish and in the neighborhood. In another instance, one lodge of the Hungarian insurance benefit association Verhovay had gradually acquired an "elite" character during the 1920s, representing the wealthier, better-established and educated members of the immigrant community.[26] For a few years during the 1930s, before it dissolved under the pressure of internal discords, the Slavonic League of Cambria County, founded by a group of well-to-do businessmen and professionals (the latter from the second generation), conducted its monthly meetings at luncheons in downtown hotels.[27] The proliferation, among all of the eight ethnic groups that made up the Slavic and Magyar community, of educational and national-patriotic societies founded to promote the knowledge of the old-country history, culture, and literature of the particular groups, also reflected the process of the differentiation of status and interests among the immigrants.

Interestingly, during the 1920s and 1930s it was often the women who were the founders of these new "interest groups." Before World War I, there were no more than 4 immigrant societies for the women (not counting rosary, sacrament, and other strictly religious groups). After 1920, 18 more were formed, often in spite of vocal opposition from the men. The women's societies in Johnstown were of four kinds (although some combined several functions at once): traditional – and most numerous – church societies, of either a religious or a social "service" character; independent insurance lodges of ethnic associations; cultural-educational groups; and national-patriotic organizations.[28] As the immigrant families became better established, children grew older, and boarders were no longer kept, women were released to some extent from their fifteen-hour workday. As a result, the number of women's clubs and societies increased.

Women from different East Central European groups seem to have followed slightly different paths of organizational and communal

Plate 13. (Top) St. Therese Slovenian Catholic Church, built in the interwar period in Morrellville, secondary immigrant settlement. (Bottom) First communion at St. Casimir Polish Catholic Church, 1920s. Collection of Anthony Cyburt.

Plate 14. Immigrant funeral in East Conemaugh, 1930s. Collection of Walter Wegrzyn.

Plate 15. Sokol's running contest, Cambria City, 1920s. Collection of Ann Novak.

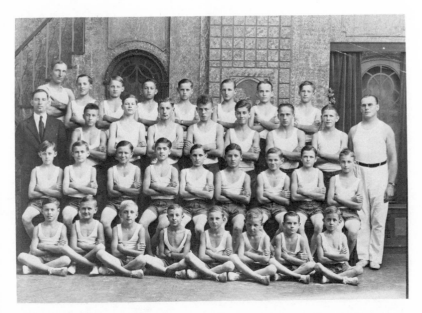

Plate 16. Junior Sokol, Cambria City, 1920s. Collection of Ann Novak.

Plate 17. Yugoslavia Singing Society, Johnstown, 1930s. Collection of John Langerholc.

Plate 18. St. Francis' Slovak Theatrical Group, 1930s. Collection of Ann Novak.

Plate 19. Hungarian Weekend Orchestra, Johnstown, 1919. Collection of Ann Karaffa.

activities. The Rusyn, Ukrainian, Hungarian, and Croatian women apparently focused their activities predominantly on the church and church-related events, with "Ladies' Aid" societies that cooked community suppers and sponsored holiday sales, bazaars, and weekend picnics. The Polish women were definitely the most active in national-patriotic groups. The role and position of women in the Polish patriotic tradition and national movement had already been strong in Europe, and in America, too, the women's organizations of this type were early established nationwide and could be imitated locally.[29] A group of Slovene immigrant women, on the other hand, during the 1920s and 1930s actively participated in the local branch of the Yugoslav Socialist party in Johnstown and formed their own branch of the traditionally progressive Slovenska Narodna Podporna Jednota (SNPJ). Characteristically, the most active there were the wives of the officers of the SNPJ men's lodges, men who, in spite of all their progressivism, were at first openly reluctant to see the "old hens" involved in public activities.[30] The Slovak women, particularly those from the better-off Morrellville section, preferred community cultural affairs: educational societies, dramatic clubs, dance group, and choirs. The Serbian women were instrumental in the secession from St. Nicholas parish in 1935, actively opposing the priest in the militant Kolo Srbskih Sestara. After the establishment of the new parish, however, they again confined their activities mostly to social-religious "service" functions.[31]

The network of youth organizations reflected the same two general tendencies characteristic of the immigrant communities in the interwar period. During the 1920s and 1930s a total of 33 East Central European youth organizations and clubs were formed (not counting the parochial school religious societies): 7 associations of sociocultural and national-patriotic character; 9 of an artistic and recreational nature; and 17 sports teams.[32] The umbrella organizations such as the Polish, Slovak, and Hungarian clubs or sports leagues demonstrated, as did their adult counterparts, the increasing solidification of ethnic group boundaries. On the other hand, "special interest" groups – theater, dance, choir, scouts, and patriotic-educational societies – were founded at local parishes and by ethnic associations and expressed the simultaneous diversification of interests and lifestyles of the second generation.

Much of the content of all these activities was "national": Plays, songs, dances, educational programs, anniversary meetings and celebrations had as their major themes the history and culture of the old country. Their format, however, was already "American," with elections, ballots, reports of proceedings, and contests, unknown to the peasant tradition of East Central Europe. Together they gave a uniquely "ethnic" character to immigrant communal life.

Like their incorporation into local society, the integration of immigrant workers into the class structure was also taking place through "ascriptive inclusion" – that is, through mediating ethnic collectivities and through an intensification of segmental attachments. Ethnic ties and identities served as the organizing principle in the mobilization of "proletarian awareness" among the East Central Europeans and in their pursuit of class interests. This is illustrated in the two instances of collective political action taken in the interwar period by Bethlehem mill workers against the company as they sought to obtain recognition for the union.

The steel strike of 1919 provided an occasion for the expression of a collective awareness transcending ethnic group boundaries. For the first time since they had settled in Johnstown and became part of Cambria's labor force, the immigrants acted as members of the American working class against the company owners. Yet ethnic feelings and perceptions of ethnic divisions deeply and indissolubly permeated their class identity and class resentment. The immigrant strikers held their own meetings in the foreign colonies, and they picketed together at the mill gates in national groupings. Their experience as "proletarians" involved in the class struggle was shared with other East Central European workers in daily meetings at homes, in neighborhood bars, and in the club halls where debates over the course of political action were conducted in the immigrants' native tongues. Significantly, the two small and short-lived branches of the Socialist party – the Slovenian and Polish branches – that existed in Johnstown for a few years after World War I had restricted ethnic group membership and conducted their meetings in the mother tongue of the members.[33]

The course of another steel strike at Bethlehem eighteen years later once again confirmed the strength of ethnic identities in the class consciousness of Johnstown's mill workers. In fact it was to these that the CIO organizers and the national labor press ascribed the ineffectiveness of the strike action in the city. From the beginning of the strike, in mid-June of 1937, until its conclusion six weeks later, the deep chasm dividing the "foreign" and "American" labor force at the Bethlehem mills prevented concerted action by the workers. A survey of the ethnic origins of a sample taken from among the loyal, antiunion workers, supporters of the company's Employee

Representation Plan, reveals that 75 percent of them were either native-born Americans or men of western European background. A similar inspection of a membership sample of the "back-to-work" movement formed in the mills under the aegis of the Citizens' Committee yields identical results. On the other hand, 70 percent of the strikers were East Central European, Italian, and Mexican workers, mostly young men of the second generation employed predominantly as unskilled laborers in the "foreign" Bethlehem plants.[34] (The class consciousness of the immigrant and second generation East Central European workers will be discussed in more detail and in a somewhat different context in Chapters 7 and 8.)

The crystallized ethnic loyalties and the segmented group networks that emerged in the immigrant communities during the interwar period were, at one and the same time, reactions to the constraining social conditions under which the immigrants lived and creations of the immigrants themselves as they sought to domesticate their assigned territory and establish a milieu within which they could effectively conduct their everyday affairs and strive to realize their desired goals. In Chapter 6 we will see how they continued their adaptation in Johnstown after World War I within the framework provided by the larger local society, and, within it, by their own ethnic communities.

6   *For bread with butter*

Chapter 4 presented the ways in which the peasant-immigrants adjusted to American industrial society during the initial years of their stay in this country. We will now examine the perceptions of opportunity, and the aspirations, of those who stayed in America for good and lived in Johnstown between the two world wars. We will also look at their accomplishments in homeownership, area of residence, and employment, as well as at the differences in their household strategies and life-styles as these were influenced by individual and family situations and preferences. Most of the chapter deals with the decades following the end of World War I, and the concluding section concerns the years of the Depression.

During the interwar period, the immigrants' evaluative framework came to comprise a prism of sorts, with simultaneous counterreflections of four distinct perspectives involving both time and space: that of the old-country village; of the initial years of their stay in this country; of the immigrant community in which they lived; and of that part of the outside American world accessible to them from their position in the social structure.

Their worldviews and attitudes formed a conglomerate of orientations made up of heterogeneous elements. This mixed bag of attitudes and behavioral patterns contained at bottom, as it were, ready-to-use insecurity and fatalism. Over and above these, a more positive orientation was expressed in the immigrant families' deliberate, active search to achieve the goals that were defined within the range of opportunities expandable from within, but limited without, and centered on material possessions and reputation as symbols of a good life and high social status. It contained, too, a small dose of cautious and guarded optimism generated by latent but cognitively and emotionally significant comparative reference to the old-country experience, strongly embedded in practicality and realism.

As in the earlier period, in their economic maneuvers the immigrants relied on family collectivism and on the continuing partial fusion of kinship/ethnic and work/occupational spheres. These strategies facilitated the achievement of goals that the immigrants desired. At the same time, however, they generated conflicts and ten-

182

sions in their everyday lives resulting from the precariousness and uncertainty of existence in that segment of Johnstown's socioeconomic structure that they collectively occupied.

Their continuously insecure existence was not conducive to the disappearance of the old peasant attitude of uncertainty about tomorrow and the basic concern with survival. This *negative wish*, fraught with anxiety, had continued as an important component of the orientation of the immigrants after the war. Faced with recurrent periods of industrial slumps and unemployment that wiped out their savings and reduced their standard of living, they "retreated" into traditional fatalism. This deeply entrenched attitude never disappeared from their worldview and was ready to use whenever needed as a psychological defense and coping mechanism that made them not only accept losses and failures as a natural part of existence but also encouraged them to hang on in times of adversity and stubbornly try again when things improved. At the other end, there was a *positive want*, like that of the workers encountered by Whiting Williams during his travels around American factories: to be "getting on, doing a little better than merely holding on . . . The main thing [was] the sense of motion . . . the satisfaction in the distance travelled rather than in the point arrived at."[1]

While the immigrants' opportunities for vertical mobility through personal educational and occupational advancement had remained severely limited, the gradual expansion of consumption standards in the ethnic communities served as a mode by which they were integrated into the American sociocultural system.[2] Despite the slowdown in the development of Johnstown's economy following World War I, the general progress in consumer technology and in the overall standard of living, and the gradual trickling down into the ethnic communities of American mass-produced goods and consumption patterns, increased among the immigrant families the number of wants satisfiable by market mechanisms and further immersed their households in an environment of increasing technological complexity. This, in turn, raised the ceiling of consumption and expanded the material goals that they perceived as desirable and accessible. If the strategy of the immigrant households during their first years in America can be described, in Sol Tax's phrase, as "penny capitalism," during this second phase it was "quarter" or even "dollar capitalism" – an expansion of the basically similar pattern.

In this context, steady work (the fundamental desire of the immigrants), seen as the equivalent of a combined income of all employable family members, continued to be perceived by the East Central Europeans as the means of accumulating the amount of surplus capital needed to secure the family's survival during times of unemployment and also to elevate their life-style as much as possible above the subsistence level. As before, their active reliance on the interpenetration of kinship/ethnic and work/occupational roles was an adaptive response to the ascriptive labor policies of the Bethlehem Company. Also, however, and at the same time, the immigrant households purposefully used their particularist orientations and tactics to achieve the desired goals. As the immigrants' capacity to exploit the material opportunities available in their environment somewhat expanded, the range of sought-after values achievable within the class and ethnic boundaries of their communities also broadened: first a larger apartment, then a house, then a house in a better neighborhood further away from the mills, then a larger house with an annex, running water, a bathroom, a piano, a radio, washing and sewing machines, window curtains, and "American" furniture.

In the second phase of their adaptation in America, the peasant-immigrants' attitude toward work had become further fragmented. The dreary hardship and insecurity of their lives sustained a residue of the old peasant ethos of labor conceived as the mandatory toil of humanity and as an end in itself. Simultaneously, however, the expanding material opportunities and the immigrants' striving to maximize their gains further fostered instrumentalization of their perception of work. Calculating rewards for each hour of labor, many of them chose harder, more difficult jobs that offered additional pay, and asked their bosses for extra hours of work.[3] At the same time, though, they also learned to slow down on the job, adopting the proletarian mores of exhausted industrial laborers acting in self-defense.[4] With the passage of time, the peasant-immigrant laborers developed an "ethnic" work ethic that entailed at the same time a manner of thinking – toward maximizing gain in exchange for a more difficult and longer-lasting type of work – and a particular pace of activity: Once on the job they desired, the immigrants worked furiously when the boss was around and slowed down when he was not watching.[5]

The immigrants judged the opportunities existing within their reach, as well as their failures and accomplishments, from a complex of related perspectives constructed out of collective and individual memory and experience. One such perspective, by this time dim and remote but still ever-present in immigrant thinking, was the old-country reference: In comparison with their memories of life in European villages at the end of the last century, their American existence, however constrained and insecure, still appeared better to the immigrants. "There we had nothing to hope for; here there was at least a little something for us, and for our children," was a common motto repeated by East Central Europeans in Johnstown as well as by others, in letters, memoirs, and diaries.

The second superimposed perspective that the immigrants used in evaluating their present situation was the reference to the initial years of their stay in America. Here again the comparison was, for most of them, favorable to the present. Their lives during the 1920s, although difficult and uncertain, were nevertheless somewhat easier, more affluent in terms of possession of material objects, and more comfortable than those of the newcomers at the beginning of the century.

The third overlapping perspective through which the immigrants viewed and evaluated their current position and that with the passage of time had become the most relevant, was that of their own local ethnic community in Johnstown. The world of goods available within the limits of "foreign colonies" – a somewhat better life that was already enjoyed by others in the immigrant community – formed in the minds of the immigrants the basic reference framework within which they construed and measured their own goals and desires, and coped with and resolved the built-in tensions. The field of maneuvers accessible to immigrants was fixed from without and confined to the space delineated by their structural position in the city. But from within, this space was seen as expandable and as containing options that the immigrants used actively in various combinations in a deliberate effort to attain an approximation of the "good life." These options included the search, through kinship and ethnic networks, for a better job: if possible, better-skilled, as there appeared in the mills more of the mechanized tasks; if not, then more remunerative, either within the same or another Bethlehem department or with a different local manufacturer. They included, too, overtime work and moonlighting at night and during weekends. They also involved increasing the total family income by entering into the labor market all employable members of the household, keeping boarders, renting out part of a newly purchased house, reducing household expenditures through extensive reliance on home production of food from gardens and domestic animals, on women's abilities to prepare and preserve food and to sew and weave, and on men's old-country skills in carpentry, masonry, and other households repairs. As we shall see, maneuvering within these options to reconcile different values that the immigrants held caused them no small amount of pain and frustration.

The fourth parallel perspective through which the immigrants perceived their situation was that of the outside local American world. Despite the immigrants self-absorption within their ethnic communities, in comparison with the earlier period of their stay in the city, when most of them saw themselves as sojourners, the outside American world was more intensely present by the 1920s in the consciousness of East Central Europeans who had made America their permanent home.

Since they were now of Johnstown more than of the old-country village, and since their ties with the latter became increasingly indirect and symbolic, the immigrants perceived the local American world as closer to them and more immediate. Unavoidably they saw it as privileged: It had more money and more material objects; better jobs; nicer neighborhoods; bigger homes; and access to political power. It was also remote and turned inward on itself. Yet however distant, after a few decades of living in America, this outside world had nevertheless become "domesticated," as it were, by the immigrants. Some of what it possessed, especially material objects, as well as its extrinsic cultural patterns, such as forms of recreation and ways of conducting communal affairs, were partially replicated in the ethnic communities and incorporated into ethnic culture. At the same time, this intensified presence of the American world in the perceptions of immigrants was introducing a new element into their mental relationship with their ethnic communities. To apply Geertz's metaphor, the immigrants, though strongly "held by" these communities, were now also, if mostly symbolically, "holding" them themselves.[6] They could now not only quite concretely imagine themselves living an "American life" but could also, if they had really wanted to (which most of them didn't), have actually tried to move into this realm by breaking all ties with their ethnic community by changing their names and learning good English in order to pass, for instance, as "John Smith" somewhere in Colorado.

This new "American" component in the immigrants' perceptive framework had also generated some ambivalence and tension. On the one hand, it was the world from which new goods and consumer patterns of urban industrial society trickled into the ethnic communities and that, by its technological development, also expanded the range of material goods accessible to immigrant families. On the other, however, controlling both goods and power, the "superior"

American world set fixed limits on their opportunities to enjoy a still better, easier, more comfortable life. It raised expectations, at the same time frustrating them through structurally built-in class and ethnic obstacles.

Before we move on to examine the economic maneuvers that East Central European families in Johnstown used during the 1920s in order to realize their goals, we should see how and by what concrete standards the immigrants defined the "good life." A statement by Thomas B., a seventy-six-year-old immigrant from Croatia, renders the sense of responses given by most of the older-generation informants to my inquiries about their image of a "good life" in Johnstown during the 1920s: "a healthy family, steady job, and respect among people."[7] For the parents of a second generation Rusyn, this ideal was "steady employment so that the family could have [both] bread and butter."[8]

I argued earlier that the immigrants desired "steady work" as a means rather than an end in itself. They perceived it as an instrument to enable their families to survive and at the same time to accumulate some surplus capital to be turned into a life better than in the old country – the "bread with butter." After World War I, when most of the immigrants finally decided to make, or resigned themselves to making, America their home, the "bread with butter" to be achieved through a steady income lost its immediate old-country reference. Now the "good life" was conceived of, sought after, and consumed in the context of opportunities that existed in Johnstown, within the framework of options accessible to "foreigners." "After the [first] war," eighty-four-year-old Anthony C. divided the adaptation of East Central Europeans in Johnstown before World War II into three phases: the beginning of the century, the 1920s, and the Depression: "If one did not drink, did not gamble, and if all family contributed and lived thriftily, one could get things here and make good, better than in the beginning."[9]

Immigrant memoirs from the 1920s permit an estimate of the meaning for East Central Europeans of a *decent life* in America in dollar values. Although this information comes from immigrant laborers in other American cities, it can also be applied to Johnstown's families. During the 1920s an income of $40 to $45 a week was considered "good money" by East Central Europeans. "On my weekly wage of $45," writes a Polish worker from Lowell, Massachusetts, "with my wife [without outside employment] we could live *dostatnio* – abundantly."[10] Another immigrant memoirist from Brooklyn, New

York, was paid $24 a week as a subway laborer, while his wife worked for $16 a week in a candy factory, "and so we prospered well."[11] On the other hand, to survive on $15 to $22 a week was *"ledwo życie"* – "hardly a life."[12] In Johnstown, as indicated by my informants' accounts of their spendings in the interwar period, *dostatni* life could have been realized even more cheaply. Considering the average cost of living in Johnstown during the 1920s and the reliance of the immigrant households on subsistence plot farming and gardening, we arrive at an annual income of about $1,600 to $1,700 that the local East Central European family would have considered as the threshold from which a "good life" could begin. At the other extreme, a yearly income of $700 to $800 was, for the immigrants, barely enough to exist on.[13]

The immigrants' image of a "good life" involved several components: first and foremost, savings, a necessary safety net against the economic uncertainty of working-class existence. A few hundred dollars to house and feed the immigrant family for a couple of months if there was no work at all seemed to have been perceived as the required limit for the minimal feeling of safety. Our Polish immigrant from Lowell, to whom a $45 weekly income appeared sufficient to live comfortably, in the same context mentions with satisfaction his "[considerable] savings of $800."[14] As we shall see shortly, such a sum was just about enough to permit an East European household in Johnstown to barely survive through the year.

With savings set aside, a "good life" in the eyes of most immigrants also involved the possession of a house. At the close of the 1920s, the purchase of a home in one of the immigrant sections of Johnstown required on the average between $3,000 and $4,000 (see Table A.10 in the Appendix). If borrowed in toto, the expected annual expenditure to service the purchase of a $3,500 house was between $500 and $550. This included the mortgage – that is $350 a year in principal payments, spread equally over ten years, which, I calculate, was the average period of time the immigrants needed to repay their home loans; annual interest payments at 5 to 6 percent, amounting to an average of $100 a year for ten years; and approximately $50 to $100 a year for real estate taxes, home insurance (if desired), and do-it-yourself repairs. If spread over a longer period of fifteen years, payments could be reduced by $100 annually.[15]

The style of life was the third component of good existence as seen by the East Central Europeans. It embodied a rather peculiar combination of persisting peasant habits and new, mass consumption patterns of urban industrial society typical of an emergent ethnic working-class subculture, fused with imitations of old-country "gentry" airs and behavior. For the peasant-immigrant workers who remembered well the poor village fare with its monotonous rotation of "borscht and potatoes," the amount and quality of food they consumed in America was an important requirement of the "good life." For Anthony C., an old Polish mill worker, a good, comfortable standard of living for an immigrant family in Johnstown during the 1920s meant a monthly food expenditure of about $50 to $60, not counting what was consumed "from the house," that is, food grown and processed at home.[16]

The possession of American-style clothing and consumer goods was another component of living in style á la immigrant. "There is still debt on the house," wrote a Polish memoirist, "but food we have always [plenty], . . . and we are dressed according to the local [American] people."[17] Besides dress that looked "American" and not "foreign," the ideal of the good life for East Central Europeans also meant the enjoyment of at least some of the furnishings and household appliances produced by the industrial society. Its styles and fashions in consumption goods trickled down to the immigrant homes through women who saw the things in the windows of downtown stores when they went shopping and in the American homes in which they worked as servants and cooks. The range of mass-produced material goods desired by the immigrants was delimited by income brackets that they perceived as sufficient for a family to lead a more or less dostatnie życie. It permitted, for instance, credit payments for household furniture of over $100 a year, and the purchase of linoleum for the floor, a sewing machine, a wash boiler, and lace curtains or draperies for the windows. A higher income – or more rigorous savings on a total family income of $1,600 to $1,700 – could allow for a victrola, an item considered prestigious in the immigrant communities, and perhaps a tub for the bathroom. Still more income above the level required for "comfortable savings" of a few hundred dollars, house payments, and abundant food, would have permitted the purchase of a used automobile costing around $150 (a new one could be bought for about $500) or, for instance, a fur for the wife: At the end of the 1920s such a fur could be had for about $75.[18]

Finally, a good life as seen by the immigrants also involved some degree of participation in the ethnic community's networks and institutions, as well as contributions to its welfare. It was in this area of communal participation that peasant-immigrant workers eagerly imitated the style of the old-country gentry. For their dances and picnics and for ethnic celebrations, the immigrants "looked to the revels and balls the [old-country] gentry held in the provincial casinos as a model for their own social evenings . . . It was not the traditions, customs and folk costumes of their peasant heritage [or their new worker's status], but the egret-feathered hat and . . . gold-braided gala dress traditional to the landed gentry."[19] Anxious that "Božeuchovaj, l'udia poveda že sme žobrači": "God forbid that people say we are beggars!" – poor immigrant families often avoided such gatherings or even Sunday Mass in the neighborhood ethnic parish if they could not give for *kolekta* (the collection). On the other hand, as late as the 1920s and 1930s a generous style of giving in the parish and at social events in the immigrant communities, public gifts of money, and donations sent to the European village for church bells or holy paintings evoked comparisons with the *pan baron*, reassuring those who displayed such behavior of a sense of self-worth and satisfaction.[20]

We will now look at the tactics used by immigrant families in Johnstown during the 1920s to achieve the closest possible approximation of what they perceived to be a "good life." We shall begin by examining the different income sources available to the immigrant working-class households and the means that they used to supplement or augment them, and then compare their income with their expenditures, savings, and investments.

During the 1920s, no less than 90 percent of the East Central European men in Johnstown were employed as manual workers. Most of them worked as ordinary laborers – unskilled or general operatives. From among the Slavic and Magyar immigrants recorded in the 1900 census who were still present in town in 1920, 84 percent were classified as ordinary laborers; in 1925 the figure was 75 percent.[21]

As in the earlier period, the male breadwinner was the major provider for the immigrant family. After the period of rapid fluctuations in industrial production following World War I, by 1924–5 the average wages of laborers employed in the steel and iron industry became more or less stabilized for the rest of the decade. In Pennsylvania, the average entrance wages paid in the second half of the 1920s to a common laborer employed in the mills ranged, depending on the department, from as low as $.30 an hour to as high as $.50 an hour.[22] The customary full-time hours of work also varied significantly: For instance, in Johnstown some plants worked on a 8:4 (44) schedule, some others 8:8 (48), 10:7 (57) and 10:9 (59).[23] The average full-time monthly earnings of unskilled mill la-

Table 6.1. *Full-time and actual monthly and annual earnings of mill workers and miners, 1925–1929*

	Average Monthly Earnings		Average Annual Earnings	
Occupation	Full-time	Actual	Full-time	Actual
Mill Laborer	$ 68–118	$ 57–98	$ 816–1,416	$ 684–1,176
"Pick" miner	101–123	83–101	1,212–1,476	996–1,212
Better-skilled mill worker (service shops, manufacturing shops)[a]	135–142[b]	112–118	1,620–1,704	1,346–1,415
Machine cutter (coal miner)	$163–191	$134–157	$1,956–2,292	$1,608–1,884

[a] I excluded most of the highly skilled occupations in steel production, those of heaters, rollers, blowers, and melters who earned over $50 a week, because these jobs, with few exceptions, were practically inaccessible to East Central Europeans.
[b] Minimum was paid for jobs in service shops, maximum for jobs in manufacturing shops.
Source: Compiled from U.S. Bureau of Labor Statistics, "Wages and Hours of Labor," *Monthly Labor Review*, (September 1929), 132–5; ibid., (October 1929), 168–70; Commonwealth of Pennsylvania Department of Labor and Industry, *Union Scale of Wages and Hours of Labor*, Special Bulletin No. 20 (1926), 21–83; ibid., No. 22 (1927), 12–89; Paul F. Brissenden, "Earnings of Factory Workers 1899 to 1927: An Analysis of Payroll Statistics," in U.S. Bureau of the Census, Census Monographs, No. 10 (1929), 96–7.

borers covered, then, a substantial range, from $68 to $71 (the lowest-paid common laborer usually worked a fifty-seven to fifty-nine hour week) to as much as $110 to $118. The average full-time wages paid in Pennsylvania to coal miners (loaders) and hand-and-pick miners ranged, depending on the job performed, from a minimum of $101 a month to $123 (combined averages for 1926 and 1929, based on twelve starts in a half-month period).

Owing to the fluctuations in industrial production, the actual earnings received by the mill workers and miners was of course substantially lower. By the mid-1920s the actual average wages of laborers employed in the iron and steel industry were approximately 17 percent less than full-time earnings. In the Pennsylvania coal mines the average loss was about 18 percent (data for 1929).[24] Table 6.1 compares the full-time and actual earnings of the less- and better-skilled mill laborers and coal miners in the late 1920s. It shows that the actual earnings ranged, for the mill laborers, from as low as $57 a month to $98 a month; for the hand-miners, the range was from $83 to $101.

The discrepancy between the full-time and actual wages could, however, be somewhat reduced by extra earnings. The actual loss of income caused by sickness or injury was partially covered by workers' insurance organizations. During the 1920s East Central European benefit societies in Johnstown paid their members a little over $.70 a day for each workday lost.[25] A more substantial source of extra income for a worker to balance the loss resulting from fluctuations in industrial production was work on Sundays and holidays. In Johnstown, the rates paid to the mill workers for overtime work ranged in the mid-1920s from 1 to 1.5 times the regular rate, depending on the department.[26] In the coal mines, the workers paid by the car or tonnage were more independent and could arrange their weekday schedules, extending the overtime hours by four to five hours a day. For instance, an inspection of payroll records of the small Harve-Mack Coal Company in neighboring Indiana County reveals that during the randomly selected period from January to March of 1925, a number of loaders and hand-pick miners made up to $40 over our estimated maximum monthly wage average in their category, which meant a few hundred dollars more a year.[27]

Another source of possible supplementary earnings used by a number of Johnstown's immigrant laborers in order to make up for the loss of wages from current occupations was substitute employment in times of slackened work at Bethlehem. Commonly on such occasions the temporarily laid-off men took up assorted jobs on nearby farms or in the local construction industry. The latter paid the unskilled laborers in the area rates higher than the average received in the mills: $0.70 an hour for a 8:4 (44) shift, which amounted to average weekly earnings of $30.80 for full-time work.[28] This substitute employment on the farms and in local construction was easier to get for the workers employed in those Bethlehem departments where the seasonal slackening of production occurred in the summer months: in the basic steel and rolling mills, iron and steel forging departments, and in the foundries,[29] all of which employed large numbers of immigrant workers.

All these facts concerning full-time and actual earnings in different Bethlehem departments and in the coal mines, hours of labor, seasonal shifts in production, overtime prospects and working conditions, as well as personalities of the bosses and their treatment of people were obviously known to the workers. The latter factor was of high importance at a time when no regulations defended the workers and when ascriptive considerations routinely took precedence over those of individual skill and performance.[30]

Since the Bethlehem Company employment records were destroyed by the floods, I could not calculate the proportion of voluntary resignations among the total work separations by the East Central European mill workers. Instead, we can use as an approximation the most common voluntary resignation rate as reported nationwide for selected American factories. In the period 1924–9 it averaged 30 percent, accounting for nearly 70 percent of total separations (including layoffs and discharges).[31] My analysis of labor mobility based on a sample of 150 East Central European miners during the 1920s as recorded in the employment records of two small independent coal mines near Johnstown: Berwind White in Windber, and Johnstown Coal and Coke in Beaverdale – reveals a similar rate: 60 to 70 percent voluntary resignations in the total number of separations.[32] Voluntary resignations by Bethlehem Company mill workers covered a large number of inside transfers from shop to shop or between plants, which the company employment office recorded separately as "resignations" and "accessions."[33] The workers who quit their current jobs of their own accord did so either because they disliked their jobs, because they wished to avoid transfer to work that they considered worse in terms of earnings, hours, or distance from home, or because they had a chance of obtaining a more rewarding position, either financially, or in terms of working conditions, or both.[34]

In seeking a good or a better job, immigrant workers at Bethlehem Steel relied as before on the replication of private-communal kinship and ethnic networks inside the mills. A relative, a fellow immigrant from the ethnic community, a German mill worker acquaintance from the plant or from the church provided the necessary "social resources" – ties and connections – or what the Poles in Communist Poland today aptly refer to as "shoulders." "You had to know somebody to get anywhere [at Bethlehem]": This conviction of a Rusyn mill worker was repeated by virtually all of my Johnstown informants. "For [good] jobs . . . you got them through individual contacts."[35] The natural "shoulders" were other East Central Europeans: "John K., a Rusyn, he worked in the employment bureau at Bethlehem. Although most good positions were taken [by native-born Americans and those of Western European background], it helped us 'Hunkies' when he heard about good openings."[36] "Some of our people [Lutheran Slovak] got into better positions in the mills because they were acquainted with the German workers, and this through the church activities."[37] Also helpful in immigrant "occupational careers" was the collective befriending of a group by the boss in a particular department, turning to one's advantage the company's ascriptive labor policy: "Different parts of the mill took different nationality groups; the boss would take you if you were this or that nationality."[38]

For most of the immigrant families, the earnings of the head of the household constituted the major source of income. Unfortunately, for the interwar period there is no statistical data comparable to those collected at the beginning of the century in Johnstown by the Immigration Commission on the sources of earnings in the immigrant families. As in the earlier period, the economic strategy in most of the immigrant households in Johnstown was what one second generation Pole expressed to me as a maxim of his own parents: "Never depend on one income." His own family conformed to this rule in the fullest, with the father employed at two jobs, as a coal miner and fixer of old houses, the mother weaving and raising chickens, and himself and his three adolescent brothers helping the father with house repairs.[39]

Certainly not all East Central European households in Johnstown employed all of their members in multiple jobs, but most of them relied on some combination of financial resources. By 1920, the offspring of the immigrants recorded in the 1900 census as small children and infants were already adult and working. Among the 217 Slavic and Magyar working-class households that had persisted in Johnstown until 1925 for whom information could be collected, in that year 28.1 percent of the families had only one person gainfully employed; 45.6 percent had two; 18.0 percent had three; 6.5 percent had four; and 1.8 percent had five or more people gainfully employed outside the home. The average number in my sample of adult persons of both sexes employed per each household in 1925 was two, not counting the contributions from wives keeping boarders and selling the products of their gardens, sewing, weaving, and so on.[40]

The kinship/ethnic "shoulders" and personal ties and connections were utilized by the immigrants to bring their sons into the mills so that they could work side by side with their fathers and relatives. "I became a machinist, and so, like me, my sons became ones, too"; "[In the 1920s], I got into the rigger department because my father and brother worked there . . . If you did not know anybody [at

Bethlehem], you were lost"; "I got myself hired in the mechanical department [where] my future father-in-law was a gang leader."[41] The earnings of the young men employed in the Bethlehem Company mills and coal mines hovered around the lower bracket of the average (actual) wage for the immigrants, estimated earlier at $57 a month.

The young women worked as servants, maids, cooks, and laundrywomen in American homes; as laborers in the local cigar factory; as salespersons in immigrant stores; or, if they had a little more education, as cashiers and clerks. Like their male peers', the jobs of the Slavic and Magyar women were arranged through personal connections. In the later 1920s, the average full-time earnings of young East Central European women in Johnstown ranged from $20 to over $40 a month, with work in domestic service much more unstable, though more readily available.[42]

The younger children also contributed to the household economy. In 1926, the Pennsylvania Department of Labor reported 9.2 percent (233) of the total number of fourteen- to fifteen-year-old population in Johnstown employed in the city industries, a proportion much lower than in the eastern section of the state, with its numerous textile and clothing factories more "suitable" for children's work.[43] The number of gainfully employed adolescents in Johnstown was in reality much higher, since despite the attempts of the schools to prevent the practice, the immigrant families routinely "corrected" the age of their fifteen-year-olds to fit the required sixteen-year-old school-leaving limit. The fourteen- to fifteen-year-old boys working in the mills under the supervision of their elders or as messengers, mailboys, or couriers at Bethlehem Steel Company offices usually made between $20 and $30 a month.[44] Having lost one job, a child quickly found another. According to a 1926 report of the Pennsylvania Bureau of Women and Children, for over 60 percent of the children employed in manufacturing, the period of unemployment lasted no longer than three to four weeks. Still younger children employed themselves selling baskets of vegetables from their family's gardens to the neighbors at $0.10 to $0.15 apiece, picking strawberries, and performing other tasks on the farms in Westmont at $0.60 to $1.00 a day, working as shoeshiners downtown, at $1.00 to $1.50 for a twelve-hour day. If lucky and persistent, during the season a twelve- or thirteen-year-old could contribute up to $20 a month to the family budget.[45]

There were in Johnstown no significant opportunities for the gainful employment of married women. As in the earlier period, during the 1920s the women, the wives of the steelworkers and miners, mostly stayed at home. The lack of outside employment reinforced traditional family roles in the East Central European households. One of them was for the women to contribute to the household economy by keeping boarders, sewing, weaving, tending to gardens and poultry, or even running small farms on the hills surrounding the city. A housekeeper received between $25 and $30 a month from a boarder during the 1920s, counting room, meals, and laundry. This amounted to an additional net income of about $180 to $240 a year, after subtracting the average cost of the boarder's food, gas, and electricity.[46] The immigrant families who already lived in their own houses often rented out part of them. Thus, for a three-room apartment in a house in a foreign colony, a homeowner received approximately $10 to $12 a month, depending on the facilities. In one year, it meant an additional income of $120 to $144. The whole half of a two-family house in Morrellville rented for $20 to $30 a month, bringing an annual income of $240 to $360 from a full-year occupancy.[47]

Many immigrant women sewed clothing for themselves and for their own children: underwear, blouses, trousers, skirts, and dresses. Those who were skilled at this art also sewed for the neighbors, selling the garments which could be made in a day, for $0.50 to $2.00 apiece. Some women supported their whole families by professional sewing of more expensive dresses for the "Americans." If there were regular orders, they made "pretty good money": about $100 or even more, a month.[48]

As has been mentioned, women made a systematic contribution to the family budget through the reduction of food expenditures. After World War I, the household economy of the East Central Europeans not only retained but even solidified its residual "worker-farmer" characteristics. While the men worked at Bethlehem, the women grew vegetables in backyard gardens or in plots on the hills and kept rabbits and chickens. In fact, the families that had moved out of the primary foreign colonies to the higher sections of town expanded their gardens or added cultivated plots on the hills.[49] The keeping of cows and pigs was also permitted beyond the limits of town. Many immigrant households took advantage of this in continuing their "worker-farmer" economy: "Right across the street, one block away [from us] the animals were permitted, [so people kept them] in shanties": As a boy during the 1920s, John B. helped Slavic women with cows and pigs for a little money; "at occasions, people would get together to butcher [a pig]; it was some kind of a minifestival."[50] Some immigrant families purchased larger pieces of land on the surrounding hills – 2 or even 4 acres that they cultivated and used for the cattle, their own as well as those of others, who paid them for the service. From such families, of which there were in the city a sufficient number for most of my informants to name several offhand, many Johnstowners – East Central Europeans as well as Americans – purchased milk and potatoes.[51]

The persistence through the interwar period in Johnstown of small plot farming among East Central European households facilitated the preservation in their economic behavior of the traditional peasant reliance on payments and services in kind. Although money was recognized by the immigrants as the dominant means of exchange and used as the instrument for economic calculation, in times of unemployment, when it was temporarily lacking, they reverted to a "support exchange system," trading in home-raised chickens, eggs, fresh vegetables, and home-baked products.

Moonshining, often involving an effort of the entire household, was another popular if illegal way of supplementing the family income during the 1920s. "I was bootlegging, like most people around here," recalls an old Rusyn woman from East Conemaugh: "If only you kept chickens, you were already a suspect, as you needed grain. But there was almost no risk involved: If they caught you, they only confiscated the chickens and grain."[52] The alcohol thus produced was sold mostly to neighbors for $.10 to $.15 a glass. A hard-working bootlegger in the foreign colony who "sold moonshine by gallons" could make a few hundred dollars a week.[53]

There were other ways in which the immigrants expanded their family income: for instance, playing music at ethnic dances, picnics, weddings, and christenings that took place every weekend in the foreign communities in Johnstown and the vicinity. During the 1920s, the musicians at such occasions were paid $3 apiece for a day's playing, plus extras for special numbers: approximately $2 each. If they played regularly, and if their audiences were not too parsimonious with tips (some threw buttons and nails into the base drum instead of nickels and dimes), musicians could make about $300 a year more.[54]

To keep their heads above the level of *ledwo zycie* and, in particular, to try to raise the standard of living to a level of relative material comfort, it was necessary for most of the East Central Europeans in Johnstown to use a combination of available resources in a concerted fund-raising strategy. A few typical versions of the immigrant family budgets in Johnstown during the 1920s will illustrate this situation.

They are grouped in five categories, from the minimum survival level to the level of relative comfort as defined by the immigrants themselves.

Trimmed radically to the barest subsistence, with minimal food and shelter, minimal provision for clothing, and nothing for household furnishings, health insurance, personal care, recreation, and participation in communal life besides the obligatory annual church dues, the annual expenditures in the mid-1920s of an immigrant household in Johnstown, consisting of seven people (two parents and five children, including two to three adult ones) amounted to about $700.00 to $750.00. They included the following: $450.00 for food (37.50 a month, or $9.37 a week); $120.00 to $180.00 rent (at about $10.00 to $15.00 a month) for a two- to three-room apartment in the foreign colony tenement rows (without hot water); $40.00 for the barest minimum of heat and light (Johnstown used cheap natural gas; in the peasant tradition, many a struggling immigrant household heated only the kitchen in colder months and concentrated all family activities there); $20.00 for household operation; $30.00 for clothing (mostly fabric to sew at home and occasional ready-made items purchased on sale); about $30 for alcohol for the man (2 glasses of whiskey at $0.15 twice a week on weekends); and a minimum of $12.00 yearly for church dues.[55]

Although food expenditures constituted the largest item in the survival budgets of immigrant households in Johnstown, they were significantly lower than the food costs of low-income families in bigger cities in which supplementary subsistence farming was not readily available. Calculating the expenditures made on food by the immigrants in Johnstown, I included only the items that they regularly purchased: salt, sugar, tea, coffee, lard, flour, and meat, and also butter, milk, and potatoes (those who had their own animals and who farmed on the hills had these products "for free"). Other articles were made or processed at home.[56] This dependence of the immigrant worker-farmer families in Johnstown on the fruit and vegetables gathered by women from gardens and plots and on the products prepared by them at home reduced spending on food in the subsistence-income households by as much as 40 to 50 percent in comparison with the expenditures of the "standard American urban working class family." According to a report of the U.S. Commission of Labor Statistics, such an average American family, consisting of husband, wife, and five children (of whom two to three were adult) would have had to spend, by the mid-1920s, a minimum of $825.00 to keep themselves adequately nourished.[57] Similar results yield a comparison of the minimum expenditures on nourishment in East Central European households in Johnstown with the University of Chicago Council of Social Agencies' estimate of necessary food expenses in families of unskilled Chicago workers in 1925. The estimate was based on the Chicago budget, which provided the "minimum normal standard" for family existence. The food, it specified, "must meet the recognized dietetic standards in furnishing protein, fuel, minerals and salt in necessary quantities (as provided in specially calculated tables)." According to the report, "The food cost . . . for a man at hard muscular work in a family where bread is bought is estimated at $14.30 per month."[58] In Butler, Pennsylvania – one of twelve places in which the cost of living was investigated in 1926 by the National Industrial Conference Board – the average minimum annual cost of food to maintain "a fair American standard of living" for a working-class family of four was estimated at $544.00.[59] In that same period in Johnstown, approximately seventy miles southeast of Butler, subsistence-level expenditures on food for an East Central European family of four did not exceed $300.00, and the average minimum cost of food for an adult, working, East Central European man per day was $0.24, or about $7.00 a month.

The sum of $700.00 for annual expenditures in the survival budget still exceeded by a few dollars the minimum actual yearly earnings of a common foreign laborer in the mills who received the lowest rate of $0.30 an hour. For a family supported exclusively by the income of a breadwinner in this category—perhaps a mill worker, the wife of a drunkard, or a widow with minor children—life was miserable, a continuous struggle with unending debts and constant embarrassment caused by an inability to participate, systematically and visibly, in the social and religious life of the community.

We will now look at immigrant family budgets typical of four different levels of affluence. Table 6.2 shows possible combinations of resources that East Central European households in Johnstown could have used during the 1920s to accumulate different amounts of annual incomes.

A budget of a family whose income was slightly above the minimum level (marked in the table as *I*) might include some limited provisions for such additional items as household furnishings, health and life insurance, church donations and education for children in the parochial school, and some recreation and participation in ethnic institutional networks. Together with food, rent, fuel, and

Table 6.2. *Estimated annual funds of immigrant families in Johnstown*

Contributor	Group I				Group II				
	1	2	3	4	1	2	3	4	5
Main breadwinner									
Principal job[a]	$700	$700	$700	$700	$700	$1,000	$700	$700	$8
Extra employment	200				200				
Adult son (spending allowance excluded)[b]							600	600	
Adult daughter (spending allowance excluded)		150				150			3
Adolescent son employed part-time (spending allowance excluded)			100	200	100				
Wife (sewing, weaving, other)				100	200		50		
Minor children	50	50	100						2
Boarder			200						2
Total	$950	$900	$1,100	$1,000	$1,200	$1,150	$1,350	$1,300	$1,4

[a] In actual earnings (two-month employment loss subtracted).
[b] Conservatively, I took the lowest unskilled income bracket ($684 in actual ea(r)ings; see Table 6.1) as the average for young laborers, sons of immigrants.

light, for a seven-member family such expenditures would require a minimum annual income of about $900.00 to $1,100 (there were also intermediate versions between this bracket and the $700.00 survival limit). It would have included $450.00 to $550.00 for food; $150.00 to $200 for rent on an apartment; about $50.00 to $100.00 for clothing and household furnishings (in different combinations); $60.00 for light and heat; $20.00 for household operation; $25.00 for health and life insurance (for husband and wife, both in an ethnic association), $30.00 to $50.00 for church and parochial school, including a minimum of $12.00 for church dues, $6.00 in expected donations, and up to $20.00 for extra contributions, as well as $12.00 tuition for the children ($0.50 a month per child for the first two children, each additional child free); $6.00 for participation in ethnic societies (husband and wife, $0.25 monthly dues per member); $25.00 for recreation (picnics, dances, $0.25; theater tickets, $0.15);

by income sources (1920s)

Group III						Group IV				
1	2	3	4	5	6	1	2	3	4	5
$700	$800	$900	$1,000	$800		$700	$850	$900	$1,000	$850
	200			200						200
600	600	600	600		(2) 1,200	(2) 1,200	600	600	600	
250		200		150	200		200	150		100
				150				150		150
	50				50	100				
									50	
			200		200				200	(2) 400
$1,550	$1,650	$1,700	$1,600	$1,500	$1,650	$1,900	$1,750	$1,800	$1,850	$1,700

$50.00 for alcohol (allowing two glasses of whiskey at $0.15 a glass on weekends, two glasses of beer a night on weekdays, at $0.25 for six glasses); $20.00 for personal care; and $25.00 for medical treatment.

Existence on the income of $900.00 to $1,100.00 was also terribly insecure. Since, as the workers were acutely aware, "one never knew what one was going to make (for the year)," the possibility of a family skidding to the bottom survival level without any protection in the form of savings remained concretely present. To the family at this income level, everyday life presented a constant pressure from the unwelcome alternatives with almost no space for maneuvering. To maintain a somewhat more elevated standard of living, with more money spent on food, a slightly larger apartment with running water, and some on clothing and recreation, would not leave any money for savings. Such a prospect motivated most families to keep their standard of living close to the survival level in order to put away $100 to $150 a year. In this income group, the tension between the desire to raise and keep one's family above the level of economic subsistence at a somewhat more comfortable standard and the desire to participate in communal activities and meet expected social obligations was particularly painful. Either one participated in the social life of the group, paid to the ethnic societies, and donated to the community church and the parochial school and institutions, or else one painstakingly accumulated small savings in order to achieve a somewhat more relaxed existence in the future. For instance, like many other East Central European churches in Johnstown, St. John Byzantine Catholic Ukrainian church coped during the 1920s with constant financial difficulties, unable to meet payments on its $16,000.00 outstanding debt for the construction of a new building. "These years," writes the church's monographist, "constituted the most difficult and trying period for our parish. About 40 families of weak faith left the true church to form an independent church of their own. Other families became members of the neighboring foreign churches."[60] Although the ostensible reason for the split was religious discord between the Byzantine Rite and Orthodox factions within the Ukrainian group, many immigrant families left the church in order to escape the demands for increased donations that would have diminished their savings. The Catholic Slovak community in Johnstown boasted the oldest and largest parochial school among "foreigners." This position of leadership, however, exacted a heavy financial toll from the parishioners, since the upkeep of the school demanded a sum of $8,000.00 a year, for which the tuition received for 1,000 pupils and the external subsidies were insufficient. The erection of a new Rusyn Greek Catholic Church building in Cambria City in 1920 required an extra loan from the parishioners of $18,000.00 – that is, an average of about $20.00 a family beyond the usual dues and collections of about $17.00 a year for each family.[61] A number of immigrant households that did not possess the money to participate in the communal life or to pay for the necessary services, in order to preserve their self-esteem and reputation, used the defensive tactic of making traditional payments in kind, offering the products grown in their gardens and made at home.

The tension between the desire to accumulate surplus capital for family needs and "participatory pressures" increased with the expansion of the range of material goods available to the immigrants as they became more integrated into American consumer society. To some extent, the option of retreating into the privatized ethnic circles at the edges of the organized immigrant networks – an option

created by the incipient process of gradual shifting of the immigrants' position vis-á-vis their communities from "being held" toward "holding" – provided the opportunity to overcome some of
this conflict and ambivalence.

At the next highest level of affluence we have the annual budget
of a working-class immigrant household whose annual income
ranged between $1,150 and $1,400 (marked as *II* in Table 6.2). In
this income group, a seven-member family with two to three adult
children could have afforded the following expenditures: about $500
to $600 for food; $240 to $300 for rent ($20 to $25 a month for a four-
to five-room house); $75 to $100 for clothing; $50 for household fur-
nishings; $75 for light and heat; $20 for household operation; $25
for health and life insurance; $50 to $75 for church and school; $25
to $50 for recreation; $35 to $50 for alcohol; $25 for medical treatment;
$20 for personal care; and $25 for ethnic societies, gifts sent to Europe, presents, etc.[62]

In this income group, existence continued to be uncertain, since
the acquired status above the minimum level could easily be lost –
for instance, by a prolonged illness or injury to one of the contrib-
utors, if there was no substitute. But it nevertheless offered more
space for maneuvering, and a choice of one option was not so absolutely exclusive of others. Thus, a family with an annual income
of about $1,150 to $1,400 could deliberately select a strategy of half
measures, and, after setting a goal of $20 in monthly savings, keep
on using the money as it came, some for slightly better food, some
for an extra donation to the church or for a membership in an ethnic
society. A study of the economic situation of Polish immigrant workers in selected American cities during the 1920s and 1930s reported
that before the Depression, over 40 percent of the unskilled laborers
had savings in the bank, and among the skilled workers this proportion was 80 percent.[63] In Johnstown, I was told repeatedly that
during the 1920s, "unless [a man] was lazy, or a drunkard or a
gambler, or if wife was not thrifty, a lot here had some [little]
savings"[64] Most such immigrant families belonged to this group of
small savers, accumulating about $100 to $200 a year, then using
some of it up, and then continuing again to save.

Another option for a household with an annual income of about
$1,400 was to take life as it came and to maintain their style of life
at a somewhat elevated level as long as they could, with more abundant food on the table, more ready-made, fashionable "American"
clothing, paying for a $5 commemorative Mass for a relative instead
of a silent one for $1, treating others occasionally to whiskey or beer

and music at picnics and national celebrations, or sending $10 or even $20 to Europe to show one's good fortune to the poor relatives.[65]

A family could also decide to reduce its standard of living in order to maximize savings. More affluent immigrant budgets could be trimmed significantly by cutting down on the items of lesser importance. Expenditures on food and purchased clothing and furniture could, if the family wished, be cut back to the barest minimum. Voluntary donations for church and money orders to Europe could be reduced, totally eliminated, or in the case of the church, substituted for with occasional payments in kind offered to the parochial school and to the pastor's kitchen. Recreation could be restricted to a few annual outings. At the cost of increasing the tension between incompatible commitments, if annual expenditures could be cut down to a sacrificial $1,000 or less, an immigrant household with a total income of $1,400 could, if not prevented by unexpected expenses, extra layoffs, and slowdowns at work, put aside up to $400 a year.

The minimum income that would allow a family willing to exist at the survival level, with no savings, to service the purchase of a home in one of the immigrant sections was $1,400. In order to do this, however, some previously accumulated capital beyond the "safety net" needed for a down payment must have been available, or money would have to be borrowed from friends or relatives or from a lending institution. A number of immigrants who decided to purchase a home on this minimum income subsequently balanced their budgets by renting out part of it for a yearly return of $120 to $200. Others reduced the expense from the very start by buying only a lot, for $600 to $900, and then erecting the house with the help of friends (the carpentry skills that many immigrants had learned in the old country came in very handy).

Now we turn to the next highest family income of $1,500 to $1,700 a year, marked in Table 6.2 as *III*. If all the contributions continued at a steady rate – that is, if there were no income losses beyond the standard two months loss of wages that we have already subtracted from the men's full-time earnings; if the children who looked for employment quickly found it; if boarders paid on time or the wife found good customers for her products, a thrifty home-owning family with an annual income of $1,600 and home-grown foodstuffs could accumulate savings at a rate of about $150 a year. At this level, it could purchase food for about $600 a year to supplement home-grown products, service the annual payments on the home of $500 (plus $100 for gas, heat, and household operation); purchase (either with cash or on credit) about $150 worth of home appliances and clothing (the adult working children having their own allowances of $50 to $100 a year that they could spend on dress and recreation); pay for life insurance and personal care; and participate in the social and religious life of the community to the tune of $100 to $150. Yet for households in this category, a wedding, a christening, or a funeral, a sickness, or other events entailing expenses would require the family to reduce its standard of living or draw on its savings.

Finally, by making a concerted effort, an immigrant household could have aimed at realizing a collective annual income of over $1,700 (marked *IV* in Table 6.2). On such income, if it remained steady, a thrifty immigrant family could have put aside $1,000 in a couple of years.

We have seen what the East Central Europeans considered to be a "good life," what opportunities existed in Johnstown to allow them to achieve some approximation of that goal, and what the sacrifices and tradeoffs were. We will now look at the actual accomplishments of the immigrant families during the decade following World War I. Unfortunately, systematic data on the central components of the immigrant image of a "good life": the amount of savings, the material objects possessed, and regularity of communal participation, are not available. But I have gathered information about homeownership as well as about residential and occupational patterns among the immigrants, and also about church contributions by families of different economic standing. I have also made an estimate of the total annual wage earnings of the families of immigrant laborers who persisted in Johnstown between the 1900 census and the mid-1920s.

Although the growth of homeownership among immigrant families was restrained by the continuing housing shortage in Johnstown and by the precarious economic position of most of the Slavic and Magyar households, the number of families that owned their own homes nevertheless increased systematically in the interwar period. The proportions of homeowners in the decade preceding the Great Depression among the immigrants – persisters and returnees, and in particular occupational categories – are given in Table 6.3. By 1930, over one-third of the persisters had owned their own homes. (The overall proportion of residents of the City of Johnstown who owned their own homes in 1930 was 40 percent.) On the other hand, the percentage of homeowners in that year among the returnees was only half that for the persisters.

Table 6.3. *Proportion of homeowners among East Central European male immigrants (persisters and returnees) and in different occupational groups, 1920–1930 (in %)*

	1920	1925	1930
Persistence			
Persisters (heads of households)	27.0 (114)[a]	30.0 (112)	35.0 (101)
Returnees	10.0 (13)		16.0 (15)
Occupation (employed persisters only)			
Ordinary laborers	20.5 (88)		24.2 (47)
Skilled workers	28.4 (9)		36.8 (7)
Employed in business and services	35.1 (12)		48.0 (13)
Residents of City of Johnstown	36.4		40.1

Note: Numbers in parentheses represent *N*. The number of homeowners among female-headed families was too small for tabulation. Immigrant homeownership rates for particular nationality groups in the period 1920–40 are presented in Table A.3 in the Appendix. The numbers, however, are much too small to warrant meaningful comparisons.
[a] In July 1920, *Chranitel*, a Rusyn-language newspaper published in Johnstown by St. Mary Greek Catholic parish, reported the rate of homeowners among its parishioners as 22 percent (of the total of 759 families reporting), pp. 9–12.
Source: East Central European foreign-born male population from manuscript schedules of 1900 census, traced in the 1920, 1925, and 1930 Johnstown city directories; see also Table 3.4 in this book.

The proportion of homeowners was, expectedly, higher among the immigrant entrepreneurs and the skilled mill workers than among ordinary laborers. On the average, the homes of the latter were also less expensive. Inspection of a sample of 145 real estate transfers recorded by the East Central Europeans in the county Recorder's office during the decade 1920–1930 indicates that in most cases the buying and selling prices of immigrant homes ranged from $2,700 to $3,800, with the transactions conducted by ordinary laborers concentrated in the lower bracket.[66] Table 6.4 presents the average tax valuations of homes owned by the immigrants in different occupational categories in 1920, 1925, and 1930–1. On the average, during the decade of the 1920s the tax values of the homes

Table 6.4. *Average tax valuations of immigrant homes, by homeowner's
sex and occupation, 1920, 1925, 1930–1931*

	1920	1925	1930–1
Males			
Ordinary laborers	$1,900	$2,050	$2,250
Skilled workers	2,300	2,700	3,090
Employed in business and services	3,100	3,370	3,340
Females (widows, boardinghouse keepers)	1,500	2,480	1,950
Average for all categories	$2,200	$2,650	$2,660
N (total entries 1920–30/31) = 1,850			

Note: For 1920 and 1925, my calculations were based exclusively on "new
acquisitions," i.e., only the names of homeowners who appeared in a given
ward after the time of my previous checking: after 1915 for the year 1920,
and after 1920 for the year 1925 (if an immigrant had previously owned a
house in a different ward he or she would be counted as "new" in the
current one). Also, since the tax valuation volumes for 1930 for some wards
and boroughs were missing at the time of my research, I had to use the
listing of 1931 homeowners as published in the *Johnstown Tribune*. In a regular section entitled "County Assessments" it enumerated all homeowners
for that year, not just the "new acquisitions."
Source: Cambria County Commissioner's Office, Ebensburg, Pa., "Precepts
of the Assessors: Annual Enumeration of All Persons, Properties and Things
Subject to Taxation," 1920, 1925, 1930, wards 9–11, 14–21 in Johnstown,
boroughs of East Conemaugh, Franklin, Brownstown, Lower Yoder. Also
"County Assessment" (for the year of 1931), *Johnstown Tribune*, January 27,
1932–December 1, 1932.

of ordinary East Central European male laborers were about 35 to 40
percent lower than the values of homes owned by immigrants employed in ethnic businesses and services. In comparison with the
skilled mill workers, the values of laborers' homes were on the average 20 to 25 percent lower. The same table also shows that the
average value of homes owned by women (as calculated for the
whole decade 1920–30) was approximately 30 percent lower than
the average value of homes owned by men.

The largest group among employed immigrants, the ordinary laborers, was by no means economically homogenous. By 1925 most
of them still did not own their own homes. Among those who did,
at one extreme over 10 percent possessed only small, poor houses
– huts almost – valued at less than $1,000. At the other extreme, a
similar proportion owned homes that were valued for tax purposes

at over $3,000. The homes of the majority fell into the tax categories between $1,000 and $3,000: In the lower bracket, these were the homes near the mills, without electricity and running water; in the upper one they were somewhat bigger and better-equipped houses higher up on the hills (tax valuation of homes owned by ordinary laborers in the period 1920 – 30 are shown in Table A.11 in the Appendix).

Besides homeownership, place of residence in the city was another indication of the achievement of the family. From about the time of World War I, the immigrant families were moving in increasing numbers out of the original "foreign colonies" near the mills into higher areas of the city and the surrounding boroughs. By 1930, as many as 56 percent of the immigrant families settled in Moxham, and 60 percent of those in Morrellville were homeowners, as compared with a mere 28 percent in old Cambria City.[67]

In the secondary ethnic settlements the immigrants paid on the average $1,000 more for their homes than in the primary colonies. Even the homes of ordinary laborers in the new, "better" sections of town were more valuable than those in the old "foreign colonies" near the mills. By 1930, over 60 percent of the ordinary laborers' homes in the primary sections were tax valued at less than $2,000; the respective proportion in the areas of secondary settlement was about 40 percent. (The average tax valuations of immigrant homes in primary and secondary ethnic settlements in Johnstown between 1920 and 1930 are shown in Table A.12 in the Appendix.)

We will look, finally, at the contributions paid by the immigrants to their ethnic parishes. In July of 1920, *Chranitel*, a newspaper published by St. Mary's Rusyn Greek Catholic Church in Cambria City, printed a list of donations by particular families (the paper ceased to appear after one year or else the subsequent issues were lost). In just two special collections during that year for the construction of a new church building – *kolekta* and *fundacia* – the parish, numbering 877 members (750 families and 127 single people), acquired a sum of $27,000.[68] Divided equally among the parishioners, this would have meant a contribution of slightly over $30 per "collective" (family) or individual member. Their contributions, however, varied greatly, from nothing to well over $100. Table 6.5 compares the amounts given in two collections by St. Mary's parishioners (renters and homeowners) as noted in *Chranitel's* list of donors. Thus, among the parishioners taken as a whole, about one-fourth made no contribution at all; one-half donated less than $30; and about one-fourth gave amounts ranging from $30 to more than $100. Among the

Table 6.5. *Donations by St. Mary's Greek Catholic Church parishioners (renters and homeowners), 1920 (in %)*

Amount of Contribution	All Parishioners	Renters	Homeowners
0	23.4 (205)	27.7 (198)	4.3 (7)
$1–14	21.7 (190)	23.7 (169)	12.9 (21)
$15–29	30.5 (268)	31.2 (223)	27.6 (45)
$30–49	8.0 (70)	3.4 (24)	28.2 (46)
$50–99	10.0 (88)	10.4 (74)	8.6 (14)
$100 and over	6.4 (56)	3.6 (26)	18.4 (30)
Total	(877)	(714)	(163)

Note: Figures in parentheses represent *N*.
Source: Compiled from *Chranitel*, July 1920, pp. 9–12.

homeowners, the proportions were different, however: Only a few made no contribution at all; well over one-third paid between $30 and $99, and nearly one-fifth donated over $100.

Obviously, even in the same budget group, different families could have had different motivations for giving more or less to their church. Among those who contributed nothing, in the category of renters, there must certainly have been families simply unable to spare even a few dollars from their tight survival budgets. There were also those who had some limited funds but decided to eliminate the participation in communal giving in order to accumulate savings. Among the owners, those who only contributed a few dollars may have found that having purchased a house, they had no money left for extras; or, having accumulated some capital, they may have chosen to use their funds differently.[69] However, considering the importance of communal (church) participation in the immigrants' image of a "decent life" as well as the actual pressure to participate exerted directly by the pastor and indirectly by community members through status evaluations, it can probably be assumed that on the whole the immigrant families' contributions to the welfare of the parish more or less corresponded to their overall economic standing.

We can now present an estimate of the general distribution of the East Central European working-class households in Johnstown in the mid-1920s in terms of total annual family income from wages. The figures are calculated for the year 1925 and cover a total of 217 working-class immigrant families (persisters) that were already present in Johnstown at the time of the 1900 census. My estimate of total family income involves only the wage earnings of the gainfully employed adult members of the households; the income received from boarders, the earnings of minor children, and the selling of garden and domestic products is not included.

I grouped the occupations of the adult, gainfully employed men and women persisters recorded in the 1925 city directory, ascribing to each a dollar score reflecting average actual earnings as estimated earlier in this chapter. In order not to overestimate their incomes, the lower wage brackets were used.[70] Households (43) whose heads and members worked in a family business were excluded, since in too many cases it was impossible to get an accurate approximation of their total annual income.

The proportions of East Central European working-class families in various annual wage income categories in 1925, in relation to the number of adult family members employed, are shown in Table 6.6. Clearly, the dependence on one wage earner drastically reduced the income of immigrant households. Three-fourths of the families with only one adult wage earner subsisted on a survival budget of less than $1,000 annually. The employment of two adult persons reduced this proportion to slightly over one-tenth. Two-thirds of the two-worker households were in the $1,000 to $1,600 income bracket, permitting a slightly more comfortable, though still insecure, economic existence below the threshold of what the immigrants defined as a "good life." The employment of three or more adult members of the household located the majority of immigrant families in the *dostatnie* category.

The proportions of East Central European working-class families in various categories of annual wage income, in relation to the sex and occupation of the head of household, are shown in Table 6.7. Expectedly, the female-headed immigrant families lived a more strained economic existence: About one-half of such households, as compared to less than one-fourth of the male-headed ones, subsisted on a survival income of less than $1,000 annually. We can add that in almost 50 percent of the female-headed families in 1925, there was only one adult person gainfully employed on the outside, whereas in the male-headed household this proportion was only 25 percent.

Not surprisingly, life was much more difficult economically for the families of ordinary laborers than for the families of skilled workers. About 30 percent of the ordinary laborers' families were merely "survivors," and another 40 percent were located in a financial

Table 6.6. *Estimated average annual wage income of immigrant working-class families, by number of adult members gainfully employed, 1925 (in %)*

Avg. Annual Wage Income	Number Employed					Total Families in Income Category
	1	2	3	4	5 and over	
Less than $1,000	75.4 (46)	11.1 (11)	5.1 (2)	(0)	(0)	27.2 (59)
$1,000–1,600	9.8 (6)	66.7 (66)	15.4 (6)	(0)	(0)	35.9 (78)
$1,600–2,000	11.5 (7)	13.1 (13)	17.9 (7)	14.2 (2)	(0)	13.4 (29)
Over $2,000	3.3 (2)	9.1 (9)	61.6 (24)	85.8 (12)	100 (4)	23.5 (51)
Total	28.1 (61)	45.6 (99)	18.0 (39)	6.5 (14)	1.8 (4)	100 (217)

Note: Figures in parentheses represent *N*. Table includes both male- and female-headed families. Cell percentages are calculated from column totals (*N*). Marginal row and column percentages are calculated from the grand total (*N* = 217).
Source: East Central European population from manuscript schedules of 1900 census, traced in Johnstown city directory for 1925.

Table 6.7. *Distribution of estimated total annual family income of East Central European working-class households, by sex of head and occupation, 1925 (in %)*

Total Family Income	Occupation of Female Head			Occupation of Male Head		
	Homemaker	Laborer	Total	Ordinary Laborer	Skilled Worker	Total
Less than $1,000	48.0 (12)	49.9 (3)	48.4 (15)	28.2 (44)	(0)	23.7 (44)
$1,000–1,600	28.0 (7)	16.7 (1)	25.8 (8)	41.7 (65)	16.7 (5)	37.6 (70)
$1,600–2,000	8.0 (2)	16.7 (1)	9.7 (3)	6.4 (10)	53.3 (16)	14.0 (26)
Over $2,000	16.0 (4)	16.7 (1)	16.1 (5)	23.7 (37)	30.0 (9)	24.7 (46)
Total	(25)	(6)	(31)	(156)	(30)	(186)

Note: Numbers in parentheses represent N. Total N for table is 217.
Source: East Central European population from manuscript schedules of 1900 census, traced in Johnstown city directory for 1925.

bracket that made possible a life above the level of mere survival but below that of the "good life." In the group of skilled workers, most families had an estimated total income above the "good life" threshold.

In 1925, the majority – almost two-thirds of the male- and female-headed working-class families who had persisted in town since 1900 – existed on a collective annual income of less than $1,600, which was below the threshold of a "good life" as seen by the immigrants. Of this number, "survivors" – families struggling on subsistence incomes below $1,000 a year – constituted more than one-fourth. At the other extreme, more than one-third of the households enjoyed a more relaxed economic existence on total family incomes above $1,600; of this number, about one-tenth fell into the category of $1,600 to $2,000 annual wage income and nearly one-fourth received more than $2,000 annually.

My calculations of family income refer to immigrant families who were already living in Johnstown at the time of the 1900 census and who by 1925 had adult, fully employable children. In order to obtain a gross estimate of the size of the lowest income category for the whole of the East Central European population in the city, I made the following calculation. In the 1920s about 3,000 East Central European families were living in Johnstown. From the 1920 census I calculated that 56 percent of the total number of foreign-born families in the city had only one gainfully employed worker. (In nearby Pittsburgh, a steel town similar to Johnstown but large enough for the census to provide more detailed information about particular nationality groups, the proportion of East Central European households with only one gainfully employed worker was about 50 percent.)[71] In Table 6.6 we saw that 75 percent of the Slavic and Magyar working-class families with only one adult wage earner subsisted on a survival income of less than $1,000 a year. Working-class families constituted approximately 90 percent of the total East Central European population in Johnstown, and the remainder were families of immigrant businessmen. If we assume that annual incomes in this latter group, including households with only one gainfully employed worker, were over $1,000, it can be conjectured that no less than 40 percent of the total number of foreign-born East Central European families present in Johnstown in the mid-1920s existed on a combined household income of less than $1,000 a year. This estimate, it should be repeated, however, does not include additional income that the families may have received from boarders and from part-time jobs of minor children.

The world of the East Central European families in Johnstown during the 1920s was more "feasible" and more "expandable" than in the earlier period, and certainly more so than in the old country. But at the same time, for most, economic existence retained its fundamental characteristic from the past: insecurity. With one year better, one worse in the mills, and with the constant tension and conflict among different exigencies of everyday life, the immigrants' existence, despite all of their efforts to maintain and even improve the family's standard of living, was fraught with uncertainty.

Membership in the middle-income group, and even in part of the higher-income category in the immigrant communities was fluid. My 1925 estimate of the distribution of family incomes indicates the approximate size of particular financial strata, but a number of immigrant households were moving from one income segment to another, depending on their current earning potential and on seasonal economic fluctuations. Those currently occupying the middle financial position – above the survival level and below that of the "good life" – had had before their eyes not only a vision of a better existence in the income group above them but also that of the struggle for survival below. Similarly, with the exception of those few firmly established at the top of the immigrant financial hierarchy, the families currently in the more elevated income brackets saw through their inner eyes the prospect of skidding – to the striving middle, and down below, among the survivors. The deep-seated attitude of old peasant fatalism, sustained by the hardship and insecurity of industrial existence in America, lay beneath this awareness.

The immigrants learned to look for and "help luck" when it was there. In good industrial conditions the family actively utilized its kinship/ethnic networks in a collective work effort and consumed, and if possible, accumulated some extra capital. But the immigrants retained a realistic readiness to accept failure as a normal and natural part of human existence. Wrote *Chranitel*, the Rusyn newspaper in Johnstown, quoting Scripture:

> Sčastja takoje, jak drabina
> Skol'ko stepenov pojdeme do hory,
> Stolko často treba zyjti znov do doly
> Zivot naš takyj
> Jak plavanije morskoje
> Koli volny to podnosjat nas
> Do hory, to kidajut nas dolu

(St. Ambrosius)

Zivot jest dorohoju
Kotora vedet nas to čerez
Doliny, to čerez hory

                                                        (Gregorius)[72]

[Happiness is like a ladder:
As many steps as we move up,
Often that many we have to descend again.
Our life is like swimming at sea:
Now the waves take us upward,
Then throw us downward again . . .]

[Life is a road that leads us
Now through the valleys, and then
Through the mountains.]

The most faithful way to depict the uncertainty or the "fluctuating" quality of immigrant existence would be to make year-to-year comparisons of actual family budgets. Since no such data exist, occupational shifting can be used as one substitute measure. The immigrants' occupational status and mobility in the interwar period will be discussed in more detail in the following chapter devoted to the internal social stratification of the East Central European communities. Here I will only briefly note the general tendency.

In comparison with the earlier period, the proportion of immigrant men who were already living in Johnstown in 1900 and were still present in town in the interwar period, and who had also been recorded as holding positions above the lowest occupational level at least once at my four checkpoints in 1915, 1920, 1925, and 1930, increased considerably, from 29 to 45 percent (see Table A.13 in the Appendix). But even if it became generally easier for the immigrants to rise occupationally above the lowest skill level, still, about 40 percent of the "achievers" were found to have held their elevated positions only once. The degree of impermanence of the immigrant occupational achievement is further illustrated by the almost equal proportions of occupational elevations and skidding. The average overall rate of occupational *ascents* – elevations recorded after 1915 and still held by 1930 – was 53 percent. At the same time, however, the rate of occupational *descents* – elevated positions acquired after 1915 but lost before or by 1930 – was a high 47 percent.[73]

One more measure of the "fluctuating" quality of the existence of East Central European families in Johnstown in the interwar period was the turnover in homeownership. The shifts in immigrant homeownership, calculated in two sets of three-way comparisons, between 1915, 1920, and 1925, as well as 1920, 1925, and 1930, are shown in Tables A.14 and A.15 in the Appendix. The average rate of home losses from one five-year checkpoint to the next, between 1915 and 1930, was approximately 15 percent. At the same time, the average proportion of new acquisitors – that is, of the homeowners recorded at particular checkpoints who had not owned a house at an earlier date – was, for that period, also about 15 percent.

What, then, the immigrants saw happening around them in their ethnic communities and what they saw as the "nature of things" in America was, like the *Chranitel*'s parable, the ups, downs, and ups again of the human fate. For Johnstown's immigrants, their colonies were neither "ghettos of opportunity," as the consensus historians would have it, nor "ghettos of despair," as described by the radical school, but both. This mixture of hope and insecurity, the simultaneous perception that it was feasible, if costly and difficult, to somewhat improve the family standard of living by a collective effort of its individual members, and that all of the painfully achieved gains could be easily lost due to a turn in external conditions, formed the essence of the immigrants' worldview. It was rooted in the traditions of their peasant culture and religious faith and perpetuated by the realities of their American working-class existence.

The Great Depression provided a spectacular confirmation of the immigrants' view of life as *morskoje plavanije* – swimming at sea in an alternation of highs and lows – and strongly brought to the fore their latent fatalism. The reaction of most of the families to the Depression was a mixture of resignation and a determination to hold on and survive despite all: "We were not surprised by hard times . . . It was normal, it happened to us before in 1922 and 1923": Andy A.'s father was a miner, and his family suffered from prolonged hardship during the coal strike in the early 1920s.[74] And, from another Johnstown immigrant: "In the Depression [almost] everybody around us lived like we did, so what else could we do, we survived on what was available, and hanged on."[75]

Immigrant households survived during the 1930s on earnings from part-time odd jobs taken by family members in Johnstown and other cities, often at considerable distance; by using up family savings and taking small loans from friends and relatives; by buying on credit at neighborhood stores; by using relief and government programs; and by reducing regular expenditures for food, clothing, and utilities.

With the drastic curtailment of employment in the steel plants, wage payments to the mill workers declined sharply, falling by 54 percent between the summer of 1929 and mid-year 1931. In the fall of that year both Bethlehem Steel and U.S. Steel cut wages further by 10 percent, reducing the average earnings of the mill workers from $36.07 a week, for 1925, to $25.90. By the spring of 1932, with local manufacturing production at its lowest since the onset of the Depression, the average weekly earnings in the Johnstown steel industry dropped to $12.77, a full 50 percent.[76] Over the next two years, for periods of up to several months in a row, only a little over one-half of the foreign-born laborers in Johnstown worked full-time, and the remainder either took turns in the mills two or three times a week (about one-fourth of the labor force) or remained unemployed (another quarter).[77]

The unskilled laborer employed part-time brought home no more than $8 to $10 a week.[78] After about a two-year period of improved industrial conditions and increased wages, 1937 and 1938 witnessed another acute slump, and with the decrease in steel orders the actual wages of thousands of Johnstown laborers backslid to an irregular $10 to $12 a week.[79] Those who did not have a more or less steady job in the mills came to the gates daily "at 7 A.M., and some were picked out for work, [others] returned at 3 P.M., the second shift, and again at 11 P.M. – one had the best chances then. If you came three times like this, you had a [good] chance to be picked out."[80] At the same time men searched for odd seasonal jobs around the area, on large potato farms owned by Bethlehem Company at the outskirts of Westmont Borough, where a day's work paid a dollar, or painting houses and helping with carpentry for private contractors, a job that brought $.50 an hour as long as it lasted.[81] The relief programs – WPA, CWA, FWPA, CCC – introduced by the Roosevelt administration were also implemented in Johnstown, where they were put to use to employ men in sewer construction projects, in street repair, and in river dredging.

With thousands of men either totally idle or employed only part-time, the Depression brought onto the labor market in Johnstown increased numbers of women seeking work, the wives of mill workers and young single women who had previously stayed at home. In 1934, out of 1,769 unemployed women seeking work in Johnstown, over 50 percent were looking for gainful employment for the first time.[82] For the East Central European women, work as cooks, maids, and servants in American homes and in downtown hotels and restaurants – jobs that during the Depression paid $3 to $5 a week – was the most common employment, if rather irregular.[83]

Unable to find employment in Johnstown, many a young man or woman traveled to bigger cities where work was easier to find. Between 1930 and 1934, the city of Johnstown lost 5,000 people: Of this, a number relocated from the city proper to the surrounding boroughs, but many left town altogether in search of work.[84] For the East Central Europeans, New York became a job mecca of sorts during the Depression, and they developed there efficient informal networks of placement. A round-trip railroad excursion to New York that went every second week cost $2; those who did not have the money regularly rode the freight trains, jumping onto them from the fields after the trains had left Johnstown.[86] In New York, young women worked "for the Jews": in private homes as maids and cooks, or in Jewish restaurants and small factories; all of this was arranged in a chain pattern, with those already employed finding placement for others. Thus employed, young women received food and board plus $25 to $35 a month, of which they either sent or brought home a significant part to Johnstown and handed to their parents.[85] Young men usually found jobs in New York restaurants washing dishes and cleaning tables; if lucky, with tips they could earn $18 to $20 a week, a sum that was considered then "very good money." Others went to the factories in Cleveland and Detroit.[87] When work in the Johnstown mills picked up in 1936, many of them returned, only to resume their travels when it slackened again in 1937 and 1938.[88]

For a great number of immigrant families, however, despite an average 15 percent decrease in the overall cost of living between 1929 and 1935,[89] all of these combined financial resources were still insufficient to make ends meet on a pre-Depression level. Virtual elimination of clothing and household expenditures, a drastic reduction in food spending and trimming of diet was used by the East Central European households as a means of coping with the bad times.[90] During the 1930s, most of the foodstuffs consumed by immigrant families were prepared at home, shopping being limited to buying once-a-week big specials on leftover meats and dairy products announced in the *Johnstown Tribune* (usually a group of neighbors purchased one copy at $.02 apiece) and in church bulletins and notices of special events.[91] Credit in the neighborhood stores was used very widely: "Most families bought groceries on paper. All purchases were recorded on slips kept near the cash register. On pay days all or part of the bill was paid."[92] Particularly stricken households "made everything at home," living on a rotation of soup and noodles, with an occasional addition of milk and eggs "earned" by a day's work on nearby farms.[93] Unable to pay the water bill ($4 for a three-month period), jobless family members "paid" it by working at the North Fork Dam (owned by the Bethlehem Company).[94]

By the mid-1930s, almost one-fifth of the population of Cambria County received some kind of relief in kind: flour, powdered milk, sugar, or in food orders, at about $4 a week for a family.[95] Because local relief records were destroyed by the floods, I could not estimate the proportion of East Central European families on relief. My informants admitted that immigrant households accepted "food given out by the government" but usually denied that they took relief in cash.[96] However, a 1937 survey of housing conditions in Johnstown conducted by the U.S. Department of Labor contained some information on the "concentration of relief" in particular city sections. All primary "foreign colonies" were classified in the report as "heavy on relief," and secondary East Central European settlements were classified as "heavy" to "moderately heavy."[97]

The records collected by the Department of Labor investigating the housing conditions of Johnstown's labor force during the Depression permit an estimate of the average global family income that the households had at their disposal in the mid-1930s. According to this report, in the areas of primary immigrant settlement in the city (which also housed American families), the average income was found to range from $780 to $1,500 a year. In sections of secondary settlement, again with a number of American residents, the total family income ranged from $860 to $1,900.[98] Another government investigation of family budgets of Johnstown's residents, conducted in 1934–5, also included East Central European households. A calculation of the combined family income for that period in the immigrant homes indicates an average income of slightly less than $900 annually per household, ranging from a minimum of $507 (for a family composed of two women, both employed as seamstresses) to a maximum of $2,323 (for a family of nine members, with seven adults gainfully employed for at least part of the year).[99] Taking into account a 15 percent reduction in the overall cost of living by the mid-1930s in comparison with 1929, we may conclude that in terms of my pre-Depression income estimates, the majority of Slavic and Magyar families in the city struggled to get by on a total annual income of about $1,000 – that is, at close to the survival level. This income was sufficient to get by on only at the price of a radical trimming of expenditures for food and other items. Families at this level lived with a persistent sense of uncertainty about tomorrow and an unceasing conflict between individual and family desires, on the one hand, and the demands of communal participation on the other.

Different families chose different ways of coping with these tensions. Even within the limitations of severely restricted funds, the households differed from one another in preferences and life-styles. As indicated in the 1934–5 study of expenditures by Johnstown's working-class families, in about 40 percent of the investigated Slavic and Magyar households, annual expenditures exceeded total money receipts for the year (the average overspending was $47). However, besides expenditures on clothing, home furnishings, and transportation, which can be considered as necessary elements of existence (transportation costs reaching in some families as much as $100, apparently needed for travel for longer distances in search of work), nearly one-half of the excess spending was on recreation. Expenditures for this item in six- to eight-member households with young adults ranged from $20 to $30 to over $200 in a year.[100] "With no work," my informants described their daily preoccupations during the Depression, "people sat at home or played. They went to dances, and picnics, or they played billiards."[101] In a similar account a Pole, a part-time steelworker at the Bethlehem Company, said, "In the mills then, people worked only three to four days a week at best. So every night they attended the Polish Hall, weekends they had picnics . . . Were we depressed? Yes and no, because it was a general situation, like a national disaster."[102] One picnic organized by the Slovenian Workers' Home in July of 1935, with nearly 100 families participating brought $382 in *dohotki* (income): $.10 admission per person, and $.05 for a glass of beer. In that same period, the average monthly income from the bar in the Slovenian Club (with about 140 dues-paying members) ranged between $160 and $180.[103]

It was only those immigrant households in which one member at least was lucky to have secured and kept steady, well-paying employment at Bethlehem Steel or that had several adult members employed more or less constantly and contributing to the family income that managed to purchase a house during the 1930s. Fewer than one-tenth of the 1930 immigrant renter-persisters had become homeowners by 1940.[104] But although home acquisition among the immigrant families became significantly less frequent than in the preceding decade, the overall rate of retention remained unchanged. Most of the families stubbornly held on to their homes through the bad years, even at the price of radically reducing their food and all other expenditures to the barest survival level.

Inspection of a list of over 1,000 houses owned by people with identifiably Slavic and Magyar names appearing in the 1940 precepts of the tax assessor reveals that a little over 10 percent of the houses were "sold to county" for unpaid taxes. By comparison, in the areas of the city where the "Americans" lived, the average proportion of home losses reported in that year was 6 percent.[105] An average of one-fifth of East Central European homes "sold to county" for unpaid taxes had a notation indicating that they were subsequently "redeemed"; the respective proportion in the native-born American sections of town was 13 percent. The rate of recorded home losses in the more expensive secondary settlements, inhabited mostly by younger families and relatively recent homeowners, was twice as large (16 percent) as that in the cheaper primary "foreign colonies" (8 percent), populated mostly by older, less affluent immigrants. At the same time, the immigrant families in the secondary settlements seemed to have been better prepared to more quickly redeem their possessions. As noted in the tax lists, 27 percent of the immigrant homes, as opposed to 12 percent in the primary "foreign colonies," were subsequently redeemed.[106]

All in all, the prolonged industrial depression of the 1930s forced the majority of the immigrant families to reduce their living standard to the survival level or only a little above it, with all of the accompanying tensions, conflicts, and insecurities. Although leveling down, the same depression deepened the already existing socio-economic distinctions in life-styles and general well-being between the more successful, better-established minority and the remaining mass of "ordinary" immigrant families either struggling at the survival level or trying to maintain their standard of living in the intermediate stratum. The following chapter reconstructs the internal social stratification in the East Central European communities in Johnstown as it emerged in the beginning of the century and crystallized in the subsequent decades.

7 Internal social stratification in the immigrant communities

The impressive body of quantitative data related to societal stratification and mobility collected in recent years by ethnic and urban
historians measures the position of immigrants on the stratification
ladder of the larger and dominant society and according to its criteria
of status and achievement. In the last few years, some disappointed
users of such uniform ranking have been postulating an "intrinsic"
treatment of the immigrants' socioeconomic attainment in American
society in order to bring out the felt and lived meaning of their
experiences, perceived and evaluated in terms of their own cultural
and social priorities.[1]

Postulation of an "intrinsic" interpretation of ethnic mobility and
stratification is theoretically justified. Highly differentiated complex
societies contain considerable diversity of stratification subsystems.
In such societies, segmented by caste, class, religion, and ethnicity,
or by some combination of these factors, particular segments de-
velop an internal stratification that either replicates in a full or shortened form the hierarchy of the larger society or possesses its own
particular dimensions and characteristics. This multiplicity as a feature of stratification systems in complex societies requires that the
social positioning and mobility of members of the larger society and
of its subsegments be described simultaneously in both perspectives.

Conditions prevailing in Johnstown throughout the first half of
the century provide the empirical rationale for such an approach.
In the ascription-based ethnic-divisive Johnstown society, the paths
of status achievement were contained within the ethnic segments.
Adapting to this situation, as they strove to achieve the goals that
they valued, the immigrants created in their communities internal
social ladders on which they moved up and down. By and large,
transmission between the immigrant and the outside American
stratification systems started operating in Johnstown more systematically only after the Second World War.

Chapters 3 and 5 located East Central Europeans in the socio-

This chapter appeared in an abbreviated version in the *Journal of Social History*, Fall
1982, 75–107.

economic and political structure of the larger Johnstown society. Against this background, we will now reconstruct the internal social stratification system of the immigrant communities as it emerged at the beginning of the century and crystallized during the 1920s. The focus on the emergence of intraethnic social stratification in no sense negates the simultaneous process of class formation cutting across the immigrant communities and of the proletarianization of the great majority of immigrants in their adjustment to industrial life in this country. Rather, I would like to propose a complementary model for the treatment of stratification and the related problems of status and achievement, different from that used in social historical studies of ethnicity, especially in the mobility analyses.[2] My discussion leaves several unanswered questions. As proposed here, a historical model for treating the range of issues related to social adaptation, mobility, and success of peasant-immigrants in urban industrial society is not a finished product. It is, rather, a trial balloon, an invitation extended to ethnic and labor historians as well as to urban and community sociologists to search for a better understanding of the meaning of the experience of peasant-immigrants as industrial workers in urban society.

This chapter examines different components of the internal social stratification of the East Central European communities in Johnstown before World War II and reconstructs the allocation and movement of the immigrants on this ladder. The unequal distribution of goods and values among different positions in social groups creates a hierarchy of rank or social stratification. It has two basic dimensions between which there is a continuous feedback, so that they operate as "lagged functions" of each other. One can be termed resources, involving factors such as income, occupation, education, organizational membership, and formal and informal political "connections." Another is rewards, involving life-styles, personal or family autonomy, and power. Social stratification involves, on the one hand, the actual distribution of resources and rewards and, on the other, perceptions of it held by the group members.[3]

In order to describe the actual distribution of social positions in the group studied, we must specify the components of social standing as perceived by its members. Reconstruction of conceptions and images people have of their stratification system is important if we are to understand the "social arithmetic" they use to assess, weigh, and combine various elements of resources and rewards in the attainment of social well-being.[4]

In reconstructing the criteria of the internal social stratification system in the immigrant communities in Johnstown, I apply the standards of differentiation employed by the people themselves – the approach used by sociologists and social anthropologists who study local communities.[5]

After reconstructing from the conceptions of the immigrants the internal social stratification system of their communities in Johnstown before World War II, I then treat it as *real* – that is, I examine the objective interrelations of its particular components and their relative weight or "lifting power" in the allocation of status. I then present the actual distribution of immigrants on the particular status dimensions that they themselves specified and in the overall internal stratification of the immigrant communities. Next, I discuss the openness and stability of the immigrant social system as well as the transmission of status from this system to the larger society. In the conclusion of this chapter, I return to the immigrants' perceptions of the social structure of their own as well as the larger American system, presenting their evaluations of opportunities to advance on the internal social ladder in their communities, as well as their images of the external, dominant social order.

My information about the basic components of the social stratification of the immigrant communities in Johnstown, the determinants of membership in particular strata, and the means of mobility between them came from a group of informants consisting of 35 immigrants and older representatives of the second generation born in Johnstown at the beginning of the century. I asked them a series of questions most commonly used in studies of social stratification in small communities: Were there any "classes" (strata) in your community? How many? Who were the highly respected? Who were the leaders? How did they achieve their positions? How did one gain recognition in the community? How did one lose it? Were there any exceptions? Deviants? Outcasts? Was any particular behavior expected of the "elite" in the immigrant community? Did they conform to these expectations? How did one "make it" into the higher stratum of the group? How did one advance in the community? Was there a transfer possible between the immigrant hierarchy and the larger American society? Who were the ones who did transfer?

In a deliberate attempt to elicit from the informants as many ideas as possible on a wide range of topics associated with the internal group stratification, I applied neither the formalized interview schedules nor the quantitative techniques used for measurement of prestige. Instead, I used a minimally structured interview with open-ended questions.[6]

This study deals with the past, and an attempt to extract from my informants the type of point-by-point ranking of particular positions in their old group social hierarchy could not have rendered meaningful results. I was also aware of "loading the dice" by the very posing of strata-suggesting questions. Most of my informants were quick to enumerate the bases of social differentiation within their groups during the time I was interested in. The fact that most of them were able to answer my inquiries easily suggests that the evidence that I collected as to the basic dimensions of the internal social stratification system in the immigrant communities is not just an artifact of the method used but reflects social reality as it indeed appeared to their members.[7]

The immigrants were also asked to enumerate members of their "upper strata." Their listings, persuasive as they were through their very repetition, were subsequently checked in real estate records, tax assessment books, and business guides; on gravestones in immigrant cemeteries; among lists of officers in ethnic organizations and societies, parochial boards, and committees; among speakers at immigrant banquets and celebrations; and finally in the local newspapers, which made occasional references to East Central European leaders in the "foreign colonies." In addition, I checked the material from 115 tapes with life stories of retired East Central European coal miners and steelworkers from Johnstown and vicinity, collected in 1975-7 for the University of Pittsburgh at Johnstown Ethnic History Project, for information pertaining to problems of intragroup social stratification and mobility of immigrant workers.

Finally, there is the important problem of general instability of status and of changes in status patterns occurring over time. In presenting components of the immigrant social stratification system in Johnstown as it emerged at the beginning of the century and crystallized during the 1920s, I will point out the general direction of changes in the configuration and relative importance of particular status components that occurred during that period. A more serious problem, concerning the assessment of status distribution and mobility up and down the internal social stratification ladder, results from what in earlier chapters I called the "fluctuating reality" of immigrant existence in America. I tried my best to account for this fact in the interpretations; the fluidity of the immigrant stratification system, particularly in its middle portions, makes the model more "solid" at the extremes, and vague and ambiguous in between them.

The broadest categories in which the immigrants perceived the social structure in Johnstown during the first decades of this century were those of *their own* versus *American*. Counterposing these two categories, the immigrants usually adopted the designation employed in the dominant local society: "us foreigners," as opposed to the generalized out-group, physically and socially distant. The latter was conceived of diffusely in both class and ethnic terms: The "Americans" implied also the "rich," "the bosses," "those from the hills." The East Central Europeans' perception of internal social stratification within the dominant world was substantially flattened. In principle, they saw above them a large vaguely differentiated class of "Americans" composed of native-born and Western European people, now seen as one category, now as separate groupings "above at the top." Depicted in thick strokes, the social structure in Johnstown appeared to the immigrants as a "divided" system with clearly drawn distinctions between the American world and their own, and – within the latter – with two broad categories: the upper stratum, or the immigrant elite, and a lower one composed of "poor and ordinary people." By the 1920s, however, there crystallized in the immigrant communities a third, intermediate stratum, much more diffuse and open-ended.

The internal social stratification of the immigrant communities represented a fundamentally classless but nonegalitarian system.[8] In comparison with the more complex and differentiated larger society, the immigrant status ladder was much shorter. Whereas the occupational structure of the larger society in Johnstown contained a wide range of positions, from unskilled laborers to wholesale merchants, bank presidents, and chief surgeons, in the immigrant communities it "ended" at the level of a neighborhood storeowner or a family doctor or druggist (the latter of whom were from the second generation). Educational distribution, which in the larger Johnstown society covered a full range up to university degrees, in the immigrant communities extended from illiteracy to a few years of village school or night English classes. Similarly, in comparison with the larger society, the income ladder in the immigrant communities was considerably shorter, ranging from the meager annual earnings of unskilled mill laborers to those of "big" ethnic merchants in foreign colonies who made "over $5,000 a year."

My informants identified altogether ten factors that differentiated their communities and made for internal social stratification. Seven of these factors, explicitly enumerated by the immigrants constitute the resource dimensions of societal stratification: (1) "seniority," or length of time spent in the United States (2) ethnic organizational membership and participation; (3) occupation; (4) economic standing; (5) education; (6) American political connections; and (7) "moral virtue" (character). Cutting across these are three other factors that form the reward dimensions of the system: (8) life-style (residence, consumption patterns, intragroup social circles); (9) personal (family) autonomy; and (10) power. These were not mentioned by my informants as distinctive status criteria but in connection with particular resources, as their "signs" or "natural functions" of sorts. They are listed separately for the purpose of greater analytical clarity.

Figure 1 presents the stratification system of the immigrant communities in Johnstown. What by the standards of the dominant system constituted vaguely differentiated lower strata of Johnstown's society, in the perception of immigrants was divided into upper, middle, and lower societal levels. The immigrant merchants and store owners in the "foreign colonies"; the leaders of ethnic societies who were educated in the history and literature of their national groups; the newly established homeowners in secondary immigrant settlements: All those who by immigrant standards filled the middle and upper ranks in the immigrant stratification system, still occupied positions close to the bottom of the stratification system of the larger society.

We will now present the particular status dimensions in the immigrant communities and discuss their interrelations and relative weight.

"Seniority" or length of time spent in the United States. At the turn of the century, during the years when hundreds of peasant-immigrants were arriving in Johnstown, when the foreign colonies were taking shape and the immigrant labor gangs were being formed in the mills, when churches were being constructed and national societies organized – experience, initiative, and personal skills were at a high social premium. The pioneers – those who had arrived earlier and were already established in Johnstown – were naturally respected and looked up to by the newcomers. In the economically undifferentiated group of peasant-immigrants, the "seniority" of the founders of the national societies, of the church builders and members of organizing committees, had thus served as a source of prestige, elevating the old-timers to high status positions.[9]

"The [immigrant] workers whom I found in Steelton acted as though they belonged to two caste systems" – noted a Slovenian writer in his memoirs from the beginning of the century – "the

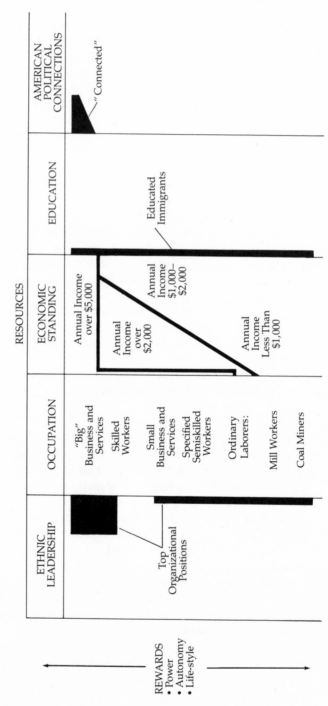

Figure 1. Immigrant social stratification in the interwar period. *Note:* "Seniority" and "moral virtue" are omitted from diagram, the former because it gradually became transformed into one of the five factors, the latter because it could not be graphically represented. In addition to "big" businessmen of the immigrant generation, the top occupational stratum in East Central

caste three times larger than the other one included the green-horns, or in the Slovene, the 'grinarji.' Of course, the class division was greatly affected by the older immigrants who were by now 'mangling' the English language . . . They had steady work, or their own 'ples' [place: job in a factory] . . . They felt 'something more.' The real Americans made no distinction. To them all of us were 'green' and 'ripe' Hunkies."[10]

Although they carried themselves high, the "old-timers" helped recent arrivals from the village or friends of friends to find houses to live in and a "ples" in the mill. The profits from this exchange were mutual. Those who provided the service were rewarded with power and prestige among their own; the recipients gained jobs, which, if they were better than others available to immigrants, they then tried to keep within their group.[11]

The "old-timers" also organized the immigrant societies: drew up lists of members, collected dues, chaired meetings. Once recognized as leaders, they were usually reelected to offices in consecutive years. The group social hierarchy, based on "seniority" enhanced by greater employment stability – relative, of course, to the day-laborer position of greenhorns – and by organization leadership to some degree perpetuated itself during the initial years of the immigrants' stay in Johnstown. With the passage of time, "seniority" alone without the supporting factor of economic standing lost importance as a status factor in the social stratification of East Central European communities.

Ethnic organizational membership and public participation. In each group, organizational networks developed in response to the needs of the immigrants as they settled in the new environment. Throughout the whole period under study, from the turn of the century until World War II, the officers of immigrant societies, church boards, and various cultural and national committees possessed significant prestige in the East Central European communities, holding leadership positions in the immigrant group and acting as its representatives on the outside.

Obviously not all among a total of 140 East Central European organizations that existed in Johnstown during the 1920s were equally prestigious in the eyes of the immigrants. The highest status was enjoyed by the branches of large national organizations: the Greek Catholic Union, the Croatian Fraternal Union, the Slovene National Benefit Society, the Polish National Alliance, the Polish Roman Catholic Union, the Serb National Federation, the Hungarian Verhovay, the Slovak Evangelical Union, the Russian Brotherhood, the Slovak Jednota, the Ukrainian National Association, and the umbrella clubs and organizations representing a federation of ethnic societies. Within these there also existed subtle differences in prestige. Intense status competition colored the organizational life of all East Central European communities in Johnstown from the first years of their existence. Not surprisingly, there was among my informants little agreement as to the prestige ranking of particular branches of the established national societies. Only three among the many branches of various ethnic organizations that existed in the 1920s and 1930s seem to have been widely regarded as being more prestigious or elitist than others. Two of them were already mentioned in Chapter 5 as "status societies": lodge No. 15 of the Hungarian Verhovay and the Slovak St. Francis Lodge of the Jednota in Morrellville. In addition, the Poles pointed to the old Polish National Alliance Lodge No. 832 in Minersville. Whereas the first two owed their prestige to their "professional" membership (immigrant businessmen, dealers in real estate, and since the 1930s, also a handful of second generation doctors and lawyers) the third owed it to an unusually active leadership and to established connections with the American political world outside.[12]

Prior to World War I, "seniority" and ethnic organizational leadership constituted two major status resources that reinforced each other, rewarding those who possessed them with a degree of power and influence in the immigrant communities. In the 1920s and 1930s, when wealth and occupational standing became the decisive factors in immigrant social stratification, economic position and leadership in more important ethnic organizations became closely related. In order to reach the top level of the immigrant status hierarchy, ethnic involvement and public participation were a necessary condition though, as we shall see shortly, not a sufficient one. "People who were officers of Jednota, who mingled, and went to [ethnic] conventions . . . they were looked up to . . . If you had business but did not come outside [kept to yourself], then you were not so respected": This opinion of a Slovak was repeated by representatives of virtually all other ethnic groups included in the study.[13] A person of acknowledged wealth who did not participate in the immigrant communal networks, did not attend social gatherings and national celebrations, and was not seen at public group meetings did not enjoy high status in the community. But, said a Hungarian, himself an influential member of the immigrant elite, "It almost never happened, as these things somehow went together."[14]

At the beginning of the century, when the churches and societies were just being formed, over 70 percent of the elected officers were laborers, most often old-timers with some knowledge of English and a steady *ples* in the mill.[15] With the passage of time, most of the more prestigious immigrant societies in the communities came under the direction of small merchants, real estate dealers, and saloon keepers. In the 1920s and 1930s, between 60 and 70 percent of the top officers of the major East Central European organizations in Johnstown were immigrant entrepreneurs – a proportion many times larger than their approximately 10-percent share in the total East Central European immigrant population in the city after World War I.[16] Even among the officers of the Slovene Socialist Lodge in Johnstown, active during the 1920s and 1930s, successful immigrant businessmen occupied 45 percent of the top positions and were unanimously granted a high leadership status.[17] In some groups, however, the leadership had remained in the hands of the workers. For instance, a small Ukrainian Orthodox community had only one entrepreneur in its midst; similarly, membership of the "officer corp" of the Slovak Evangelical Union and of the Polish National Alliance lodge in Moxham was almost exclusively working class, simply because there were no businessmen in these groups.[18]

Significantly, before the Second World War there were among the officers of ethnic societies in all immigrant communities no more than a handful of skilled workers – less than their approximately 10-percent share in the East Central European population by the mid-1920s. "Some skilled workers from here [immigrant communities] had changed their names," recalls an officer of one of the leading Croatian societies: "Without it, they had small chance at Bethlehem [Steel]."[19] It was probably between these two "status-lifting" factors – an elevated occupational position in the mill and public ethnic participation – that there was the greatest tension and, for most immigrants, the hard choice to make of giving up one for the other. Those among the minority of skilled mill workers who had been active in immigrant organizations were rewarded with high status for their elevated occupational position, good English, and ethnic leadership combined. About those who kept apart, explained a Slovene, "People would say, 'He's Slovenian, but it's a shame.'"[20]

The remaining 30 to 40 percent of the top officers of the major immigrant societies in the interwar period were laborers. As far as I was able to determine, however, most of them apparently possessed some distinguishing characteristics that elevated them to these positions – either education and refinement (i.e., as defined in the immigrants' terms), or high economic standing. Practically all of the more influential immigrant societies in Johnstown had among its leaders at least one "educated" person (education as a status factor in the immigrant stratification will be discussed separately). In the Polish and Hungarian communities – two groups that came from societies in Europe that possessed large and self-conscious, status-displaying noble classes – an assumed "nobility" of style and bearing played a role in gaining prestige. "He was just a mill worker," a Pole explained to me, pointing to one face in a group photograph of officers of the Polish Roman Catholic Union from the 1920s, "but he was more like a *szlachta* [gentry]; you can see this by looking at his face that he was smart."[21] The Hungarians made similar comments in discussing the positions and backgrounds of leaders in the local church and Verhovay. As many as 7 of them – two retail merchants and 5 mill workers, all of them of peasant background – were described as "typical Hungarian higher class."[22] Other laborers holding organizational positions in the immigrant communities between the wars tended to be more affluent and economically well established. Among the workers who were officers of more important immigrant societies at the end of the 1920s, over two-thirds were homeowners (the proportion for the whole East Central European population was about one-third).[23]

An interesting problem in the immigrant status hierarchy is the "lifting power" of leadership in women's organizations. A number of immigrants pointed to women who "often were powers behind their husbands in [ethnic] politics, pushing them [to compete for leadership]."[24] Their wives' participation in more prestigious women's societies additionally enhanced the family status. "This was a well-respected family: She [the wife] was very active in organizing different events around the church." Similar comments were more likely to come from Poles and Serbs and from immigrants from the secondary settlements, more ethnicized/"Americanized," rather than from people who lived in the primary foreign colonies (see the discussion of women's societies and residential group differentiation in Chapter 5). Frequently the officers of women's organizations were the wives or relatives of male ethnic leaders: Such, for instance, was the case with the Slovene Naše Sloga, the women's branch of the Slovenska Narodna Podporna Jednota, the women's Rusyn Lodge No. 116 of the Greek Catholic Union, the Russian Orthodox Lodge in East Conemaugh, or the cultural clubs in St. Francis Slovak parish in Morrellville that had women leaders. On the other hand, a good proportion of the top officer positions in the Kola Srbskih Sestara – the Serbian Sisterhood Circles – in both St. Nicholas and St. Petka parishes, as well as that of Kótko Polek – the Women's Circle of the Polish National Alliance – active in the 1920s and 1930s, were filled by women unrelated to the male leaders.[25]

An estimate of the total number of available top-status positions in East Central European organizations in Johnstown in the interwar period can only be tentative, since there was no consensus among the informants as to the prestige ranking of their societies. In all 8 East Central European ethnic groups, the post of pastor automatically placed its holder among the top ethnic leaders. In the 1920s there were 20 East Central European priests in Johnstown (3 mission churches shared pastors with the mother parishes). These posts, however, were not open for status competition from the community but were filled from outside. As for the ethnic organizations, I will count only the more prestigious, largest, and best-established ones, each with 3 top positions: president, vice-president, and secretary. This calculation yields a total of about 80 top organizational positions for all 8 East Central European groups in the city. Lesser positions on church boards and ethnic committees numbered approximately 200 (sports clubs, youth clubs, singing groups, dance groups, and strictly religious societies excluded).

Occupation. In the first years of the immigrants' stay in this country, when most of them were sojourners, jobs in the Cambria Company mills or in nearby coal mines were important to maximize savings to be taken back to the village and turned there into material possessions. As the immigrants settled permanently in Johnstown, occupational position gained importance as a factor in social stratification in their local communities. As the number of immigrants grew, the need for trade and services increased; by the mid-twenties there were in Johnstown proper and the surrounding areas approximately 250 East Central European business and service enterprises, a twenty-fold increase since the turn of the century. With technological progress in the steel industry, there appeared at Bethlehem Steel more jobs for operatives, comprising various semiskilled tasks. Even though most of the better-skilled jobs were taken by native-born Americans and western Europeans, some also became available to Slavic and Magyar workers.

Occupational status in the immigrant colonies in Johnstown carried meanings typical for small communities, or "urban villages." Rather than an outcome of combined educational and income levels – the definition prevailing in the large modern society – occupational position among East Central Europeans was measured in terms of

material rewards, personal (family) autonomy, and power: the ability to make others dependent upon one's professional services. As
it was crystallizing as a stratification factor, during the first decades
of this century, occupational status was related primarily to power.
With the passage of time, prestige became associated with wealth,
personal independence, and a more affluent, "American" life-style.
"The most important [person] here was so and so," explained Peter
K. in Cambria City, when asked to name the factors that made people important in the community. "All he had at first was a horse
and a buggy, but everybody needed him for hauling and moving,
since people then moved around a lot." Or from another account:
"A baker brought the merchandise to people [his status was therefore lower], while a butcher had people come to him, [so he enjoyed
higher prestige]."[26] Through the professional services they rendered, people in elevated occupational positions were able to exercise a significant degree of control over the individual and communal affairs of the immigrants. Persistence in the immigrant
communities of the peasant tradition of payment in kind for business
and professional services, exacerbated during the years of economic
depression, additionally strengthened this control. With money the
dominant form of exchange in the industrial society of which the
immigrants were already a permanent element and whose basic
rules they had by now internalized, payments in kind were, as we
saw earlier, used as a defensive tactic – a substitute for the "real
thing." Such payments were accepted by those who provided services when money was lacking, but they evoked in the donors a
sense of embarrassment and indebtedness. In the mills, elevated
occupational placement of an individual meant not only increased
material rewards and a more affluent life-style for his family but also
the ability to serve as a "shoulder" for others. Since the "careers"
of the immigrants at Bethlehem Steel depended on such particularist
devices, better jobs, especially if held more permanently, gave their
holders considerable influence among immigrant fellow workers.

  In order to reconstruct the occupational status ranking in the immigrant communities as it crystallized during the 1920s, I used a
procedure somewhat different from that applied by Theodore
Hershberg, Michael Katz, Stuart Blumin, et al., in their comparative
study of occupational hierarchy in five nineteenth-century American
cities.[27] First I compiled a list of the occupations which, as I previously learned from the interviews and from other sources (1925 city
directory and business guide), were actually performed by the
immigrants. The list numbered 48 positions.[28] Instead, how-

ever, of ranking the occupations myself, as did Hershberg and his colleagues, I asked 19 of my informants from Johnstown to do so. Since the ranking had to be projected far back into the past, one could not expect the respondents to scale the whole list of 49 positions. Instead I asked them what occupations were "at the top," and noted their answers. I then inquired about the next-to-the-top positions, and the next, and so on, each time noting the answers as they came spontaneously. In this way, four occupational classes emerged, with "big" entrepreneurs at the top; skilled workers second but "removed" from the ladder, as it were; smaller shopkeepers and store clerks third; and ordinary laborers at the bottom. I then inquired about the remaining occupational positions, asking my respondents to assign them to particular classes. In this process, a fifth intermediate status category appeared of workers above, common laborers, holding better, mechanized jobs in the mills.[29]

Table 7.1 is a list of occupations grouped in five status categories as ranked by the East Central Europeans themselves. Of the total of 48 occupations, they spontaneously listed 25. The placement of some occupations caused some hesitation: Store owners, grocers, and butchers were placed either in Class I – the top category – "if [they were] rich," or in Class III – the third highest – "if [their] business was small." Occupational status in the immigrant perceptions was closely related to economic standing and apparently construed in personalized terms as a reputational attribute, rather than as a formal attribute of position.[30] I eventually asigned "big" store owners, grocers, and butchers to the first category as "merchants" (the designation that the city directories used to denote businessmen of greater economic stature), and "ordinary" ones to the third. "Saloon keeper" was unanimously ranked as top in wealth and in power over the men but low in prestige, "particularly in the eyes of the women [wives]" – a jigsaw puzzle of male and female status rankings of occupations to be figured out by stratification sociologists. Hesitantly, I assigned this occupation to the top category.

Among the skilled occupations, the status of plasterers, paperhangers, and painters – the occupations of only a few in a steel town – seems to have been perceived by immigrants as lower than that of electricians or mechanics.

The third occupational class seems a mixed bag. The majority of my informants put "smaller" butchers, grocers, and store owners at the top; clerks and salesmen in the middle; and barbers, shoemakers and bartenders at the bottom. Had one wished to multiply occupational classes, this category could probably have been sub-

Table 7.1. *Status ranking of immigrant occupations*

I	II	III	IV	V
Priest*	Blacksmith*	Baker*	Brakeman	Laborer (mill)*
	Boiler maker*	Barber	Craneman	Coal miner (pick)*
Banker (immigrant)*	Carpenter*	Bartender	Conductor	
Merchant*	Electrician*	Butcher*	Driver	
Saloon keeper*	(Gang) foreman*	Clerk (store)	Fireman	
Undertaker*	Machinist*	Confectioner*	Hoistman	
	Mechanic*	Constable	Machine operator	
	Millwright*	Grocer*	Switchman	
	Molder*	Jeweler*	Watchman	
	Painter	Photographer		
	Paperhanger	Salesman		
	Plasterer	Shoemaker		
	Plumber*	Steamship agent		
	Rigger*	Storeowner*		
	Stonemason	Theater owner		
		Tailor*		
		Tobacconist		

Note: I is the highest category, *V* the lowest. Occupations within categories I–V are not ranked, but listed alphabetically. Asterisks mark the occupations that my respondents listed spontaneously.
Source: Interviews, 1925 city directory and business guide.

divided into three. I "forced" all of these occupations into one status group, following Hershberg and his colleagues' classification. There was also a problem with the constable. My informants kept placing this occupation separately, ranking it high in terms of power and connections, although below the top occupations. I put it in the third category.

Although grouped together with ordinary mill laborers, the pick coal miners had been perceived in the immigrant communities as lower in occupational status owing to the character of their work. About half of my informants did not know what to do with the "watchman": "Not too important"; "Did not count"; "Cleaner job"; "Better watchman than coal miner" – since this occupation clearly did not fit into other categories, it was placed in the fourth.

Their internal occupational ladder as it presented itself to the East Central Europeans in Johnstown during the interwar period, looked, then, somewhat as follows:

Class I   "Big" businesses and services in ethnic neighborhoods
Class II   Skilled occupations in the mills and elsewhere
Class III Small businesses and services in ethnic neighborhoods
Class IV   Better jobs in the mills (cleaner, lighter, mechanized)
Class V   Common mill labor and coal mining

Probably the most peculiar feature of the immigrant social stratification system was the "bulging out" of the skilled category (Class II) toward the larger American society. As we have seen earlier, the skilled workers tended to avoid participation in ethnic organizational activities, an important dimension of immigrant social stratification. A handful of electricians, carpenters, or mechanics who were found to be in the immigrant generation were awarded status for skills, income, and the "American" prestige that went with their occupations. But those who deliberately avoided associating with their ethnic group and its communal life, who kept to themselves and visibly aspired to the "higher" American world, parroting its airs and behavior, were set apart from the immigrant community. When asked to rank the skilled occupations in the 1920s and 1930s, my informants, thinking apparently about the concrete persons who held them, were often at a loss: "[They] just did not fit into our scale, as [they] kept away from our crowd," or "[They] were somewhere in between, neither here nor there." In an interesting discussion of occupational prestige in the present-day black American subculture, Paul Siegel reported a "theoretically awkward" phenomenon of blacks allocating occupational status according to the

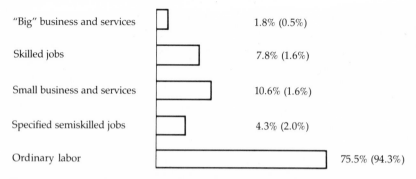

Figure 2. Occupational distribution of male immigrants, 1925. *Note:* Data based on the occupational distribution of immigrant male persisters in Johnstown since 1900; figures in parentheses are for the foreign-born East Central European men as recorded in the 1900 census.

pattern prevailing in the white dominant society and not as based on their own location and experience in this system.[31] Half a century ago, East Central Europeans in Johnstown created in their communities their own system of social stratification that they used to allocate status. But the "bulging out" of the skilled category in their social ranking indicates that they were conscious of the external, dominant occupational hierarchy and that in their evaluations they applied a double measure of sorts.

Before presenting the distribution of immigrants on their five-step occupational ladder, it should be reemphasized that although the ladder was structurable into segments, it was rickety, particularly in the middle, where the immigrants moved back and forth by little steps quite close to each other as they shifted between jobs that were basically similar yet different enough in pay and conditions to give them a sense of motion.[32] The occupational movements of the immigrants will be presented in more detail later in this chapter. In static representation, their occupational distribution by the mid-1920s was as shown in Figure 2.[33]

Unfortunately, by 1925 the numbers of particular nationality group members among the persisters from 1900 – the population that served as the basis for my tabulations – were already too small for meaningful statistical comparisons. A few general comments seem warranted, however. First, a relatively small but closely knit group of Hungarians had maintained its connections with the German community in town. An album commemorating the twenty-fifth anniversary of St. Emerich's Hungarian Catholic Church, published in 1930, carried several announcements by businessmen with distinctly German names. (I found no similar advertisements in other groups' jubilee albums, although contacts with Germans, particularly of a religious nature, were also maintained by a small community of Slovak Lutherans in the city.)[34] Having maintained their contacts with the German mill workers higher up in the Bethlehem Company's pecking order, the Hungarians appear to have had a larger proportion of skilled laborers than had the Slavic groups, especially in the machine and carpentry shops, where they "pulled in others" (Hungarians).[35] Second, unique to this group was a particular sociocultural trait, a transplant from old-country relationships. Unlike all other East Central European groups, the Hungarians counted as "theirs" the Jewish Hungarian businessmen and professionals: dentists, druggists, and physicians in Cambria City, whom they placed within their occupational ladder, side by side with the Hungarian Christians. The Hungarian Jews in Johnstown not only served the Christian community but also took an active part in Hungarian cultural and national celebrations and even in church events. In no other East Central European group in the city – although they all dealt regularly with Jewish businessmen and sought their professional services – did social and cultural relations reach such a degree of closeness.[36]

A third observation also concerns the continuation of old-country patterns in the immigrant communities in America. Polish and Ukrainian immigrants from southern Galicia, as well as Rusyns and Slovaks from the other side of the Carpathians, often shared common pioneers in Johnstown. This territorial and cultural affinity was also reflected in the "content" of these groups' occupational hierarchies, in that they occasionally claimed the same top entrepreneurs as "theirs." In the case of the Ukrainians, it was not done without resentment toward the Poles, whom they perceived as "uppity snobs" – a carryover from the European dominant–subordinate relationship between the two groups. The Rusyn-Slovak claims were emotionally neutral. When one and the same merchant was claimed by both groups, it was explained that "He was a Slovak Rusyn," or "It was a Rusnak family from Slovakia."

Economic standing (wealth). Initially insignificant as a status dimension, since the immigrants settling in Johnstown around 1900 were all equally poor, in the differentiated East Central European communities that had developed by the 1920s, it was ultimately economic position that stood out as the basis of status and power.

As it crystallized during the 1920s, this status dimension was most closely related to occupational position, and then, at the upper echelons of the immigrant social stratification, to ethnic leadership and "American connections." Wealth, defined by immigrant standards, brought rewards in terms of elevated life-style and family autonomy and, through rendering of services and organizational leadership, also control over the affairs of the immigrant community as well as its individual members.

The economic rank of a family was not measured solely by income defined in terms of a given amount of money received annually. Rather it reflected a combination or "weighted average" of various possessions, financial as well as material, displayed in public and partly "invested" in the community and evaluated by it. Although "it could not be proved how much money they [wealthy immigrants] had, as they kept a tight lip about it, we all knew [that they were rich] because they lived high – wine, dine, and all."[37]

Defining economic standing in the immigrant community, my informants included "the showmanship – the front you put on for others" as an important element of status.[38] Walter W. described the external signs of elevated economic standing that projected and generated prestige in the Polish community. They included all, or at least some, combinations of the following: property ownership; nice, "advanced" furniture (that is, more modern and "American" than that possessed by most immigrant households); a telephone ("It was a big thing, then, people had to come to you and ask please to let them use it"); dress ("a golden watch, a vest, a hat"; "Children of the 'big shots' were better dressed and had more toys"); an automobile ("Only the rich ones had it; they would loan a car to people for a wedding or a funeral"); food ("They ate much better"); the style of family celebrations ("They threw big weddings and baptisms"); generosity toward others ("with alcohol and cigars in bars and [on] other occasions"); and community patronage (donations, sponsorship).[39]

The last two elements were very important. Spending some wealth on others – whether on individuals or on the community as a whole – resulted not only in social rewards such as prestige but also in influence over people. As we have noted earlier, the ability to give donations to the church was particularly rewarding for immigrant status seekers. In 1914, a small Slovak Lutheran congregation purchased a property on which to erect its church. Four immigrants – Andrew Liptak, John Kocis, John Baran, and John Hliboky – all of them mill workers, donated toward this end over $200 each, for which they were honored with elaborate memorial plaques fastened to the church pews. In 1920, six parishioners of St. Mary's Greek Catholic Church – Joan Francuz, Helena Jartim, Michael Mikula, John Staruch, Paul Chubar, and John Chema – donated $1,000 each "na novu cerkov" (for the new church), and their names were known all over the foreign colony and repeatedly published in *Chranitel*, the local Rusyn newspaper. Six other parishioners donated over $500 each and had their names read from the pulpit during High Mass.[40]

Whereas family wealth and ethnic patronage both constituted elements of status in the East Central European communities, for most immigrants the effort to realize the two at the same time involved an unwelcome tension. Anthony C., a member of an old and influential family in Cambria City, explained: "To be involved in the [ethnic] community and to increase your [material] fortune worked often against each other. If one went outside, took part, treated others, and so on, it helped popularity but took away money. If you sat at home, [saved money], and did not participate, there was no [high] respect."[41]

In Chapter 6, which described the realization by the immigrant working-class families of what they defined as a "good life," I presented data on the distribution of their collective annual incomes and on homeownership. We will now complement this information by adding data on the economic position of the immigrant minority – the entrepreneurs – and then present an estimate of the content and size of particular economic strata for all of the East Central European communities in Johnstown in the late 1920s.

It is admittedly difficult to estimate the incomes of the entrepreneurs: store owners and business people in the ethnic communities. By the late 1920s, they constituted about 10 to 12 percent of the employed Slavic and Magyar foreign-born male population in Johnstown. The revenues of this group ranged quite widely, depending on the size and prosperity of the enterprises, both subject to annual fluctuations. To get some estimate of their incomes, I looked at the amount of mercantile taxes paid in the interwar period by Slavic and Magyar businessmen in Johnstown and inspected records of thirty bankruptcy cases filed by them in that same period. With good – that is, more or less regular business – and few delinquent or uncollectible debts owed to the merchant on open accounts, a small bakery or a general store in the foreign colony could bring, on the average, a "spendable" income of $1,500 to $2,500 annually, after one has subtracted overhead expenses (store rent and utilities, taxes and insurance, wages for employees) and the capital needed to purchase merchandise. A larger grocery or a butcher store brought between $2,500 and $5,000 in net revenues, depending on the steadiness of work at Bethlehem's mills and coal mines. The income of the most successful immigrant retail merchants, established tavern keepers, "big" butchers, and undertakers was higher.[42]

A more systematic measure of economic standing of immigrant businessmen is provided by Dun & Bradstreet's credit ratings. Although they do not give information about the actual income of the firms, we can assume that it was generally proportional to the size of the enterprise. Inspection of Dun & Bradstreet's records for a total of 217 Slavic and Magyar enterprises in the city that were rated between 1925 and 1929 reveals that the majority (60 percent) were small businesses with an average "pecuniary strength" – that is, (current) surplus of assets over liabilities – estimated at less than $2,000. One-fourth (25 percent) were valued at $2,000 to $5,000, and the remainder (15 percent) at over $5,000.[43]

On the basis of all the above data, and from the information gathered from interviews and from comparing data given in the city business guides with tax and real estate records, we can make the following estimate of the approximate size and content of particular economic strata in the immigrant communities in Johnstown before the Depression. At the very top of the immigrant economic hierarchy there was a total of no more than 60 to 70 families that by immigrant standards were considered rich: approximately 30 to 40 of them were headed by entrepreneurs with estimated annual incomes of about, or over, $5,000; the rest were mill workers, multiple homeowners. With an undiminished need for housing in the immigrant colonies, dealing in real estate was a good business that brought considerable profit. As a separate occupation, it did not appear in the immigrant communities until the mid- or late 1930s: Before that time, real estate operations were conducted by immigrants "on the side." For instance, Mihal M., a mill worker, during the twenty years after 1897, accumulated seven houses in one of the immigrant sections of town, for which he paid a total sum of $15,750. Of those, he had sold four by 1933 for the same sum of $15,750, and he rented the remainder to his countrymen. Andy M., a store owner, between 1907 and 1923 purchased eight houses for a total sum of $17,727, renting them all to immigrant families. Mike P., first a saloon keeper, then an ordinary mill worker, during the seventeen years from 1909 to 1926 bought six houses for a total sum of $9,225, later selling two of them for $5,400, keeping two for himself (one apparently to be rented), and transferring two to his children.[44]

Together, the families of the richest immigrant businessmen, some of whom also dealt in real estate, and those of multiple property owners constituted approximately 2 percent of the total number of foreign-born East Central European households in Johnstown in the mid-1920s. The class below this consisted of property-owning immigrant families with annual incomes of over $2,000. This group was composed of households of better-off shopkeepers and owners of prosperous service establishments, of families of skilled workers established in their jobs, and of a number of households of ordinary laborers, particularly those of homeowners in the secondary immigrant settlements, where several members contributed to the collective family income. I calculate that this group constituted approximately 20 percent of the total number of foreign-born East Central European families in the city.[45]

The next class below consisted of immigrant homeowning families with annual incomes of between $1,000 and $2,000. At the bottom were renting families with annual incomes around the "survival" level – that is, below $1,000, families wholly unable to meet the requirements of "showmanship" that indicated elevated economic standing in the immigrant community. In Chapter 6 I estimated that about 40 percent of the total number of East Central European immigrant households in the mid-1920s struggled with such a situation. This group was composed for the most part of families of unskilled laborers with only one breadwinner and of female-headed households; most immigrants in this category resided in the primary foreign colonies.

Education. In Chapter 1 we saw what kind of education was appreciated by the peasants and what types of "learned men" were respected in the village. The immigrants' life in America, with its unceasing economic insecurity and physical exhaustion, had not fortified in them a striving for formal education. The semicaste sociocultural system in Johnstown additionally inhibited development among the immigrants of a widespread concern with schooling. Their place, the immigrants knew as well as did the "Americans," was at the open-hearth and blast furnaces and in the coal mines, not in the offices. Even if they had possessed some formal schooling, in all likelihood they would have worked in the mill. There were, in fact, in the "foreign colonies" a few educated immigrants who had completed seven or eight grades in Europe and who worked as laborers at Bethlehem Steel.

This situation perpetuated in the immigrant culture elements of the old peasant approach to learning. And so the education that they did value and respect was conceived of as a combination of simple literacy – most often self-taught in the old country or acquired through night school in Johnstown – and wisdom gained from experience, a knowledgeability about the "things of this world" that could be put to use in advising neighbors on the important matters of life. "My father was an educated man," said Anna C., a Johnstown-born Pole. "He could read and write. He was a cook in service [in Poland], and he traveled everywhere with the house[hold]."[46]

This conception of education contained an additional element: the assumed "gentry" airs and bearing, most clearly detectable among the Poles and Hungarians – peasant-immigrants from countries with deeply entrenched native aristocratic cultures. The "cultured" people in their communities were those who carried themselves in what the immigrants remembered as the style of the old-country gentry. Such bearing, however, if not supported by what most immigrants considered education – literacy, and some knowledge of history, geography, and politics – was scorned and ridiculed by community members. Those, on the other hand, who combined all of these virtues, were looked upon with respect.

This brings us to three other components of the immigrants' notion of education that gradually emerged as their communities were "ethnicized" after World War I. First, as the immigrants became increasingly aware of their collective identities – linguistic, cultural, and historical – they came to bestow social prestige on people who were versed in their ethnic groups' national past and heroes. Another component of education as seen by the immigrants was a command of English, a factor of increasing importance since they had made Johnstown their permanent home. Good English facilitated better occupational placement in the mills; those holding offices in ethnic organizations also needed it for contacts with the outside American world.

A third component in the immigrants perception of learning was the gradually emerging approval of formal schooling for children, seen as a vehicle for some social and economic elevation. This incipient attitude, however, was hesitant and half-hearted. Even though slightly expanded, the opportunities for advancement in Johnstown for the second generation had remained severely limited by class and ethnic ascription, and most immigrant parents were aware of this situation. The fulfillment of the primary, and realizable, goal of the immigrant families – to accumulate the maximum possible amount of financial and material resources – required, as we have seen, a combined effort of all employable members. Keeping children at school for a prolonged period of time not only did not bring visible rewards in terms of economic success; in fact, it significantly decreased, if not annihilated, the family's choice to accomplish this dominant purpose.[47] Yet after the First World War a new attitude toward formal education for children began to appear among the immigrants. It first developed in the local immigrant elite among small merchants and ethnic organizational leaders. It was then gradually accepted among the more affluent working-class families, particularly those in the "better," secondary ethnic colonies. During the decade following World War I, a total of 143 American-born Slavs and Magyars graduated from (two) Johnstown high schools: 40 percent of them were children of immigrant businessmen, 20 percent of better-skilled workers, and 40 percent of ordinary laborers.[48] Since the late 1920s, the number of immigrant families sending their children through high school had been steadily increasing. The parents of those very few who went to college and acquired professions were rewarded with significant prestige only after the offspring had settled in Johnstown to serve the immigrant communities. On the whole, however, the attitude of parental commitment to formal schooling for children did not become prevalent among the East Central Europeans until after World War II, when they had achieved relative economic security.

As understood by the immigrants, education served in the ethnic communities as a weak status "lifter," independent of economic standing. "It was just a different kind of respect [enjoyed by the learned men]," explained a Hungarian, describing social stratification in her community.[49] The cultured and learned individuals were rewarded with leadership positions in the group organizational structures. By the 1920s each ethnic group had on the boards of its more influential societies one or two such individuals. "He was just a coal miner, but he was educated," or "He had a better job in the mill and spoke English pretty well": Such men sat on the ethnic committees together with the well-off immigrant entrepreneurs. Together with the pastors of the ethnic parishes, who as such enjoyed the status of educated men, the total number of learned immigrants in all of the Slavic and Magyar communities before World War II probably did not exceed, at maximum, 30 to 40. The influence of educated (lay) immigrants was limited and "situational": It became visible at organizational meetings and on festive occasions, at ethnic banquets and celebrations, or at the occasional conferring with "Americans" about communal matters. In everyday life, however, it remained largely inactive.

American political connections. As we have seen in Chapter 5, the number of East Central Europeans who held elected public offices in Johnstown during the interwar period was minimal. However, as the immigrant communities became a permanent element of the life of the city and as ethnic organizational leadership crystallized in them, the links to the local political establishment grew more solid and numerous. For their part, Johnstown politicians and ward party bosses "penetrated" ethnic organizational networks, seeking the cooperation of the immigrant elite to mobilize political support and socialize the civil loyalty of immigrant populations. Ethnic leaders were called upon during and after World War I to participate in the "Americanization campaign" by conducting English and citizenship classes in the foreign colonies and were instrumental in organizing ethnic "Citizens' Clubs" that sprang up in the immigrant sections in the 1920s. They also collaborated with the "Americans" in election campaigns to mobilize local votes. During its short-lived existence, the Slavonic League of Cambria County, an elitist business and professional organization, sponsored occasional lunches and dinner receptions in downtown Johnstown hotels. Attended by local American politicians, such functions created additional informal linkages between the top stratum in the immigrant communities and the local political establishment.[50]

For ethnic leaders, connections with the representatives of the city's power structure served to enhance their own position within the foreign colonies. When individual and communal matters arose that had to be taken before the municipal or borough governments, ethnic leaders could mobilize their "American connections," acting as spokesmen for their respective groups.

In the immigrant colonies, the "American connections" were to an extent valued for their very "Americanness." But unless those who possessed them used their connections to facilitate services to the community and its particular members, their mere association with the "Americans" would not have lifted their status position to the upper echelons of the immigrant stratification system. In fact, the opposite was true: Assuming "American" airs and ostentatiously maintaining "American" contacts at higher social levels without simultaneous ethnic participation and sponsorship usually annoyed immigrant public opinion, evoking an attitude of rejection and distance.[51]

As a status factor in the immigrant stratification system, the "American connections" were a derivative of a combination of economic standing, occupational position, and ethnic organizational leadership. Together with these, they generated a significant degree of control over communal affairs as well as over the potential service seekers among individual members of immigrant communities. The number of immigrants who during the 1920s and 1930s had either themselves held local political office as aldermen, justices of the peace, or members of borough councils or else possessed well-established connections with local politicians did not exceed 25 to 30 (not counting the priests).

"Moral virtue" (character). Last but not least, certain moral virtues or character traits constituted an element in the overall reputation of immigrants and their families within their communities. To enjoy a good reputation, a family had to conform to a few agreed-upon images: Both the man (husband, father) and the woman (wife, mother) should be hard workers, each in his or her prescribed domain. A lazy person had low status. The woman, in addition, should be thrifty; the man should not be a drunkard or a gambler. Willingness to work, thriftiness, and self-restraint were valued in the peasant-immigrant working-class culture as virtues in themselves and were prized as such. At the same time, they were seen as practical and instrumental values. Describing the ways in which one had gained and lost status in the immigrant communities before World War II, my informants pointed to such flaws of character as laziness ("He was not a hard worker, bummed from job to job"); extravagance ("She spent money on clothing, wasn't thrifty at home"); and self-indulgence ("Everyone drank a little, but he just never stopped") as the causes of many a family's continuing poverty or skidding on the ethnic socioeconomic ladder.[52]

These basic "reputational requirements" applied to all members of the immigrant communities and served for upward and downward adjustments of their overall status in the group social hierarchy. The positions at the top of the ladder carried with them a set of additional moral obligations of a social nature: charity, compassion, readiness to provide assistance, public identification with one's group and its people. Recreating the social stratification of the immigrant communities as it existed before World War II, my informants mentioned these factors as the qualities that were needed to elevate a well-off store owner, a prosperous undertaker, a real estate dealer, or an officer of an ethnic society to a position of acknowledged prestige and respect in the group. The status of those who did not meet such group expectations was still acknowledged by the rank and file but not without qualifications and resentment. For instance, an affluent leader of a Rusyn community, with well-established contacts in the local political establishment, who during the Depression bought out the houses of those unable to meet payments on their property, was at the same time recognized as a leader and sought after for his services, and strongly condemned for his greedy behavior. Similar condemnation of the selfishness displayed in hard times by some of the acknowledged "big fish" came from the Croatian community.[53] The existence of social obligations tied to high-status positions in the immigrant colonies was more readily acknowledged by the rank-and-file members than by the elite. Not surprisingly, the former much more often also perceived a discrepancy between group norms and reality.

This completes our review of the basic status components of internal stratification system in the immigrant communities. We will now use all this information to estimate the size of particular strata. The task is relatively easy in the case of the upper immigrant stratum. When the basic status components – economic standing, occupation, ethnic leadership, and "American connections" – are considered, in none of the eight ethnic groups did the proportion of upper-rank families in the total immigrant population in Johnstown between the two wars exceed 2 to 3 percent. The most successful entrepreneurs and ethnic leaders, the priest, occasionally also the local artist, perhaps a musician who conducted the church choir and weekend orchestra brilliantly; or the "scholar" versed in an ethnic group's national past who enjoyed a well-earned fame for his patriotic speeches delivered at banquets and celebrations – those were the members of the immigrant elite. This group was also clearly defined in the perceptions of the immigrants themselves. My informants were virtually unanimous in enumerating the members of the upper stratum in their communities.

It is admittedly much more difficult to draw the contours of the middle stratum, which was fluctuating and diversified in nature. In the case of the upper stratum, and, for that matter, of the lower one as well, the defining criteria overlapped, thus forming one virtually homogeneous group of people. In contrast, the intermediate stratum

Plate 20. Immigrant stores in East Conemaugh, 1920s. Collection of Walter Wegrzyn.

"*Starý musí,
Mladý môže*"

.... hovorí naše príslovie.

Keď v rodine vašej potre-
bovať budete *pohräbníka*

zavolajte

JÁN
MOSKAL

413
BROAD ST.

Telefon **691**

Automobily na krstiny
a veselia.

Jubilejný

Program

Dietok

Osadnej

Školy

Sv. Štefana Kr.

DŇA

15. apríla, 1934

o 8. hod. večer.

8

Plate 21. Immigrant business advertisement, St. Stephen's Slovak Catholic Church *Jubilee Album*, 1934.

Plate 22. Immigrant homes, Morrellville, interwar period.

Plate 23. Second generation, Morrellville, 1930s. Collection of Michael Tumbas.

was filled with families with nonuniform characteristics. Nor did consensus exist among the immigrants themselves as to the "content" of the middle stratum. My informants variously pointed to lesser businessmen and owners of service establishments in the foreign colonies who "had more than the rest" but could not stand comparison with the "truly successful"; to those who had secured for themselves better jobs in the mills; to homeowners who had "bettered themselves on the scale" and moved into the more desirable sections of town; or else to officers of ethnic societies who were "just coal miners" but enjoyed a higher prestige in the community because of their devotion and social activism.

Estimates of the size of the immigrant middle stratum will, then, differ depending upon the scope of the definition. If we include in this group only the families of lesser entrepreneurs, of more affluent workers who held good jobs in the mills, and of ordinary laborers with top positions in ethnic societies, the approximate size of the intermediate stratum did not exceed 20-odd percent. If, however, the middle group also contains the homeowning families of ordinary laborers – a group that by immigrant standards was considered successful – and all of those active in ethnic societies in lesser posts, the proportion increases to between 33 and 40 percent by the end of the 1920s.

Finally, by any reckoning the lower stratum comprised the majority of immigrants in the city – 60 to 75 percent – consisting of families of ordinary, "unconnected" rank-and-file mill workers and coal miners who struggled to support their families and tried to put away some money for the purchase of a home. The shape of the overall immigrant stratification system in the interwar period is shown in Figure 3.

Beyond the question of size, social stratification in a large, complex society as well as in its subsegments involves problems of stability – that is, the persistence in particular strata of the same individuals (families) over an extended period of time – and of openness – that is, movement into and out of the strata. In an expanding structure, the upper and middle strata may be increasing in size by taking in people from lower echelons of the stratification system (openness), while at the same time retaining their earlier members (persistence). Or, they may retain their established members without providing wider channels for interstratum mobility.

During the period following World War I, as the status dimensions crystallized in East Central European communities, three simultaneous processes, noted already in earlier chapters, were affecting immigrant social stratification. First, the avenues of material and occupational achievement available to the immigrants, although restricted by class and ethnic ascription, had nevertheless expanded somewhat, with property ownership as well as the chances for occupational elevation to desirable business and "better," more mechanized positions in the mills increased over the earlier period. Also, with the expansion of ethnic organizational networks, the number of offices available increased. These developments led to further social differentiation of the immigrant communities that had begun before World War I. In addition, during the second phase of their stay in Johnstown the immigrants' chances of maintaining their elevated socioeconomic positions had also improved, especially for those more firmly established in the foreign colonies. At the same time, the ethnic officers who had proved themselves active and effective leaders had become more firmly established in their organizational positions. These processes had led to the crystallization of the upper stratum and to the increasing "retention" of its mem-

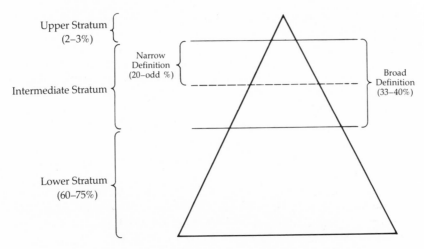

Figure 3. Overall stratification of status in immigrant communities.

bership. However, its size had remained stable, its growth restricted by the stagnant economy of the city, the ethnic-ascriptive promotion policies of the Bethlehem Company, and despite all growth, the limited number of leadership positions in ethnic organizations. Third, although the opportunities for status elevation in the immigrant colonies had increased, the expanding intermediate stratum was characterized by a high degree of fluidity. In comparison with the upper stratum, the intermediate one was easier to enter, but the positions in it were much more insecure, reflecting the precariousness of the existence of most immigrant families whose economic welfare directly depended on the regularity of production in the local mills and coal mines.

A complete interpretation of the immigrants' mobility up and down their internal stratification ladder would require a combined accounting for all status dimensions. The data available are insufficient for such analysis. Chapter 6 presented information on the acquisition and losses of homes in the interwar period, as well as on the occupational shifting and the unstable financial condition of most of the working-class families. I have, however, no systematic data about immigrants' savings and accumulated material possessions, which, together with property and income, accounted for a family's overall economic standing. The following discussion of the immigrants' status mobility is therefore necessarily limited to only two components of their stratification system: ethnic leadership, and occupation.

The total number of available top and lesser positions in the more influential ethnic organizations during the 1920s and 1930s hovered, as we have seen, around 300. My checking of lists of officers for a sample of 14 local branches of the better-established ethnic associations and church committees for the period from 1920 to 1940 revealed that the leadership positions circulated among a limited number of people – about 20 per organization – who alternately took different offices. In addition, the same top immigrant activists often simultaneously held office in different organizational boards and committees in their groups. For instance, in the Slovak Lutheran group, we find on the board of St. John's Church between 1920 and 1940 a total of only 17 names. Meanwhile, of the 6 top officers of Lodge No. 239 of the Slovak Evangelical Union in Johnstown in that same period, 5 were members of the parish committee. Four other immigrants from the parochial board held high offices in the competing Lodge No. 197.[54]

We may conclude that the total number of persons who held office in the immigrant organizations of higher status was probably also no greater than about 300 – the number of posts available. The immigrant leadership group was not closed, but it was stable. Advancement within the ethnic organizational ranks was possible if one was willing to work hard at gaining and keeping popularity in the immigrant community; in the records of the societies that I checked, new names appeared regularly alongside the old established ones. But in all groups, the "personnel core" of ethnic leadership remained virtually unchanged during the whole interwar period.

As for occupational mobility, we saw earlier that in terms of occupational characteristics the immigrants had in the interwar period continued to "lag behind" the occupational distribution of the employed male population of Johnstown as a whole, and that most of the time their efforts at occupational achievement involved horizontal or only slightly upwardly inclined maneuvers within the category of ordinary labor: between unskilled and various unspecified semiskilled jobs. Still, between 1915 and 1930, as many as 45 percent of the male immigrants who were already present in town at the beginning of the century had been recorded as holding occupational positions above this level at least once at my four checkpoints in 1915, 1920, 1925, and 1930. In the first phase of their residence in the city, the difference in the frequency of occupational elevations between the immigrant persisters and the returnees was quite pronounced. It had disappeared in the second phase. Among all present in Johnstown between 1915 and 1930, persisters constituted 73 percent and returnees 23 percent; their proportions among the occupational "achievers" were similar: 76 and 24 percent, respectively (see Table A.13 in the Appendix).

Quite frequently these elevations were one-time accomplishments accounting for 40 percent of the total, and about one-third of them were more "solid" – that is, recorded at three or four of my checkpoints.[55] It seems to have been easier for a man to maintain his position in ethnic business and services, where 40 percent of all occupational achievements in this category were "solid" ones, than in the skilled mill occupations, where the respective proportion was 30 percent. Shifts from the lowest-level manual labor in Bethlehem Company mills and coal mines to immigrant businesses and services constituted the most frequent type of immigrant occupational movement in the interwar period, accounting for 50 percent of the total number, whereas movements to the skilled positions totalled 25 percent.

Among the total number of occupational moves recorded between 1915 and 1930, *ascents* – cases of better jobs acquired after 1915 and kept by 1930 – constituted 53 percent and *descents* – drops by 1930 to the lower occupational levels – 47 percent. The ratios of upward to downward mobility did not differ significantly in shifts between particular occupational categories. Among all transfers between the lowest-level manual jobs and skilled positions, the ascents constituted 45 percent and the descents 48 percent (the remaining 7 percent were those who shifted to specified semiskilled and business positions). For moves between the lowest-level manual jobs and business service occupations, the proportion of ascents was 57 percent and of descents 43 percent.

Since employment in business and services in the immigrant communities, if successful, offered the best chance of moving to the upper immigrant stratum, let us look somewhat more closely into the mobility patterns of this group in the interwar period. They indicate, on the one hand, a great amount of continuous motion into and out of the small-business stratum and, on the other, the persistence in it of a small group of established, secure entrepreneurs.

To trace these processes, I conducted two analyses. First, in order to estimate the growth or decline in the volume of business conducted by immigrant entrepreneurs who stayed on in this profession between 1915 and 1930, I used Dun & Bradstreet's evaluations of the "pecuniary strength" of their businesses. Second, in order to assess the rate of movement into and out of this group, I traced all entrepreneurs with recognizably Slavic and Magyar names through the city business directories at six checkpoints: 1915, 1920, 1925, 1929, and (during the Depression) 1933 and 1937 (the latter is the only volume between 1933 and 1940 that was saved from the floods).

Dun & Bradstreet's credit records provide full information for 106 East Central European entrepreneurs in Johnstown who maintained their businesses between 1915 and 1930. Of this number, the credit ratings of slightly over 35 percent remained unchanged, with the "pecuniary strength" of the great majority of businesses valued within the $1,000 to $2,000 bracket. Another 40 percent had improved their financial standing, with two-thirds moving into the category of $2,000 to $5,000; and the remainder placed in the over $5,000 bracket. Finally, the businesses of about 25 percent of the immigrant entrepreneurs either declined in volume or alternately decreased and expanded.[56]

As for business turnover, from Johnstown business directories I compiled a list of 583 Slavic and Magyar names of entrepreneurs who operated in town between 1915 and 1937. The average gross rate of business turnover – the disappearance of names from the business directories from one checkpoint to the next – in the period from 1915 through 1929 was 43 percent.[57] The decade 1915 to 1925 witnessed the most intense immigrant movement into small business: Almost 70 percent of the Slavic and Magyar names appearing at each subsequent checkpoint were new entries.

By the mid-1920s, there were approximately 250 East Central European enterprises of various kinds in Greater Johnstown. This was apparently too many for the consumer capacity of the immigrant communities in the city, and so in the second half of the decade the immigrant entrepreneurial population had stabilized somewhat, with 35 percent new entries among all those listed in the 1929 business directory. Between 1929 and 1937, the total number of East Central European entrepreneurs in the city decreased by 20 percent, with over one-third of the names of Slavic and Magyar entrepreneurs listed in the 1929 business directory having disappeared by 1937.[58]

Was it possible to move from the internal social ladder of the immigrant community into the stratification system of the outside American society? Did connective links exist between the middle and upper strata in the East Central European communities and the upper-lower and lower-middle ranks in the larger dominant system? Could a person who moved to the middle or to the top of the immigrant status hierarchy "slide" onto the outside American ladder and continue the upward movement? By and large, the answers are negative. The metaphor of a tree and tree climbing used by Norbert Wiley to describe the multiplicity of stratification systems in ethnically pluralist societies applies well to the situation in Johnstown before World War II. The immigrant and dominant systems in the city can be pictured as a tree, the former as one of its limbs, the latter as its trunk: "The limbs," writes Wiley, "are like strata, leading gently upward but primarily outward and away from [the trunk and] all chance of serious ascent."[59] In such a situation, Wiley maintains, mobility is both possible and impossible. Climbing up the side, or "ethnic," branch of the tree precludes movement in the dominant dimension, which is along the trunk up to the top of the tree.

One way for the Johnstown East Central Europeans to get to the trunk of the stratification tree was through the skilled occupations, if one "hopped" from the ethnic limb by cutting most ties with the immigrant community. There were some East Central Europeans who did just that (their case was discussed earlier in this chapter), but their number was small.

There were also among the Slavs and Magyars in Johnstown before World War II a few (from the second generation) who succeeded in entering the dominant white-collar world of business and finance. But in the opinion of the "successful" themselves, despite the displayed attitude of the appropriate "deference, service, and acquiescence, [which was] the only way to act for a foreigner [toward the downtown business establishment]," they still had not been accepted "on the equal basis."[60] To the "Americans," native-born and Western European alike, the "foreigners" – Slavs and Magyans – collectively occupied the lowest echelons of the local societal structure. Their leaders and representatives, however affluent, educated, and influential in terms of immigrant values, had been just that and no more: *representatives* of the "foreign colony," individuals who had to be dealt with, who deserved an occasional mention in the local paper, but who did not really belong to the same social and cultural world.

In ascription-based, ethnic-divisive Johnstown society, East Central Europeans realized their status achievement within the ethnic subsegments by moving up on the ladders of the internal stratification systems that they created in their communities and that reflected their cultural values. The transmission belt between the immigrant and the dominant American stratification structures did not start operating in Johnstown on a larger scale until the 1940s, and even then haltingly and not without resistance.

And finally: How did the immigrants evaluate their own stratification ladder and chances of economic success and status improvement within their own communities? How did the social structure of the immigrant communities affect the social consciousness of their members? Did they find it open and "just"? Did a higher or lower status position in the immigrant hierarchy affect their perceptions and attitudes? And, finally, what were the immigrants' feelings about the dominant American system in Johnstown?

The East Central Europeans tended to perceive their own stratification system as it had crystallized during the 1920s as continuous in its lower and middle parts and then as increasingly discontinuous, with the top connected to the base by few and narrow passages. Their evaluations of the chances of advancement within the immigrant social hierarchy were generally accurate – that is, they corresponded to the actual opportunity structure as it existed in the immigrant communities.

To those placed in the late 1920s at the lower levels of their group stratification, the positions at the top of the ladder appeared rather remote. As they saw it, a chance for "ordinary people" to move to the uppermost immigrant stratum was, in the interwar period, severely limited. Unless one was blessed with a sudden stroke of unusual fortune, "It was possible, but highly unlikely." Their evaluation of the situation was quite correct, for by that time the elite in immigrant communities had indeed become rather closed, and the opportunities for many more additional businesses (or, for that matter, for skilled careers in the mill) were limited. As one of my informants, who pointed to a general decline in Johnstown's economic expansion and to the stabilization of the numerical growth of East Central European communities in the city after World War I put it, "There was [in the foreign colonies] only so much need for the businesses."[61] As much as they valued the autonomy and prestige associated with conducting a business, the immigrants realistically perceived the high risks associated with it and the difficulty of maintaining an enterprise dependent on the irregular payments of customers employed in the mills and coal mines: "With the exception of big fish [established immigrant businessmen], so many started and failed." And from the daughter of a Serbian storekeeper who repeatedly closed down his business to work in the mill, only to reopen it later and close down again: "People bought on credit, and [for months] did not pay, so it was hard to make out."[62]

From below, the status cleavages and symbols of wealth, power, and prestige within the East Central European communities were usually seen with sharp clarity. On the other hand, some members of the immigrant upper stratum tended to negate the importance of these inequities with an almost "ideological" zeal: "[We] always treated everybody the same way, and many of our friends were coal miners." And yet to those coal miners they looked and behaved differently – dressed differently, ate differently, and carried themselves differently: "Mrs. H., R., and M., here in the parish, the wives of [our] big shots, always carried themselves *vysoko* (high)"; "The upper class [in the community], they turned up their noses."[63]

The prevailing attitude of the "ordinary" people in the immigrant communities toward their upper strata was also ambivalent, with alternating feelings now of pride and identity, now of envy and resentment, depending on the situation. When represented in the outside and also at solemn ethnic occasions or festive group celebrations – annual picnics, elections, church jubilees – the immigrant community called upon its elite and let it play its role with popular approval. In such instances the status cleavage dividing the group temporarily disappeared: The "big shots," who were usually perceived as a distinct group in itself, were then seen by the rest as "ours," people made of the same piece as Slovaks, Croatians, Rusyns, or, more broadly, the "Slavish" or the "foreigners." Yet the everyday attitudes of the rank-and-file members of the East Central European communities toward their upper strata also contained a discernible element of resentment against the rich and the "lordly." In fact, this resentment appears to have been more focused and more concrete than the diffuse, generalized feeling toward the "Americans" who "lived on the hills." It is possible that in an environment like Johnstown's, with prolonged ethnic separateness and limited social contact between the immigrant and native segments of the population, a part – how significant remains to be ascertained in further research – of the class-based resentment felt by the poor and powerless toward the wealthy and influential circulated *within* the bounds of immigrant communities, directed at their familiar "domestic" elite, without transferral to the dominant but socially and culturally distant upper stratum on the outside.[64]

The immigrants' perception of the middle stratum was also accurate. They thought it was possible for a family to advance into the middle ranks in the immigrant community. With some luck and initiative, the process could even be speeded up, if not always made permanent, through successful maneuvering using the informal networks of "ties," "shoulders," and "connections" extending between their families, ethnic neighborhoods, and the Bethlehem Company's mills and coal mines. Without such fortuitous circumstances, advancement out of the bottom socioeconomic stratum of the immigrant community could be achieved only through slow, painstaking material accumulation gained by inconspicuous, concerted effort of the whole family: "Well, if your wife was thrifty, she baked at home, kept chickens in the garden, sewed for the children – you did not spend too much, then, because everything was so cheap. If you had other people working in the family and if you did not drink in bars and saved your money, you could get somewhere, like buy a house."[65]

Even though in comparison with the "Americans" outside and with their own upper stratum in the local communities most immigrants saw themselves as "poor and ordinary," the superimposed reference framework of the old-country village and their first years in this country, ever-present in the immigrants' evaluation of their accomplishments, gave even the nonmobile a sense of movement – of an improvement in life-style and material condition.[66] This comparative perspective, extrapolating the current circumstances of the immigrants' existence out of the context of urban industrial society and into the one of a socioeconomic order still largely premodern, dulled the local, that is, American-based class resentments felt by the peasant workers of the immigrant generation.

This brings us to the final point of this chapter: the immigrants' perceptions of the dominant American social system and their position in it. The discussion will focus on the largest, working-class segment of the immigrant communities and use David Lockwood's distinction between three ideal types of workers' social consciousness: (1) the traditional form of the *proletarian* variety whereby the image of society takes the form of a dichotomous, two-valued power model; (2) the other traditional variety of the *deferential* type whereby the perception of social inequality is one of prestige or status hierarchy; workers displaying this type of social imagery defer to their superiors socially and politically, and they perceive the unequal social order as legitimate and do not question the privileged position of the dominant class; (3) the *privatized* type, whereby social consciousness approximates what may be called a "pecuniary" model of society in which social divisions are seen mainly in terms of differences in income and material possessions, and where work attachments are primarily instrumental, viewed as a means of acquiring extrinsic rewards, whereas community relationships are basically privatized, the workers' daily existence home-centered and socially isolated.[67]

Like their worldviews in general, the peasant-immigrants' perceptions of American society were profoundly ambivalent, composed of different attitudes that coexisted alongside each other, molded by past experience as much as by current environment and situations. The social consciousness of peasant-immigrant workers in Johnstown before World War II represented, simultaneously though in different proportions and intensity, the elements of all three Lockwoodian types: deferential, proletarian, and privatized. Intextricably fused with ethnic perceptions, they spread over the immigrants' lives in a mixed and diffuse manner and, meshed with each other, jointly informed their class-ethnic consciousness.[68]

The deferential imagery of the social order held by the peasant-immigrants had its roots in their experience as commoners in the deference societies of eastern Europe, where the upper class (landlords and gentry) was perceived and treated as the traditionally legitimated, naturally superior order. The "Hunky" workers in Johnstown did not view their position vis-à-vis their American employers as fundamentally different from that which they had occupied in Europe. Writes Bell about the Slovak immigrants in Braddock, Pennsylvania, at the beginning of the century: "In the old country the Slovaks had been . . . a nation of peasants and shepherds . . . from the beginnings of time whom the centuries had taught patience and humility. In America they [are] all this and more."[69] In the eyes of the immigrants: poor, uneducated, unskilled, without knowledge of English, dressed in a rural fashion, the "Americans" in Johnstown were not completely unlike the *pany* (landlords) in Europe. They were uppity, urbanely clothed, genteelly mannered, moving with ease in a world that to the peasants appeared bewildering: people of a superior species. This attitude surfaced repeatedly in the accounts of their initial years in America related to me by the immigrant generation: "They were advanced, Americans, and we were poor backward peasants"; "Those from the hills were superior, the elite"; "We considered them something better, like lords."[70] The reinforcing message of the world naturally and from times immemorial divided into the categories of rulers and subordinates also came powerfully from the pulpits of immigrant churches. Said a 1921 editorial in Johnstown's *Chranitel*: "God has created His world and

His creatures according to His Almighty Will. There is a place in it for the rich and the mighty, and a place for the honest and poor, hard-working folks. All will be rewarded in Heaven for their earthly struggles."[71]

Semicaste social divisions and the cultural aura in Johnstown sustained this deferential component of the immigrants' perceptions. The workers' deferential imagery has been linked by Lockwood to employment by small firms.[72] Recent studies, however, indicate that it may not be the size of the workplace but rather the organization of industry and the industrial subculture that influence the workers' consciousness.[73] Johnstown's mills and coal mines were the places where immigrants came into the closest relation with representatives of the dominant class-ethnic system, and its pattern reflected the ascriptive hierarchical bases of the town's social structure. They were hired to labor gangs, assigned to particular duties during the daily work process, paid, transferred, and laid off by the shop bosses. The bosses were native-born Americans or Welsh, German, or Irish – "those from the hills," representing the dominant system vis-à-vis the "Hunky" laborers whom they controlled and "kept in their place." Immigrants' employment, their daily job assignments, and their remuneration depended on deferential personal relations with the shop bosses and on "connections" with the gang leaders in other departments who could be resorted to for transfers to avoid layoffs or to secure a better-paying position within the range of lower-skilled tasks reserved for the foreigners.[74]

Local politics was another context in which the immigrants came into personal contact with the "Americans," and in this sphere, too, the pattern of the relationship mirrored the dominant ascriptive hierarchy. The interaction usually took place at election time, when native-born Americans, or, even more frequently, German and Irish ward bosses – "patriarchs" – appeared in bars and halls in the foreign colonies to sign up "Hunky" votes in exchange for a liberal distribution of drinks. Such personalized, particularist relations between immigrant laborers and their factory and political bosses standing in lieu of the American establishment stabilized the segmented social and cultural order and the workers' perceptions of it through the mechanism that Howard Newby has called "the deferential dialectic" between distance and intimacy, founded on the conception of the "natural" order of things.[75]

Yet the acceptance by peasant-immigrants of the legitimacy of the class-ethnic structure of inequality did not entail, as postulated in

Lockwood's deferential type, a vision of the dominant system as a continuous hierarchy of statuses. They saw it is "divided," the image reinforced, again, by their preindustrial experience. In Europe, peasants perceived the social order as fundamentally discontinuous: "There is not equality among angels in heaven; there will never be any on earth," went a saying in the Galician villages: "A peasant is always a peasant, a gentleman a gentleman: Amen."[76] Their image of American society was likewise discontinuous. As pointed out at the beginning of this chapter, the broadest categories in which peasant-immigrants perceived the social structure in Johnstown were those of their own group – "foreigners," "ordinary people" – versus "Americans" – "the rich," "the bosses," "those on the hills," the generalized dominant class conceived of diffusely in ethnic and economic terms. Kracha, the immigrant hero in Bell's *Out of This Furnace*, thus lectured young Mike Doberjack: "I've been in America long enough to learn that it is run just like any other country. In Europe your emperors and dukes own everything and over here it's your millionaires and your trusts."[77]

But although the immigrants had been aware of the deep opposition between themselves and the "Americans," in their everyday lives in Johnstown this perception was dulled and inactive. The nonunion, captive city of Johnstown, dominated by one powerful industrial employer, with its prevalent nativist climate and practice in the workplace and in political life, did not enhance a sustained "proletarian consciousness" among the workers. The "occupational solidarity" of the immigrants, and their "work comradeship" – the distinctive characteristics of Lockwood's proletarian type – had been expressed and realized in the daily experience of East Central Europeans in Johnstown through segmented ethnic attachments. The fusion between kinship ethnic and work spheres in the life-worlds of immigrants only further segregated them from their American fellow workers.

Social perceptions of the immigrant laborers came closest to the ideal proletarian type during the occasional conflicts on the shop floors and in particular during the steel strikes of 1919 and 1937 against the Bethlehem Company that sharpened their class consciousness and gave it a conflict focus through intensified awareness of a common situation and of shared interests with fellow workers. Still, even on these occasions, the proletarian consciousness of the immigrant laborers was mobilized and expressed through particularist ethnic identities, and their collective class action was inherently mediated through ethnic group membership. Most of the time, however, the proletarian feelings of the immigrant laborers "floated free," diluted by other attitudinal components.

The third kind in Lockwood's typology is the privatized worker: a family-centered person who perceives work primarily in instrumental terms as a means of acquiring pecuniary rewards and material prosperity. As we have seen earlier, this motif was particularly pronounced in the attitudes and behavior of peasant-immigrant workers as they strove, through collective family efforts and by utilizing the replicas of ascriptive-kin networks in the workplace, to carve out the maximum amounts available from the limited opportunities that existed for them in Johnstown and to realize the desired goals.

In Europe, because of the nature of their labor, peasants conceived of work primarily in the privatized context of an individual household rather than larger class ramifications. The instrumental motivation of their migration to America sustained this basic orientation. As long as they saw themselves as sojourners, the primary goal of the peasant-immigrants was the maximization of monetary gains to be taken back to the home country. After they settled in this country for good, the immigrants' family-oriented pursuits had largely retained the same fundamental purpose: to accumulate as much income as possible, first and foremost as a safety net against economic insecurity, and secondly in order to achieve the closest approximation to what their community defined as a "good life."

In its acquisitive pecuniary outlook, family-centeredness, and instrumental orientation toward work and work roles, the immigrants' social consciousness represented important elements of Lockwood's privatized type. However, in his typology these characteristics are associated with social disintegration, alienation, and uprootedness, as contrasted with the "communal sociability" of proletarian workers, firmly integrated into traditional local communities. Lockwood's privatized worker is an economically minded social isolate; peasant-immigrants were, rather, instrumentalists-participators. They were immersed in close-knit, embracing communities based on shared birthplace, language, and religion that sustained their group awareness and solidarity. At the same time, these ethnic communities upheld, through socially approved norms and expectations concerning the conduct of their members, the immigrants' basic cultural orientation of familism, material accumulation, and instrumentalism in occupational and economic pursuits.[78]

It has been argued, in the debate on the socialization of subordinate classes into the value system of dominant groups in western societies, that the former do not actually hold the "official" ideology, as the consensus theorists maintain, but that their acceptance of the existing order is essentially of a pragmatic and noncommittal nature.[79] The immigrants in Johnstown before World War II perceived the larger American system as dominant and superior because it controlled goods, power, and privileges. It evoked in them, as did the dominant class itself, confused feelings of indifference and resentment, combined with a mixture of pragmatic and normative acquiescence. In terms of the relation between the "foreigners" – the subordinate group – and the dominant "American" one, the stratification system in Johnstown was based on what Edward Shils has termed a "coerced consensus."[80] The "consensus" component came from the immigrants' acknowledgment of the superiority of the American world, founded on a generalized conception of the world as naturally divided into leaders and followers, and stabilized in the pattern of their personal encounters with the "Americans." The "coercion" component, founded on their economic and political dependence within the dominant structure, evoked in the immigrant workers attitudes of both resentment and realistic pragmatism and resignation.

As we shall see in the last chapter of this book, the perceptions of the immigrant children – the native-born generation – while composed of basically similar elements, were, however, mapped differently, forming, as in a turned kaleidoscope, a familiar yet different composition.

8 The second generation

This chapter can be read as a postscript to the preceding ones. The second generation in this study are sons and daughters of the East Central European immigrants, born in America shortly before or after 1900.[1] They have been present throughout this book as we examined the economic maneuvers and social adjustments of the immigrant families to the structural conditions and cultural aura of Johnstown before World War II. The semicaste sociopolitical organization of the city funneled most of the daily activities of second generation East Central Europeans into their ethnic communities. Within these communities, the lives of the second generation were centered on their families.

The immigrant children in Johnstown continued to live with their parents long after they reached adulthood, and when they finally set up their own independent households, most of them chose to reside in close proximity to their parents, with whom they maintained close contact. Of the second generation Slavic and Magyar men recorded by the 1900 census in Johnstown, two-thirds still lived with their parents in 1920. By 1930, almost one-fourth of them, all men thirty years old or more, still lived in the parental households.[2] An inspection of city directories for the late 1930s reveals, particularly in secondary ethnic settlements, a distinct clustering of the same family names within street blocks, in all likelihood parents and their adult, independent children. In 1937, among the American-born male heads of East Central European households, 60 percent were found to reside in the same ward as their parents and an additional 30 percent in adjacent wards or in areas close enough so that the distance could be traveled on foot. In 1940, this combined parent-children "proximity rate" was 75 percent.[3]

Like their parents', the existence of American-born Slavs and Magyars in Johnstown was tempered by the severe economic realities of their time and place. In a sustained effort to direct and mold their lives as much as possible, they tried to carve out and appropriate in their pursuits whatever limited space was available. Their lives were made up of elements basically similar to those that formed the world of their parents, and, like theirs, were also split and ridden with cleavages. But they were not identical. This last chapter post-

266

script shows the different "mapping" of the second generation's life-worlds to which differently placed emphases gave particular coloring and configuration that influenced their reactions and outlooks.

For the immigrant generation who arrived in America as adults, the chasm between the old world from which they came and the new one was at the root of the alienation and nostalgia they experienced. Without knowledge of English and without industrial skills, the immigrants were confined, and confined themselves, to the realm of tightly knit communities of their peasant-immigrant countrymen.

In Johnstown, where the economic and social conditions sustained ethnic divisions and weakened class integration, a very substantial portion of the existence of the second generation was still lived inside the walls of their ethnic communities, replicated in neighborhoods and in the workplace. In comparison with the immigrants, however, for the sons and daughters of immigrants the "walls" inside which they lived were much more transparent and permeable. They revealed on the outside an American world that reached them directly through the English language, school, newspapers, recreation, and contacts with their American peers.

For the second generation, American-born children of immigrants, their condition as American industrial laborers, *here and not there*, was the sole reality they knew from experience that had for them a directly personal, emotional, and cognitive meaning. In this reality, in Johnstown before World War II, they occupied a definite place circumscribed by class and ethnic constraints. Together with their parents, in a concerted family effort, they pursued their goals and purposes within it and played off against the constraining "walls" by ways and means described earlier in this book. But the close presence of the world outside the now transparent walls of their ethnic communities created considerable pain and frustration in their existence. The axis of the tensions informing the life-worlds of the second generation was the incompatibility between, on the one hand, perceived and partially internalized American norms of equal opportunity and universalist achievement based on individual ability, skills, and performance, and rights of citizenship, and, on the other, the reality of particularism and class/ethnic near-ascription.[4] Two institutions in particular – the school and the workplace – generated and sustained in the American-born immigrant children alternating feelings of frustration, anger, and resignation.

At the beginning of the century, when the numbers of southern and East Central European settlers in America increased yearly at a rapid rate, the school superintendent of Cambria County, joining in with a chorus of voices across industrial America, announced the urgent necessity of assimilating the newcomers; otherwise, he warned, "the very life of the nation will be jeopardized," threatened by the "dregs" brought into western Pennsylvania by the "rapid development of our coal fields and the enlargement of the Cambria Steel plant." The local schools, stated the superintendent, faced a tremendous task of Americanizing these people, who were "as a rule ignorant, immoral and lacking those traits which constituted good citizenship."[5]

As everywhere else in Pennsylvania, Johnstown was swept up in the school reform and Americanization movement, and the immigrant children at the beginning of the century were taught the natural superiority of American civilization and its fundamental values of freedom, equality, and personal achievement.[6] My second generation informants remembered well being told as children in the classroom "America is the best country on earth"; "America is the land of opportunity for all"; "You can become what you want"; and "Don't be a coal miner."[7] Equally ingrained in the memory of those who attended the public schools in Johnstown was another recollection – of recurrent feelings of embarrassment and inferiority to the "American" children, caused by difficulty with the English language (in the early grades), "foreign" dress, and "unpronounceable" names.

As late as the 1930s teachers in the junior high school in Morrellville, attended by many immigrant children from secondary ethnic settlements, classified the national background of their students under the misnomer "Slavish."[8] "At school I went as Tomas," recalls Mike T., whose given name is distinctly Serbian, "because the teacher would not pronounce or spell my own." Echoes his wife, "My name was Tomasovich, but the teacher spelled it Tumoski, she did not bother to get it right."[9] Casmira G., a second generation Polish-American, did not know English when she entered public elementary school: "It was very hard. By the second grade I already spoke English but never raised my hand or anything – I was afraid I'd make a mistake . . . American children called us 'Hunky' . . . We felt inferior. I quit [school] because I was embarrassed, always embarrassed about everything and myself. Many of our [people] quit school early because we were all sort of scared, those [American] kids were more advanced, they knew more from home, like music or American history."[10] And a similar recollection from Joseph H., born at the beginning of the century to a Slovak immigrant family: "We did not like school, dropped out as soon as possible."[11]

A comparison of immigrant children's attendance at public and parochial schools in the city at the beginning of the century indicates that although only 5.5 percent of those enrolled in the American public schools continued their education beyond the sixth grade, the proportion was nearly 20 percent for children attending their "own" parochial schools. It is probable, considering the recollections of my second generation informants from their school years, that the reason why the children quit public school early was a painfully felt alienation from the dominant cultural system. As a matter of fact, we may speculate that attendance at public schools could have "cost" the children increased tension resulting from an even more acute perception of the chasm between the ideal of universalist achievement and the reality of particularism and class/ethnic near-ascription. On the other hand, the immigrant parochial school placed more emphasis on moral-religious and national education than on personal accomplishment based on ability and skill. Although it did not inculcate strong "American" values, it at least spared the children an increased burden of frustration, of which their lives were full enough in any case.[12]

The discrepancy between the dominant ideology of equal opportunity and the practice of particularism and class/ethnic near-ascription in the school experience of the children of the second generation continued throughout the interwar period. In junior high school, they were almost automatically placed in vocational or commercial rather than college courses: nearly 70 percent of the East Central European students entering junior high schools in Johnstown before World War II were thus allocated.[13] Those few who desired the college course had to struggle for it: "Your [East Central European] name was enough to put you in vocational course, [and] a hassle was needed to get you into the college one."[14] As late as 1935, Edward Y., the son of Polish immigrants, and William K., a second generation Slovak, had to summon help from their parents to persuade the teacher to enroll them in the higher-status program: "College course [at junior high school] was for a better breed . . . Foreign people had to fight to get in."[15]

Although *nolens volens* they partially absorbed the values of the dominant society that they were taught at school, the sons and daughters of the immigrants were at the same time keenly aware of the gulf between these ideals and their actual chances in Johnstown. This perception was summarized by Mike T., a second generation Serb, born in 1905: "At school we learned [about how man is master of his fate], but we knew that we had a double strike against us, foreign extraction and poor and uneducated parents," and he added one additional handicap – the Depression.[16] In the perceptions of the second generation, some schooling and some personal advancement were correlated, but education, the basis of individual achievement in the dominant cultural paradigm, "was not the most important [factor] for your future." By and large, success was determined by particularist considerations: "In 70 percent of cases, it mattered more who your father was, his nationality and all . . . and whom he knew, and whom you knew."[17]

With such perceptions the members of the second generation were leaving school and entering the world of work. There the chasm between the norm of achievement based on performance and ability and the particularistic criteria of ethnicity and personal connections was even more evident. The ascriptive work and promotion policies prevailing at Bethlehem Steel during the interwar period were summarized by Charles H., who was then general foreman in the mechanical department: "Second generation, sons of the Slavish immigrants, their chances for advancement were better [than their fathers'], . . . but a lot [of them] for us Americans were like the immigrants, they stayed at home with their parents . . . and spoke the old-country language." About the company's promotion policies, Charles H. said, as we noted earlier, "When there was a list of names for promotions [to the skilled and supervisory positions]: White, McKinnley, Baumgarten, Borowski, and so on, they [management] tended to scratch out the 'Hunky' ones."[18] The second generation's perception of their situation as workers corresponded with that of the company. They saw ability and performance as somewhat important but, first, blocked from above at a certain ceiling by class/ethnic ascription, and, second, conditioned on particularist "ties," "shoulders" to lean on, and "connections." "If you had ambition, you could get ahead only so far, you could advance some," but "to get a good job in the mills you had to know somebody; for [better] jobs, we did not read newspaper ads; you got them through individual contacts."[19]

This is how it was, and the second generation acted accordingly. But the generalized sense of a chasm between the dominant achievement ideology and the constraining boundaries of class/ethnic reality evoked in the immigrant children no small amount of frustration and resentment. A large part of it, however, was suppressed and "accommodated" through their immersion in the daily life of the parental household and in the dense world of ethnic communities.

Like that of the immigrants, the social consciousness of their American-born children in Johnstown before World War II represented a composite of attitudes. But the constellation of its constitutive elements was different, and they were more clearly compartmentalized into spheres of perceptions and action, rather than meshed together in one confused pattern. In terms of the Lockwoodian tripartite classification of workers' social imagery used in Chapter 7 to interpret the immigrants' perceptions of the American social order, the class/ethnic consciousness of the second generation combined the dominant, familist-instrumentalist component of the "privatized" type with a strong undercurrent of "proletarian" outlook, easily activated in the sphere of work roles and relations, and a weaker, residual "deference" element, detectable in the sociocultural and political realms.

The immigrants and second generation shared a basic community of outlooks generated by day-to-day living under the same roof and by shared work and social situations. In the ethos of East Central European households, work was conceived of primarily within the particularized family/kin context rather than in its larger social/class ramifications. This orientation was sustained by the cultural value system of the surrounding ethnic communities, which placed major emphasis on the privatized-instrumental function of the occupational activities and economic pursuits of individuals, relating them closely to family welfare. The evaluation of the character and moral standing of immigrant sons and daughters by their ethnic communities was based first and foremost on the eagerness and success with which they contributed to the material prosperity of their households. The immigrant priests admonished the second generation to "work, work for the family" as soon as possible and were ready to sign papers for underage boys to leave school and join their fathers or relatives at Bethlehem.[20]

Seen in the perspective of daily activities, instrumentalized work had for the second generation basically the same purpose that it had for their parents. It was the means, through concerted family effort, of obtaining and increasing concrete pecuniary and material rewards. In one of the Slovene homes in Johnstown I was given a pile of old issues of the *Ameriški Družinski Koledar* (American family almanac) published by the progressive social-democratic Slovenska Narodna Podporna Jednota. In an article on the second generation, using an approach highly unusual for the East Central European press in America, a Slovene author implicitly confirmed this prevalent attitude, lamenting that "[Slovene] parents . . . fail to teach their children the facts and realities of life: that there is a working class and that as a member of the working class they should think as workers – politically, socially and economically . . . Important as [proletarian consciousness] training is in the family, most youngsters are forced to go without it, for the very reason that their parents do not fully realize its necessity."[21]

Alongside or maybe "beneath" this privatized orientation there was in the worldview of the second generation a residue of fatalism that also undergirded the outlook of their immigrant parents and that the "fluctuating" quality of their own economic existence did not eradicate. This fatalistic component in the attitudes of the immigrant children, partly absorbed from the parents together with other approaches, partly reconstituted in their own experience in Johnstown, further "privatized" their outlook by detaching, as it were, their daily activities from their concrete social-class context. Viewed from a mundane perspective as the instrumental means of acquiring extrinsic rewards, labor – the lifelong, dreary, and toilsome effort that dominated man's life and made him dependent on it – was seen by the second generation ultimately as an attribute of the universal *condition humaine*. Although in no way systematic and conclusive evidence, the responses – projective associations given by some immigrant children in Johnstown Junior High School tests suggest that their deep perceptions of the world indeed differed substantially from dominant American middle-class outlooks. In 1928, in a test of mental ability given to students in Garfield Junior High School in Morrellville, a number of immigrant children chose "man" as the notion opposite to that of "strong" (other options being "small," "short," and "thin"), and selected "pity" as the feeling man usually harbors for his children (other options being "affection," "contempt," and "reverence"). Needless to add, they all flunked the test.[22]

Yet the Slovenska Jednota was not correct in its assertion that the "proletarian" outlook was totally absent from the attitudes of the immigrant children. This component was clearly present in their orientations, stronger and more focused than in the foreign-born generation. It was detectable in the young people's perceptions of their roles as industrial laborers. They did not hide their dislike for the drudgery of their labor and openly used means of avoiding physical exhaustion on the job, unlike their parents, who slowed down only when not supervised. In a routinely performed action that turned the dependence of workers against their employers, immigrant sons slowed down and "loafed" in the mill shops. The slowdown approach was practiced by workers paid fixed hourly rates. Those who worked on incentive plans "loafed" after they had accomplished their own pecuniary goals for the day: "I usually did my day-incentive in six hours" – George L., worked in the Bethlehem Company axle plant; "then I was loafing around for two."[23] The crystallization of the elements of the work ethos of the experienced industrial workers in the approach of the immigrant children was accompanied by the "proletarianization" – in the Lockwoodian sense – of their perceptions of work relations.

This became particularly pronounced during the 1937 strike at Bethlehem Steel in which the second generation workers participated en masse. "You are not going to call us 'Hunky' no more": This theme recurred in my second generation informants' accounts of the motives for East Central Europeans' participation in the collective labor action against the company.[24] As they told about their perceptions of labor and economic relations in Johnstown before World War II, their recollections contained a distinct note of sustained anger and assertiveness, absent in the immigrant accounts. Their opinions were also rendered in language different from that of their parents, with terms such as "exploitation" and "domination" used to describe their position as "Hunky" workers in Johnstown. Most often, these references appeared in the context of discussion of the prolabor legislation of the Roosevelt administration and particularly of the 1937 strike at Bethlehem Steel.

The members of the second generation were aware of the difference between the constellations of their own and their parents' class/ethnic perceptions. "The immigrant generation," said Pete K., who was born in 1911 in Cambria City, a son of a mill worker, "they did not realize too much that they were exploited, or [if they did] it was natural for them. Even in 1919 [during the steel strike] many of them were [simply] led by the organizers. Us, we were different. [During the 1937 strike] we knew what we were fighting for."[25] This difference in the mapping of immigrant and second generation class/ethnic consciousness, most pronounced in their perceptions of work roles and relations, manifested itself in occasional conflicts at home between parents and children. "Think what you like, but keep your mouth shut": Their life in Europe as well as in this country had taught peasant-immigrants to keep away from public affairs.[26] The second generation saw things differently, at least regarding their lives as industrial workers. During the organizational drive for the

1937 strike in Johnstown, exchanges such as the following, related
by a second generation Rusyn, must have taken place in many immigrant homes. When young Mike N. and his friends were signing
up for the union and getting ready to join the strike, his old foreign-
born father, himself a laborer at Bethlehem Steel for many years,
repeatedly warned them: "You will lose jobs." To this, Mike replied:
"Dad, we don't care . . . We don't want to live like Hunkies anymore, like you immigrants, treated like trash."[27] After the union
had finally been established in Johnstown, the second generation
became more assertive, even outright defiant of the employers: "I
remember one day, with a buddy we took off to Niagara Falls for a
weekend, despite the fact that we were supposed to report to work
. . . Our fathers would never do that, they were afraid we'd lose
jobs [and tried to dissuade us from going]. But we weren't afraid
[like them] anymore, we had the backing of the union."[28]

The social consciousness of the second generation also contained
a deference component since they learned from their parents at
home a philosophy of the "natural order of things on this earth" –
the message, as we have seen earlier, reinforced in teachings received from the immigrant churches, which urged "hard-working
creatures of God" to exercise humility and patience suitable for their
condition planned by "Almighty Providence." In comparison with
the immigrant generation, however, the deference component in
the orientations of their American-born children had become reduced in impact and scope. But it was still present and seems to
have retained its greatest influence in their cultural perceptions and
those related to the public, political sphere of the dominant system.

Immersed in their ethnic communities, the second generation accepted as natural the separateness of their own and the "American"
sociocultural worlds. They generally perceived things "American,"
as well as "American" social circles (clubs, associations, neighborhoods, social activities), as culturally "advanced" and "superior."
In the sphere of public life, the American-born Slavs and Magyars
in Johnstown clearly perceived a gulf between the universalist norm
of citizenship and the excluding practice of near-ascription, but their
attitude, although resentful, was on the whole generally acquies-
cent. To my question whether and in what way they had thought
of themselves as "Americans" and members of American society
before World War II, most of them pointed to their ethnic identities
and to their participation in ethnic organizational networks and public activities. With the exception of a few from the ethnic elite, such
as the professional men who belonged to the Slavonic League,

"American politics" was, in the apparently shared opinion of the immigrant children, a matter "for Americans, better suited for it." All in all, although the immigrant children in Johnstown before World War II shared with their parents essentially similar, if differently composed, worldviews, their social consciousness seems to have been emotionally rawer and therefore more uncomfortable. They pursued their goals through the available channels vacillating between recurrent feelings of anger, frustration, and acquiescence that stemmed from the insoluble tensions inherent in their position as the American-born children of peasant-immigrant "Hunkies" located at the bottom of the social structure in a small, autocratic, and ethnically divided steel town.

We will now examine a little more closely the ways in which the second generation adjusted to and at the same time appropriated the social and economic space that they occupied in Johnstown. First, we shall see what their life goals or aspirations were, and, second, examine some of their accomplishments and their own perceptions of these achievements.

The aspirations people have do not represent a constant set of goals; as they move through life their goals are redefined to correspond more or less to the actual conditions of their existence. I attempted to reconstruct the life goals of the second generation as they were modified from the time of their adolescence until they had reached middle age in the 1940s. My informants, in their own accounts of the past, made a sharp distinction between the time before the Depression and the 1930s. I will accept this distinction and present the aspirations of the immigrant children in these two phases that they themselves perceived as significantly different.

The life goals of the second generation men and women, like those of their immigrant parents, were, first and foremost, characterized by profound realism and tempered by the class and ethnic position that they occupied in Johnstown society. Like that of the immigrants, the image of a "good life" of the children centered on family, work, material possessions, and the local ethnic community. Fundamentally similar to those of their parents', the aspirations of the second generation, however, did not simply replicate but expanded upon them.

Peter S., an American-born Slovak, gave this summary characterization of the life goals of his generation during the 1920s: "[We wanted] what the parents wanted, but more, more of everything."[29] As they listened to their immigrant parents telling how they had lived when they came to this country at the beginning of the century, the second generation thought it "The Stone Age." John B., a Rusyn born in East Conemaugh before World War I, remembers many such conversations: "When parents told children how they lived, they'd answer: 'But you had lived in the Stone Age!' and parents say: 'We wish you'd never have to live like this.' "[30] The generalized negative reference to the quality of life of the immigrant parents, expressed in the desire "to have a better life than they had," recurred in most of my conversations with the American-born Slavs and Magyars in Johnstown.

To the immigrant children, a "life better than the parents'" consisted of three major components: work – its quality and remuneration, and the material standard of existence it allowed for; "good family"; and "respect among people." Let me briefly comment on each of them.

Not surprisingly, the most important element in the second generation's image of a good life was work performed by the man, the major breadwinner in the family. It was judged by its steadiness, quality, and the remuneration it brought. Most of the young men followed their older relatives to the mills. The desire that man's work be steady was reiterated by the American-born generation as often as it was by the immigrants: Some measure of steadiness was synonymous with regular income; without it life was unceasingly insecure, and it was impossible to maintain for any long period of time whatever surplus capital one managed to accumulate. The income desired by the second generation mill workers was, of course, "as much as you could get there," but full-time wages of a better-skilled worker, averaging about $6 a day for a nine-hour shift in the mill in the mid 1920s, appears to have been considered as "very decent pay" by the young men.[31]

Although perceived as the prerequisite for a "better life," steadiness of employment and income at Bethlehem – the two most fundamental considerations for the immigrant – were not all that their children aspired to in their work. More than their fathers, they also considered its quality. Louis M., superintendent at the Bethlehem Company in Johnstown during the 1920s, compared immigrants and their sons: "The children did not want the [kind of] work their fathers did – dirty, mostly menial – [they] wanted better jobs, cleaner, mechanized, with some skills."[32]

As we saw in Chapter 7, in the eyes of the immigrant generation, ownership of a successful business in the East Central European communities enjoyed the highest prestige, with skilled industrial occupations "bulging out," as it were, to the outside, "neither here nor there" from the point of view of the immigrant status hierarchy. The second generation acknowledged the status hierarchy as it functioned in the communities of which they were part and in which the immigrants occupied the leading positions. But in their own perceptions, the occupational status ladder was represented a little differently, more closely resembling that of mainstream American society.

First, as they conceived of it, the occupational hierarchy had lost its "bulge" and straightened out, with skilled occupations placed right within it. Second, in comparison with the immigrant status ladder, it was expanded by two additional categories absent in the representations of their parents: professions and mainstream clerical occupations. Shortly before World War II, professionals in the East Central European communities in Johnstown numbered no more than thirty-odd second generation people: a few doctors, dentists, and druggists, some lawyers, and a small group of teachers. The professions were assigned the highest prestige (women professionals – teachers and nurses – did not "count" in the dominant male hierarchy; they will be discussed separately later). Such prestige was apparently accorded on a double basis: reputationally to particular people for their overall social performance in the community, and to the whole category in accordance with its "class" characteristics. This superimposition reflected the half-way location of the second generation's worldviews, extended, as it were, between the parental "urban village" perceptions of social status and those prevailing in modern industrial society.

The place second from the top was given by the American-born generation to skilled mill occupations, which outranked ownership of an ethnic business. Recollecting the ambitions of the young men in the 1920s, my respondents pointed to "advancement" and "prospects" in the mills rather than "opening an independent business," the career highly valued by the immigrant generation. This rearrangement of prestige allocation came from a realization of the limited opportunities and high risk of failure in ethnic businesses: In the 1920s and 1930s, the immigrant communities were in fact, as we saw in Chapter 7, saturated with immigrant enterprises, and the turnover, particularly among the new entries, was considerable. At the same time, the men of the second generation had, more than their immigrant fathers, been acculturated to the American industrial world and in particular to the position that they occupied in it. In Chapter 7 I used Norbert Wiley's notion of a "stratification tree" to show that the career of an ethnic businessman led upward but in a sense away from the main "prestige trunk." From the class position occupied by the second generation men in the steel town, the natural avenue up the tree, however narrow and limited, led through advancement in industrial jobs.[33]

Next in rank after the skilled occupations in the mills, in the view of the second generation men, came mainstream clerical jobs, together with the ownership of a retail business. If "weeny," or tiny, as my informants described it, the latter was placed below steady clerical employment; if prospering, above it.[34]

The American-born men wanted to have jobs "better than their fathers'." This meant, if not skilled occupations or office work – and these jobs, they were aware, were in scarce supply for "foreigners" – mill jobs with better conditions, cleaner and lighter, of which, with the mechanization of the steel industry, there was an increasing number. These were preferred over work in the worst Bethlehem Steel departments: "The Coke plant was bad, but had a better pay; fabrication shops were better"; "[We wanted] jobs as far as one could get [ahead], with a clean, light work, not like father's pick and shovel"; "above the menial level."[35]

A steady, well-paid, good-quality job for the man of the family was the first element of a "life better than fathers'" to which the second generation aspired. The second component had to do with the style of life and the material standard of existence. In their accounts of what they wanted from life, food – an important anchor point in the images of peasant-immigrants – was absent. The second generation knew about hunger in Europe only from stories told by their parents and, at least before the Depression, took food for granted. As with their aspirations concerning work, the second generation's goals related to the material quality of life had been basically an expansion of the parental values, formed and shaped by the mass American culture. An exchange between Dobie and Julie in Braddock, Pennsylvania, as related in Thomas Bell's *Out of This Furnace*, reflects the content and the horizon of those aspirations, also shared by young people in nearby Johnstown: Julie says, "If I had a sewing machine I could make a lot of my own clothes . . . In a way, we'll really save money." Dobie answers, "I'd rather we got an electric refrigerator first." Julie: "We need so many things. Refrigerator, sewing machine, vacuum cleaner, good silverware." Dobie: "Sure takes a lot of machinery to keep house nowadays, don't it." Julie: "If you want to live nice."[36]

To have a decent, clean, not too hard job in the mills; to be able

to afford clothes, recreation, a car (by the late 1920s a used Model
T touring car could be had in Johnstown for about $150); a "good
family"; and, in the future, a house with nice furniture and the
necessary "machinery" – these were basically the life goals of the
younger generation.

Besides a better job for the man – less tiring, steadier, and bringing
money to be used to buy material possessions – the second generation's vision of the "life better than fathers'" contained an additional element: They wanted fewer children than their parents
had. In the peasant tradition, the immigrants simply had their children: They were considered a gift of God, and, at the same time,
to have many of them was seen as an element of the family collective
economic strategy. In the perceptions of the second generation, children, yes, came naturally, and there should be several of them –
but only to a point. Too many were seen not as an economic asset
but as a liability. In the economic strategies of their own families,
the second generation deliberately adjusted the number of children
to cope with hardships and to improve the material standard of the
household. The immigrant mothers never talked openly with their
daughters about the intimate side of married life. What Mary U., a
second generation Slovene, learned from her mother before she got
married in 1921 was typical for others in her generation: "She
[mother] told me the facts of life: Watch yourself, keep yourself clean
and dry feet, and you will be all right."[37] But the American-born
women that I talked to admitted that they themselves, as well as
their friends, had to some extent planned their families. "Many immigrants had ten children and more; with us [second generation] it
was four or at most five, and no more." "The times were hard; we
did not want any more and were careful." "Four children and that
was it – who wants more? We had a difficult life. So I was careful,
did nothing *gac* but was careful." "In the 1920s, there was a Doctor
P. downtown; [second generation] foreign women went to him, and
he taught them, and they had no more babies. One learned from
another." "[Second generation] parents had half the number of children the immigrants had; although they often gave excuses of
health, they planned a little in their heads, wanted to have it a little
better in life, better clothing, and house, not to have so many children – How the parents struggled with it."[38] And indeed, they had
fewer children than their parents; whereas the average number of
children in the immigrant families in Johnstown was 6.5, the second
generation had an average of four.[39]

The second generation saw the quality of work and of life-style that they desired for themselves as an expansion of what their parents had had. The image of a "good family" and "respect among people" – two important life goals that they usually enumerated in one breath, together with the first two – were generally perceived by the second generation as a continuation of their parents' lives. Telling how, as young people in the 1920s and 1930s, they imagined having a "good family," the second generation men and women fundamentally identified with the style of home life and ways of raising children practiced by the immigrant generation, except that some of them thought that the parents had been "a little too strict." "Respect among people," a value of a social nature, was seen by them as a function of good steady work, decent family income, and life-style and compliance with the patterns of conduct accepted in their ethnic communities. As they perceived it, the expected conduct involved, in essence, a quiet, clean, thrifty, church-going household with hard-working members, of a type fundamentally similar to that valued by immigrants. In terms of the expectations of everyday social and cultural behavior at home and in the community, the second generation by and large followed their parents.

The functioning of the East Central European households during the Depression and the contributions of the second generation to the economic survival of their families has already been discussed in Chapter 6. The experience of the 1930s had a radically "trimming" impact on the aspirations and life goals of the second generation, who were at that time in the young phase of their adult life, either recently married or with small children of their own.

The aspirations of peasants-immigrants as they were leaving Europe and after they settled in America formed, as we saw earlier, a "continuum of desiderata" extending, within a range fixed from the outside by their structural location and their cultural values, from a minimum – the "negative want" – to the most positive imagined state of affairs. The Depression "pushed" the desires of the great majority of second generation people far back toward the minimum state or the "negative want," while other wishes and goals that they might have harbored, less attainable or simply unrealistic under the circumstances, were for the time being suppressed or eliminated from consciousness and became latent.

The hardships of the Depression forced many Slavic and Magyar households in Johnstown back to the "Stone Age" of the early years of the immigrants' stay in America, giving the second generation a bitter taste of the experience they had heard about in their parents' stories. Their sense of deprivation was slightly eased by the residue of fatalistic acquiescence remaining in their attitudes, a ready-made element of their parents' worldview and part of the atmosphere of the home that they had absorbed as they grew up. This fatalism also facilitated somewhat the readjustment of aspirations and the reduction of life goals: "Our parents lived like that; we knew hard times from before, it did not surprise us so much," was a common reaction to the Depression among the immigrant children.[40] The fact that it affected virtually everyone around them made the experience easier: "Everybody was in it like us, [so we coped]."[41]

Nevertheless, in the 1930s the range of aspirations of the American-born generation had narrowed to one predominant consideration: work. "Work in the mills was [then] the biggest dream of everybody":[42] This recollection of Charles M., a second-generation Rusyn, was repeated by all who told about their lives in Johnstown during the Depression. "In the Depression time, nobody was thinking what they wanted [from life]: everybody wanted work."[43] The Depression also radically reduced the income aspirations of the mill workers. In the 1920s young men considered the $6 a day earned in the mills a good wage, but now $19 a week became "fabulous pay."[44] When there was nothing in the way of work to be had in Johnstown, young people traveled to other places and made their money at odd jobs (see Chapter 6). When conditions improved, they usually returned to Johnstown and went back to the mills: "Then there was another slump, and so we lived from year to year."[45] Year by year during the 1930s, with their aspirations to a "life better than the fathers'" buried and set aside, preoccupied mostly with getting a job and with holding onto it as long as possible in order to keep their heads above water, the younger generation, like everybody else, waited for the "national calamity" to go away.

We now turn to the actual accomplishments of the second generation in the interwar period. As with the immigrants, the information available does not account for all elements of what they valued as a desirable life: Most of all we lack systematic data on their material possessions and life-styles, the crucial components of their aspirations.

Without Bethlehem Company records, it was impossible to reconstruct the actual jobs that the second generation men held in the mills according to wage rates and quality. As for the immigrants, occupational data for their American-born sons came from the city directories. As noted before, by routinely assigning a summary label

of "laborer," the city directories distorted the finer distinctions between unskilled and various kinds of unspecified semiskilled jobs
that had been most important to the employed in their evaluations
of particular assignments and in the choices they made between
them. Approximate as these figures are, I present them so that the
situation of the immigrant children can be compared with that of
their parents. I also examine the impact of the socioeconomic position of fathers on their children's occupational status; residential
and homeownership mobility among the second generation; and
their participation in ethnic activities.

In Chapter 5 we saw that in terms of their occupational characteristics, between 1920 and 1949–50 the American-born sons of the
immigrants had been unable to match the occupational distribution
of Johnstown's male employed population as a whole. That comparison demonstrated what should have been, and what actually
was, the rate of their mobility in the city's occupational structure
between two time points spanning thirty years. It did not tell us
about their occupational pursuits in between. Let us now fill some
of this gap, using the same approach as with the immigrants: that
is, tracing the shifts in individual careers of the second generation
workers.

From the total of 933 American-born men recorded by the 1900
census (35 percent of whom had already left Johnstown for good
before the end of World War I), I traced the group of 225 of those
who had been present in Johnstown at least twice between 1915 or
1920, and 1949 (the checkpoints in between were 1925, 1930, and
1940). This time span, covering the years of the Depression, extends
from the period around which the majority of the second generation
had begun working to the time when they were fifty years old or
over, already past middle age.

Women get married and "disappear" from records. Of the total
number of 509 American-born East Central European women recorded by the 1900 census, I traced 192, those who appeared in the
Johnstown city directories, either as "girls at home" or as gainfully
employed persons, at least once at my checkpoints between 1915
and 1949.

We shall begin with the men, for whom the information is more
systematic. In comparison with the immigrants, their sons were
more occupationally mobile, intensely moving up, down, and side-
ways along the occupational spectrum. Apparently it was also
easier for the second generation than for the immigrants to maintain
their elevated occupational positions once attained. Their occupa-

tional movements were not only more intense and somewhat more solid, but also more "dispersed" than those of their fathers, indicating some broadening of the available occupational opportunities. However, the decade of the Depression had a pronounced negative impact on the occupational curricula of these workers, and it was only after 1940 that they "recouped" to the pre-Depression level.

Data on the pursuits of the occupational "achievers" – men who had risen above positions of ordinary laborers in the mills and mines at least once at my checkpoints – are given in Table A.16 in the Appendix. Thus, of the 225 American-born East Central Europeans present in Johnstown between 1915–20 and 1949, including both persisters and returnees, almost two-thirds – 65 percent – achieved occupational positions above the lowest occupational level at least once. Of this number, 34 percent were found to have held their elevated positions at only one of my checkpoints, and 45 percent three or more times.

The immigrant sons present in Johnstown between 1915–20 and 1949 were also more spatially mobile than their fathers had been, with the proportion of returnees larger (53 percent) than that of persisters (47 percent). Among the occupational "achievers" the proportion of returnees was 46 percent, and of persisters 54 percent, suggesting that moving into and out of Johnstown did not have a strongly detrimental impact on the occupational accomplishments of the movers relative to those of the persisters.[46] A not unimportant factor that most likely helped returnees to quickly get reabsorbed into the job network in Johnstown was that they had been born and raised in the city and had "connections" that could be activated upon return.

While most upward shifts by the immigrants were direct transfers involving only two occupational levels, 42 percent of the sons' movements were "mediated" – that is, involved more than two occupational categories.[47] The proportion of "mediated" transfers in the second generation's occupational movements was about 70 percent among those found to have held elevated positions at three or more of my checkpoints. The "mediated" transfers appeared also to have been more successful, in that a greater proportion of immigrant sons in this group, as compared to the direct-shifters, had maintained their positions above the lowest skill level through my subsequent checkpoints.

The relative success of achiever-mediators among the second generation suggests a hypothesis. The information that movements involving several different occupations were more successful in terms

of permanence of occupational achievement does not warrant conclusions as to the motives and personalities of the persons involved.
It could well have been that others who had moved directly from
unskilled jobs to higher levels and failed were also trying, unsuccessfully, to establish themselves in other pursuits, and so the data
tell us only the fact that it was difficult for an East Central European
worker in the interwar period to retain a better-skilled job. Without
deciding the matter, since the data at hand do not permit it, it may,
however, be suggested that in these generally unfavorable conditions, where the odds were against them, those who were prepared
to try anything that came along – the more unsettled ones, in fact
– moving and shifting around from job to job and trying their "luck"
at all opportunities that presented themselves might have had a
better chance at sustained occupational elevation above the lowest
skill level.

Despite an impressive "achievement rate" of 65 percent, the occupational turnover among the second generation men was intense.
The overall rate of occupational *ascents* – the proportion among the
achievers of those who had acquired their elevated positions after
1915 or 1920 and were later found above the lowest-skill level – was
55 percent for the whole group of "achievers." At the same time,
the rate of *descents* – the proportion of those who had held elevated
jobs in 1915 or 1920 but were subsequently found working as ordinary laborers – was a high 45 percent.[48]

This high proportion of occupational "descents" in the career
chains of the second generation was in large part a result of the
Depression. A closer inspection of the periodization of occupational
achievement of the immigrant sons shows, on the one hand, the
interruptive impact of the decade 1930–40 on their careers and, on
the other, the *recoup* after 1940. Thus, 75 percent of the total number
of recorded occupational elevations of second generation men occurred either before or after the Depression.

The destructive impact of the Depression on their careers and the
subsequent *recoup* in the 1940s are seen clearly when their occupational distribution is compared with that of their fathers before
and after the 1930s (see Table A.17 in the Appendix). In 1925, nearly
40 percent of the second generation, as opposed to 25 percent among
the immigrants were found to hold occupations above the level of
ordinary laborer. Five years later, however, the respective proportions were about 25 percent in each group. The Depression "pulled
down," as it were, the second generation to the occupational level
of their immigrant fathers, destroying whatever advantage the sons

had over the immigrants resulting from the upgrading of labor in the mills, their knowledge of English, and better industrial skills. It was only by 1949 that the proportion of immigrant sons employed above the level of ordinary laborer again reached 40 percent.

Now to the occupational pursuits of the second generation women. The presentation will be rather brief, since the available data are very fragmentary. The old Johnstown city directories routinely underenumerated women, and in all likelihood the number of gainfully employed second generation East Central Europeans was systematically underestimated, especially if they worked as domestic servants or clerks in immigrant businesses. The young unmarried women who lived with their families were listed in city directories as "girls at home," but often they were not enumerated at all. And so clearly the total of 129 second generation Slavic and Magyar women (of 509 recorded in the 1900 census) listed in city directories as gainfully employed at one or more of my checkpoints between 1915 and 1949 represents but a small fraction of the total proportion of young women – persisters from the 1900 census – who had ever worked for income. Such incomplete data inform us neither how many East Central European women in Johnstown actually held jobs outside their homes, nor how long they worked. The information gathered from city directories tells us, most of all, what jobs they held.

The overall occupational distribution of the second generation women listed as gainfully employed at least once at my checkpoints between 1915 and 1949 shows a predominance of clerical and sales occupations, which account for about one-half of all cases recorded. Approximately one-fifth each were domestic servants and factory workers, and the remaining one-tenth were professionals (teachers and nurses) and "mediated" cases involving transfers between two or three occupational categories. The occupational distribution of the gainfully employed second generation women at the consecutive checkpoints between 1915 and 1949 is shown in Table A.18 in the Appendix.

The occupational accomplishments of the second generation sons and daughters were not independent of their fathers' positions. The pattern of fathers' influence on the careers of second generation men and women is illustrated in Tables A.19 (sons) and A.20 (daughters) in the Appendix.

Table A.19 shows three pairs of odds-ratios derived from comparing fathers' and sons' occupations in the period 1915–49, from about the time most of the second generation entered the labor market to their last job recorded in this study. The odds-ratios are computed by comparing fathers' and sons' occupational status: (1) at time points fifteen or more years apart; (2) at time points five years apart; and (3) at concurrent time points. Calculations are made for two sets of occupational comparisons: blue- versus white-collar occupations, and unskilled and unspecified semiskilled versus specified semiskilled and skilled occupations.[49]

First and foremost all odds-ratios derived from these comparisons are greater than 1, indicating a positive association between fathers' and sons' occupational position. Predictably, the vast majority of sons of fathers who were ordinary laborers worked at the same occupational level. All sets of comparisons also indicate a high rate of intergenerational skidding, reconfirming the profound instability of the economic situation of the East Central Europeans in Johnstown.

The order and magnitudes of the estimates also suggest two further patterns: (1) For both blue- and white-collar and within the blue-collar comparisons, fathers' position has a stronger impact on sons' occupational location in comparisons made at concurrent time points than in those involving longer time periods; (2) the influence of fathers' on sons' occupational position is stronger in blue- and white-collar comparisons than within the blue-collar ones. These findings should be accepted cautiously, because of the small sizes of the samples on which they are based.[50] Yet the observed differences seem significant substantively in that they have interesting methodological implications.

First a comment on the tendency of fathers' position to exert more influence on sons' occupational pursuits in comparisons concurrent in time as opposed to those covering longer time periods. Moving from concurrent comparisons of fathers' and sons' occupations to those fifteen or more years apart reduces the odds-ratio by approximately one-half in both comparisons (blue- and white-collar, 7.4:3.3, and within the blue-collar 3.4:1.6). For the immigrants who had achieved elevated occupational positions, their superior status was, as we have seen earlier in this book, inherently precarious and unstable, achieved one year, lost the next in the incessant flow of *morskoje plavanije* – "swimming at sea" – that comprised the work experience of East Central Europeans in Johnstown. In this context, the "influence of the father's occupational status" meant his very concrete ability – or lack of it – to channel his sons *here and now* into particular departments, shops, labor gangs, or ethnic businesses.

And, particularly in the mills, continuously governed by ascriptive-particularist criteria in hiring and promotion, with the "careers" of the workers dependent on lucky chains of personal influence and contacts, the instability of the immigrants' occupational achievement practically eliminated any long-term influence of the once-elevated status of fathers on their sons' subsequent positions.

Another parallel reason for the weak association between fathers' and sons' positions in the mills may be the fact that jobs were often allocated to sons by members of their "social resource" networks other than their fathers: by relatives employed at Bethlehem Steel, as well as by friends and *kums* who funneled jobs to the young, thus deflecting, or, rather absorbing, part of the fathers' influence. In view of our knowledge about the collectivist employment strategies on which the immigrant groups relied during the first half of the century, it may be suggested that for the purpose of intergenerational mobility studies the definition of "father" should be broadened to include other members of the kinship/ethnic units who could have served in lieu of the parent himself.

The second pattern suggested by the results in the table is that the association between fathers' and sons' occupations is stronger in blue- and white-collar comparisons than within the blue-collar ones (the average odds-ratios calculated from all three time panels are 5.1. and 2.0, respectively). The composition of the "white-collar" sample in my study makes this finding partly self-evident: A considerable proportion of the second generation men employed in white-collar occupations worked in family businesses. For this group, the influence of parental status quite literally meant its "inheritance."[51] In this context, more interesting appears the fact that even in the comparison at concurrent time points, half of the sons of white-collar fathers – that is, ethnic businessmen – were found employed in manual jobs. It was suggested in Chapter 4 that the resumption by immigrants of ordinary manual labor after having held for some time a better-skilled blue-collar position or white-collar one in ethnic business or services should more properly be called "shifting" rather than "skidding." To account for historical situations such as the one described in this book, involving high impermanency of occupational achievement and collectivist family tactics in employment and work, we should also, perhaps, work out and operationalize a concept of "*inter*generational shifting."

The impact of fathers' occupations on daughters' careers is illustrated in Table A.20 in the Appendix. A combined odds-ratio was calculated by comparing fathers' and daughters' status, at concurrent time points, in blue- and white-collar categories, as recorded at each of six checkpoints between 1915 and 1949 when both daughter and father were listed in Johnstown city directories as gainfully employed. The table shows an equal distribution of daughters of blue-collar fathers between manual and white-collar occupations. Over 80 percent of the daughters of white-collar fathers, however, had clerical, sales, or professional occupations, whereas fewer than 20 percent were employed as blue-collar workers, either as domestic servants or as factory laborers. As with immigrant sons employed in white-collar occupations, this high capacity of white-collar fathers to confer similar status on their daughters is explained in part by a considerable proportion of daughters who worked in family businesses as clerks, cashiers, or bookkeepers.

Before we move on, we will look briefly at the second generation women in the professions: teachers and nurses. An exact count is impossible because of the gaps in local records, but between 1915 and 1940 there were apparently in Johnstown about 50 to 60 of them altogether, approximately 30 to 35 teachers and 20 to 25 nurses.[52] Although the majority of the young women pursued employment only for the period of time before they were married, those in the professions worked for a longer time. Of the 13 women teachers who started working in Johnstown public schools before the Depression, one-half worked for ten or more years.

For an East Central European immigrant daughter in Johnstown during the 1920s and 1930s to continue formal education beyond the age of fifteen or sixteen required either that her parents be affluent enough to afford giving up her help in the household or her financial contributions, or – if they were not economically secure – that they saw genuine value in occupational careers for women.

Of the 22 women teachers whose fathers' occupations I was able to identify, one-half were daughters of manual workers. I talked with a few of the second generation women who taught in Johnstown schools before World War II. They all happened to be Serbs; there were then in the whole Serbian community in Johnstown about 6 or 7 young women who became teachers. As they tell it, their desire to pursue a teaching career was, at least in their cases, supported by their mothers against their fathers' will and strengthened by role expectations that formed in their peer group (all of these women were friends and lived close to each other).[53]

The commitment to a teaching career by these women in a sociocultural environment in which formal education was not highly val-

ued and where the roles of women and men in the family were
traditionally defined, entailed a considerable price. "The men were
afraid of girls like that . . . The educated girls often had problems
with marriage, it was difficult to find a husband at their level, and
they were proud."[54] And a similar opinion from a second generation
man: "When a girl became a teacher, it was a good chance she'd
stay single. And many did. Men stayed away from them. Not so
with nurses, they were not so remote, and not so with secretaries,
because they kind of waited for a husband."[55]

This completes our examination of the work and occupational accomplishments of the younger generation. Now to two other important components of their idea of a "good life": relocation into
the better, more prestigious neighborhoods in the city, and homeownership. As we have seen, during the 1920s two-thirds of the
adult second generation traced from the 1900 census still lived in
the parental households; by 1930, this proportion was one-fourth.
The analysis that follows is limited to the American-born Slavic and
Magyar men recorded as household heads in city directories between 1920 and 1949.[56]

In their residential movements, the second generation closely resembled their parents, relocating from the old immigrant colonies
near the mills into the more prestigious neighborhoods on the hills
surrounding the city where new ethnic communities sprang up. By
1940, of the total of 294 American-born male heads of households,
both persisters and returnees, about 30 percent lived in the primary
immigrant colonies, 60 percent in secondary ethnic settlements, and
about 10 percent in mixed neighborhoods.

A comparison of the occupational distribution of those who stayed
in the foreign colonies, those who had already lived in secondary
ethnic settlements, and those who relocated there between 1930 and
1940 suggests that the men who moved from the old immigrant
sections into the more prestigious neighborhoods on the hills were
moderately "on the make," improving their life situations in terms
of occupational and residential status. Thus by 1940 the proportion
of ordinary laborers, among the American-born men who did not
move away from the foreign colonies after 1930, was 84 percent, as
opposed to 74 percent among those who were already living in secondary ethnic settlements, and 69 percent among the "movers,"
men who relocated from the primary to the secondary settlements
between 1930 and 1940. It may be added, too, that the lowest pro-

portion of ordinary laborers (40 percent) was found among the minority group residing in nonethnic, mixed neighborhoods in Johnstown.

The process of home acquisition among the immigrants' sons was slower, delayed by the Depression. By 1930, among all of the second generation male heads of households, persisters as well as returnees, traced from the 1900 census, the proportion of homeowners was only 14 percent. In 1940, it was 19 percent, falling much behind the overall rate for the city of 35 percent. The ending of the Depression and the wartime industrial prosperity made it possible for more Johnstowners to accumulate enough savings to invest in a home. Also helpful were changes in the real estate market that introduced easily available, long-term, low-interest mortgages with low down payments, and low-cost building construction aimed at working-class buyers.[57] And so during the 1940s the overall homeownership rate among American-born Slav and Magyar men doubled, reaching 39 percent in 1949. Among the persisters – men who were present in Johnstown in 1930 – it was 45 percent, a proportion corresponding to the general rate reported for the city by the 1950 census.[58] (The shifts in homeownership among the second generation male heads of households between 1930 and 1949 are shown in Table A.21 in the Appendix.)

We turn now to the last aspect of the immigrant children's conception of a "good life": social participation and respect. As in the lives of their parents, their worldviews had two anchors: family and work. Both were defined, lived, and evaluated in the context of the local ethnic communities in which most of them resided. For most of the second generation, their membership in the ethnic communities was natural and self-evident. In comparison with their immigrant parents, however, the American-born, English-speaking children of the immigrants had more and broader contacts with their American peers in school, sports, shared recreational facilities, and finally in the workplace, despite the continuing ethnic segmentation. In comparison with the immigrant generation, the American-born children were to a greater extent "holding," rather than being "held by," their ethnic communities. As experienced by the second generation, the "walls" separating the ethnic communities and the outside American world had become transparent. More fundamentally, their position in American society and in the ethnic communities had been that of "hyphenates," people belonging "here" and "there" at the same time, just as the immigrants had belonged simultaneously to the old world in Europe and to their "foreign colonies" in America.

Although the walls that surrounded them had become transparent and partly permeable through broadened contacts and exchanges, the ethnic communities had nevertheless continued to "hold" the second generation who, reciprocally, "held" them through everyday participation. Social respect – high reputation and good standing among people that constituted an important component of the image of a successful life in the perceptions of the second generation – was ultimately realized and enjoyed in their daily lives first and foremost in the ethnic communities through private and organizational activities. We will focus here briefly on the latter, since it was the sphere that seems to have generated some tension for the second generation.

As we have seen in Chapter 7, participation and leadership in ethnic organizations had been perceived by the members as an important element of prestige. Had the immigrant children before World War II ascended to status positions in the ethnic organizational network? For the most part, they had not: The American-born generation took over ethnic leadership in Johnstown only after the war. Through the 1930s, with the exception of the short-lived elitist Slavonic League, in which the representatives of second generation professionals were prominent, the established ethnic associations of the East Central Europeans in Johnstown had been dominated by the immigrants: The Slovak Jednota, Slovak Lutheran Union, Hungarian Verhovay, Serb National Federation, Ukrainian National Association, Polish Roman Catholic Union, Polish National Alliance, Slovene National Benefit Society, Croatian Fraternal Union, Greek Catholic Union, and the Russian Brotherhood had on their rosters by the end of the 1930s no more than one or at most two officers of the American-born generation. The actual leadership and authority remained firmly in the hands of the immigrants. In fact, attempts by members of the second generation to get themselves elected to ethnic offices and to assume leadership positions were usually met with reluctance and often open resistance by the immigrants.

My American-born informants in Johnstown from practically all nationality groups confirmed this opinion: "They [the immigrants] were very strict and kept a [tight] hand on those societies. They called [us] young men 'snots'"; "Immigrants did not want the second generation to participate [as officers] in ethnic societies except maybe [to organize] picnics."[59] The immigrants' rejection of the second generation's attempts to assume leadership positions in ethnic organizations seems to have produced no overly strong tension in the lives of the former: "[They did not want us], so we turned elsewhere, to sports, to our own things and social life."[60] Nevertheless, it added one more element of current frustration to their daily lives, this time generated not from without but from within the ethnic communities themselves.

The long-range impact of this situation became visible only later, in the postwar years when the foreign-born generation started passing away and there were no impatient crowds of second generation members ready to take over their posts. It is possible that the closing off in the 1930s and 1940s of ethnic group leadership to the American-born generation, then more eager to assume organizational functions, was one of the contributing factors in the observed privatization of ethnicity in the postwar era, in which participation and social contacts have been reduced to narrow circles of personal friends, and large organized networks have served increasingly as the *decorum* utilized at symbolic occasions to manifest the group's public existence.

Interestingly, the second generation women in Johnstown seem to have been absorbed into the leadership network of Slavic and Magyar women's organizations with greater ease, possibly because the positions in women's societies were not considered as a source of power in the immigrant communities and served primarily as supportive, supplementary status lifters. Relatively recent, since most of them were established in the interwar period, in order to survive they also needed a sustained membership body, which the founding immigrant mothers drew in a large part from the second generation.

And so we come to the conclusion of this unavoidably selective interpretation of the life-worlds of the second generation before World War II. We have seen what were the fundamental values that they thought worth striving for and have mapped the basic tensions that structured their existence. We have also reviewed some of their accomplishments. How did their perceptions of their situations and life goals relate to where they stood at the end of the 1940s?

The chief aspiration of the second generation was to acquire "more, more of everything" than their parents had. The "more" included better jobs, material possessions, and an elevated standard of living. The industrial and technological advances after World War I made possible at least a partial realization of these goals, achieved through familism, as the primary economic strategy, and reliance on kinship ethnic networks for job advancement. But the structural limitations of Johnstown and its semicaste normative system set rigid constraints on the opportunities of the immigrants' children. Their lives were filled with frustrations and tensions – hard lives, with built-in resignation and insecurity. Just when they entered their fully adult lives, the Depression forced most of them to struggle for survival and to abandon ambitions to achieve a "life better than the parents'," although their disappointments were somewhat eased by the fact that the "calamity" affected the whole country.

After the Depression, their situation improved considerably, with the nationwide upturn in the economy and technological progress, and also as a result of the unionization of local mills which regulated and increased wages and reduced the role of particularist criteria in job promotions. "It was a hard life for us in those years, and particularly in the Depression it was the worst. After that . . . it was a different epoch, much easier, in the forties and later" – this assessment was shared by most of the second generation in Johnstown who told about their past.[61]

By 1949, 40 percent of the American-born men traced in this study since the beginning of the century held better-skilled manual or white-collar jobs. Most still worked as "laborers," although probably most of them acquired mechanized jobs in the mills. After the war, over two-thirds of those traced from the 1900 census resided in higher-status secondary ethnic settlements or in mixed neighborhoods in the city. The end of the Depression and the beginning of good years for the steel industry, bringing to Johnstown regular orders and steady production, together with changes in the real estate market favorable to lower-class buyers, facilitated the realization of the goal that was so important in the ethnic working-class culture: homeownership. Between 1940 and 1950 the homeownership rate among the second generation in Johnstown more than doubled, reaching parity with that for the whole city. Finally, nationwide growth of mass-produced consumer technology made available to the immigrant children more, and more modern, material goods which either had not existed in their childhood or had been out of the reach for their parents.

How did the second generation perceive their position and evaluate their accomplishments? In his classic account of working-class life in America, *Automobile Workers and the American Dream*, Eli Chinoy interprets the workers' emphasis on "economic security," "small goals in the factory," and "constant accumulation of personal [material] possessions" (rather than on formal education and occupational advancement) as defensive rationalizations of failure and substitutes for success: "Most workers do not explain their failure to rise in terms of forces beyond their control. In order to convince themselves that they are getting ahead and that they are not without ambition, workers apply to the ends they pursue the vocabulary of the [American] tradition of opportunity."[62]

To interpret the perceptions of the immigrant generation, in the conclusion of Chapter 7 we used the distinction between pragmatic and normative acceptance of social order proposed by Michael Mann in his essay *The Social Cohesion of Liberal Democracy*.[63] Translated into this framework, Chinoy's thesis reads as follows: (1) The workers basically lack pragmatism in their assessment of their low position in the existing social order: "Most workers do not explain [their situation] in terms of forces beyond their control." (2) They display a virtually complete normative assimilation of the dominant [middle-class] values: The workers "defensively rationalize" their "failure to rise," in the culturally prescribed mode, through education and vertical occupational mobility by grasping at "substitute success." Conducted in the 1950s, Chinoy's study, as he himself explicitly points out, dealt with nonethnic native-born American workers. Clearly, his interpretation does not adequately represent the worldviews of the children of the East Central European peasant-immigrants.

Deep pragmatism underlay the orientations of the second generation Slavs and Magyars in Johnstown before World War II. As we have seen, they were acutely aware of the constraints that the social and economic conditions of the time and place in which they lived exerted on their life opportunities.

They did perceive the norms of mainstream society through the "transparent walls" between their ethnic communities and the dominant world, and they partially internalized these norms, which penetrated their lives in various ways. This unavoidable, if only partial, absorption of the dominant American norms and expectations – in particular that of personal worth tested in individual performance and talents – although strongly counterbalanced by a pragmatic assessment of the external ethnic/class obstacles, nevertheless affected to some extent the second generation's perceptions of their position and accomplishments. As they told about their lives in Johnstown before World War II, there was in their accounts a detectable trace of a normative acceptance of the dominant opportunity ideology: "We did not have much chance [to become educated and

move up in the American world,] . . . [yet] one has to earn everything in life, you earn when you try; [if] you don't, you're worth
nothing."[64]

These confused expressions of the immigrant children reflected,
however, not an invasion of "false consciousness" – replacement
of ethnic working-class values by the dominant middle-class ones
– but rather the segmentation of reality into two spheres: the dominant American world and the ethnic community, each "ruled," as
it were, by different perceptions. The perception of the "external
obstacles," partially angry and rebellious, partially resigned and ac-
quiescent, depending on the realm of life, was applied virtually
unanimously by my Johnstown informants to the dominant American world and their position in it. On the other hand, regarding
the accomplishments within their own ethnic communities and according to their cultural standards and expectations, the second generation more readily perceived an individual and his or her capa-
bilities – or more precisely, a family collective – as active agents in
striving for success.

Their assessment of the chances available within their ethnic
working-class habitat was informed by down-to-earth realism. It expressed a qualified acknowledgment of the opportunity for slightly
upwardly inclined movement that accurately defined the space
within which they could and did move, searching to realize valued
goals. Their values, focusing on economic security, better work in
the factory, accumulation of material possessions, and the possession of a reputable family, respect, and prestige in the ethnic community, were not simply "defensive rationalizations" by people who
had failed in society. With a sharp sense of the external constraints,
and at the cost of uncomfortable tension and pain, the second generation nevertheless genuinely conceived of, felt, and pursued these
values qua achievements. In their ethnic working-class communities, with the nourishing cultural background of the parental households, the values that informed their images of a "good life" and
mobilized them to maneuver within the restricted environment to
carve out from it the maximum achievable, possessed their own
autonomy. These values played a vital part in sustaining them; they
were also authentic – that is, felt and lived genuinely.

The second generation knew their world and its rules. They actively maneuvered within it, appropriating from it as much as possible, using a battery of collective family strategies practiced by their
immigrant parents and adding their own devices to make them more

efficient: residing with their parents after marriage, then setting up their own households in close proximity; slowing down their pace of work in the mills to avoid exhaustion, and working overtime when they needed more capital; chain-traveling to other cities when one of them got a good job and could serve as a "shoulder" for others; circulating between occupational levels in Johnstown when opportunities appeared. Reacting to the reality in which they functioned, and at the same time sustaining it by their practices, the second generation conceived of and pursued their achievements as primarily particularist and collective endeavors, mediated by and conditioned on a concerted family effort and a continuing fusion of kinship/ethnic and work/occupational roles, rather than as individual performances in formal education and vertical occupational advancement as prescribed in the cultural paradigm of the dominant American society.

The increasing social and economic differentiation within their ethnic communities was, as the immigrant children saw and acknowledged, "empirical proof" that the realization of *some combination* of the life goals valued in the East Central European working-class culture: more money; better (cleaner and lighter) work; home-ownership; material possessions; and residence in more prestigious sections of the city had been achievable through "particularist efforts" by profiting from whatever skills and talents were possessed by an individual and his or her family collective, mediated by connections and networks of informal contact.

However, while actively sought and cherished, the achievements of the second generation, as defined in terms of their values and preferences, were not to be taken for granted. The instability of the industrial world on which they depended for their livelihood, and the mediation of one's success through the sustained good fortune or personal favors of others – the "shoulders" – had taught the immigrant children to accept their achievements with caution, always ready to face yet another stroke of adversity. "It was possible for us to get somewhere in Johnstown, to get some, like savings, or a house, a better material life. You could live well if it worked, but then you never knew – something comes, and you have nothing . . . have to start all over again."[65] This evaluation of the life situations of East Central Europeans in Johnstown, expressed by a second generation Slovak, was echoed over and over again in my conversations with men and women from all of the other groups.

Their perceptions were informed simultaneously by a sense of having achieved "some," as they cautiously put it, the hard way, in spite of all adversity, so that it was thus even more genuinely felt as an accomplishment, and by a deep-running resignation and sense of disappointment. Evaluating their experience, the immigrant children were unable to separate the feelings of accomplishment and frustration, achievement and failure, since the two had been inextricably meshed in their life-worlds.

Conclusion

The aim of this book was to show how social processes of broader scope and longer *durée* are realized in the course of people's everyday actions, in the continuous interplay between them and their environment. We have seen how, through continuing adaptation, by alternately expanding and contracting their goals in response to situational exigencies, East Central European families in Johnstown domesticated and appropriated their environment.

In particular, this study has traced the slow process of social change as it was realized through the interpenetration of traditional and new elements in the behavior and attitudes of peasant-immigrants and their children in industrial America during the first half of this century. Concurrent with this process, contained in and at the same time containing it, the American working-class and civil-national society were assuming their contemporary form and character.

These processes were "becoming" through the everyday lives of people, in their adaptive decisions made with reference to specific environmental contexts with particular constellations of relationships. These, as we saw, were not favorable to the people who were the subjects of this study. From the turn of the century through World War II, the autocratic character of Johnstown, its limited structural opportunities, its ascription-based normative system, as well as the immigrants' own "supply" characteristics – their lack of English, industrial skills, and urban experience – severely limited the opportunities available to them as they pursued their goals. The unstable production and labor conditions in the steel industry on which the overwhelming majority of them depended for their livelihood made their existence continuously uncertain. As they strove to realize their goals, East Central European families approached their situations differently, selecting from a limited range of opportunities the paths and means suitable to their individual circumstances, tastes, and preferences. But the lives of most of them were shot through with frustration and tension, as the continuous "fluctuations" in their insecure existence brought now disappointment, now a little promise and hope, and again resignation.

298

Both immigrants and their American-born children, "Hunky" laborers in Johnstown, were realists who saw their situation as it was, hard and restricted. They responded to it by purposefully maneuvering within the available space, utilizing a battery of resources fit for the conditions and supported by Johnstown's social organization. These resources comprised familism as a collective economic strategy; reliance on the fusion of kinship/ethnic and work roles and on particularist tactics in job procurement and occupational advancement; the creation of an internal group stratification ladder on which they could move to acquire status; and ethnicization as the way to public participation and self-inclusion in the local American society.

As the immigrants coped with and adapted to the industrial world, some elements of traditional peasant attitudes and behavior, functional and effective under the new conditions, were strengthened and sustained, and some new ways and approaches emerged and solidified. Perceiving their situation in America and evaluating accomplishments and failures, they simultaneously used the multiple-reference framework of the European village and the foreign colonies in Johnstown. The worldviews of peasant-immigrant-workers thus formed a multifaceted entity consisting of different attitudes and practices in which old and new components coexisted alongside each other, informing their perceptions and daily activities.

The life-worlds of American-born East Central Europeans were also kaleidoscopic, composed of similar elements but mapped and allocated differently, ridden with tensions and ambivalences. They sharply perceived the chasm between the norms of equal opportunity, universalist achievement, and citizenship propounded in the dominant American ideology, and the reality of class/ethnic ascription in which they lived. They partially absorbed these norms and partially rejected them, applying different "rules" to different aspects of their situations. They perceived the ethnic working-class world that they inhabited as limited without by class and caste constraints but, within, expandable in terms of values that they considered important. Their life goals were primarily focused on the collective well-being of the family and home and on participation and respect in the ethnic community. They conceived of their daily labors primarily in instrumental terms as a means to maximize these values. But at the same time their attitudes contained a distinct background layer of ready-to-use fatalism and resignation, in part acquired from their parents' old peasant philosophy of life, in part also sustained and regenerated by the daily reality of their experience as American industrial workers. This approach coexisted with the attitude of proletarians who saw the industrial world as exploitative and reacted against it by the use of devices to alleviate their hard and dreary labor and by adjusting their daily work activities to their own current needs and priorities.

This multitude of attitudes and behavioral patterns formed the essence of the life-worlds of these ethnic working-class Americans, and it was with these many-layered, ambiguous *Weltanschauungen* that they entered the postwar era. As they have become increasingly integrated into the mainstream of American society, so have their hybrid worldviews, thus making their particular contribution to the notion of "modern mind" imply not a consistent arrangement of homogeneous, well-fitting attitudes but rather a cognitive and emotional ambiguity, often painful and uncomfortable to the bearers, with an inherent variety of outlooks and ideas patched together in a crazy-quilt mosaic.

Notes

Introduction

1 Josef Barton, *Peasants and Strangers: Italians, Rumanians and Slovaks in an American City, 1890–1950* (Cambridge, Mass.: 1975); John Bodnar, "Immigration and Modernization: The Case of Slavic Peasants in Industrial America," in *American Workingclass Culture: Explorations in American Labor and Social History*, ed. Milton Cantor (Westport, Conn.: 1972), 333–61; *Immigration and Industrialization: Ethnicity in an American Mill Town, 1870–1940* (Pittsburgh, 1977); and *Workers' World: Kinship, Community and Protest in an Industrial Society, 1900–1940* (Baltimore, 1982); John Bodnar, Roger Simon, and Michael Weber, *Lives of Their Own: Blacks, Italians and Poles in Pittsburgh, 1900–1960* (Urbana, Ill.: 1982); Paula Benkart, "Religion, Family and Continuity among Hungarians Migrating to American Cities," Ph.D. thesis, John Hopkins University, 1975; Branko Colaković, *Yugoslav Migrations to America* (San Francisco, 1973); William Galush, "Faith and Fatherland: Dimensions of Polish-American Ethnoreligion, 1875–1975," in *Immigrants and Religion in Urban America*, ed. Randall M. Miller and Thomas D. Marzik (Philadelphia, 1977), 84–103; Caroline Golab, *Immigrant Destinations* (Philadelphia, 1977); Victor Greene, *The Slavic Community on Strike: Immigrant Labor in Pennsylvania Anthracite* (Notre Dame, 1968), and *For God and Country: The Rise of Polish and Lithuanian Ethnic Consciousness in America* (Madison, 1975); Edward R. Kantowitz, "Polish Chicago: Survival through Solidarity," in *The Ethnic Frontier: Group Survival in Chicago and the Midwest*, ed. Melvin G. Holli and Peter d'A Jones (Grand Rapids, 1977), 180–209; Helena Znaniecki-Lopata, *Polish Americans: Status Competition in an Ethnic Community* (Englewood Cliffs, N.J.: 1976); Joseph Parot, "The American Faith and the Persistence of Chicago Polonia," Ph.D. thesis, Northern Illinois University, 1971; Julianna Puskaś, *From Hungary to the United States, 1880–1914* (Budapest, 1982); Irwin Sanders and Ewa Morawska, *Polish-American Community: Survey of Research* (Boston, 1975); Timothy Smith, "Immigrant Social Aspirations and American Education, 1880–1930," *American Quarterly* (Fall 1969), 522–49; "New Approaches to the History of Immigration in Twentieth-century America," *American Historical Review* (July 1966), 1265–80; "Religion and Ethnicity in America," *American Historical Review* (December 1978), 1155–86; and "Lay Initiative in the Religious Life of American Immigrants," in *Anonymous Americans: Explorations in Nineteenth-century Social History*, ed. Tamara Hareven (Englewood Cliffs, N.J.: 1971); Mark Stolarik, *Slovak Migration from Europe*

301

to North America, 1870–1918 (Cleveland, 1980), and Growing Up on the South Side: Three Generations of Slovaks in Bethlehem, Pennsylvania, 1880–1976 (Bethlehem, Pa: 1985); Olivier Zunz, The Changing Face of Inequality: Urbanization, Industrial Development and Immigrants in Detroit, 1880–1920 (Chicago, 1982).

2   John Bodnar, "Materialism and Morality: Slavic-American Immigrants and Education, 1890–1940," Journal of Ethnic Studies (Winter 1976), 1–21; "Immigration, Kinship and the Rise of Working-class Realism in Industrial America," Journal of Social History (Fall 1980), 23–47; Workers' World; Bodnar, Simon, and Weber, Lives of Their Own; David Hogan, "Education and the Making of the Chicago Working Class, 1880–1930," History of Education Quarterly (Fall 1978), 227–71; Daniel Luria, "Wealth, Capital and Power: The Social Meaning of Homeownership," Journal of Interdisciplinary History (Autumn 1976), 261–83; Virginia Yans-McLaughlin, Family and Community: Italian Immigrants in Buffalo, 1880–1930 (Ithaca, N.Y.: 1977).

3   Arthur L. Stinchcombe, Theoretical Methods in Social History (New York, 1978); Charles Tilly, As Sociology Meets History (New York, 1981); Philip Abrams, Historical Sociology (Ithaca, N.Y.: 1982); Theda Skocpol, "Sociology's Historical Imagination," in Vision and Method in Historical Sociology, ed. Theda Skocpol (New York, 1984), 1–22. Skocpol's book also provides a compendium with an annotated bibliography on comparative and historical sociology.

4   Norbert Wiley, "The Current Interregnum in American Sociology," paper presented at the annual meeting of the American Sociological Association, Detroit, August 31–September 4, 1983.

5   For instance, to quote from among only the most renowned studies, S. N. Eisenstadt, The Political Systems of Empires: The Rise and Fall of Historical Bureaucratic Societies (New York, 1963); Reinhard Bendix, Nation-building and Citizenship: Studies of Our Changing Social Order (New York, 1964), Work and Authority in Industry (Berkeley, 1974; orig. 1956), and Kings or People: Power and the Mandate to Rule (Berkeley, 1978); Barrington Moore, Jr., Social Origins of Dictatorship and Democracy: Lord and Peasant in the Making of the Modern World (Boston, 1966); Charles Tilly, The Vendée (Cambridge, Mass.: 1964), and From Mobilization to Revolution (Reading, Mass.: 1978); Charles Tilly, Louise Tilly, and Richard Tilly, The Rebellious Century, 1830–1930 (Cambridge, Mass.: 1975); Eric J. Hobsbawm, Industry and Empire: The Making of Modern English Society (New York, 1968); Immanuel Wallerstein, The Modern World-System: Capitalist Agriculture and the Origins of the European World-Economy in the Sixteenth Century (New York, 1974); Perry Anderson, Lineages of the Absolutist State (London, 1974), and Passages from Antiquity to Feudalism (London, 1974); Theda Skocpol, States and Social Revolutions (Cambridge, 1979); J. Rogers Hollingsworth and Ellen J. Hollingsworth, Dimensions in Urban History: Historical and Social Science Perspectives on Middle-Size American Cities (Madison, 1979); Ira Katznelson, City Trenches,

Urban Politics and the Patterning of Class in the United States (New York, 1981); David M. Gordon, Richard Edwards, and Michael Reich, *Segmented Work, Divided Workers: The Historical Transformation of Labor in the United States* (Cambridge, Mass.: 1982). The contributions of Eisenstadt, Bendix, Tilly, Wallerstein, Anderson, and Moore are analyzed and evaluated in Skocpol, *Vision and Method in Historical Sociology.* For theoretical statements on "macro"-sociological approaches to history, see Stinchcombe, *Theoretical Methods in Social History,* and Tilly, *As Sociology Meets History.*

6   Anthony Giddens, *Profiles and Critiques in Social Theory* (Berkeley, 1982), Chap. 1, "Hermeneutics and Social Theory"; Fernand Braudel, *On History* (London, 1980), pt. 2, "History and Sociology"; E. P. Thompson, "The Poverty of Theory or an Orrery of Errors," in E. P. Thompson, *The Poverty of Theory and Other Essays* (London, 1978); Michael Merrill, "Interview with E. P. Thompson," *Radical History Review* (Winter 1976), 1–12; James Henretta, "Social History as Lived and Written," *American Historical Review* (December 1979), 1293–1322; Clifford Geertz, *The Interpretation of Cultures* (New York, 1973), pt. 1, "Thick Description: Toward an Interpretive Theory of Culture"; Pierre Bourdieu, *Outline of a Theory of Practice* (New York, 1977), Chap. 1, "The Objective Limits of Objectivism." Also Peter L. Berger and Thomas Luckmann, *The Social Construction of Reality: A Treatise in the Sociology of Knowledge* (New York, 1967); and Alain Touraine, *Production de la société* (Paris, 1973).

7   Braudel's work, enormous in the scope of its thematic concerns as well as the epochs it covers, and informed by the underlying notion of the *longue durée,* can hardly be labeled simply as "microscopic." At the same time, his attention to "the lowest level of history" – that is, to the "structures of daily life" – justifies placing him in this group: See *The Mediterranean and the Mediterranean World in the Age of Philip II,* 2 vols. (London 1972–3); *Capitalism and Material Life, 1400–1800* (New York, 1973); and *Civilization and Capitalism, 15th–18th Century,* 3 vols. (New York, 1979). Reconstruction of the process of "structuration" – of the emerging new patterns of social relationships (figurations) and the corresponding transformations of the human psyche as these emerge in the everyday cultural practice of acting persons, also constitutes the basis of Norbert Elias's analysis of the evolution of Western "civilized" society (*The Civilizing Process,* 2 vols. [Oxford, 1978]). For a small and unavoidably arbitrary sampling of sociohistorical studies that trace social processes through the pursuits of "mankind [more than] waist-deep in daily routine," in Braudel's phrase, see, e.g., Herbert Gutman, *Work, Culture and Society in Industrializing America* (New York, 1976); Emmanuel Le Roy Ladurie, *Montaillou: Cathars and Catholics in a French Village, 1294–1324* (London, 1978); Tamara K. Hareven, *Family Time and Industrial Time* (Cambridge, 1982); E. P. Thompson, *The Making of the English Working Class* (London, 1963); Aileen Kraditor, *The Radical Persuasion, 1890–1917: Aspects of the Intellectual History and the Historiography of Three*

American Radical Organizations (London, 1981), esp. Chap. 10, "Epilogue: John Q. Worker"; David A. Corbin, *Life, Work and Rebellion in the Coal Fields* (Urbana, Ill.: 1981) Also Barrington Moore, Jr., *Injustice: The Social Bases of Obedience and Revolt* (White Plains, N.Y.: 1978), pt. 2, "An Historical Perspective: German Workers, 1848–1920." For a review of recent contributions to the field of microhistorical sociology, see Skocpol, "Emerging Agendas and Recurrent Strategies in Historical Sociology," in *Vision and Method in Historical Sociology.*

8   Giddens, *Profiles and Critiques in Social Theory*, 39.

9   Florian Znaniecki, *The Method of Sociology* (Chicago, 1934); Alfred Schutz, *On Phenomenology and Social Relations* (Chicago, 1970); Geertz, *Interpretations of Cultures.*

10 W. I. Thomas and Florian Znaniecki, *The Polish Peasant in Europe and America*, 2 vols., 2nd ed. (New York, 1958). The lasting contribution of Thomas and Znaniecki's analysis lies less in the theoretical interpretation than in the actual documentation of the intertwining of the old and the new elements in the peasant culture as it was being transformed at the turn of the century, first in Poland, then in America. Contrary to the authors' predictions, the peasant-immigrants in America did not quickly become "modern individualists," nor did their family organization "rapidly disintegrate." Rather, the urban industrial environment nurtured in the immigrant working-class culture a combination of traditional and new elements. For an assessment of Thomas and Znaniecki's work, see Herbert Blumer, ed., *Critiques of Research in the Social Sciences: An Appraisal of Thomas and Znaniecki's "The Polish Peasant in Europe and America"* (New York, 1939); in particular reference to Polish-Americans: Znaniecki-Lopata, *Polish Americans.*

11 For a discussion of this "concert performance" as the aim of historical sociology, see Abrams, *Historical Sociology*, Chap. 10: "Theory, Questions, and Some Limits of Historical Sociology."

12 Skocpol, "Sociology's Historical Imagination," 17.

13 Mustafa O. Attir, Burkart Holzner, and Zdenek Suda, eds., *Directions of Change: Modernization Theory, Research and Realities* (Boulder, Colo.: 1981); Reinhard Bendix, "Tradition and Modernity Reconsidered," *Comparative Studies in Society and History* (April 1967), 292–346; Herbert Blumer, "Industrialization and the Traditional Order," *Sociology and Social Research* (January 1964), 129–39; S. N. Eisenstadt, "Social Change, Differentiation and Evolution," *American Sociological Review* (June 1964), 375–86; "Social Transformation in Modernization," *American Sociological Review* (October 1965), 659–73; *Tradition, Change and Modernity* (New York, 1973); and "Post-Traditional Societies and the Continuity and Reconstruction of Tradition," *Daedalus* (Winter 1973), 1–29; Clifford Geertz, ed., *Old Societies and New States: The Quest for Modernity in Asia and Africa* (New York, 1963); Eugene Gendzier, "Modernity and Development," *Theory and Society* (June–December 1979), 139–55; Joseph R. Gusfield, "Tradition and Modernity: Misplaced Polarities in the

Study of Social Change," *American Journal of Sociology* (January 1967),
357–63; Bert F. Hoselitz and Wilbert Moore, *Industrialization and Society*
(New York, 1963); Jessie G. Lutz and Salah El-Shakhs, eds., *Tradition
and Modernity: The Role of Traditionalism in the Modernization Process* (New
Brunswick, N.J., 1982); Leon Mayhew, "Ascription in Modern Societies," *Sociological Inquiry* (Spring 1968), 105–21; John J. Poggie, Jr., and
Robert N. Lynch, eds., *Rethinking Modernization* (Westport, Conn.:
1974); Philip M. Hauser, "Observations on the Urban–Folk and Urban–
Rural Dichotomies as Forms of Western Ethnocentrism," in *The Study
of Urbanization*, ed. Philip M. Hauser and Leo F. Schnore (New York,
1965), 503–19; Allan Schnaiberg, "Measuring Modernism: Theoretical
and Empirical Explorations," *American Journal of Sociology* (November
1970), 399–426.

14   It is impossible to enumerate even a small fraction of these studies. For
a few of the most renowned accounts relating to the "developing" societies: Bert F. Hoselitz, "The City, the Factory, and Economic Growth,"
American Economic Review (May 1955), 166–93; Janet Abu-Lughod, "Migrant Adjustment to City Life: The Egyptian Case," *American Journal of
Sociology* (July 1961), 22–32; Gerald Breese, *Urbanization in Newly Developing Countries* (Englewood Cliffs, N.J.: 1966); A. L. Epstein, "Urbanization and Social Change in Africa," *Current Anthropology* (October
1967), 275–96; James C. Abegglen, *The Japanese Factory* (Glencoe, Ill.:
1958). Studies also abound on the persistence of traditional ways and
orientations in various segments of contemporary American society:
Milton Gordon, *Assimilation in American Life: The Role of Race, Religion
and National Origin* (New York, 1964); Stanley Lieberson, "Suburbs and
Ethnic Residential Patterns," *American Journal of Sociology* (May 1962),
673–81; *A Piece of the Pie: Blacks and White Immigrants since 1880* (Berkeley,
1980); Herbert Gans, *The Urban Villagers* (Boston, 1962); Gerald Suttles,
The Social Order of the Slum: Ethnicity and Territory in the Inner City (Chicago, 1968); Nathan Glazer and Daniel P. Moynihan, *Beyond the Melting
Pot: The Negroes, Puerto Ricans, Jews, Italians and Irish in New York* (Cambridge, Mass.: 1963); Eugene Litwak, "Occupational Mobility and Extended Family Cohesion," *American Sociological Review* (February 1960),
5–23; Alvin Gouldner, *Patterns of Industrial Bureaucracy* (Glencoe, Ill.:
1954); Everett Hughes, *Men and Their Work* (Glencoe, Ill.: 1958); David
Brown, *The Mobile Professors* (Washington, D.C.: 1967); Mark S. Granovetter, *Getting a Job: A Study of Contacts and Careers* (Cambridge, Mass.:
1974); William H. Whyte, *The Organization Man* (New York, 1956); James
Coleman, *Community Conflict* (New York, 1957); Angus Campbell,
Philip E. Converse, Warren E. Miller, et al., *The American Voter* (New
York, 1964); Elmora M. Matthews, *Neighbor and Kin* (Nashville, Tenn.:
1966); Leonard Blumberg and Robert R. Bell, "Urban Migration and
Kinship Ties," *Social Problems* (Spring 1959), 328–33; Thompson Peter
Omari, "Factors Associated with Urban Adjustment of Rural Southern
Migrants," *Social Forces* (October 1956), 47–53; Kenneth L. Wilson and

Alejandro Portes, "Immigrant Enclaves: An Analysis of the Labor Market Experiences of Cubans in Miami," *American Journal of Sociology* (September 1980), 295–319; Ivan H. Light, *Ethnic Enterprise in America: Business and Welfare among Chinese, Japanese, and Blacks* (Berkeley, 1972); Edna Bonacic and John Modell, *The Economic Basis of Ethnic Solidarity: Small Business in the Japanese American Community* (Berkeley, 1980).

15 Barton, *Peasants and Strangers;* Bodnar, "Immigration and Modernization: The Case of Slavic Peasants in Industrial America"; Bodnar, Simon, and Weber, *Lives of Their Own;* Greene, *The Slavic Community on Strike,* and *For God and Country;* Gutman, *Work, Culture and Society in Industrializing America;* Hareven, *Family Time and Industrial Time;* Hogan, "Education and the Making of the Chicago Working Class"; John Modell and Tamara K. Hareven, "Urbanization and the Malleable Household: An Examination of Boarding and Lodging in American Families," *Journal of Marriage and the Family* (August 1973), 467–80; David Montgomery, *Workers' Control in America: Studies in the History of Work, Technology and Labor Struggles* (Cambridge, 1979); Daniel Rodgers, "Tradition, Modernity and the American Industrial Worker," *Journal of Interdisciplinary History* (Spring 1977), 655–67; Rudolph J. Vecoli, "Contadini in Chicago: A Critique of *The Uprooted,*" *Journal of American History* (December 1964), 404–17; Yans-McLaughlin, *Family and Community;* Zunz, *Changing Face of Inequality;* David Brody, *Steel Workers in America: The Non-Union Era* (Cambridge, Mass.: 1960); Gordon, Reich, and Edwards, *Segmented Work, Divided Workers;* Tamara K. Hareven, "The Dynamics of Kin in an Industrial Community," *American Journal of Sociology,* Special Issue S84 (1978), 151–75; Gabriel Kolko, "The American Working Class: Immigrant Foundations," in *Main Currents in Modern American History,* ed. Kolko (New York, 1976), Chap 3; Elisabeth H. Pleck, "Two Worlds in One: Work and Family," *Journal of Social History* (Winter 1976), 177–95; Virginia Yans-McLaughlin, "Patterns of Work and Family Organization: Buffalo's Italians," *Journal of Interdisciplinary History* (Autumn 1971), 299–314.

16 The "situational" approach to ethnicity has its more and its less radical versions. The former takes whatever attributes are associated with particular ethnic groups to be primarily situational, generated and sustained by external structural (economic or political) conditions. See, e.g., Fredrik Barth, ed., *Ethnic Groups and Boundaries: The Social Organization of Cultural Differences* (Boston, 1969); Leo Despres, ed., *Ethnicity and Resource Competition* (The Hague, 1975); William L. Yancey, Eugene P. Ericksen, and Richard Juliani, "Emergent Ethnicity: A Review and Reformulation," *American Sociological Review* (June 1976), 391–403; Charles Ragin, "Ethnic Political Mobilization: The Welsh Case," *American Sociological Review* (August 1979), 619–35; "Class, Status and 'Reactive Ethnic Cleavages': The Social Bases of Political Regionalism," *American Sociological Review* (June 1977), 438–50; Nelson Kasfir, "Ex-

plaining Ethnic Political Participation," *World Politics* (March 1979), 365–88; Kenneth McRoberts, "Internal Colonialism: The Case of Quebec," *Ethnic and Racial Studies* (April 1979), 293–318; François Nielsen, "The Flemish Movement in Belgium after World War II: A Dynamic Analysis," *American Sociological Review* (February 1980), 76–94; Joanne Nagel and Susan Olzak, "Ethnic Mobilization in New and Old States: An Extension of the Competition Model," *Social Problems* (December 1982), 127–43; Joanne Nagel, "A Structural Theory of Ethnicity," paper presented at the annual meeting of the American Sociological Association, San Antonio, August 27–31, 1984; Cynthia Enloe, "The Growth of the State and Ethnic Mobilization: The American Experience," *Ethnic and Racial Studies* (April 1981), 123–36; Eric M. Leifer, "Competing Models of Political Mobilization: The Role of Ethnic Ties," *American Journal of Sociology* (July 1981), 23–47; Michael Hechter, "The Political Economy of Ethnic Change," *American Journal of Sociology* (March 1974), 1151–78; Michael Hechter, Debra Friedman, and Malka Appelbaum, "A Theory of Ethnic Collective Action," *International Migration Review* (Summer 1982), 412–34; Alejandro Portes, "The Rise of Ethnicity: Determinants of Ethnic Perceptions among Cuban Exiles in Miami," *American Sociological Review* (June 1984), 383–98.

A "moderate" interpretation, which also informs the present study does not reduce individual and collective expressions of ethnicity to purely situational phenomena with no cultural anchorage but rather combines in one embracing account an analysis of the context, or the external activators of ethnic behavior and attitudes, and of their specific cultural form and content. See, e.g., Nathan Glazer and Daniel P. Moynihan, Introduction, in Nathan Glazer and Daniel P. Moynihan, eds., *Ethnicity: Theory and Experience* (Cambridge, Mass.: 1978), 1–26; M. Elaine Burgess, "The Resurgence of Ethnicity: Myth or Reality?", *Ethnic and Racial Studies* (July 1978), 265–86; Stephan Thernstrom, Ann Orlov, and Oscar Handlin, eds., *Harvard Encyclopedia of American Ethnic Groups* (Cambridge, Mass.: 1980); Andrew Greeley, *Why Can't They Be Like Us? America's White Ethnic Groups* (New York, 1971); Charles F. Keyes, "Towards a New Formulation of the Concept of Ethnic Group," *Ethnicity* (March 1976), 213–18; Sandra Wallman, ed., *Ethnicity at Work* (London 1979); John W. Bennett, ed., *The New Ethnicity: Perspectives from Ethnology* (St. Paul, 1975). A similar approach also informs such sociohistorical studies of immigration and ethnicity as Yans-McLaughlin's *Family and Community*, Bodnar, Simon, and Weber's *Lives of Their Own*, and Hareven's *Family Time and Industrial Time;* Humbert S. Nelli, *Italians in Chicago, 1880–1930;* Rudolph J. Vecoli, *The People of New Jersey* (Princeton, 1965); Greene, *For God and Country.* For a critical review of "primordial" and "situational" ("mobilizationist") approaches to ethnicity, see James McKay, "An Exploratory Synthesis of Primordial and Mobilizationist Approaches to Ethnic Phenomena," *Ethnic and Racial Studies* (October 1982), 395–421; also John Higham, "Current Trends in the

Study of Ethnicity in the United States," *Journal of American Ethnic History* (Fall 1982), 5–15.

17 Lloyd I. Rudolph and Suzanne Hoeber Rudolph, *The Modernity of Tradition: Political Development in India* (Chicago, 1967). Similar ideas are also found in Eisenstadt, "Post-Traditional Societies and the Continuity and Reconstruction of Tradition"; Clifford Geertz, "The Integrative Revolution: Primordial Sentiments and Civil Politics in the New States," in *Old Societies and New States*, 105–58; Poggie and Lynch, *Rethinking Modernization;* Lutz and El-Shakhs, *Tradition and Modernity: The Role of Traditionalism in the Modernization Process.*

18 See, e.g., Charles Tilly and C. Harold Brown, "On Uprooting, Kinship and the Auspices of Migration," *International Journal of Comparative Sociology* (September 1967), 139–64; Bonacic and Modell, *Economic Basis of Ethnic Solidarity;* Light, *Ethnic Enterprise in America;* Wilson and Portes, "Immigrant Enclaves: An Analysis of the Labor Market Experiences of Cubans in Miami"; Leifer, "Competing Models of Political Mobilization"; John S. MacDonald and Leatrice D. MacDonald, "Chain Migration, Ethnic Neighborhood Formation and Social Networks," *Millbank Memorial Fund Quarterly* (January 1964), 82–97; Marta Tienda, "Familism and Structural Assimilation of Mexican Immigrants in the United States," *International Migration Review* (Fall 1980), 383–9; Wallman, *Ethnicity at Work;* Cummins, *Self-help in Urban America;* Yans-McLaughlin, *Family and Community;* Hareven, *Family Time and Industrial Time;* Golab, *Immigrant Destinations;* Bodnar, Simon, and Weber, *Lives of Their Own.*

19 Cf., for instance, Bodnar, "Immigration and Modernization"; Barton, *Peasants and Strangers;* Bodnar, Simon, and Weber, *Lives of Their Own.* On the prevalence of security over achievement concerns among the immigrant working class, see Stephan Thernstrom, *Poverty and Progress* (Cambridge, Mass.: 1964), esp. Chaps. 4, 5, and 7.

20 Among the most renowned expositions of this argument, see Talcott Parsons, *Structure and Process in Modern Societies* (Glencoe, Ill.: 1965); *The System of Modern Societies* (Englewood Cliffs, N.J.: 1971); Karl W. Deutsch, "Social Mobilization and Political Development," *American Political Science Review* (May 1961), 493–514; Gabriel A. Almond, "A Development Approach to Political Systems," *World Politics* (Summer 1965), 183–214; Oscar Handlin, *Boston's Immigrants, 1790–1880: A Study of Acculturation* (Cambridge, Mass.: 1941; rev. ed., New York, 1970); Robert E. Park, *Race and Culture* (Glencoe, Ill.: 1950); Thomas Sowell, *Ethnic America: A History* (New York, 1981). For a review of the "assimilationist" literature, see Charles Hirschman, "America's Melting Pot Reconsidered," *Annual Review of Sociology* 9 (1983), 397–423.

21 Studies on "reactive ethnicity" cover a wide variety of settings, from postcolonial nation states to local ethnic communities in Canada, the United States, and Western Europe. See, e.g., Raymond L. Hall, ed., *Ethnic Autonomy: Comparative Dynamics, the Americas, Europe and the Developing World* (New York: 1979); Michael T. Hannan, "The Dynamics

of Ethnic Boundaries in Modern States," in John W. Meyer and Michael
T. Hannan, ed., *National Development and the World System* (Chicago,
1979), 253–75; Nagel and Olzak, "Ethnic Mobilization in New and Old
States"; Cynthia Enloe, *Ethnic Conflict and Political Development* (Boston,
1973); Ragin, "Ethnic Political Mobilization"; Kasfir, "Explaining Ethnic
Political Participation"; Michael Hechter, *Internal Colonialism: The Celtic
Fringe in British National Development, 1536–1966* (Berkeley, 1975); Hechter, Friedman, and Appelbaum, "A Theory of Ethnic Collective Action"; Leifer, "Competing Models of Political Mobilization: The Role of
Ethnic Ties"; Frances Henry, Introduction, in Frances Henry, ed., *Ethnicity in the Americas* (The Hague, 1976), 1–7; Saskia Sassen-Koob, "Formal and Informal Associations: Dominicans and Colombians in New
York," *International Migration Review* (Summer 1980), 179–92; Richard
Sinnott and E. E. Davis, "Political Mobilization, Political Institution-
alization, and the Maintenance of Ethnic Conflict," *Ethnic and Racial
Studies* (October 1981), 398–414. For a critical review of ethnic mobilization–reactive ethnicity literature, see Suzan Olzak, "Contemporary
Ethnic Mobilization," *American Review of Sociology* 9 (1983), 355–74.
22 Bodnar, Simon, and Weber, *Lives of Their Own*. See also Bodnar, *Workers'
World*, and *Immigration and Industrialization*; Greene, *For God and Country*; Yans-McLaughlin, *Family and Community*; Rudolph J. Vecoli, "European Americans; From Immigrants to Ethnics," in William H. Cartwright and Richard L. Watson, Jr., eds., *The Reinterpretation of American
History and Culture* (Washington, D.C.: 1973), 81–112. On segmentation
and group particularism in the maturing of America as a "society of
interrelated but insular parts," see Robert H. Wiebe, *The Segmented Society: An Introduction to the Meaning of America* (Oxford, 1975), esp. Chap.
2, "The Units of Life."
23 In particular, this book is indebted for insights and approaches to two
now-classic sociohistorical studies: Gutman's *Work, Culture and Society
in Industrializing America*, and E. P. Thompson's *The Making of the English
Working Class*. It also profited from others: Brody, *Steel Workers in America*; "The Old Labor and the New: In Search of an American Working
Class," *Labor History* (Winter 1979), 111–26; and *Workers in America:
Essays on the Twentieth Century Struggle* (New York, 1980); Cantor, *Amer-
ican Workingclass Culture*; Gordon, Edwards, and Reich, *Segmented Work,
Divided Workers*; Melvyn Dubofsky, *Industrialism and the American
Worker, 1865–1920* (Arlington Heights, Ill., 1965); James R. Green, *The
World of the Worker: Labor in Twentieth-century America* (New York, 1980);
Susan Hirsch, *Roots of the American Working Class* (New York, 1980);
Kraditor, *Radical Persuasion*; Kolko, "The American Working Class: Im-
migrant Foundations"; Montgomery, *Workers' Control in America*; "To
Study the People: The American Working Class," *Labor History* (Fall
1980), 485–512. Among the sociological studies of social class images
and representations, the following were particularly useful: Elisabeth
Bott, *Family and Social Network* (London, 1957); Anthony Giddens and

David Held, eds., *Classes, Power and Conflict* (Berkeley, 1982); David Lockwood, "Sources of Variation in Working Class Images of Society," *Sociological Review* (November 1966), 249–67; *The Black-Coated Worker: A Study of Class Consciousness* (London, 1958); and "The New Working Class," *European Journal of Sociology*, 1, (1960), 148–259; John H. Goldthorpe, "Attitudes and Behavior of Class Assembly Workers: A Deviant Case and a Theoretical Critique," *British Journal of Sociology*, 17 (1966), 227–44; John H. Goldthorpe, David Lockwood, Frank Bechhoffer, et al., *The Affluent Worker: Industrial Attitudes and Behavior* (London, 1968), and *The Affluent Workers in the Class Structure* (Cambridge, 1969); Martin Bulmer, ed., *Working-class Images of Society* (London, 1975); Howard Newby, *The Deferential Worker: A Study of Farm Workers in East Anglia* (London, 1977; Frank Parkin, *Class Inequality and Political Order* (London, 1971), and Parkin, ed., *The Social Analysis of Class Structure* (London, 1974); Michael Piore, *Birds of Passage: Migrant Labor and Industrial Societies* (Cambridge, Mass.: 1979); Kenneth Roberts, F. G. Cook, S. C. Clark, et al., *The Fragmentary Class Structure* (London, 1977); Daniel Rodgers, *The Work Ethic in Industrial America, 1850–1920* (Chicago, 1974); Michael Mann, "The Social Cohesion of Liberal Democracy," *American Sociological Review* (June 1970), 423–39; and *Consciousness and Action in the Western Working Class* (London, 1973); Howard H. Davis, *Beyond Class Images: Explorations in the Structure of Social Consciousness* (London, 1979). Also Lillian B. Rubin, *Worlds of Pain: Life in the Working-Class Family* (New York, 1976) and John Gaventa, *Power and Powerlessness: Quiescence and Rebellion in an Appalachian Valley* (Oxford, 1980).

24 Clifford Geertz, *Islam Observed: Religious Development in Morocco and Indonesia* (Chicago, 1968), 15.

25 Geertz, *Interpretations of Cultures*, 25.

26 Clifford Geertz, *The Social History of an Indonesian Town* (Cambridge, Mass.: 1965), 153.

27 Emily Balch, *Our Slavic Fellow Citizens* (New York, 1910); Margaret Byington, *Homestead: The Households of a Mill Town* (New York, 1910); John Fitch, "Wage Earners of Pittsburgh," *Charities and the Commons* (March 6, 1909); Peter Roberts, *The Anthracite Coal Communities: A Study of the Demography, The Social, Educational and Moral Life of the Anthracite Regions* (New York, 1904), and "The New Pittsburghers: Slavs and Kindred Immigrants in Pittsburgh," *Charities and the Commons* (January 2, 1909).

28 Robert K. Merton and Elinor Barber, "Sociological Ambivalence," in *Sociological Ambivalence and Other Essays*, ed. Robert K. Merton (New York, 1980), 3–32.

29 Quoted after Charles Bosk, *Forgive and Remember* (Chicago, 1979), 204.

30 John Sharples and Ray M. Shortridge, "Biased Under-enumeration in Census Manuscripts: Methodological Implications," *Journal of Urban History* (August 1975), 419–36; Robert G. Barrows, "Instructions to Enumerators for Completing the 1900 Census Population Schedule," *His-*

torical Methods Newsletter (September, 1976), 201–12; Charles Stephenson, "Determinants of American Migration: Methods, Models in Mobility Research," *Journal of American Studies* (August, 1975), 189–97; Frank Furstenberg, Jr., Douglas Strong, and Albert Crawford, "What Happened When the Census Was Redone: An Analysis of the Recount of 1870 in Philadelphia," *Sociology and Social Research* (April 1979), 475–506; Thernstrom, *The Other Bostonians*, Epilogue, 289–302, and "Notes on the Historical Study of Social Mobility," in *Quantitative History*, ed. Don Karl Rowney and James Q. Graham, Jr. (Homewood, Ill.: 1969); Richard Jensen and Charles Dollar, *Historian's Guide to Statistics* (New York, 1971); Howard Chudacoff, *Mobile Americans* (New York, 1972), 25–6, 42, 57, 179; Peter Knights, *The Plain People of Boston, 1830–1860: A Study in City Growth* (New York, 1971), 4, 127–39; Thomas Kessner, *The Golden Door: Italian and Jewish Immigrant Mobility in New York City, 1880–1915* (New York, 1977), Introduction and Chaps. 3, 5, and 6.

31 Having no other large body of demographic data for 1900 against which to verify the accuracy of census information, I attempted a gross homemade estimate. I calculated the frequency on the forms of census takers' annotations that mention boarders, e.g., "John Kowalski, Marianna Kowalski [children listed] . . . *and several boarders* [names illegible or unspecified] or [refused to give information]." I found over 50 such notations for the wards inhabited by East Central Europeans. Taking 5 as the average number of boarders per immigrant household (cf. Chap. 4) adds about 300 more people. This figure, I think, should be at least tripled to account for cases of purposeful or inadvertent underreporting of the actual number of boarders by the immigrant informants, errors by the enumerators, and for the obvious undercounting of American-born women. All in all, it seems entirely likely that the 1900 manuscript schedule reported no more than 80 to 85 percent of the East Central European residents in the city. In verifying the national origin of the immigrant households listed in the 1900 manuscript census, I used parochial and organizational records, whenever possible referring to the 1910 manuscript census enumeration (available since 1982), which specified the mother tongue of residents (in linking personal data in the two sets of schedules, when in doubt I ascribed to boarders the national origin of the head of the household).

32 On the shortcomings of city directories as a source of information see Sidney Goldstein, *Patterns of Mobility, 1910–1950: The Norristown Study* (Philadelphia, 1958), 90–123; Chudacoff, *Mobile Americans*, 127–39; Kessner, *Golden Door*, Introduction and Chaps. 5 and 6. One problem with the early twentieth-century directories was the not infrequent misspelling of Slavic and Hungarian names by the enumerators, so that matching them took a considerable amount of labor. I did not use SOUNDEX, as clumsy and hopelessly time consuming, relying instead on my own East European ear. Thus, in doubtful cases I first prepared a list of possible variants of the names in question: *Chowanec, Howanec,*

Chowanicz, Howanicz, etc., and then checked the first names of their carriers as well as of their wives and children (if present), referring, if necessary, to the parochial and ethnic organizational records. In the course of this procedure, by the way, I located a certain number of second generation children of Johnstown's immigrants born in the United States in or before 1900 who were not recorded by the 1900 census. Unfortunately, I can give no numerical estimate of error resulting from the census and city directory misspellings: Aware of the possibilities of omitting people who were still present in Johnstown or else of checking a Mike *Howanec* as present when the name was in fact that of a different Mike *Chovanicz,* misspelled, I tried my conscientious best to minimize the number of those cases, but unavoidably a certain proportion must have remained undetected.

33 Florence R. Kluckhohn and Fred L. Strodtbeck, *Variations in Value Orientations* (Evanston, Ill.: 1961).

34 Estimates from data compiled from *Twelfth Census of the United States: 1900, Population,* vol. 1, Table 82; ibid., *Manufactures,* vol. 7, vol. 1, Tables 76, 106, 108; U.S. Congress, *Reports of the Immigration Commission: Abstracts of Reports of the Immigration Commission,* vol. 1, 61st Cong. 3rd sess., Sen. Docs. 747; p. 145, 782–85; *Thirteenth Census of the United States: 1910, Population,* vol. 1, Tables 2, 26–28; *Fourteenth Census of the United States: 1920, Population,* vol. 2, Tables 11, 17; ibid., *Abstract of the 14th Census of the United States: 1920,* Tables 71, 73, 76.

35 Hollingsworth and Hollingsworth, *Dimensions in Urban History.*

36 Bodnar, *Immigration and Industrialization.*

37 Yancey, Ericksen, and Juliani, "Emergent Ethnicity: A Review and Reformulation."

38 For instance, Theodore Hershberg, Michael Katz, Stuart Blumin, et al., "Occupation and Ethnicity in Five Nineteenth-century Cities: A Collaborative Inquiry," *Historical Methods Newsletter* (March–June 1974), 174–216; John T. Cumbler, *Working Class Community in Industrial America: Work, Leisure and Struggle in Two Industrial Cities, 1880–1930* (Westport, Conn.: 1979); Hollingsworth and Hollingsworth, *Dimensions of Urban History,* Chap. 2, "Empirical Case Studies: Eau Claire, Zanesville and Green Bay"; Michael Weber and Ewa Morawska, "East Europeans in Steel Towns: A Comparative Analysis," *Journal of Urban History* (May 1985), 280–313.

Chapter 1: Backgrounds

1 John Bodnar, Roger Simon, and Michael Weber, *Lives of Their Own: Blacks, Italians and Poles in Pittsburgh, 1900–1960* (Urbana, Ill.: 1982); Caroline Golab, "The Impact of Industrial Experience on the Immigrant Family: The Huddled Masses Reconsidered," in *Immigrants in Industrial America, 1850–1920,* ed. Richard L. Ehrlich (Charlottesville, Va.: 1977); John T. Cumbler, *American Working-class community: Work,*

Leisure and Struggle in Two Industrial Cities, 1880–1930 (Westport, Conn.: 1979); Olivier Zunz, *The Changing Face of Inequality: Urbanization, Industrial Development and Immigrants in Detroit, 1880–1920* (Chicago, 1982).

2 Timothy Smith, "Religion and Ethnicity in America," *American Historical Review* (December 1978), 1155–86; Josef Barton, *Peasants and Strangers: Italians, Rumanians and Slovaks in an American City, 1890–1950* (Cambridge, Mass.: 1975), and "Migration as Transition: An Illustration from the Experience of Migrant Miners to North America," paper presented at the annual meeting of the American Historical Association, Washington, D.C., December 28–30, 1982; Paula Benkart, "Religion, Family and Community among Hungarians Migrating to American Cities, 1880–1930," Ph.D. thesis, Johns Hopkins University, 1975.

3 Sol Tax, *Penny Capitalism: A Guatemalan Indian Economy* (Chicago, 1963).

4 Ibid., 204–6.

5 Krystyna Duda-Dziewierz, *Wieś Małopolska a Emigracja Amerykańska.Studium Wsi Babica pow.Rzeszowskiego* (Warsaw, 1938), 30.

6 S. N. Eisenstadt, *Tradition, Change and Modernity* (New York, 1973), 5, 14, 99, 129, 146; Daniel Lerner, *The Passing of Traditional Society* (Glencoe, Ill.: 1958), 45, 78; David McClelland, *The Achieving Society* (New York, 1961), 174.

7 The figures represent the average for specific countries. Within the same region, however, there were considerable variations in land distribution. In Slovakia, for instance, at the end of the last century 80 percent of the peasantry in the Spiš province owned holdings smaller than 5 hectares, whereas in the Turiec province the proportion was 54 percent; in Nitra, 63 percent; in Trenčin and Zvolen, 62 percent; in Liptov, 71 percent; see Jan Hanzlík, "Začiatky Vhysťahovalectva zo Slovenska do USA a Jeho Priebeh až do Roku 1918, Jeho Pričiny a Našledky," in *Zčiatky Ceskej a Slovenskej Emigracie do USA*, ed. Josef Polišenský (Bratislava, 1975), 71; see also Ladislav Tajtak, "Východoslovenské Vysťahovalectvo do Prvej Svetovej Vojny," *Nové Obzory*, 3 (1961), 227. In Slovenia, the proportion of smallholders (less than 5 hectares) among peasants ranged from over 60 percent, in the districts of Celje, Maribor Gorica, Brežice, Ljutomer, and Pluj, to about 30 percent in the districts of Velikovec and Celovec; see *Gospodarska in Družbena Zgodovina Slovencev* (Lubljana, 1970), 1:177. In Congress Poland, the proportion of peasant holdings less than 5 hectares ranged at the beginning of the century from slightly over 30 percent in the counties of Skierniewice and Lowicz, to over 70 percent in those of Kutno, Radom, Sieradz, and Wieluń; see Witold Nowosz, "Tradycyjne Gospodarstwo Chłopskie i Jego Przemiany," *Prace i Materiały Muzeum Archeologicznego i Etnograficznego w Łodzi*, 1 (1976), 114. The disproportions in the patterns of peasant landownership reflected not only regional differences within particular countries but also national discrimination against minorities. For instance, almost two-thirds of all

dwarf-holdings (less than 3 hectares) in the Hungarian part of the Austro-Hungarian Empire belonged to non-Magyars; in Transylvania, 70 percent of such holdings were owned by Rumanian peasants, and in Slovakia 69 percent of dwarf lots were held by Slovaks. On the other hand, over 60 percent of the estates over 50 hectares in these provinces were in the hands of the Magyars (Ivan Berend and Győrgi Ránki, *Underdevelopment and Economic Growth: Studies in Hungarian Social and Economic History* (Budapest, 1979), 91.

8   Zbigniew Stankiewicz, "The Economic Emigration from the Kingdom of Poland Portrayed on the European Background," in *Employment-seeking Emigrations of the Poles World-wide XIX and XXC,* ed. Celina Bobińska and Andrzej Pilch (Krakow, 1975), 33.

9   After Jerome Blum, *The End of the Old Order in Rural Europe* (Princeton, 1978), 418. At the beginning of the century the birthrates in selected eastern European countries were as follows: Subcarpathian Rus', 43.7; Galicia, 44.1; Croatia-Slavonia, 39.3; Slovakia, 36.9; Hungary, 36.7; in western Europe the birthrates hovered around 30.0. See E. Pamlenyi, ed., *Social-economic Researches on the History of East Central Europe* (Budapest, 1970), 89; Stanisław Szczepanowski, *Nędza Galicji w Cyfrach* (Lvov, 1905), 56; Toussaint Hočevar, *The Structure of the Slovenian Economy, 1948–1963* (New York, 1965), 83; W. P. Kopczak and S. I. Kopczak, *Naseljenje Zakarpatja za 100 Let* (Lvov, 1977), 37; Jan Svetoń, *Obyvatel'stvo Slovenska za Kapitalizmu* (Bratislava, 1958), 323; Ion Aluas, "Industrialization and Migration of the Transylvanian Peasantry at the End of the Nineteenth Century and the Beginning of the Twentieth Century," *East European Quarterly* (January 1970), 502; Julianna Puskaś, *From Hungary to the United States, 1880–1914* (Budapest, 1982), 45–6; Irena Kostrowicka, Zbigniew Landau, and Jerzy Tomaszewski, *Historia Gospodarcza Polski XIX i XX Wieku* (Warsaw, 1978), 159.

10 Compiled from: Svetoń, *Obyvatel'stvo Slovenska,* 72–3; B. Il'ko, *Zakarpatske Selo na Pocatku XXst., 1900–1919* (Lvov, 1973), 120–1; *Polish Encyclopaedia,* S. V. "Economic Life of Poland," 3:216–18; 344–5; 413–14; Władysław Rusiński, "The Role of Peasantry of Poznań (Wielkopolska) in the Formation of the Non-Agricultural Labor Market," *East European Quarterly* (January 1970), 515; Ryszard Turski, *Między Miastem a Wsią.Struktura Społeczno-Zawodowa Chłopów-Robotników w Polsce* (Warsaw, 1965), 75–85.

11 Franciszek Bujak, *Maszkienice.Wieś Powiatu Brzeskiego:Stosunki Gospodarcze i Społeczne* (Krakow, 1901), 51, 120, and *Galicja* (Lvov, 1914), 1:393.

12 Bujak, *Zmiąca.Wieś Powiatu Limanowskiego: Stosunki Gospodarcze i Społeczne* (Krakow, 1903), 62–3.

13 Compiled from Elżbieta Kaczyńska, *Społeczeństwo i Gospodarka Północno-Wschodnich Ziem Królestwa Polskiego w Okresie Rozkwitu Kapitalizmu* (Warsaw, 1974), 31–3; Aluas, "Industrialization and Migration of the Transylvanian Peasantry," 504; Tajtak, "Slovak Emigration and

Migration in the Years of 1910–1914," *Studia Historica Slovaca*, 10 (1978), 55–64; I. Szabó, ed., *A Magyar Parasztság a Kapitalizmus Korában, 1848–1914* (Budapest, 1965), 2:321–71; Puskaś, "Emmigration from Hungary to the United States before 1914," *Studia Historica Academiae Scientiarum Hungariae* (1975), 10–17; Berend and Ránki, *Hungary: A Century of Economic Development* (New York, 1974), 24–6; Ireneusz Ihnatowicz, Antoni Mączak, Benedykt Zientara, *Społeczeństwo Polskie od X do XX Wieku* (Warsaw, 1979), 459–66.

14   Compiled from Ihnatowicz, Mączak, and Zientara, *Społeczeństwo Polskie*, 459–66; Benjamin Murdzek, *Emigration in Polish Social-Political Thought, 1870–1914* (New York, 1975), 314–89; Golab, *Immigrant Destinations* (Philadelphia, 1977), 80, 86–7, 99; Leopold Caro, *Emigracja i Polityka Emigracyjna ze Szczególnym Uwzględnieniem Stosunków Polskich* (Poznań, 1914), 20–31; Zanna Kormanowa and Irena Pietrzak-Pawłowska, eds., *Historia Polski* (Warsaw, 1978), vol. 2, pt. 1, "1850/64–1900," 216–19; Imre Ferenczi and Walter F. Willcox, *International Migrations*, 2 vols. (New York, 1929–31), 1:126, 225–6, 588–91, 727, 786–90, and 2:349–52, 377–89; Andrzej Pilch, "Migrations of the Galician Populace at the Turn of the Nineteenth and in the Twentieth Centuries," in *Employment-seeking Emigrations of the Poles*, 78–80, 84–8, 93–7; Stankiewicz, "The Economic Emigration from the Kingdom of Poland," in Bobińska and Pilch, *Employment-seeking Emigrations of the Poles*, 37–48; Adam Galos and Kazimierz Wajda, "Migrations in the Polish Western Territories Annexed by Prussia, 1815–1914," in Bobińska and Pilch, *Employment-seeking Emigrations of the Poles*, 63–75; G. S. Rabinowitch, "The Seasonal Emigration of Polish Agricultural Workers to Germany," *International Labour Review* 25 (1932).

15   Compiled from Berend and Ránki, *Hungary: A Century of Economic Development*, 26; Puskaś, *From Hungary to the United States*, 14–28; Ferenczi and Willcox, *International Migrations*, 1:416–20.

16   Compiled from C. A. Macartney, *The Habsburg Empire, 1790–1918* (London, 1968), 755, n.2; Ferenczi and Willcox, *International Migrations*, 1:233, 588–91; 878–81, and 2:401–3, 413–14, 429–32; Richard Pfaunder, "Die Grundlagen der nationalen Bevölkerung gesentwicklung Steiermarks," *Statistische Monatschrift* (1907), 557–92; Wilhelm Hecke, "Binnenwanderung und Umgangssprache in den Oestereischen Alpenländern und Südländern," *Statistische Monatschrift* (1913), 323–92, and "Binnenwanderung and Umgangssprache in den nördlichen Ländern Oestereichs," *Statistiche Monatschrift* (1914), 653–723.

17   Compiled from Josip Lakatoš, *Narodna Statistika* (Zagreb, 1914), 62; Kaczyńska, *Społeczeństwo i Gospodarka*, 137–40; Stankiewicz, "Economic Emigration from the Kingdom of Poland," 37–41, 50; Pilch, "Migrations of the Galician Populace," 78–80.

18   The fourth type – interurban migrations – is not included in this discussion, which focuses primarily on movements of directly rural origins.

19 Bujak, *Zmiąca*, 70–1.

20 Mark Stolarik, *Slovak Migration from Europe to North America, 1870–1918* (Cleveland, 1980), 10–15; Tajtak, "Slovak Emigration and Migration in the Years 1900–1914," 55–60; Il'ko, *Zakarpatske Selo*, 71–82. Also, two contemporary Hungarian micromonographs dealing with local rural migrations: "A kis jenöi uradalom Arad úrmegyében" (Pest, 1914), and Kukats Jozsef, "Vasoh község monografija," *Magyar Gazdák Szemleje* (1906).

21 As quoted in Barton, *Peasants and Strangers*, 43–4. See also three contemporary Rumanian community monographs dealing with village migrations: Romul Simu, *Monografia Comunei Orlat* (Sibiu, 1895); Ioachim Munteanu, *Monografia Economica-Culturala a Comunei Gura Riului* (Sibiu, 1897); N. Carpisan, *Monografia Comunei Rahan* (n.p., 1897).

22 Murdzek, *Emigration in Polish Social-Political Thought*, 69–117.

23 Stanisław Pawłowski, *Ludność Rzymsko-Katolicka w Polsko-Ruskiej Części Galicji* (Lvov, 1919), 33–4; Il'ko, *Zakarpatske Selo*, 71–82.

24 Bogdan Stojsavijević, *Povijest Sela:Hrvatska-Slavonija-Dalmacja, 1848–1918* (Zagreb, 1973); Vesna Mikačić, "The Significance of the Regional Aspect of Migration: The Example of Yugoslavia," in *Emigration from Northern, Central and Southern Europe: Theoretical and Methological Principles of Research* (Krakow, 1984), 235–45.

25 Tajtak, "Slovak Emigration and Migration," 57–8; Puskaś, *From Hungary to the United States*, 56–63.

26 Compiled from Pilch, "Migrations of the Galician Populace," 92–3, 96–9; Macartney, *Habsburg Empire*, 755, n.2.

27 Maria Misińska, "Podhale Dawne i Współczesne," *Prace i Materiały Muzeum Archeologicznego i Etnograficznego w Lodzi*, 15 (1971), 33–4; also Jan Kantor, "Czarny Dunajec," *Materiały Antropologiczno-Archeologiczne i Etnograficzne*, 9 (1907), 150–61; Hanzlík, "Začiatky Vysťahovalectva zo Slovenska," 61–3.

28 Compiled from Ferenczi and Willcox, *International Migrations*, 1:92, 225–6, 233–5, 239, 689–91; 2:349–52, 377–89; and Murdzek, *Emigration in Polish Social-Political Thought*, 369; Rabinowitch, "The Seasonal Emigration of Polish Agricultural Workers to Germany"; Jerzy Zubrzycki, "Emigration from Poland in the Nineteenth and Twentieth Centuries," *Population Studies*, (March 1953), 248–63; Kormanowa and Pietszak-Pawłowska, *Historia Polski*, vol. 2, pt. 1, pp. 107–10; Caro, *Emigracja i Polityka Emigracyjna*, 31; Galos and Wajda, "Migrations in the Polish Western Territories," 61–70; Rusiński, "Role of the Peasantry of Poznań," 522; B. Szczepański, "Wychodźstwo Sezonowe i Emigracja Zamorska z Terenu Ziemi Kaliskiej w Końcu XIX i na Początku XX Stulecia," *Rocznik Kaliski* (1974), 101–23; Aluas, "Industrialization and Migration of the Transylvanian Peasantry," 506; Svetoń, "Slovenské Vysťahovalectvo w Období Uhorského Kapitalizmu," *Ekonomićky Casopis*, vol. 4, pt. 2 (1956), 179. The estimates are based on the reports of German job agencies and "foreign (immigration)

bureaus." The actual numbers of East Central European seasonal peasant-workers in Germany were probably higher, possibly by as much as one-fourth: A number of them never reported to the registration offices, since they worked every year for the same farmers by private arrangement.

29 Caro, *Emigracja i Polityka Emigracyjna*, 61–7.

30 Berend and Ránki, *Hungary: A Century of Economic Development*, 25–90, and *The European Periphery and Industrialization, 1780–1914* (New York, 1982); Anna Zarnowska, *Klasa Robotnicza Królestwa Polskiego, 1870–1914* (Warsaw, 1974); Kormanowa and Pietrzak-Pawłowska, *Historia Polski*, vol. 2, pt. 1, 375–565; Doreen Warriner, ed., *Contrasts in Emerging Societies: Readings in the Social and Economic History of South-Eastern Europe in the Nineteenth Century* (Bloomington, Ind.: 1965), "General Introduction: Contrasts and Comparisons."

31 *Polish Encyclopaedia*, s.v. "Prussian Poland," Chap. 3, "Industry," 106–28.

32 Tajtak, "Slovak Emigration and Migration," 46–50; Berend and Ránki, *Underdevelopment and Economic Growth*, 94.

33 Hočevar, *Structure of the Slovenian Economy*, 44–9, 86–9; Branko Colaković, *Yugoslav Migrations to America* (San Francisco, 1973), 25–7; Mikačić, "The Significance of the Regional Aspect of Migration," 235–45.

34 Vladimir Dedijer, Jvan Božić, Sima Cirković, et al., *History of Yugoslavia* (New York, 1974), 361–3; Igor Karaman, *Privreda i Društvo Hrvatske u 19.Stoljeću* (Zagreb, 1972), 316–21, 379; Joel M. Halpern and Barbara Kerewsky Halpern, *A Serbian Village in Historical Perspective* (New York, 1972), 48–56; Il'ko, *Zakarpatske Selo*; Aluas, "Industrialization and Migration of the Transylvanian Peasantry," 501–25.

35 Berend and Ránki, *Underdevelopment and Economic Growth*, 141–3, 148–9. Also Ervin Pamlényi, ed., *A History of Hungary* (New York, 1973), 346.

36 Tajtak, "Slovak Emigration and Migration," 46; Svetoň, *Obyvatel'stvo Slovenska za Kapitalizmu*, 82, 108; Kaczyńska, *Dzieje Robotników Przemysłowych w Polsce pod Zaborami* (Warsaw, 1970), 113–19; *Polish Encyclopaedia*, 3:419–29, 539.

37 Kaczyńska, *Dzieje Robotników Przemysłowych*, 83; *Polish Encyclopaedia*, 3:108, 113–15, 163; Kormanowa and Pietrzak-Pawłowska, *Historia Polski*, vol. 2, pt. 1, 220–7; Kostrowicka, Landau, and Tomaszewski, *Historia Gospodarcza Polski*, 177–202; Karaman, *Privreda i Društvo Hrvatske*, 316–34.

38 Berend and Ránki, *Underdevelopment and Economic Growth*, 93–4.

39 Ihnatowicz, Mączak, and Zientara, *Społeczeństwo Polskie*, 359–66. Also Turski, *Między Miastem a Wsią*, Chaps. 1–3.

40 Compiled from Berend and Ránki, *Hungary: A Century of Economic Development*, 77–9. Also Rácz István, "Parasztok elvándorlása afaluból," in *A Parasztság Magyarországon a Kapitalizmus Korában, 1848–1914*, 2 vols., ed. Szabó István (Budapest, 1965); Hanak Péter, ed., *Magy-*

arország Története (Budapest, 1978), vols. 6–7, *1890–1918;* B. Kenéz, *Városok Fejlödése és Jelentödése* (Budapest, 1905), as quoted in Tajtak, "Slovak Emigration and Migration," 61.

41 Kormanowa and Pietrzak-Pawłowska, *Historia Polski,* vol. 2, pt. 1, pp. 406–13; Zarnowska, *Klasa Robotnicza Kròlestwa Polskiego,* 110–16, 154–65; Edward Pietraszek, *Wiejscy Robotnicy Kopalni i Hut.Dynamika Przemian Społeczno-Kulturowych w Sierszańskim Ośrodku Górniczym w XIX i XX Wieku* (Wroclaw, 1966); Turski, *Między Miastem a Wsią,* provides a good bibliography on this issue in relation to Polish territories at the beginning of the century.

42 Compiled from Kormanowa and Pietrzak-Pawłowska, *Historia Polski,* vol. 2, pt. 1, pp. 220–8, 633–44; Danuta Dobrowolska, *Górnicy Salinarni Wieliczki w Latach 1880–1939* (Wroclaw, 1965), 78–109; Lakatoš, *Narodna Statistika, 5;* Cvetko Kostić, *Seljaci Industriski Radnici* (Belgrade, 1955); Stojsavljević, *Povijest Sela;* Pavlo Blaznik, Bodo Grafenauer, and Sergij Uilfan, eds., *Zgodovina Agrarnih Panog* (Lubljana, 1970); Kaczyńska, *Dzieje Robotników Przemysłowych,* 117–32, and *Siła Robocza w Przemyśle Ciężkim* (Warsaw, 1977), 125; Zarnowska, *Klasa Robotnicza Królestwa Polskiego,* 111–39; Berend and Ránki, *Hungary: A Century of Economic Development,* 79–82.

43 Kaczyńska, *Dzieje Robotników Przemysłowych w Polsce,* 119–25; Zarnowska, *Klasa Robotnicza Królestwa Polskiego,* 111–31; Kormanowa and Pietrzak-Pawłowska, *Historia Polski,* vol. 2, pt. 1, 221–3, 368, 644; Turski, *Między Miastem a Wsią,* Chap. 2; Berend and Ránki, *Hungary: A Century of Economic Development,* 80–1; František Bielik, ed., *Slovenské Vysťahovalectvo.Dokumenty III.Korešpondencja z Rokov, 1893–1939* (Martin, 1976), 6–18; Tajtak, "Slovak Emigration and Migration," 46, 56–61; *Gospodarska in Družbena Zgodovina Slovencev,* 122–4; Kostić, *Seljaci-Industrijski Radnici;* Halpern and Halpern, *A Serbian Village in Historical Perspective.* For a general discussion of "peasant-workers" as a social category, see Corrado Barberis, *Gli Operai-Contadini* (Bologna, 1970); also Barton, "Migration as Transition: An Illustration from the Experience of Migrant Miners to North America."

44 W. Długoborski, "Peasant Economy in the Coal and Smelting Regions of Middle-East Europe before and during the Early Period of Industrialization," paper presented at the International Colloquium on Peasant Economies before and during the Early Period of Industrial Revolution, Białowieża-Białystok, Poland, September, 1973.

45 Compiled from Pilch, "Migrations of the Galician Populace," 97–8; M. Myška, *Počatky Vytvareni Délnicke Tridy v Zelazarnach na Otravsku* (Ostrava, 1962), 77–86, and "Fossores ex Galicia.Udział Emigrantów z Galicji w Formowaniu się Klasy Robotniczej w Górnictwie Węglowym w Drugiej Połowie XIX Wieku," *Małopolskie Studia Historyczne,* 3–4 (1966), 65, 70–3.

46 Bujak, *Maszkienice, Wieś Powiatu Brzeskiego:Rozwój od R.1900 do R.1911* (Lvov, 1914), 86–91.

47 Pilch, "Migrations of the Galician Populace," 94–9.

48 Hočevar, *The Structure of the Slovenian Economy*, 82–4; Tajtak, "Slovak Emigration and Migration," 57–9. Lakatoš, *Narodna Statistika*, 61–2; Ferenczi and Willcox, *International Migrations*, 1:92, 588–91, 724–27 and 2:413–14, 429–32.

49 Pilch, "Migrations of the Galician Populace," 92–4.

50 Kaczyńska, *Dzieje Robotników Przemysłowych*, 107; Kormanowa and Pietrzak-Pawłowska, *Historia Polski*, vol. 2, pt. 1, 407–9.

51 Berend and Ránki, *Hungary: A Century of Economic Development*, 26, 79.

52 Józef Okołowicz, *Wychodźstwo i Osadnictwo Polskie Przed Wojną Świa-tową*, (Warsaw, 1920), Chap. 23; Lakatoš, *Narodna Statistika*.

53 Tajtak, "Slovak Emigration and Migration," 58–9; also Július Mésároš, *Dejiny Slovenska II.od Roku 1848 do Roku 1900* (Bratislava, 1968), 408.

54 Hanzlík, "Začiatky Vysťahovalectva zo Slovenska," 63–4.

55 Ferenczi and Willcox, *International Migrations*, 1:92, 126–8, 225–6, 233–5, 239, 689–91, 724, 786–90, and 2:349–52, 377–89; Galos and Wajda, "Migrations in the Polish Western Territories," 66–7.

56 *A Statistical Abstract Supplement: Historical Statistics of the United States, Colonial Times to 1957* (Washington, D.C.: 1961), Tables C88–100, C115, C133, C218–83; Emily Balch, *Our Slavic Fellow Citizens* (New York, 1969), 74, 244, 261–3, 280–1, 436–8, 452, 460–6; Priscilla Fishman, *The Jews in the United States* (New York, 1973), 33; Ferenczi and Willcox, *International Migrations*, 1:195–205, 230–95, 384–95; Puskaś, "The Process of Overseas Migration from East-Central Europe, Its Periods, Cycles and Characteristics: A Comparative Study," in *Emigration from Northern, Central and Southern Europe*, 33–55; Bobińska and Pilch, *Employment-seeking Migrations of the Poles*, 41–8, 61–5, 83–91; K. Englisch, "Die Oesterreichische Auswanderungsstatistik," *Statistische Monat-schrift*, (February-March, 1913); H. Chmelar, *Höhepunkte der österrei-chischen Auswanderung aus den im Reichstrat vertreteten Königsreichen und Ländern in den Jahren 1905–1914* (Vienna, 1974); I. Rácz, *A Paraszti Mig-rácio és Politikai Megitélése Magyarországon, 1849–1914* (Budapest, 1980); František Bielik and Elo Rákoš, ed., *Slovenské Vysťahovalectvo Do Roku 1918.Dokumenty I* (Bratislava, 1969).

57 For general estimates of the return flow to East Central Europe during the first two decades of this century, see J. D. Gould, "European Inter-continental Emigration. The Road Home: Return Migration from the U.S.A.," *Journal of European Economic History* (Spring 1980), 41–113; Charles Price, "Methods of Estimating Size of Groups," *Harvard En-cyclopedia of American Ethnic Groups*, Appendix A, 103; W. Schlag, "A Survey of Austrian Emigration to the U.S.," in *Oesterreich und die An-gelsaechsische Welt*, ed. O. Hietsch (Vienna, 1961), 141. For particular countries, see Puskaś, *From Hungary to the United States*, 16–28; Frances Kraljic, "Croatian Migration to and from the United States between 1900 and 1914," Ph.D. thesis, New York University, 1975, 4, 30, 46, 56, 64; George Prpić, *The Croatian Immigrants in America* (New York,

1971), 441; Ivan Cižmić, "Iseljavanje iz Hrvatske, 1880–1914g," unpublished essay (n.d.), 18–23; Tajtak, "Slovak Emigration and Migration," 50, 84, and "Východoslovenské Vysťahovalectvo do Prvej Svetovej Vojny," 234–9; Bielik and Rákoš, *Slovenské Vysťahovalectvo. Dokumenty I. Do Roku 1918* 1:30–1; Svetoń, "Slovenské Vysťahovalectvo v Obdobi Uhorského Kapitalizmu," 178–9; Stolarik, "From Field to Factory: The Historiography of Slovak Immigration to the United States," *Slovakia*, 38, nos. 51–2 (1978–9), 85; Branko M. Colaković, *Yugoslav Migrations to America* (San Francisco, 1973), 52; Andrzej Brożek, *Polonia Amerykańska 1854–1939* (Warsaw, 1977), 22, 226–7; Marek M. Drozdowski, "Działalność Polonii Amerykańkiej w Walce o Niepodległość Polski w Latach, 1910–1918," in *Polonia Wobec Niepodległości Polski w Czasie I Wojny Swiatowej* (Wroclaw, 1977), 65; Adam Wałaszek, *Reemigracja Ze Stanów Zjednoczonych do Polski Po I Wojnie Swiatowej, 1919–1924* (Warsaw, 1983), 5–14.

58   Duda-Dziewierz, *Wieś Malopolska a Emigracja Amerykańska*, 79–85.
59   Bujak, *Maszkienice . . . Rozwój od R.1900 do R.1911*, 91–3.
60   Maria Niemyska, *Wychodźcy po Powrocie do Kraju* (Warsaw, 1936), 67–8.
61   Blum, *End of the Old Order in Rural Europe*, 432.
62   Gyula Illyés, *Puszták Népe* (Budapest, 1936), 55–6.
63   Blum, *End of the Old Order in Rural Europe*, 433.
64   On peasant banks, loan and credit agencies and cooperatives, see, for Austria-Hungary generally, J. Buchinger, *Der Bauer in der Kultur-und Wirtschaftsgeschichte Oesterreichs* (Vienna, 1952), 252–9; for Slovakia, Vladimir Zuberec, "Formovanie Slovenského Agrárneho Hnutia w Rokoh 1900–1918," *Historický Casopis* 2 (1972), 305–46; for Hungary proper, Berend and Ránki, *Underdevelopment and Economic Growth*, 87–96; for Romania, D. Mitrany, *The Land and the Peasant in Rumania* (London, 1930), 377–84; for Croatia-Slavonia, Stojsavijević, *Provijest Sela*, 334–47; for Subcarpathian Rus', Ivan Bryk and Mykhailo Kotsiuba, *The Ukrainian (Ruthenian) Co-Operative Movement in Galicia* (Lviv, 1913), and Il'ko, *Zakarpatske Selo*, 91–6; for Slovenia, Hočevar, *The Structure of the Slovenian Economy*, 59–64, and *Gospodarska in Družbena Zgodovina Slovencev*, 639; for Poland, *Polish Encyclopaedia*, 3:194–214, 310–38, 508–30; for Russia, A. B. Petersen, "The Development of Cooperative Credit in Rural Russia, 1871–1914," Ph.D. thesis, Cornell University, 1973, 132–3; Blum, *End of the Old Order in Rural Europe*, 433.
65   On the high interest rates on loans in East Central European villages, see Hočevar, *Structure of the Slovenian Economy*, 60–1; Balch, *Our Slavic Fellow Citizens*, 179–80; Murdzek, *Emigration in Polish Social-Political Thought*, p. 153, and pp. 255–6, n. 24; Il'ko, *Zakarpatske Selo*, 109–15.
66   Benkart, "Religion, Family and Community among Hungarians Migrating to American Cities, 1880–1930," 18; Bujak, *Maszkienice . . . Rozwój od R.1900 do R.1911*, 125–6. The peasants were indebted not only for unpaid taxes but also, and as a matter of fact even more often, for

new material purchases. The taxes charged to peasant households differed quite widely from region to region, but, for instance, in Zakarpatje, on a 4-hectare piece of land, two horses, two cows, and two pigs, a peasant paid at the beginning of the century 147 kronen ($30); a landless peasant (cottager) with one cow and one pig paid 66 kronen ($13) (after Il'ko, *Zakarpatske Selo*, 104).

67 Murdzek, *Emigration in Polish Social-Political Thought*, 151–3. For the figures on capital brought into Hungary by seasonal peasant-workers before the First World War, see Puskás, *From Hungary to the United States*, 77.

68 Bujak, *Maszkienice.Wieś Powiatu Brzeskiego*, 49–50, and *Maszkienice . . . Rozwój od R.1900 do R.1911*, 105.

69 Stanislaw Hupka, *Ueber die Entwicklung der westgalizischen Dorfzustände in der Z. Hälfte des 19. Jahrhunderts* (Teschen, 1911), quoted in Caro, *Emigracja i Polityka Emigracyjna*, 77.

70 William I. Thomas and Florian Znaniecki, 2nd ed., *The Polish Peasant in Europe and America* (New York, 1958), 1:164–6.

71 Ibid., 190.

72 Quoted after ibid., 173.

73 Ibid., 47. On the persistence of traditionalist, precapitalist attitudes toward work and gain among agricultural laborers employed on farms in eastern Europe at the turn of the century, see also Max Weber, *The Protestant Ethnic and the Spirit of Capitalism* (New York, 1958), 59–62.

74 Ibid., 174–5.

75 Bujak, *Limanowa.Miasteczko Powiatu Zachodniej Galicji* (Krakow, 1902), 70–1.

76 Okołowicz, *Wychodźstwo i Osadnictwo*, 390; Caro, *Emigracja i Polityka Emigracyjna*, 177–9, 273; Murdzek, *Emigration in Polish Social-Political Thought*, 155, 160. A present-day Slovak historian argues, however, that (at least in Slovakia) peasant seasonal migrations did not increase local farm wages "as claimed by the burgeois observers" (Svetoń, "Slovenské Vysťahovalectvo v Období Uhorského Kapitalizmu," 190).

77 Jan Słomka, *From Serfdom to Self-government: Memoirs of a Polish Village Mayor, 1842–1927* (London, 1941), 57.

78 Berend and Ránki, *Hungary: A Century of Economic Development*, 82–4.

79 These and the following calculations (see n. 80) are based on the information that peasant seasonal workers saved approximately 60 to 70 percent of their earnings. I compiled the data from Bujak, *Maszkienice.Wieś Powiatu Brzeskiego*, 49–50, and *Maszkienice . . . Rozwój od R.1900 do R.1911*, 104–5; *Polish Encyclopaedia* 3:217, 345; Mésáros, *Dejiny Slovenska*, 2:345.

80 Compiled from Bujak, *Maszkienice.Wieś Powiatu Brzeskiego*, 49–50, and *Maszkienice . . . Rozwój od R.1900 do R.1911*, 102–3; Macartney, *Habsburg Empire*, 717; Mésáros, *Dejiny Slovenska*, 431–2; *Polish Encyclopaedia*, 3:220, 345–6, 539–40; Okołowicz, *Wychodźstwo i Osadnictwo*, 279–80; Misińska, "Podhale Dawne i Współczesne," 40; Irena Lechowa, "Tra-

dycje Emigracyjne w Klonowej," *Prace i Materiały Muzeum Archeologicznego i Etnograficznego w Lodzi*, 3 (1960), 51.

81 Thomas and Znaniecki, *Polish Peasant*, 1:700.

82 Ibid., 187.

83 Zofia Wygodzina, *Kobieta Wiejska jako Czynnik Gospodarczy i Kulturalny* (Lvov, 1916), 7, 11, 13–14; Słomka, *From Serfdom to Self-government*, 81; Blum, *End of the Old Order in Rural Europe*, 119.

84 May N. Diaz and Jack M. Potter, "The Social Life of Peasants," in *Peasant Society*, ed. Jack M. Potter, May N. Diaz, and George M. Foster (Boston, 1967), 155.

85 East Central European peasant societies generally held women in low esteem. Their low status was reflected in proverbs and sayings, strikingly similar in different parts of the regions. So, for instance, a proverb popular among the South Slavs said that at the birth of a girl, "Even the fire weeps," and female children were looked upon as "alien bone." Up north, in Poland, there was a saying, "Wash her, brush her, watch her, and even pay for her – you must to get rid of her." In Russia, a peasant proverb favorably compared household animals with a girl: "Better a goat in the house than a daughter." Although in all East Central European peasant societies the culturally defined status of men was superior to that of women, and although it had been the man who was the outwardly acknowledged head of the family, the actual position of women differed somewhat from region to region. The further north, the more frequent were the occurrences of nominal rather than factual domination by the man in the peasant household. Among the South Slavs, women in the peasant family customarily carried heavy loads, walking behind men who traveled empty-handed or rode mules, and at home women were not supposed to sit down and rest from work for a minute or sit with the men at the table. If they did, they were promptly rebuked with a derisive remark from the men and a comment such as "[They are] sitting as if they were men." Among the Northern Slavs, however, even though women stayed put at home, bound by their household duties and apparently uninterested in other matters, exceptions to this rule were not infrequent. In practically every village one could usually find a few "token" women, married, who managed their households, performing the role prescribed for the husbands, or who knew better how to handle financial matters and conduct and win litigations (very common among peasants), or who even habitually drank vodka with men in the tavern and smoked a pipe. Such cases were commented on and ridiculed by local public opinion, but they constituted an accepted part of social life of the village.

The highest compliment, however, that one could pay to a woman in peasant society was "Ona je vredna": "She is (both) willing and able to work hard." The ability and eagerness to work was the first commandment in the peasant family ethos, binding all members, regardless of sex. The division of labor between men and women in the peasant household was clearly defined and sanctioned by tradition. Beside tending to children, doing housework, weaving, cooking, and spinning, women took care of the livestock and garden and did much of the labor in the fields, such as working the root crops, reaping, raking, and making haystacks – activities considered to be the domain of the women. "Babski" – female – was also the business of selling eggs, cheese, butter, and other minor produce in the market; it was carried out by the women independently, and they made their decisions without interference from the head of the household. Women were entitled to keep the money obtained for the produce sold in market use it for household needs (not for themselves, however). See Stanisław Ciszewski, *Zeńska Twarz* (Krakow, 1927), Prace Komitetu Etnograficznego PAU, no. 4, 1; M. Kostomarow, *Oczerki Domasznej Zizni i Iravov' Wielikorusskogo Naroda* (Petersburg, 1887), 156; Dinko Tomasić, *Personality and Culture in East European Politics* (New York, 1948), 58–9; Wincenty Witos, *Moje Wspomnienia* (Paris, 1964), 1:129–32.

86   Słomka, *From Serfdom to Self-government*, 57.
87   Bujak, *Maszkienice, Wieś Powiatu Brzeskiego*, 46, 55, and *Maszkienice . . . Rozwój od R.1900 do R.1911*, 77–81. On female seasonal laborers in Denmark, see Eugeniusz Kruszewski, *Problemy Osadnictwa Polaków w Danii, 1893–1939* (London, 1980), 35, 81. For instance, 82 percent of all Polish agricultural workers in Denmark before World War I were women (20 percent of them were less than sixteen years old; 56 percent were sixteen to twenty years of age).
88   Svetoń, *Obyvatel'stvo Slovenska*, 162.
89   Compiled from Bujak, *Maszkienice, Wieś Powiatu Brzeskiego*, 49–51, 55–7, and *Maszkienice . . . Rozwój od R.1900 do R.1911*, 92–3, 102–4; Ferdynand Kuraś, *Przez Ciernie Zywota* (Częstochowa, 1925), 38–9.
90   Słomka, *From Serfdom to Self-government*, 122. Also Maria Librachowa, ed., *Dziecko Wsi Polskiej* (Warsaw, 1934), 29–30, 152–92; Z. Mysłakowski, *Rodzina Wiejska Jako Srodowisko Wychowawcze* (Warsaw, 1931), 71, 120.
91   Słomka, *From Serfdom to Self-government*, 122.
92   Svetoń, "Slovenské Vysťahovalectvo," 190; also Mésároš, *Dejiny Slovenska*, 2:345, 431–2.
93   Bujak, *Maszkienice, Wieś Powiatu Brzeskiego*, 43–6, and *Maszkienice . . . Rozwój od R.1900 do R.1911*, 68.
94   Kruszewski, *Problemy Osadnictwa Polaków w Danii*, 94. Before World War I, peasant boys and girls working in Denmark saved, on the average, $20 to $25 from an eight- to nine-month season, "a sum impossible for them to earn at home" (ibid., 102).
95   Władysław Orkan, *Listy ze Wsi* (Warsaw, 1925), 1:77. Students of modern urban-industrial societies often overlook the existence in peasant communities of a complex status stratification system and tend to min-

imize its impact on everyday lives and personal relations in the villages. The evidence of existing and felt status inequalities in rural communities is abundant in historical as well as anthropological literature. On the general issue of preindustrial stratification systems, see M. G. Smith, "Pre-Industrial Stratification Systems," in *Social Stratification and Mobility in Economic Development*, ed. Neil J. Smelser and Seymour M. Lipset (Chicago, 1966), 141–76; also Bernard J. Siegel, ed., *Studies in Peasant Life: Biennial Review of Anthropology* (Stanford) 1961, 1963, 1965, 1967. On social organization and status differences in European villages, see Julian Pitt-Rivers, "Social Class in a French Village," *Anthropological Quarterly*, 32 (1960), 1–14; Sydel F. Silverman, "An Ethnographic Approach to Social Stratification: Prestige in a Central Italian Community," *American Anthropologist* (August 1966), 899–922; Leonard Moss, "Estate and Class in a Southern Italian Hill Village," *American Anthropologist* (April 1962), 287–301; Robert T. Anderson and Gallatin Anderson, "Changing Social Stratification in a Danish Village," *Anthropological Quarterly*, 33 (1960), 98–105; Robert T. Anderson and Gallatin Anderson, "The Indirect Social Stratification of European Village Communities," *American Anthropologist* (October 1962), 106–25. On social stratification in East European rural communities in the late nineteenth and early twentieth centuries, see Tibor Kolossa, "The Social Stratification of the Peasant Class in Austria-Hungary: Statistical Sources and Methods of Research," *East European Quarterly* (January 1970), 420–39; Tomasić, *Personality and Culture in East European Politics*, 28–38; Kopczak and Kopczak, *Nasjelenje Zakarpatja za 100 Let*; Halpern and Halpern, *A Serbian Village in Historical Perspective*; Olive Lodge, *Peasant Life in Yugoslavia* (London, 1919); Hoćevar, *Structure of the Slovenian Economy*, 44–105; Doreen Warriner, ed., *Contrasts in Emerging Societies: Readings in the Social and Economic History of South Eastern Europe in the Nineteenth Century* (Bloomington, Ind.: 1965); Joseph Obrebski, *The Changing Peasantry of Eastern Europe* (Cambridge, Mass.: 1976); Irene Winner, *A Slovenian Village: Zerovnica* (Providence, 1971), 41–7. Excellent accounts of the complex societal organization in peasant communities in eastern Europe can also be found in literary fiction such as, for instance, Władysław Reymont's *The Peasants* (New York, 1924–5) or Jan Holocek's *Our People* (Chicago, 1938).

96 Bujak, *Zmiąca,Wieś Powiatu Limanowskiego*, 62–3.

97 Bujak, *Maszkienice . . . Rozwój od R.1900 do R.1911*, 17–25, 83.

98 Edward Steiner, *The Immigrant Tide, Its Ebb and Flow* (New York, 1980), 283

99 J. Cvijić, "Studies in Yugoslav Psychology," *Slavonic Review* (1930), 383–4; M. E. Durham, *Some Trial Origins, Laws and Customs of the Balkans* (London, 1928), 175: cited in Tomasić, *Personality and Culture in East European Politics*, 28, 191. Similar observations in Asen Balikci, "Quarrels in a Balkan Village," *American Anthropologist* (December 1965), 1456–70.

100 Witos, *Moje Wspomnienia*, 1:85–6. Also Władysław Orkan, *Komornicy* (Lvov, 1899); Reymont, *The Peasants;* Holocek, *Our People;* Emil Lengyel, *Americans from Hungary* (Philadelphia, 1948), 114–16, 137. On status competition among Polish peasants, see also Helena Znaniecki-Lopata, *Polish Americans: Status Competition in an Ethnic Community* (Englewood Cliffs, N.J.: 1976), particularly 19–20.
101 Witos, *Moje Wspomnienia*, 1:178.
102 Ibid, 94.
103 Smith, "Immigrant Social Aspirations and American Education, 1880–1930," *American Quarterly* (Fall 1969), 523–44.
104 After Józef Chałasiński, *Młode Pokolenie Chłopów* (Rome, 1946), 43–8; Thomas and Znaniecki, *Polish Peasant*, 1:290, 2:1360–6.
105 Thomas and Znaniecki, *Polish Peasant*, 1:738, n. 10. On the function of education in Slavic peasant culture, see John Bodnar, "Materialism and Morality: Slavic-American Immigrants and Education, 1890–1940," *Journal of Ethnic Studies* (Winter 1976), 1–21; Stolarik, "Immigration, Education and the Social Mobility of Slovaks, 1870–1930," in *Immigrants and Religion in Urban America*, ed. Randall M. Miller and Thomas D. Marzik (Philadelphia, 1977), 103–17.
106 Orkan, *Listy ze Wsi* 2:41. Similar observations in Stanisław Pigoń, *Z Komborni w Swiat.Wspomnienia Młodości* (Krakow, 1947), 97, and *Zarys Nowszej Literatury Ludowej Przed Rokiem 1920* (Krakow, 1946); also Witos, *Moje Wspomnienia*, 1:120–5, 144.
107 Thomas and Znaniecki, *Polish Peasant*, 1:297–9.
108 F. M. L. Thompson, *English Landed Society in the Nineteenth Century* (London, 1963); cf. also Howard Newby, *The Deferential Worker: A Study of Farm Workers in East Anglia* (London 1977), Chap. 1: "The Historical Context." On the East Central European variety, see Blum, *End of the Old Order of Rural Europe*, 418–20. Although bascially similar in type, "vertical" social relations were not identical in all of East Central Europe. For instance in Poland and Hungary, both with a numerous and highly self-conscious nobility class, the hierarchical order was particularly pronounced. In Slovenia, the westernmost flank of the region, by the beginning of the century it was already significantly weakened, whereas in Serbia, where there had traditionally been little domestic feudal stratification, the "deference mentality" was never deeply entrenched among peasants.

It should be noted, however, that the traditional deferential legitimation of social system in the rural regions of eastern Europe, while still widespread and persistent, was toward the end of the last century increasingly undermined by developments such as the emergence of peasant political parties, and self-educational and cooperative movements that presented the peasantry with alternatives to the existing model of social organization. On these developments in East Central Europe at the turn of the century, see Blum, *End of the Old Order in Rural Europe*, Chap. 15; J. Buchinger, *Der Bauer in der Kultur- und*

Wirtschaftsgeschichte Oesterreichs; C. A. Macartney, *Habsburg Empire,* Chap. 15; Oscar Jászi, *The Dissolution of the Habsburg Monarchy* (Chicago, 1929); David Mitrany, *Marx and the Peasant* (Chapel Hill, N.C.: 1951).

109 See Blum, *End of the Old Order in Rural Europe,* 45.
110 Tomasić, *Personality and Culture in East European Politics,* 199.
111 A. Kann, *The Multinational Empire, 1848–1918* (New York, 1950), 2 vols; Macartney, *Habsburg Empire,* Chap. 15: "Under Dualism, 1867–1903," and *National States and National Minorities* (Oxford, 1934); Jászi, *The Dissolution of the Habsburg Monarchy,* 271–82, 441–84; Robert W. Seton-Watson, *Racial Problems in Hungary* (London, 1908); Berend and Ránki, *Underdevelopment and Economic Growth,* 89–93; Paul R. Magocsi, *The Shaping of a National Identity: Subcarpathian Rus', 1848–1948* (Cambridge, Mass.: 1978). A very interesting discussion of the situation of national minorities in the Austro-Hungarian Empire in the context of its emigration policies can be found in M. Glettler, *Pittsburg-Wien-Budapest: Programm und Praxis der nationalitätenpolitik bei der Auswanderung der ungarischen Slowaken nach Amerika um 1900* (Vienna, 1980). On the multinational (ethnic) composition of East Central European villages, see Smith, "Lay Initiative in the Religious Life of American Immigrants, 1880–1950," in *Anonymous Americans: Explorations in Nineteenth Century Social History,* ed. Tamara K. Hareven (Englewood Cliffs, N.J.: 1971), 217, 222, and "Religion and Ethnicity in America," 1164; Barton, *Peasants and Strangers,* 27–48; Chałasiński, *Młode Pokolenie Chłopów,* 68–180; Kostrowicka, Landau, and Tomaszewski, *Historia Gospodarcza Polski,* 242–8; Tajtak, "Slovak Emigration and Migration," 61–80; Pawłowski, *Ludność Rzymsko-Katolicka w Polsko-Ruskiej Części Galicji.*
112 Słomka, *From Serfdom to Self-government,* 168.

Chapter 2: To America

1 Alfred Schutz, *Collected Papers,* I: *The Problem of Social Reality,* (The Hague, 1962) 1:69–71.
2 Understandably, since human motives and intentions are not easily measurable, historical economists have typically taken the same approach in studies of migrations. For an excellent review and critique of literature on this topic, see a series of articles by J. G. Gould in the *Journal of European Economic History:* "European Inter-continental Emigration, 1815–1914, Patterns and Causes" (Winter 1979), 593–681; "European Inter-continental Emigration: the Road Home: Return Migration from the U.S.A." (Spring 1980), 41–113; and "European Inter-continental Emigration: The Role of 'Diffusion' and 'Feedback'" (Fall 1980), 267–317. For a review and discussion of recent theories and literature on international labor migrations see Mary M. Kritz, Charles Keely, and Silvano M. Tomasi, eds., *Global Trends in Migration: Theory and Re-*

search on International Population Movements (Staten Island, N.Y.:1985); Paul R. Shaw, *Migration Theory and Fact: A Review of Bibliography of Current Literature* (Philadelphia, 1975); Charles H. Wood, "Equilibrium and Historical-structural Perspectives on Migration," *International Migration Review* (Summer 1982), 298–320; Lewellyn Hendrix, "Kinship and Economic-rational Migration: A Comparison of Micro- and Macro-Analyses," *Sociological Quarterly* (Autumn 1975), 534–44; Alejandro Portes and Robert L. Bach, *Latin Journey: A Longitudinal Study of Cuban and Mexican Immigrants in the United States* (Berkeley, 1984) Introduction and Chap. 1.

3 Data compiled from Franciszek Bujak, *Zmiąca, Wieś Powiatu Limanowskiego: Stosunki Gospodarcze i Społeczne* (Krakow, 1903), 60, 72, 95; *Limanowa, Miasteczko Powiatowe w Zachodniej Galicji: Stan Społeczny i Gospodarczy* (Krakow, 1902), 67; and *Maszkienice, Wieś Powiatu Brzeskiego: Rozwój od R. 1900 do R. 1911* (Lvov, 1914), 96–102; *Polish Encyclopaedia*, S. V. "Economic Life of Poland," 3:94–5; Irena Lechowa, "Tradycje Emigracyjne w Klonowej," *Prace i Materiały Muzeum Archeologicznego i Etnograficznego w Lodzi*, 3(1961), 36; Benjamin Murdzek, *Emigration in Polish Social-Political Thought, 1870–1914* (New York, 1974), 155–59; Paula Benkart, "Religion, Family and Community among Hungarians Migrating to American Cities, 1880–1930," Ph.D. thesis, Johns Hopkins University, 1975, 16.

4 Bujak, *Maszkienice . . . Rozwój od R.1900 do R.1911*, 91.

5 Leopold Caro, *Emigracja i Polityka Emigracyjna* (Poznan, 1914), 52–53.

6 From the reports of *föispánok* of Abauj-Torna, Veszprém, Bereg, Szatmár, Szabolcs, and Borsod in 1904 – quoted after Benkart, "Religion, Family and Community among Hungarians," 24–30. On the nonlinear correlations between indices of economic and demographic pressure and emigration rates from Hungary, see also Julianna Puskaś, "The Process of Overseas Migration from East-Central Europe: Its Periods, Cycles and Characteristics; A Comparative Study," in *Emigration from Northern, Central and Southern Europe: Theoretical and Methodological Principles of Research* (Krakow, 1984), 44–51, and Gould, "Inter-continental Emigration: The Role of 'Diffusion' and 'Feedback,'" 288–91 (drawing on the original data published by the Central Statistical Office for Hungary – in *Kivándorlása és Visszavándorlása, 1899–1913*).

7 Compiled from Władysław Grabski, *Materiały w Sprawie Włościańskiej* (Warsaw, 1919), 3:74–84; Florian Znaniecki, "Wychodźstwo a Położenie Ludności Zarobkującej w Królestwie Polskim," *Wychodźca Polski*, 3(1911), 9–16; Elżbieta Kaczyńska, *Społeczeństwo i Gospodarka Północno-Wschodnich Ziem Królestwa Polskiego w Okresie Rozkwitu Kapitalizmu* (Warsaw, 1974), 258–65; Joseph Obrebski, *The Changing Peasantry of Eastern Europe* (Cambridge, Mass.: 1976), 29–30, 39–40, 50–6.

8 Władysław Przybysławski, *Uniż:Wieś Powiatu Horodelskiego.Studium Społeczno-Gospodarcze* (Warsaw, 1933), 66.

9 W. Thomas and Florian Znaniecki, *The Polish Peasant in Europe and Amer-*

ica (New York, 1958), 2nd ed., 2:1488–99; Florian Znaniecki, "Statystyka Wychodźstwa," *Wychodźca Polski*, 1–2 (1911), 14–18, and "Wychodźstwo a Położenie Ludności Zarobkującej w Królestwie Polskim," 9–16; Obrebski, *Changing Peasantry of Eastern Europe*, 56; Julianna Puskaś, "Emigration from Hungary to the United States before 1914," *Studia Historica Academiae Scientiarum Hungariae*, (1975), 15–19, and *From Hungary to the United States, 1880–1914* (Budapest, 1982), 33, 38–41, 57–63; Maria Gliwicówna, *Drogi Emigracji* (Warsaw, 1937)," 502–3; Bujak, *Żmiąca*, 100. The importance of social networks regulating past and present population flows has been pointed out by students of migrations from other regions: Charles Tilly, "Migration in Modern European History," in *Human Migration: Patterns of Policies*, ed. William S. McNeill and Ruth Adams (Bloomington, 1978); John S. MacDonald and Leatrice MacDonald, "Chain Migration, Ethnic Neighborhood Formation, and Social Networks," in *An Urban World*, ed., Charles Tilly (Boston, 1974), 226–36; Grace M. Anderson, *Networks of Contacts: The Portuguese in Toronto* (Toronto, 1974); Bach and Portes, *Latin Journey*, Introduction.

10   Lechowa, "Tradycje Emigracyjne w Klonowej," 44–6; Jan Milczarek, "Emigracja Zarobkowa z Wieluńskiego," *Łódzkie Studia Etnograficzne* 19 (1977), 7–9.

11   Eugeniusz Kruszewski, *Probelmy Osadnictwa Polaków w Danii, 1893–1939* (London, 1980), 24; Gliwicówna, *Drogi Emigracji*, 507.

12   "Notes from my Village," by a Croatian schoolteacher, quoted after Emily Balch, *Our Slavic Fellow Citizens* (New York, 1969), 189. On the image of America in the eyes of European emigrants, see Merle Curti and Kendall Birr, "The Immigrants and the American Image in Europe, 1860–1914," *Mississippi Valley Historical Review* (September 1957), 203–32.

13   Louis Adamić, "The Land of Promise," *Harper's Magazine* (October 1931), 618–19.

14   Wincenty Witos, *Moje Wspomnienia* (Paris, 1964), 188.

15   C. A. Macartney, *The Habsburg Empire, 1790–1918* (London, 1968), 717; Emil Lengyel, *Americans from Hungary* (Philadelphia, 1948), 113–15. These calculations, however, are based on the expenditures of a city dweller rather than those of a seasonal peasant-worker. Routinely, peasant seasonal laborers boarded in large groups in rooms for which they paid from 20 to 30 kronen ($4 to $6, in 1900 dollars) monthly rent; individually it amounted to a contribution of approximately $.50 or less a month. Their meals consisted of coffee, bread, and sausage or bacon during the day and potatoes or gruel in the evening. Meat they ate only on Sundays. Their weekly food expenditures ranged from 1 to 5 kronen a week ($.20 to $1.00); calculation after Bujak, *Maszkienice . . . Rozwój od R.1900 do R.1911*, 96–7.

16.   Władysław Orkan, *Listy ze Wsi* (Warsaw, 1925), 1:120.

17   Some of my American colleagues – ethnic historians, mostly advocates of the "survival" thesis, as opposed to the "achievement" interpreta-

tion of peasant-emigrants' actions – suggested during our discussions that those immigrants who returned to eastern Europe were mostly "failures" and that the decision to go back more often than not reflected disappointment with both America and its "Great Promise." Without doubt, "failures" were not an uncommon cause of reemigration: "No, no, no more America for me [. . .] I am going back a beggar!", quoted in Edward Steiner, *On the Trail of the Immigrant* (New York, 1969), 340. Other contemporary sources indicate, however, that a great number of returnees to East Central European villages came home as "successes" by peasant standards. "Reports from all emigration countries," informed an American source at the beginning of the century, "concur in the statement that the standard of living of the peasants who have returned from the United States is above that of their neighbors": Isaac Hourwich, *Immigrants and Labor* (New York, 1922), 270–1. "In Austro-Hungary [. . .] the desire of the returning immigrants to invest in land," reported the Immigration Commission after visiting southern and eastern Europe, "has led to a considerable increase in its value, particularly in Croatia, Galicia and in the Slovak districts of Hungary": (U.S. Congress, *Reports of the Immigration Commission, Emigration Conditions in Europe*, 61st Cong., 3rd sess., Sen. Doc. 748 (Washington, D.C.: 1911), 413. In Croatia, for instance, as a result of increased demand by the returning "Amerikanci," the price of a *yoke* (1.5 acres) of land went up from $80 to about $400 during the fifteen years preceding World War I: Balch, *Our Slavic Fellow Citizens*, 183. In fact, in the East Central European villages the very term *Amerikanci/Amerykany* to the present day denotes opulence and well-being. A study of American reemigration conducted in Babica (Galicia) showed that of the total number (83) of reemigrants before the First World War, 34 percent indeed returned as "failures"–i.e., without money or with a very small amount. Of the remainder, 28 percent bought pieces of land 3 hectares or larger, 16 percent purchased pieces smaller than 3 hectares, and the rest invested their capital in new houses, farm buildings, and other material possessions. See Krystyna Duda-Dziewierz, *Wieś Małopolska a Emigracja Amerykańska.Studium Wsi Babica, pow.Rzeszowskiego* (Warsaw, 1938), 78–85.

18 The notion of the "demonstration effect" was first formulated by James S. Duesenberry, *Income, Saving and the Theory of Consumer Behavior* (Cambridge, Mass., 1949). On the role of "diffusion" and "feedback" in fostering overseas migrations from Europe, see the discussion by Gould, "European Inter-continental Emigration: The Role of 'Diffusion' and 'Feedback'," 267–317.

19 Witos, *Moje Wspomnienia*, 1:188.

20 Balch, *Our Slavic Fellow Citizens*, 471–3; Frank Sheridan, "Italian, Slavic and Hungarian Unskilled Immigrant Laborers in the United States," *Bulletin of the Bureau of Labor* (September 1907), 408.

21 Compiled from: Jan Hanzlík, "Začiatky Vystahovalectva zo Slovenska

do USA a Jeho Priebeh až do Roku 1918, Jeho Pričiny a Našledky," in *Začiatky Ceskej a Slovenskej Emigracie do USA*, ed. Josef Polišenský (Bratislava, 1975), 94; František Bielik, ed., *Slovenske Vysłahovalectvo. Dokumenty III. Korešpondencja z Rokov 1893–1939* (Martin, 1979) 3:31; Ladislav Tajtak, "Východoslovenské Vysťahovalectvo do Prvej Svetovej Vojny," *Nové Obzory* 3 (1961), 242; Murdzek, *Emigration in Polish Social-Political Thought*, 152–3; Benkart, "Religion, Family and Community among Hungarians," 12, 16. For a detailed estimate of the amount of money received in Hungary from American emigration before World War I, based on contemporary sources and statistics, see Puskaś, *From Hungary to the United States*, 77.

22 Compiled from Balch, *Our Slavic Fellow Citizens*, 140, 183; Commonwealth of Pennsylvania, *Annual Report of the Secretary of Internal Affairs 1884*: Pt. 3, *Industrial Statistics*, 12:70; Peter Roberts, "The New Pittsburghers: Slavs and Kindred Immigrants in Pittsburgh," *Charities and the Commons* (January 2, 1909), 546–7; Hourwich, *Immigrants and Labor*, 269; Edward Steiner, *The Immigrant Tide, Its Ebb and Flow* (New York, 1908), 163; Caro, *Emigracja i Polityka Emigracyjna*, 77; Lengyel, *Americans from Hungary*, 128; Jerzy Fierich, *Broniszów.Wieś Powiatu Ropczyckiego* (Warsaw, 1933), 55; *Slovenski Týždennik*, II, Pt. 29, July 18, 1913, 3–4 (quoted after Hanzlík, "Začiatky Vysťahovalectva zo Slovenska do USA," 94); David Souders, *The Magyars in America* (New York, 1922), 64; Frances Krajlic, "Croatian Migration to and from the United States between 1900 and 1914," Ph.D. thesis, New York University, 1975, 115–16, 133; Koňstantín Culeň, *Dejiny Slovákov v Amerike* (Bratislava, 1942), 1:59.

23 Compiled from G. Maior, *Political agrara la români* (Bucharest, 1906), 323; Maria Misińska, "Podhale Dawne i Współczesne," *Prace i Materiały Muzeum Archeologicznego i Etnograficznego w Lodzi* 15(1971), 52; Josip Lakatoš, *Narodna Statistika* (Zagreb, 1914), 64; Bujak, *Maszkienice . . . Rozwój od R.1900 do R.1911*, 103–4.

24 Puskaś, *From Hungary to the United States*, 54; Kaczyńska, *Dzieje Robotników Przemysłowych w Polsce Pod Zaborami* (Warsaw, 1970), 86.

25 Jeffrey Williamson, "Migration to the New World: Long Term Influences and Impact," *Explorations in Economic History*, (Summer 1974), 377.

26 Thomas and Znaniecki, *Polish Peasant*, 2:1500. Znaniecki made these observations earlier, in his Polish articles in *Wychodźca Polski* in 1911. See also *Reports of the Immigration Commission, Emigration Conditions in Europe*, 53.

27 Thomas and Znaniecki, *Polish Peasant*, 2:1496.

28 Orkan, *Listy ze Wsi*, 120.

29 *Pamiętniki Emigrantów.Stany Zjednoczone*, ed. Marek M. Drozdowski (Warsaw, 1977), 1:205, 498; 2:299.

30 Zofia Daszyńska-Golińska, "Ze Statystyki Rolniczej," *Ateneum* (Warsaw), 8(1892); "Z Demografii Współczesnej," *Ateneum* 4(1894), 103–16;

and "Własność Rolna w Galicji," *Ateneum* 7(1899), 72–108; "Badania nad Wsią Polską," *Krytyka* (Krakow), 10(1903), 10; "Własność Rolna w Austrii," *Ekonomista* (Warsaw) 4(1904), 1; "Własność Rolna w Galicji:Studium Statystyczno-Społeczne" (Warsaw, 1900). Similar observations, in relation to the conditions in Congress Poland, also in Znaniecki, "Wychodźctwo i Położenie Ludności Wiejskiej Zarobkującej w Królestwie Polskim," *Wychodźca Polski* 12(1911), 9–16; also Józef Buzek, *Pogląd na Wzrost Ludności Ziem Polskich w Wieku 19-tym* (Krakow, 1915). For the accounts of peasants-emigrants themselves, see *Pamiętniki Emigrantów.Stany Zjednoczone.*

31 Benkart, "Religion, Family and Community among Hungarians," 26–7.

32 Puskás, *From Hungary to the United States*, 27; also Gould, "European Inter-Continental Emigration. The Road Home: Return Migration from the U.S.A.," 41–113.

33 Obrebski, *Changing Peasantry of Eastern Europe*, 55–6; Duda-Dziewierz, *Wieś Małopolska a Emigracja Amerykańska*, 28–30; Puskás, *From Hungary to the United States*, 33–9.

34 Duda-Dziewierz, *Wieś Małopolska a Emigracja Amerykańska*, 47–9; also Gliwicówna, *Drogi Emigracji*, 505–6.

35 Report on emigration from Borsod County to the Hungarian prime minister, 1904, quoted after Benkart, "Religion, Family and Community among Hungarians," 27.

36 Compiled from *Reports of the Immigration Commission, Emigration Conditions in Europe*, 377; Józef Okołowicz, *Wychodźstwo i Osadnictwo Polskie Przed Wojną Swiatową* (Warsaw, 1920), 28; Tajtak, "Východoslovenske Vysťahovalectvo," 245; František Bielik and Elo Rákoš, *Slovenské Vysťahovalectvo Do Roku 1918. Dokumenty I.* (Bratislava, 1969), 1:28; S. W. Kopczak and S. I. Kopczak, *Naseljenje Zakarpatja za 100 Let* (Lviv, 1977), 154; Joseph Stipanovich, "'In Unity Strength': Immigrant Workers and Intellectuals in Progressive America. A History of the South Slav Social Democratic Movement, 1900–1918," Ph.D. thesis, University of Minnesota, 1978, 43; Jan Svetoň, "Slovenské Vysťahovalectvo v Období Uhorského Kapitalizmu," *Ekonomický Casopis*, Vol. 4, no. 2 (1956), 182; Kaczyńska, *Społeczeństwo i Gospodarka Północno-Wschodnich Ziem Królestwa Polskiego*, 144–6; Puskás, *From Hungary to the United States*, 33–9; Matjaž Klemenčcić, *Delovanje Ameriških Slovencev v Odnosu do Stare Domovine v Obdobju Druge Svetovne Vojne* (Lubljana, 1983), Pt. 2, p. 49; Ivan Cižmić, "Iseljavanje Hrvatske, 1890–1914g," unpublished essay (n.d.).

37 Stanisław Grabski, *Materyały w Sprawie Włościańskiej* (Warsaw, 1907), 1:36–45; also Puskás, *From Hungary to the United States*, 33–9; Tibor Kolossa, "The Social Structure of the Peasant Class in Austro-Hungary: Statistical Sources and Methods of Research," *East European Quarterly* (January 1970), 420–37. The following analysis of the three landless categories is a modified version of the discussion in Grabski.

38 Zbigniew Wierzbicki, Zmiąca Pół Wieku Później (Wrocław, 1963), 67–8.
39 Bujak, *Maszkienice* . . . *Rozwój od R.1900 do R.1911*, 82–5.
40 Puskás, "Process of Overseas Migration from East-Central Europe," 44–51.
41 Alfred Schutz, *The Phenomenology of the Social World* (Chicago, 1967), 87–9, and *Collected Papers*, I: *The Problem of Social Reality*, 70.
42 Puskás, *From Hungary to the United States*, 80 (a great majority of the emigrants returning to those counties before World War I had spent less than five years in America).
43 The indirect but rather convincing evidence that this was indeed the case, at least in the Polish territories, can be found in the tabulations provided by Grabski, together with his comments on the correlations between permanent and temporary emigration from different provinces of Congress Poland and on the proportion and character of the landless population. Obviously, however, much more, and more detailed, data are needed from other parts of eastern Europe before any firmer generalizations can be formulated (Grabski, *Materyały w Sprawie Włościańskiej*, 3:76–84).
44 Thomas and Znaniecki, *Polish Peasant*, 2:1499.
45 *Pamiętniki Emigrantów.Stany Zjednoczone*, 1:136.
46 Ibid., 2:414.

Chapter 3: Johnstown and the immigrant communities before World War I

1 J. Rogers Hollingsworth and Ellen Jane Hollingsworth, *Dimensions in Urban History: Historical and Social Science Perspectives on Middle-size American Cities* (London, 1979), 8–57.
2 J. J. McLaurin, *The Story of Johnstown* (Harrisburg, Pa.: 1891), 4:40–6; *Souvenir History of Johnstown, Pennsylvania, 1800–1939* (Johnstown, 1939); Henry W. Storey, *History of Cambria County, Pennsylvania*, 3 vols. (New York, 1907), and *Statistical Review of Greater Johnstown, Pennsylvania* (Johnstown, 1952), 7–8; John E. Frey, "The Bessemer Steel Industry: Johnstown's Contribution to It," *Johnstown Democrat*, Souvenir Edition, Autumn 1894, 9–10; John W. Boucher, "The Cambria Iron Company," in Pennsylvania Bureau of Industrial Statistics, *Annual Report, 1887*, E1–2; John W. Bennett, "Iron Workers in Woods Run and Johnstown: The Union Era, 1865–1895," Ph.D. thesis, University of Pittsburgh, 1977, 150–4.
3 Victor S. Clark, *History of Manufactures in the United States, 1860–1914* (Washington, D.C.: 1928), 576–7; *Johnstown Tribune*, January 17, 1900, 2.
4 William T. Hogan, *Economic History of the Iron and Steel Industry in the United States* (Lexington, Mass.: 1973), vol. 3, pt. 4, pp. 933–7.

5 Ibid., 937; Midvale Steel and Ordnance Company, *Annual Report 1916*, 16.

6 Hogan, *Economic History of the Iron and Steel Industry*, vol. 3, pt. 4, 937.

7 *Johnstown Works, United States Steel Corporation* (June 1976), vol. 4, no. 2, p. 1; "Commemorating the 75th Anniversary of Johnstown Savings Bank" (Johnstown, 1945), 1–2; U.S. Steel bicentennial, 1976, memorial album, 1; Raymond E. Murphy, *The Geography of Johnstown, Pennsylvania: An Industrial Center*, Pennsylvania State College Bulletin (1934), 20–30; U.S. Congress, *Reports of the Immigration Commission, Immigrants in Industries*, Pt. 2: *Iron and Steel Manufacturing*, Vol. 1, 61st Cong., 2nd sess., Sen. Doc. 633 (Washington, D.C., 1911), "Community A," 329.

8 Thomas C. Hopkins, "Clays and Clay Industries in Pennsylvania": Appendix, *Pennsylvania State College, Annual Report* (1897), 87–8; Murphy, *Geography of Johnstown*, 29–31; *Reports of the Immigration Commission*, "Community A," 1:329; *Johnstown Tribune*, February 24, 1908, 9.

9 "Johnstown Savings Bank," 1; Nathan D. Shappee, "A History of Johnstown and the Great Flood of 1889; A Study of Disaster and Rehabilitation," Ph.D. thesis, University of Pittsburgh, 1940, Chap. 3; *Johnstown Tribune*, November 1, 1940, 5; McLaurin, *Story of Johnstown*, 45; U.S. Bureau of the Census, *Manufactures, 1914*, 1:1281.

10 On women's employment in the steel towns, see U.S. Congress, *Report on the Conditions of Women and Child Wage Earners in the United States*: vol. 9, *History of Women in Industry in the United States*, vol. 18, *Employment of Women and Children in Selected Industries*, 61st Cong., 2nd sess., Sen. Doc. 645 (Washington, D.C.: 1913); Susan Kleinberg, "Technology and Women's Work: The Lives of Working Class Women in Pittsburgh, 1870–1900," *Labor History* (Winter 1976), 71; Corinne A. Krauze, *Grandmothers, Mothers and Daughters: An Oral History of Ethnicity, Mental Health and Continuity of Three Generations of Jewish, Italian and Slavic-American Women* (New York, 1978), and "Urbanization without Breakdown: Italian, Jewish and Slavic Immigrant Women in Pittsburgh, 1900–1965," *Journal of Urban History* (May 1978), 276–97; Elisabeth B. Butler, *Women and the Trades, Pittsburgh, 1907–1908* (New York, 1911).

11 In 1890, the Johnstown business directory had a total of 750 entries (including adjacent boroughs, and professional services), and by 1900 the number increased to 1,000. By 1910, it reached 1,750 – an increase of 75 percent over the decade. Between 1910 and 1915 business and services in Johnstown continued to grow, albeit at a slower rate of 15 percent (calculated from Johnstown city directories, for 1890, 1900, 1910, 1915); *Twelfth Census of the United States: 1900, Special Reports, Occupations*, 448–50; *Thirteenth Census of the United States: 1910, Population, Occupation Statistics*, 4:238–42.

12 Bennett, "Iron Workers in Woods Run and Johnstown," 155–9.

13 Shappee, "History of Johnstown and the Great Flood," 101; Herbert Gutman, "Two Lockouts in Pennsylvania, 1873–4," *Pennsylvania Magazine* (July 1959), 307–27; Bennett, "Iron Workers in Woods Run and

Johnstown," 210–18; John W. Giltinan, "Lockout in Johnstown, 1874," seminar paper, University of Pittsburgh, 1969; Bruce T. Williams and Michael Yates, *Upward Struggle: A Bicentennial Tribute to Labor in Cambria and Somerset Counties* (Johnstown, 1976), 4.

14 Shappee, "History of Johnstown and the Great Flood," 75–6, 528–59; Bennett, "Iron Workers in Woods Run and Johnstown," 78–85; Williams and Yates, *Upward Struggle*, 5.

15 Boucher, "Cambria Iron Company," E10–14; Shappee, "History of Johnstown and the Great Flood," 70, 97–8, 141–2, 152–4; Bennett "Iron Workers of Woods Run and Johnstown," Chap. 5.

16 McLaurin, *Story of Johnstown*, 45; Bennett, "Iron Workers of Woods Run and Johnstown," 168.

17 Shappee, "History of Johnstown and the Great Flood," 97; Bennett, "Iron Workers in Woods Run and Johnstown," 162–8.

18 *Tenth Census of the United States: 1880, Statistics of the Population*, 294, 454 (percentages based on borough estimates); after Bennett, "Iron Workers in Woods Run and Johnstown," 333, 354.

19 Katherine Stone, "The Origins of Job Structures in the Steel Industry," *Radical America* (November–December 1973), 19–67; John Fitch, *The Steel Workers* (New York, 1969), 139–43; David Brody, *The Steelworkers in America: The Non-Union Era* (Cambridge, Mass.: 1960); Peter Temin, *Iron and Steel in Nineteenth Century America: An Economic Inquiry* (Cambridge, Mass.: 1964); Frank Popplewell, *Some Modern Conditions and Recent Developments in Iron and Steel Production in America* (Manchester, England, 1906); Peter R. Shergold, "Wage Differentials Based on Skill in the United States, 1889–1914: A Case Study," *Labor History* (Fall 1977), 485–509. On the process of job restructuring at Cambria Iron Company in Johnstown, see Bennett, "Iron Workers in Woods Run and Johnstown," 20–39.

20 *Johnstown Democrat*, May 23, 1911, 5.

21 U.S. Congress, *Reports of the Immigration Commission*, pt. 2: *Iron and Steel Manufacturing*, 61st Cong., 2nd sess., Sen. Doc. 110 (Washington, D.C.: 1911), vol. 3, 31–2. Andrea Graziosi estimates the average proportion of laborers in the American steel industry in 1880 at 40 percent and in 1910 at about 60 percent: see "Common Laborers, Unskilled Workers," *Labor History* (Fall 1981), 533–4.

22 Contracting for laborers was outlawed in Pennsylvania in 1885: See Shappee, "History of Johnstown and the Great Flood," *Johnstown Tribune*, November 1, 1940, 5.

23 McLaurin, *Story of Johnstown*, Appendix, "Names of the Victims," 226–7; Johnstown City Directory, 1891.

24 On the ethnic backgrounds of my 1900 sample, see pp. 15, 398n.

25 *Reports of the Immigration Commission*, "Community A," 339.

26 East Central European population from manuscript schedules of the U.S. Census for 1900.

27 Bennett, "Iron Workers in Woods Run and Johnstown," 352–54; Shap-

pee, "History of Johnstown and the Great Flood of 1889"; *Johnstown Tribune*, November 1, 1940, 5. "Seventy nine percent of all the Welsh iron workers lived in either the first two wards of Johnstown or in Millville. Sixty nine percent of all the Irish millworkers lived in either Cambria or Millville. Sixty seven percent of all the German workers lived in either the first ward of Johnstown, Cambria, Conemaugh or Yoder." Bennett, "Iron Workers in Woods Run and Johnstown," 340–1.

28 Joel B. McCamant, "Report on the Cambria Company's Tenements, 1880," quoted in Shappee, "History of Johnstown and the Great Flood," 174.

29 Johnstown city directory, 1895.

30 In 1910, this concentration was even greater: 98 percent of all East Central Europeans recorded in the manuscript census schedules resided in Johnstown's "foreign colonies" U.S. Census, manuscript population schedules, 1910.

31 *Reports of the Immigration Commission*, "Community A," 348–9.

32 Estimated from Johnstown city directory, 1895; *Johnstown Tribune* August 22, 1893, 1; Commonwealth of Pennsylvania, Department of Labor and Industry; *Second Annual Report: 1914*, pt. 1, pp. 448–54; Commonwealth of Pennsylvania, Department of Labor and Industry, *Statistics of Production, Wages and Employees for the Year 1915*, pt. 1, pp. 470–5.

33 On the concept and application of "cultural division of labor," see Michael Hechter, "Ethnicity and Industrialization: On the Proliferation of the Cultural Division of Labor," *Ethnicity* (March 1976), 214–24, and "Group Formation and the Cultural Division of Labor," *American Journal of Sociology* (September 1978), 293–317. See also Marcia Freedman, *Labor Markets: Segments and Shelters* (New York, 1976); Richard C. Edwards, Michael Reich, and David M. Gordon, eds., *Labor Market Segmentation* (Lexington, Mass.: 1973); Michael J. Piore, *Birds of Passage: Migrant Labor and Industrial Societies* (New York, 1979), 35–49; Milton Santos, "Circuits of Work: Interdependencies in the Urban Economy," in *Ethnicity at Work*, ed. Sandra Wallman (London, 1979) 215–27; Charles M. Tolbert II, Patrick M. Horan, and E. M. Beck, "The Structure of Economic Segmentation: A Dual Economy Approach," *American Journal of Sociology* (March 1980), 1095–1116; Ronald D'Anico and Timothy Brown, "Patterns of Labor Mobility in a Dual Economy: The Case of Semi-skilled and Unskilled Workers," *Social Science Research* (June 1982), 153–75; Randy Hodson, "Companies, Industries and the Measurement of Economic Segmentation," *American Sociological Review* (June 1984), 323–34.

34 Interview with Louis Moses, retired superintendent at Cambria Iron Works, October 31, 1980.

35 *Reports of the Immigration Commission*, "Community A," 386.

36 Interview with Charles Hoover, retired general foreman at Cambria Iron Works, November 11, 1980.

37 Quoted after J. Saposs, "How the Rank and File Workers View the

Strike," unpublished report in Interchurch World Movement, *Commission of Inquiry into the 1919 Steel Strike*, Blankenhorn Papers, Archives of the Industrial Society, University of Pittsburgh, Pittsburgh, Pa., 6. The Saposs interviews, conducted in 1919, describe the events from the past that led the immigrant workers to participate in the strike.

38   Stone, "Origins of Job Structures in the Steel Industry," 39–43.
39   Calculated from *Thirteenth Census of the United States: 1910*, vol. 4, *Population*, Occupation Statistics, 4:238–42.
40   Interviews with Moses and Hoover.
41   *Reports of the Immigration Commission*, "Community A," 349.
42   There was a local YMCA, but most of its members were either native-born Americans or western Europeans; those few East Central Europeans who attended usually came, stayed, and departed in their own groups, so the interaction was very limited.
43   Quoted after Saposs, "How the Rank and File of the Workers View the Strike," 7.
44   *Reports of the Immigration Commission*, "Community A," 387.
45   Based on analysis of articles in the *Johnstown Tribune* and *Johnstown Democrat*, 1890–1915.
46   William L. Yancey, Eugene P. Ericksen, and Richard N. Juliani, "Emergent Ethnicity: A Review and Reformulation," *American Sociological Review* (June 1976), 391–403.
47   Commonwealth of Pennsylvania, Bureau of Industrial Statistics, *Annual Report of the Secretary of Internal Affairs, 1909*, pt. 3, vol. 37: *Johnstown, Pennsylvania*, 157.
48   East Central European males from manuscript schedules of 1900 census, traced in Johnstown city directories through 1940.
49   East Central European males from manuscript schedules of 1900 census, traced in Johnstown city directories, 1905 and 1910.
50   The concept of "island-hoppers" comes from Stephan Thernstrom and Peter R. Knights, "Men in Motion: Some Data and Speculations about Urban Population Mobility in Nineteenth-century America," *Journal of Interdisciplinary History* (Autumn 1970), 9–32. On the formation of local communities in the process of "island-hopping" by mobile individuals and on the island-hoppers' social and economic characteristics, see Robert H. Wiebe, *The Search for Order, 1877–1920* (New York, 1967), 2–10, 133–63; Clyde Griffen, "Workers Divided: The Effect of Craft and Ethnic Differences in Poughkeepsie, N.Y., 1850–1880," in *Nineteenth-century Cities: Essays in New Urban History*, ed. Stephan Thernstrom and Richard Sennett (New Haven, 1969), 59–63; Richard S. Alcorn, "Leadership and Stability in Mid-Nineteenth Century America: A Case Study of an Illinois Town," *Journal of American History* (December 1973), 685–702; Michael Katz, Michael J. Doncet, and Mark J. Stern, "Migration and the Social Order in Erie County, N.Y.: 1855," *Journal of Interdisciplinary History* (Spring 1978), 669–701; Edward Kopf, "Untarnishing the Dream: Mobility, Opportunity and Order in Modern America," *Journal of Social*

History (Winter 1977), 206–28; Peter J. Coleman, "Restless Grant County: Americans on the Move," *Wisconsin Magazine of History* (Autumn 1962), 16–20; Richard Hopkins, "Occupational and Generational Mobility in Atlanta, 1870–1896," *Journal of Southern History* (May 1968), 200–13.

51 The problem of ethnic (national) identity and the distinction between these two closely related groups, Rusyns and Ukrainians from the Carpathians, has been the subject of a long-standing debate among historians, linguists, and politicians. By some of them jointly referred to as "Subcarpathian Rusyns," the people inhabiting the border region northeast, south, and southwest of the Carpathian mountains have traditionally been divided into distinct ethnographic subgroups, the first two of which are found on both sides of the Carpathians: (1) the Lemkians, (2) the Hutsuls, and (3) the Boikians, in the southern lowland region. The Subcarpathian Rusyns who settled in Johnstown at the turn of the century originally identified themselves in terms of the geographic locality they came from, either south or north of the Carpathians. The Ukrainian self-identification among part of the Galician Rusyn (mostly Lemkian) immigrants in the city has developed gradually, with the emergence of churches and organizations that split the group into two segments. On the discussion of ethnoreligious differences and the emergence of separate national identities of Rusyns and Ukrainians, see Paul R. Magocsi, *The Shaping of a National Identity: Subcarpathian Rus', 1848–1948* (Cambridge, Mass.: 1978), and Magocsi, ed, *The Ukrainian Experience in the United States: A Symposium* (Cambridge, Mass.: 1979). Also Wasyl Halich, *Ukrainians in the United States* (New York, 1970); Walter Warzeski, "The Rusyn Community in Pennsylvania," and Bohdan Procko, "Pennsylvania: Focal Point of Ukrainian Immigration," in *The Ethnic Experience in Pennsylvania*, ed. John E. Bodnar (Lewisburg, Pa., 1973), 175–216 and 216–31.

52 East Central European males from manuscript schedules of 1900 census. The average number of years spent in the United States as of 1900 for the recorded representatives of different nationality groups was as follows: "Prussian" Poles, 10.6; "Russian" Poles, 5.3; "Austrian" Poles, 3.2; Magyars, 5.6; Slovenes, 5.4; Slovaks, 5.0; Croatians and Rusyns, 4.9; Ukrainians, 4.3; Serbs, 2.8. Chronologically, the Slovaks were the first to settle in Johnstown in greater numbers; apparently, by 1900, the "old-timers" were already greatly outnumbered by the more recent arrivals, which should explain a relatively low figure for this group. About one-fifth of the male Slovak residents of Johnstown recorded by the 1900 census reported that at the time of the investigation they had already been in America for more than 15 years.

53 Information based on marriage records in the immigrant parishes and on my personal interviews with the East Central Europeans in Johnstown. Unfortunately, not all the churches and not all the priests (who rotated in quick succession) recorded the actual birthplaces of the new-

lyweds, and often only the county or region was noted. *Sources*: St. Emerich (Hungarian Roman Catholic), Book of Marriages, vol. I, 1908–12; St. Mary (Rusyn Greek Catholic), Registrum Matrimonium, vol. 1, 1896–1912; St. Rochus (Croatian Roman Catholic, also served the Slovenes), Registrum Matrimonium, 1901–6; St. Casimir (Polish Roman Catholic), Marriage Register, 1902–09; St. Nicholas (Serbian Orthodox), Marriage and Baptismal Book, 1906–11; St. John the Baptist (Ukrainian Byzantine Catholic), Book of Marriages, vol. 1, 1910–24; St. John (Russian Orthodox), Marriage Records, vol. 1, 1910–17; St. Stephen (Slovak Roman Catholic), Marriage Book, vol. 1, 1901–15. Also the following interviews: #2, with Michael P. (March 9, 1981); #6, with Sophie L. (May 15, 1981); #19, with Mary U. (June 18, 1981); #38, with Andy A. (February 25, 1981), #44, with George P. (January 22, 1981); #66 (June 11, 1980) and #70 (September 6, 1980) with Walter W.; #71, with Peter H. (December 18, 1980); #88, with Anne H. (January 21, 1981).

54 Interviews: #3, with Mary P. (March 9, 1981); #4, with Nikola B. (July 14, 1981); #20, with Mary K. (June 18, 1981); #21, with Coleman N. (June 18, 1981); #38 (February 25, 1981) and #95 (July 17, 1981) with Andy A.; #66, with Walter W. (June 11, 1980). Branko Colaković makes similar observations as to the importance to the Yugoslav immigrants of the climatic and topographic resemblance of the American environment to the home country; see *Yugoslav Migrations to America* (San Francisco, 1973), 143–7.

55 Ewa Morawska, "Johnstown, Pa. – Survey of Organizations," Pennsylvania Ethnic Heritage Studies Center, Southwestern Pennsylvania Ethnic Resources Project, 2 (1980), Archives of the Industrial Society, University of Pittsburgh. By 1917 there were in Johnstown the following East Central European associations: Slovak Jednota (9 lodges), National Slovak Society (1), United Lutheran Society (2), Polish National Alliance (5), Polish Roman Catholic Union (3), Hungarian Verhovay (3), Hungarian Reformed Sick Benefit Society (2), Croatian Fraternal Union (5), Serbian National Federation (4), Greek Catholic Union (10), United Societies of Greek Catholic Religion (2), Slovak Roman and Greek Catholic Jednota (3), Ukrainian National Association (2), Ukrainian National Providence Association (1), Russian Orthodox Brotherhood (2), Slovene National Benefit Society (5), Slovene National Independent Society (1), and Slovene Benefit Society "Pomocnik" (1). The earliest chronologically was Lodge #23 of the Slovak Jednota, established in 1889. Then followed Lodge #25 of the Greek Catholic Union, and Lodge #503 of the Polish Roman Catholic Union – both in 1892. In 1893 another Jednota branch, #104, was founded, and in 1894 Lodge #5 of the Croatian Fraternal Union. In 1897, a women's lodge of the Croatian Fraternal Union was established, and another (men's) lodge, #116, of the Greek Catholic Union. In 1898, the Hungarian Verhovay, Lodge #8, and in 1899 the Hungarian Reformed Sick Benefit Society and the first local lodge of the Serb National Federation, together with another women's

lodge of the Croatian Fraternal Union. Between 1900 and 1910, 24 new branches were added to the already existing societies, and the remaining 20 were added during the second decade of the century.

56 St. Mary's Immaculate Conception Roman Catholic Church, "Births, Marriages and Deaths," vol. 1, 1860–1917.

57 "Johnstown, Pennsylvania – Survey of Churches and Organizations" Pennsylvania Ethnic Heritage Studies, Southwestern Pennsylvania Ethnic Resources Project, 2 (1980), Archives of the Industrial Society, University of Pittsburgh. The Slovaks had two churches: St. Stephen's Catholic (1891) and St. John's the Evangelist Lutheran (1903). The Hungarians also had two: St. Emerich's Roman Catholic (1905) and Hungarian Reformed (1901). The Rusyns from the southern Carpathian slopes concentrated at the opposite extremes of the city and also erected two churches: St. Mary's Greek Catholic (1895) and Holy Trinity Greek Catholic (1908). The Rusyns (Ukrainians) from Galicia, in the northern part of the Carpathians, divided their allegiance between St. John the Baptist Ukrainian Byzantine Catholic Church (1910) and St. John's Russian Orthodox parish (1908). The Croatians built Roman Catholic St. Rochus (1900), which was also attended by the Slovenes, and the Serbs built St. Nicholas Orthodox church (1906), also attended by a small group of Macedonians, Bulgarians, and Orthodox Rumanian immigrants. The Poles built St. Casimir's Roman Catholic Church (1902) and its Mission Chapel in East Conemaugh (1910). Hereafter, ethnic Roman Catholic parishes will be identified simply as Catholic.

58 The 1900 census listed 30 East Central European store owners in the city, which is 12 more than ennumerated in the "Mercantile Appraisal" that year (*Johnstown Tribune*, May 24, 1900, 6). It is possible that 12 either disappeared before the census was taken or else that their business was so very tiny – for instance, conducted from the immigrants' private quarters, such as cart hauling or dairy delivery by those at the outskirts of the borough who kept gardens and poultry – that they were not even recorded as "businesses" by the mercantile census. Information on the number of East Central European businesses in Johnstown was compiled from the mercantile appraiser's lists published annually in the *Johnstown Tribune* (the owners of two or more businesses were counted more than once). The Immigration Commission reported in 1907–8 a total of 96 East Central European businesses in the city and vicinity: 77 Slavic and Magyar, 19 Jewish: see *Reports of the Immigration Commission*, "Community A," 457.

59 Interview with Robert Gabrenya, son of the founder of the Slovenian Bank (March 18, 1980). Also Mortgagee Index, 6, 181-1/2, Recorder's Office, Cambria County Courthouse, Ebensburg, Pa.

60 Unfortunately, except for a few issues of *Cerkovnaja Nauka* from 1903, no other copies were preserved, since they were destroyed, along with many other records, in the Johnstown floods. The information about them comes from *Reports of the Immigration Commission*, "Community

A," 465–7; from David A. Souders, *The Magyars in America* (New York, 1922), 76; and *Johnstown Tribune,* October 4, 1911, 10 and April 13, 1905, 10. A listing of these newspapers is also provided in the press catalogue of the Archives of the Industrial Society, University of Pittsburgh.

61   Interview #9, with Anthony C. (October 10, 1980).

62   An excellent discussion of ethnoreligious pluralism in East Central European villages and in the immigrant communities in America at the beginning of the century can be found in Timothy Smith, "Lay Initiative in the Religious Life of American Immigrants, 1880–1950," in *Anonymous Americans: Explorations in Nineteenth-century Social History,* ed. Tamara K. Hareven (Englewood Cliffs, N.J.: 1971), 214–49, and "Religion and Ethnicity in America," *American Historical Review* (December 1978), 1155–86.

63   Interview with Rev. W. Sabo, pastor of St. Mary's Greek Catholic Church in Cambria City, September 23, 1980; also *Johnstown Tribune,* April 21, 1900, 5, and Leski Konnyu, "Hungarians in Johnstown," in *Hungarians: An Immigration Study* (St. Louis, 1967), 36.

64   *Cerkovnaja Nauka,* March 4, 26, 1903; April 18, 30, 1903; May 7, 1903; June 23, 1903.

65   "Johnstown, Pa. – Survey of Churches and Organizations," Pennsylvania Ethnic Heritage Studies, information from interview forms for East Central Europeans (Archives of the Industrial Society [AIS], University of Pittsburgh). On the ethnoreligious and institutional convergence of Rusyn and Slovak communities before World War I in the Pittsburgh area, see Mara Hlavacik, "Slovak-American Origins," unpublished report, (1978) AIS, University of Pittsburgh.

66   Interview #95, with Andy A. (July 17, 1981) and #3, with Mary P. (March 9, 1981).

67   Interview #3, with Mary P. (March 9, 1981): "We lived well with the Poles." Mary P. came from the vicinity of Krosno in Galicia; she was at first Greek Catholic, later became Orthodox: "We came from the same place, it made no difference then, Pole or Rusnak [Rusyn], and the language was mixed. But they looked down upon us a little, the Poles; also here in Johnstown they thought of themselves better." American Carpathian Citizens Club list of founding members; Polish National Alliance, Branch 1569; list of officers; "Johnstown, Pa. – Survey of Churches and Organizations," Pennsylvania Ethnic Heritage Studies.

68   St. Mary's Immaculate Conception Catholic Church, "Births, Marriages and Deaths," vol. 1, 1860–1917; Slovak Jednota, Branch 23, Membership Book, 1889–1908; *Jednota Kalendár,* 1898, 122; *Johnstown Tribune,* May 15, 1913, 17; "Schantz and Johnstown: A Souvenir for the Dedication of the Joseph Schantz Monument in Connection with the 14th Convention of the German-American Alliance of Pennsylvania" (Johnstown, June 14–16, 1913).

69   Interview #16 (June 19, 1981) and #47 (July 1, 1981), with Mary D.; #103, with Paul P. (July 21, 1983).

70 St. Mary's Immaculate Conception Catholic Church, "Births, Marriages and Deaths," vol. 1, 1860–1917; "Schantz and Johnstown"; *Reports of the Immigration Commission*, "Community A," 468.

71 "Dedication and Consecretation of St. Nicholas Serbian Orthodox Church," (Johnstown, 1964), 6; *Reports of the Immigration Commission*, "Community A," 460–1; interview #51, with Mike T. (June 5, 1981) and #88, with Anne H. (January 21, 1981).

72 "Dedication and Consecration of St. Nicholas Serbian Orthodox Church," 6–7; list of officers, from minutes, Croatian Fraternal Union Lodge #5 (Sv. Roh), July 17, 1900; George Prpič, *The Croatian Immigrants in America* (New York, 1971), 130: Prpič refers to Bozo Gojsovic – our "dynamic Serbian pioneer" – as a Croatian; for a similar reference see *Reports of the Immigration Commission*, "Community A," 460. Among the founding members of Lodge #5 of the Croatian Fraternal Union there was also a Slovenian.

73 On the role of the immigrant religious and voluntary organizations in the forming of national (ethnic) identity, see W. I. Thomas and Florian Znaniecki, *The Polish Peasant in Europe and America* (New York, 1958), 2nd ed., vol. 2, pt. 3, pp. 1511–1647; Mieczysław Szawleski, *Wychodźstwo Polskie w Stanach Zjednoczonych Ameryki* (Lvov, 1924); Konstantin Culeń, *Dejiny Slovakov v Amerike* (Bratislava, 1942), vol. 1, Chap. 9; Victor Greene, *For God and Country: The Rise of Polish and Lithuanian Ethnic Consciousness in America, 1860–1910* (Madison, 1975); Smith, "Religion and Ethnicity in America," 1155–85; Rudolph J. Vecoli, "European Americans: From Immigrants to Ethnics," in *The Reinterpretation of American History and Culture*, ed. William H. Cartwright and Richard L. Watson (Washington, D.C.: 1973), 81–112; Josef Barton, "Religious and Cultural Change in Czech Immigrant Communities," in *Immigrants and Religion in Urban America*, ed. Randall Miller and Thomas D. Marzik (Philadelphia, 1977), 3–25; Mark Stolarik, *Slovak Migration from Europe to North America, 1870–1918* (Cleveland, 1980), Chaps. 3, 5; William J. Galush, "Faith and Fatherland: Dimensions of Polish-American Ethnoreligion, 1875–1975," in *Immigrants and Religion in Urban America*, 84–103; Keith Dyrud, "The Rusin Question in Eastern Europe and in America, 1890–World War I," Ph.D. thesis, University of Minnesota, 1976; Arunas Alisaukas, "Religion, Ethnicity and the Emergence of a Lithuanian Subculture in the United States, 1870–1900," paper presented at the Hopkins Seminar in American Religious History, August 1974; Walter Warzewski, "Religious and National Consciousness in the History of the Rusins of Carpatho-Ruthenia and the Byzantine Rite Pittsburgh Exarchate," Ph.D. thesis, University of Pittsburgh, 1964.

74 *Johnstown Tribune*, April 3, 1909, 9; May 23, 1908, 9; June 24, 1913, 7; October 8, 1913, 18.

75 *Johnstown Tribune*, January 1, 1908, 6; January 6, 1908, 5; June 5, 1908, 11; June 6, 1908, 8; October 21, 1980, 10.

76 *Cerkovnaja Nauka*, May 7, 1903. I checked East Central European names

in the divorce files in the Cambria County Prothonotary's Office (Eject-
ment and Miscellaneous Docket). Between 1900 and the late 1930s about
200 East Central European cases were formally filed from the county.
In the period before the First World War, over 40 percent of all cases
that were filed by East Central European immigrants were complaints
of husbands deserted by wives. Of that number, almost one-half of the
wives were said to have run away with another man, and about one-
fourth "ran back to mother"; another one-fourth was accused of open
adultery. The most common cause for women's filing for divorce was
desertion and wife beating.

77   *Cerkovnaja Nauka*, March 4, 1903.

Chapter 4: The beginnings: strategies of adaptation

1   *Przegląd Wszechpolski*, February 15, 1895, 90.
2   Antoni Cyburt, *Historia Polonii w Johnstown*, unpublished paper in the
possession of the author. On the initial disappointment of the immigrants, see Branko Colakovič, *Yugoslav Migrations to America* (San
Francisco, 1973), 28–30, 149–50; Mark Stolarik, *Slovak Migration from
Europe to North America, 1870–1918* (Cleveland, 1980), 30; Mary Molek,
Immigrant Woman (Dover, Del.: 1976), 23, 37–39.
3   Quoted after Emil Lengyel, *Americans from Hungary* (Philadelphia,
1948), 129; also my interviews in Johnstown: #2, with Michael P.
(March 9, 1981); #3, with Mary P. (March 9, 1981); #13, with Katarzyna
C. (June 23, 1981); #52, with Janko L. (June 5, 1981).
4   Interview #13, with Katarzyna C. (June 23, 1981).
5   Oscar Lewis, *La Vida* (New York, 1968), also his *Five Families* (New
York, 1959).
6   Alex Inkeles and David H. Smith, *Becoming Modern: Individual Change
in Six Developing Countries* (Cambridge, Mass.: 1974), 6–9; and Inkeles,
"The Modernization of Man," in *Modernization: The Dynamics of
Growth*, ed. Myron Weiner (New York, 1966), esp. 149.
7   On the "irrationality" of the American factory system, see David
Montgomery, *Workers' Control in America* (Cambridge, 1979), esp. 36,
42–33, 102; Daniel T. Rodgers, *The Work Ethic in Industrial America
1850–1920* (Chicago, 1978), 159–70, and "Tradition, Modernity and the
American Industrial Worker," *Journal of Interdisciplinary History* (Spring
1977), 655–81; Tamara K. Hareven, *Family Time and Industrial Time*
(Cambridge, 1982), Chap. 6.
8   William Thomas and Florian Znaniecki, *The Polish Peasant in Europe
and America* (New York, 1958), 2nd ed, 1:196–9; also Michael Piore,
Birds of Passage: Migrant Labor and Industrial Society (New York, 1979),
52–9.
9   In his otherwise very enlightening essay, "Immigration and Modernization: The Case of Slavic Peasants in Industrial America," *Journal of
Social History* (Fall 1976), 47, and also in "Materialism and Morality:

Slavic-American Immigrants and Education, 1890–1940," *Journal of Ethnic Studies* (Winter 1976), 8, John Bodnar, having found in the Slavic foreign-language press in America at the beginning of the century repeated condemnations of the "Dollar God" and of "material excess and wantonness," infers from it a "consistent antimaterialism [permeating] the Slavic-American culture." The culture of East Central European immigrants, like most plebeian cultures in general, contained in fact a strong materialistic current, transplanted from the old country and reinforced in this one (see, for instance, the discussion in Thomas and Znaniecki, *Polish Peasant in Europe and America*, 1:156–205). Moralistic appeals of the foreign-language press were the confirmation of this tendency: There would have been no need to preach the ideal so vigorously unless it was not being practiced in actuality.

10 Colakovič, in *Yugoslav Migrations to America*, 58, reports that according to their own declarations over 60 percent of the Slovene, Serbian, and Croatian emigrants who came to this country before 1910 intended to go back home. Since this statistic also included women, many (or most) of whom were wives joining husbands in America who had more or less decided to stay, the proportion for men was probably significantly higher. On the immigrant sojourners, the distinction between sojourners and settlers, and the psychological and social implications of "sojournism," see Paul C. P. Siu, "The Sojourner," *American Journal of Sociology* (July 1952), 34–44; Robert Harney, "Boarding and Belonging: Thoughts on Sojourner Institutions," *Urban Historical Review*, (October 1978), 8–38; also Piore, *Birds of Passage*, Chaps. 2–4, and Edna Bonacic, "A Theory of Ethnic Antagonism: The Split Labor Market," *American Sociological Review* (October 1972), 547–59.

11 John Bodnar, Roger Simon, and Michael Weber, *Lives of Their Own: Blacks, Italians and Poles in Pittsburgh, 1900–1960* (Urbana, Ill.: 1982), 42, 102, 134, 143; also Bodnar, "Immigration and Modernization: The Case of Slavic Peasants in Industrial America," 53–5; Caroline Golab, "The Impact of the Industrial Experience on the Immigrant Family: The Huddled Masses Reconsidered," in *Immigrants in Industrial America, 1850–1920*, ed, Richard L. Ehrlich (Charlotteville, N.C.: 1977), 8.

12 The notion of "steady work" as a means toward, first, economic security of the family, and, second, the accomplishment of a somewhat better life, was expressed by a number of East Central Europeans I talked to in Johnstown: interviews #9 and 10, with Anthony C. (October 10, 1981, and February 23, 1981); #13, with Katarzyna C. (June 23, 1981); #37a, with John O. (March 11, 1981); #52, with Yanko L. (June 5, 1981); #62 and #62a, with Mr. and Mrs. Thomas B. (June 11, 1980); #65, with Michael N. (October 17, 1980); #71 and #71a, with Mr. and Mrs. Peter H. (December 18, 1980); #73, with Peter F. (October 2, 1980); #74, with Frances K. (October 2, 1980); #14 (UPJ), with John S.

13 On familial collectivism and the fusion of kinship/ethnic and work/

occupational roles in the adjustment of immigrants in the first half of this century, see Virginia Yans-McLaughlin, *Family and Community: Italian Immigrants in Buffalo, 1880–1930* (Ithaca, N.Y.: 1977), Chaps. 5–7; Tamara K. Hareven and Randolph Langenbach, *Amoskeag: Life and Work in an American Factory City* (New York, 1978); Tamara K. Hareven. "The Dynamics of Kin in an Industrial Community," *American Journal of Sociology* 84S (1978), 151–75; "The Role of Family and Ethnicity in Adjustment to Industrial Life," *Labor History* (Spring 1975), 249–66; and *Family Time and Industrial Time*, esp. 38–43, 73–4, 98–101, 127–9; Bodnar, Simon, and Weber, *Lives of Their Own*, Chaps. 3 and 4; Scott Cummings, ed., *Self-Help in America* (Port Washington, N.Y.: 1980). On familism and the reliance on group resources as the adjustment strategy of present-day immigrants in America, see, e.g., John S. MacDonald and Leatrice D. MacDonald, "Chain Migration, Ethnic Neighborhood Formation and Social Networks," *Millbank Memorial Fund Quarterly* (January 1964), 82–97; Marta Tienda, "Familism and Structural Assimilation of Mexican Immigrants in the United States," *International Migration Review* (Fall 1980), 383–9; Illsoo Kim, *New Urban Immigrants: The Korean Community in New York* (Princeton, 1981). Cf. also studies on internal rural–urban migration within the United States: Thompson Peter Omari, "Factors Associated with Urban Adjustment of Rural Southern Migrants," *Social Forces* (October 1956), 47–53; Leonard Blumberg and Robert R. Bell, "Urban Migration and Kinship Ties," *Social Problems* (Spring 1959), 328–33; James S. Brown, Harry K. Schwarzweller, and Joseph J. Mangalah, "Kentucky Mountain Migration and the Stem Family: An American Variation on a Theme by Le Play," *Rural Sociology* (March 1963), 48–69; Harry K. Schwarzweller and Martin J. Crowe, "Adaptation of Appalachian Migrants to the Industrial Work Situation: A Case Study," in *Behavior in New Environments: Adaptation of Migrant Populations*, ed. Eugene Brody (Beverly Hills, Calif.: 1970), 99–117.

14   Interview #51, with Mike T. (June 5, 1981); #88, with Anne H. (January 21, 1981); Cyburt, *Historia Polonii w Johnstown*; U.S. Congress, *Reports of the Immigration Commission, Immigrants in Industries*, pt. 2; Iron and Steel Manufacturing, 2 vols., 61st Cong., 2nd Ses., Sen. Doc. 633 (Washington, D.C.: 1911), "Community A," 1:454, also 332.

15   Information compiled from Commonwealth of Pennsylvania, Bureau of Industrial Statistics, *Annual Report of the Secretary of Internal Affairs: 1904*, pt. 3, 32:82–92, and 1905, pt. 3, 33:87–96; Commonwealth of Pennsylvania Department of Labor and Industry, "Cambria County," in *Second Annual Report of the Commissioner of Labor and Industry: 1914*, pt. 1, 100–1, and *Third Annual Report of the Commissioner of Labor and Industry: 1915*, pt. 1, pp. 472–3; Commonwealth of Pennsylvania Department of Labor and Industry, Office of Information and Statistics: 1914, 19; U.S. Congress, *Report on the Conditions of Employment in the Iron and Steel Industry in the United States*, vol. 3, *Working Conditions*

and the Relations of Employers and Employees, 212–14. Also Sumner H. Slichter, *The Turnover of Factory Labor* (New York, 1919), 147–53; Herman Feldman, *The Regularization of Employment* (New York, 1925), 3, 21–49, 298–9.

16 *Report on the Conditions of Employment in the Iron and Steel Industry in the United States*, 3:223. Also interview #75, with Frank G. (October 2, 1980): "When work was slack in one department, usually one to three weeks until new orders came [unless it was a more severe recession]; some people were transferred, and some laid off." In historians' reports on working conditions in American factories at the beginning of the century, estimates of the length of unemployment and of the financial losses suffered by immigrant workers are usually based on statistics as to the "number of days idle" provided by Labor Department and other censuses. In fact, this results in overestimates of both the time of actual unemployment and of the damage done to their finances, since the tendency among many immigrant workers was to move, whenever work was slack, in search of another job either within the same company or outside, leaving the city if necessary.

17 In 1906, the *Johnstown Tribune* quoted a statement from the annual report of Cambria employment records indicating an annual turnover rate of the labor force in the mills of over 100 percent: "New members admitted during the year and those reinstated upon resuming work numbered 20,713, while those lost by death and leaving the employment of the company were 19,769." (*Johnstown Tribune*, February 13, 1907, 14).

18 Bodnar, Simon, and Weber, *Lives of Their Own*, 42, 134, 143. Same in Bodnar, "Immigration and Modernization: The Case of Slavic Peasants in Industrial America," 53.

19 Slichter, *Turnover of Factory Labor*, 3–4, 18–22, 168–77; also Paul F. Brissenden and Emil Frankel, "Mobility of Labor in American Industry," *Monthly Labor Review* (June 1920), 42–3. On the intense job mobility among immigrant workers in Amoskeag Mills at the beginning of the century, see Hareven, *Family Time and Industrial Time*, Chap. 9.

20 Ivan Molek, "First Work with the Steam Boilers," in *Slovene Immigrant History, 1900–1950, Autobiographic Sketches by Ivan Molek*, ed., Mary Molek (Dover, Del.: 1979). 26.

21 On the concept and use of social networks, see J. Clyde Mitchell, "The Concept and Use of Social Networks," in *Social Networks in Urban Situations*, ed. J. Clyde Mitchell (Manchester, 1961), 1–51. On the effects of "social resources" – in particular, the so-called strong and weak ties with persons directly or indirectly linked with the individual – on his or her occupational attainment, see Mark S. Granovetter, "The Strength of Weak Ties," *American Journal of Sociology* (May 1973), 1360–80, and *Getting a Job: A Study of Contacts and Careers* (Cambridge, Mass.: 1974); Scott A. Boorman, "A Combinational Optimization Model for Transmission of Job Information through Contact Networks," *Bell*

Journal of Economics 6 (1975), 216–49; Nan Lin, John C. Vaughn, and Walter M. Ensel, "Social Resources and Occupational Status Attainment," *Social Forces* (June 1981), 1163–82, and "Social Resources and Strength of Ties: Structural Factors in Occupational Status Attainment," *American Sociological Review* (August 1981), 393–405.

22 *Reports of the Immigration Commission*, "Community A," 349; also data on the nativity of workers in particular Cambria departments, 350, 360–3. The brickyards were dominated by the Croatians, who constituted approximately 60 percent of the work force. The Ukrainians were concentrated at the Pennsylvania Railroad. At the Radiator Company the Magyars were all molders. The Slovaks constituted the majority among the East Central European blast furnace work force. The Poles predominated in the rolling mill department and in the open-hearth division. The gangs at Bessemer mills were led by the Magyars and Slovaks. The Serbs, if they worked in the mills, tended to work as riggers. "They stuck with each other, when one [from one nationality group] got a [better] job somewhere, and there was a place for more, he pulled in his chums, . . . and others were envious," recalled second generation Marianna P. as she was telling me about her father's work in the Johnstown mills at the beginning of the century (interview #92, November 21, 1980).

23 *Reports of the Immigration Commission*, "Community A," 354–7, 360–3. A large majority (about 80 percent) of the East Central European male immigrants on whom information was secured by the Immigration Commission when it visited Johnstown had made their living from the soil before coming to the United States. Only Magyars and Slovaks, about 10 percent in each group, reported previous employment in artisan trades. The Magyar group also contained a handful of men who had prior experience in iron forging acquired in Diósgyör: *Reports of the Immigration Commission*, "Community A," 354; interview with Rev. J. Benedek, pastor of the Hungarian Reformed church in Johnstown, May 23, 1980. This could have helped them to establish "connections" with better-skilled German mill workers at Cambria.

24 *Johnstown Tribune*, September 9, 1911; interview #56, with Frank S. (September 25, 1980).

25 Interview #25, with Mary K. (June 14, 1981); #41, with Paul M. (February 25, 1981); #71, with Peter H. (December 18, 1980); letter from Joseph R. to author (May 7, 1981).

26 Compiled from data collected by the Immigration Commission investigating the employment and working conditions at Cambria Steel Company in Johnstown: *Reports of the Immigration Commission*, "Community A," 354–7, 360–3, 441–6; see also David Brody, *Steelworkers in America, The Non-Union Era* (New York, 1960), 44, 107, Table 1: "Daily Wage Scale of Laborers at Cambria Steel Company, 1880–1900." Also John Fitch, "Wage Earners of Pittsburgh," *Charities and the Commons* (March 6, 1909, 1061–3; interview #9, with Anthony C. (October 10,

1980), and #43 (UPJ), with Joe N. (the latter from the collection of taped interviews by Michael Yates and Bruce Williams of the University of Pittsburgh at Johnstown; interviews from their collection will hereafter be cited as *UPJ*).

27 Interview #9, with Anthony C. (October 10, 1980).

28 Marian M. Drozdowski, ed., *Pamiętniki Emigrantów. Stany Zjednoczone* (Warsaw, 1977), 1:473–4.

29 Interview #9, with Anthony C. (October 10, 1980). On the importance of "independence" in coal mining, see Keith Dix, "Work Relations in the Coal Industry: The Hand-loading Era, 1880–1930," *West Virginia University Bulletin*, ser. 78, 7-2 (January 1978), 48–51; David A. Corbin, *Life, Work and Rebellion in the Coal Fields: The Southern West Virignia Miners, 1880–1922* (Chicago, 1981); Ellen Murray, "Why Foreign Miners Are Restless," *Coal Age* (October 13, 1917), 620–1.

30 Interview #9, with Anthony C. (October 10, 1980); letters from Anthony C. to author (September 10, 1981; June 6, 1982).

31 Interview #9, with Anthony C. (October 10, 1980), and #4, with Nikola B. (July 14, 1981). There were also jobs with more "sitting time," a consideration important for the exhausted laborers. A study of the intensity of labor in the steel industry conducted in 1912 reported that 17 to 37 percent of the regular shift time was "idle," depending on the job (however, only jobs requiring higher skills were investigated); see Sidney Koon, "Hours and Intensity of Steel Works Labor," *Iron Age* (February 1, 1921), 312–13.

32 *Report on the Conditions of Employment in the Iron and Steel Industry in the United States*, 210–14. For instance, to take one randomly selected year from the industrial statistics, in 1903 the wire department at Cambria worked only 257 days, but the iron forges worked 292, and the car and axle department and the nuts and bolts shops as many as 306. Commonwealth of Pennsylvania, Department of Internal Affairs, "Days in Operation," *Annual Report . . . 1904*, pt. 3: *Industrial Statistics*, vol. 32, *Steel Industry: Cambria County*, 82–92; ibid., *1905*, 33:87–96; ibid., 1912, 40:99–112, 329; Commonwealth of Pennsylvania, Department of Labor and Industry, *Second Annual Report: 1914*, pt. 1, "Cambria County," 100–1; "Average Days Worked," in *Report of the Productive Industries of the Commonwealth of Pennsylvania: 1916–1919*, 20. Also U.S. Congress, *Reports of the Immigration Commission, Immigrants in Industries*, pt. 1: *Bituminous Coal Mining*, 61st Cong., 2nd sess., Sen. Doc. 633 (Washington, D.C.: 1911), 68:320–1.

33 Interview #66, with Walter W. (June 11, 1980); Polish National Alliance Membership Book, Lodge #1569, Johnstown, 1907/8–24.

34 Interview #13 (UPJ), with Louis P.

35 Interview #82, with Anna C. (October 9, 1980).

36 Golab, "Impact of Industrial Experience on the Immigrant Family," 18; Bodnar, Simon, and Weber, *Lives of Their Own*, 102; Yans-McLaughlin, *Family and Community*, 175–6; Herbert Gutman, "Work, Cul-

ture and Society in Industrializing America, 1815–1919," *American Historical Review* (June 1973), 553; Olivier Zunz, *The Changing Face of Inequality: Urbanization, Industrial Development and Immigrants in Detroit, 1880–1920* (Chicago, 1982), 228–39. Somewhat inconsistently, however, the same authors who at one point state that what the immigrants made barely sufficed for mere survival often subsequently admit – commenting that "it is striking" but not discussing the implications – that a number of immigrants sent substantial amounts of money to Europe and managed over the years to put away up to $1,000, in spite of low wages and insecure employment: see Bodnar, Simon, and Weber, *Lives of Their Own*, 179.

37 *Johnstown Tribune*, January 6, 1913, 13.

38 Interview #71a, with Mrs. Pete H. (December 18, 1980); #3, with Mary P. (March 9, 1981); #20, with Mary K. (June 18, 1981); #13, with Katarzyna C. (June 23, 1981); and #10 (UPJ), with Mary R.

39 Data on rent and dues paid to ethnic societies are compiled from *Reports of the Immigration Commission*, "Community A," 408, 468. Cf. also Peter Roberts, "The New Pittsburghers," *Charities and the Commons* (January 2, 1909), 547; Margaret Byington, *Homestead: The Households of a Mill Town* (Pittsburgh, 1975), 45, 68, 206–7; Isaac A. Hourwich, *Immigration and Labor* (New York, 1922), 256–65, 269–71. The average drinking bill was calculated from the minute books of the *Slovenska Narodna Podporna Jednota*, Lodge #82, Johnstown, vol. 1, 1908–14, "pivo i viski (expens, dohotky)"; church dues are from St. Casimir's Polish Roman Catholic Church minute book, 1905–12; St. John the Baptist Ukrainian Catholic Church minute book (n.d.); St. Rochus Croatian Catholic Church minute book, 1900–5. Figures on insurance in the immigrant societies are from the minute books of the Slovak Jednota, Lodge #23, 1890–1910, and of the Polish Roman Catholic Union, Lodge #503, 1900–12. Food prices were calculated from advertisements in the *Johnstown Tribune*, April 10, 1905, 1; May 2, 1914, 15. The average loss of pay due to unemployment in a good (prosperous) year prior to World War I (assuming a worker was actually idle and did not find substitute employment) was calculated by the U.S. Congressional Commission at 13 percent (U.S. Congress, *Report on the Conditions of Employment in the Iron and Steel Industry in the United States*, 214). But immigrants who belonged to ethnic insurance societies were partially covered for sickness. For instance, for thirty days of sickness the Slovak immigrants who were members of Jednota Lodge #23 in Johnstown received before World War I about $20 (Jednota Lodge #23, minute book, 1907–8). Poles from the Polish Roman Catholic Union, Lodge #503, received a similar amount (Lodge #503, minute book 1904–12).

In 1907, the U.S. Bureau of Labor calculated that unmarried East Central European laborers were able to save as much as 60 to 70 percent of their monthly earnings – a proportion similar, by the way, to what many of them put away during seasonal migrations in Europe. A study conducted in 1903 in one Galician village in the area that sent many immigrants to Johnstown reported that out of the total number of 116 unmarried emigrants who worked in the United States at the time of the investigation, over one-third were saving 50 to 60 percent of their wages, one-third saved 61 to 70 percent, and more than one-fifth managed to put away 71 to 80 percent of the money they earned. See Frank Sheridan, "Italian, Slavic and Hungarian Unskilled Immigrant Laborers in the United States," *Bulletin of the Bureau of Labor* (September 1907), 475–7; similar information in Franciszek Bujak, *Maszkienice, Wieś Powiatu Brzeskiego: Rozwój od R. 1900 do R. 1911* (Krakow, 1914), 101–4. Also Leopold Caro, *Emigracja i Polityka Emigracyjna, ze Szczególnym Uwzględnieniem Stosunków Polskich* (Poznan, 1914), 154; Gyul Kertesz, "A Kivándorlás Szabályozása" (Budapest, 1910), unpaginated; *Entwicklung der Westgaliz. Dorfuzstände in der 2. Hälfte des XIX Jahrh.* (Teschen, 1911); quotation after Caro, *Emigracja i Polityka Emigracyjna*, 55. After inspecting the bank accounts of a sample of unmarried Slavic immigrant workers in Pittsburgh, Peter Roberts reported their average savings as $304, ranging from $200 to $437 in one year; see "The New Pittsburghers," *Charities and the Commons*, (January 2, 1909), 547. In Johnstown, information indicating similar level of savings came from Frank S. (interview #8, May 6, 1981).

40 *Reports of the Immigration Commission*, "Community A," 463, 478–9. This figure does not seem exaggerated: At that time at least 5,000 adult East Central European immigrants, capable of saving and sending home about $100 annually, were living in the greater Johnstown area (besides, the commission's estimate also included money orders sent by western European immigrants, mostly Irish and German). Estimates from other East Central European settlements in western Pennsylvania were similar: In the same year of 1907, Emily Balch found out from the local bankers in Hazelton that "two thirds of the $500,000 deposits . . . were those of the foreigners. Few of them [she was told] would deposit less than $20 a month, many as much as $50." *Our Slavic Fellow Citizens* (New York, 1969), 305. Peter Roberts reported similar findings for Slavic depositors whose records for the period 1906–7 were made available to him by a Pittsburgh banker. The average monthly savings of these Slavic immigrant laborer ranged from $20 to $40 ("New Pittsburghers," 547). In Homestead, before the depression of 1907–8 set in, over 50 percent of the total number of 3,603 Slavic immigrant families had saving accounts ranging from $100 to $1,000 (Byington, *Homestead*, 156).

41 Quoted after Lengyel, *Americans from Hungary*, 143.

42 *Reports of the Immigration Commission*, "Community A," 367. These figures represent the actual earnings of the immigrant mill workers.

43 Data compiled from interviews #36, with Henry S. (March 12, 1981); #103, with Michael J. (July 14, 1981); #4, with Nikola B. (July 14, 1981);

#41, with Paul M. (February 25, 1981); #13, with Katarzyna C. (June 23, 1981); #62–62a, with Mr. and Mrs. Thomas B. (June 11, 1980); #73, with Frank G. (October 2, 1980); #25, with Mary K. (June 14, 1981); *Reports of the Immigration Commission,* "Community A," 405–7; cf. also Balch, *Our Fellow Slavic Citizens,* 363–6; Byington, *Homestead,* 38–45, 50–7, 76–80, 138–43, 206–7.

Peter R. Shergold's, study, *Working-class Life: The "American Standard" in Comparative Perspective, 1899–1913* (Pittsburgh, 1982), provides detailed comparative data on various expenditures of American families in different income groups in Pittsburgh. Unfortunately the data for foreign-born families reported in the study lump together in one category the "Austro-Hungarians" – Austrians as well as Slavs and Magyars, which inflates the income and expenditure figures of the latter groups. For instance, the average annual expenditure for food of an "Austro-Hungarian" family is reported as $280.30 (or $23.36 a month), which is about 25 percent higher than found by Byington among the majority of Slavic "budget" households in Homestead.

The lowest weekly expenditures (store credit included) among Slavs reported by Byington in her 1907–8 study of immigrant budgets in Homestead was $10.58 for a seven-member family, and not $13.22 as quoted in Bodnar, Simon, and Weber as the "minimum subsistence level" necessary for the survival of an East European household in that town (Byington, *Homestead,* 206–7; Bodnar, Simon, and Weber, *Lives of Their Own,* 102–3). Other ethnic historians – e.g., Caroline Golab and Mark Stolarik – quote an even higher figure of $15.00 a week as the "absolute necessary minimum for the immigrant family to survive" (Golab, "The Impact of Industrial Experience on the Immigrant Family," 11–12, 18; Stolarik, *Slovak Migration from Europe to America,* 63). In Johnstown, it was possible to even further reduce Byington's minimum of $10.58 by up to 25 percent: rent in company houses was cheaper, heat and light were used only in the kitchen where all family activities concentrated and, as I will demonstrate shortly, the common use of gardens and plots significantly reduced expenditures on food. On the standard of living of immigrant households in America at the beginning of the century, see also R. J. Morrison, "A Wild Motley Throng: Immigrant Expenditures and the 'American' Standard of Living," *International Migration Review* (Fall 1980), 342–57. But Morrison combines into one category all immigrant groups, western European as well as southern and eastern European, and includes in his analysis only the households with annual earnings above $600, a sum significantly higher than the average total yearly income of most East Central European families.

44   Calculated from the data provided in the *Reports of the Immigration Commission,* "Community A," 336, 356–63, 367–9.

45   Thomas Bell, *Out of This Furnace* (Pittsburgh, 1976), 56.

46 East Central European population from manuscript schedules of 1900 census.

47 John Modell and Tamara K. Hareven, "Urbanization and the Malleable Household: An Examination of Boarding and Lodging in American Families," *Journal of Marriage and the Family* (August 1973), 467–80.

48 Modell and Hareven, "Urbanization and the Malleable Household;" Bodnar, Simon, and Weber, *Lives of Their Own*, Chap. 6; Daniel D. Luria, "Wealth, Capital and Power: The Social Meaning of Home Ownership," *Journal of Interdisciplinary History* (Autumn 1976), 261–83.

49 In the group of renters, the proportion of boarder-keeping families among the childless families, of whom one-half had already spent eight or more years in the United States at the time of the census, was 56.2 percent. Among the "older stopped bearing," of whom three-fourths had already been in the United States eleven or more years, the proportion was 60.1 percent (East Central European population from manuscript schedules of 1900 census). These statistics, however, are only for 1900. It is possible that in subsequent years the immigrants' behavior in regard to the keeping of boarders and homeownership had changed and that a significantly larger proportion of homeowners supplemented their income by taking in boarders.

50 Data compiled from *Reports of the Immigration Commission*, "Community A," 371–3. The Slovaks had the highest proportion (47 percent) of families relying entirely on husbands' earnings, and the Croatians had the lowest (18 percent). The nationality subsamples were too small, however, to permit comparative generalizations.

51 Data compiled from *Reports of the Immigration Commission*, "Community A," 371. The commission reported differences among particular nationality groups. For instance, only one-half of the lowest-income Slovak families and about two-thirds of the Magyar and Polish ones kept boarders, as opposed to 100 percent of the Yugoslavs. These groups were small, however, and so the observed differences could have been incidental rather than indicative of a more systematic pattern.

52 Ibid., 371; Emma Duke, "Infant Mortality: Results of a Field Study in Johnstown, Pennsylvania Based on Births of One Calendar Year," in U.S. Department of Labor, Children's Bureau, No. 3, Bureau of Publication #9, 1915, 47–8.

53 East Central European population from manuscript schedules of 1900 census; *Reports of the Immigration Commission*, "Community A," 408–10.

54 East Central European population from manuscript schedules of 1900 census. The numerical size of particular nationality group households was too small to permit a meaningful comparative analysis of differences in the numbers of boarders kept. Also interviews #37a, with

John O. (March 11, 1981); #41, with Paul M. (February 25, 1981); #88, with Anne H. (January 21, 1981); #58 (UPJ), with Elisabeth F.

55 Interview #59, with John B. (November 28, 1980). Similar attitudes among Italian immigrants were reported by Yans-McLaughlin, *Family and Community*, Chaps. 6–7; among French-Canadians and others, by Hareven and Langenbach, *Amoskeag*, pts. 4–5.

56 Data compiled from baptismal records collected in 9 immigrant parishes in Johnstown (St. Emerich Hungarian Catholic, St. John Ukrainian Byzantine Catholic, St. John the Evangelist Slovak Lutheran, St. Stephen Slovak Catholic, St. Mary Greek Catholic, St. Rochus Croatian Catholic, St. John Russian Orthodox, St. Nicholas Serbian Orthodox, and St. Casimir Polish Catholic). Only those who married in the church and remained members from 1900 until the 1920s were included. According to my calculations the mean age of marriage for the immigrant women was 20.5, and the mean age at the last childbirth was 34, leaving approximately fifteen years for childbearing. These statistics must be treated as gross estimates, however, because the families that I included as "persisters" could have moved out for some time and then returned with more children between my checkpoints.

The Croatian immigrant families were also found to be the most numerous in Braddock, Pa., where 37 percent consisted of ten or more persons, as opposed, e.g., to only 21 percent among Magyars; see Interchurch World Movement, *Commission of Inquiry into the 1919 Steel Strike* (New York, 1920), 100. I was unable to find a satisfactory explanation of this pattern. Personal influence of the local pastor, Rev. Father K., a strong and authoritarian figure in the Johnstown Croatian community, could have played a role, but then why three or four other pastors of the immigrant parishes, of comparable power and influence, did not "achieve" similar results through their "procreative persuasion" remain unexplained. I found nothing in the Croatian peasant tradition to account for the difference.

57 Molek, *Immigrant Woman*, 22–3.

58 Interview #26, with Casimira G. (June 13, 1981); #27, with Helen L. (June 13, 1981); #30a, with Andy A. (April 3, 1981); #10 (UPJ), with Mary R.; #54 (UPJ), with Andy B.; #62 (UPJ), with Charles Y.

59 *Reports of the Immigration Commission*, "Community A," 374.

60 Cyburt, *Historia Polonii w Johnstown*. Cyburt used the Polish expression, *"Jakijś tam nauki"* – "Some there learning."

61 See Chap. 1 of this book; also Bodnar, "Materialism and Morality: Slavic-American Immigrants and Education." See also John Bodnar, "Schooling and the Slavic-American Family," in Bernard J. Weiss, ed., *American Education and the European Immigrants: 1840–1940* (Urbana, Ill.: 1982), 78–95.

62 Cyburt, *Historia Polonii w Johnstown*.

63 Quoted after David Hogan, "Education and the Making of the Chicago

Working Class, 1880–1930," *History of Education Quarterly* (Fall 1978), 234.

64 Commonwealth of Pennsylvania, Department of Labor and Industry: *First Annual Report: 1913*, pt. 1, p. 258; Henry W. Storey, *History of Cambria County, Pennsylvania* (New York, 1907), 2:422–3, U.S. Congress, *Reports of the Immigration Commission, The Children of Immigrants in Schools*, 61st Cong., 3rd sess., Sen. Doc. 749 (Washington, D.C.: 1911), vol. 3, "Johnstown," 384–6.

65 St. Stephen's Slovak Catholic School, enrollment and attendance records (permanent roll), 1902–12. St. Stephen's are the only prewar immigrant school records in Johnstown saved from the floods. In 1906, it had 422 pupils, and their number doubled by 1915. Storey, *History of Cambria County, Pennsylvania*, 2:422; *Annual Report of the Public Schools in Johnstown, Pennsylvania* (Johnstown, 1915), 47.

66 *Reports of the Immigration Commission*, "Community A," 372.

67 For instance, in Scranton, Pa., over one-third of Polish immigrant family incomes in 1910 came from the children's earnings. See Bodnar, "Socialization and Adaptation: Immigrant Families in Scranton, Pennsylvania, 1880–1890," *Pennsylvania History* (April 1976), 160.

68 The figures for boys are compiled from *Reports of the Immigration Commission*, "Community A," 443–6; interview #6 (UPJ), with Charles B.; #47 (UPJ), with Gus M.; payroll records of the Harve-Mack Coal Company in Indiana, Pa. (UMWA Health and Retirement Funds, Richland, Pa.). For girls, interview #71a, with Mrs. Pete H. (December 18, 1980); #89, with Pauline H. (June 11, 1980); #25, with Mary K. (June 14, 1981).

69 Letter from Anthony Cyburt to author, November 23, 1981. On the relationship between child labor and immigrant homeownership strategies, see Hogan, "Education and the Making of the Chicago Working Class, 1880–1930," 242–9.

70 Duke, "Infant Mortality," 19; and *The Geography of Johnstown* (Johnstown, 1934), 36, 42. Manuscript of message delivered on March 28, 1949, over WARD Radio in Johnstown to commemorate the passing of Rev. John Martvon, the pastor of St. Stephen's Slovak Catholic church (in the possession of the author), 3; *Johnstown Tribune*, May 9, 1914, 9, and Feburary 10, 1916, 4; interview #9, with Anthony C. (October 10, 1980), and #57 (September 18, 1980); #40, with John L. (February 26, 1980); #75, with Frank G. (October 2, 1980); letter from Joseph R. to author, May 7, 1981.

71 For reassessment of the "misplaced rural – urban polarities," see R. E. Pahl, "The Rural–Urban Continuum," *Sociologia Ruralis* 6 (1966), 299–330. An interesting sociohistorical essay on the persistent symbiosis of the industrial and peasant economies and life-styles, based on a study of one village near Cologne in the Lower Rhineland in Germany, was published by Emilio Willems: "Peasantry and City: Cul-

tural Persistence and Change in Historical Perspective, a European Case," *American Anthropologist* (June 1970), 528–45. Also Herbert G. Gutman, *Work, Culture and Society in Industrializing America* (New York, 1976); E. P. Thompson, "Time, Work-Discipline and Industrial Capitalism" *Past and Present* (December 1967), 56–97. For a detailed account of the symbiosis of peasant and industrial economies in the small coal-mining towns in America during the first decades of this century, see Victor Greene, *The Slavic Community on Strike: Immigrant Labor in Pennsylvania Anthracite* (Notre Dame, 1968), 41–56.

72 "Gruba Hanka Pirog i Jej Siedmiu Bortnikow" [Big Hanka Pirog and her seven boarders] (Detroit, n.d.) (manuscript in private collection of Walter Wegrzyn in Johnstown).

73 Calculated by comparing the expenditures on food as listed in Slavic family budgets compiled by Byington in Homestead (*Homestead*, 45, 76–8, 139–40), with items listed by my Johnstown informants as grown or made at home. In 1909, a pound of fat meat (scraps and cuts), the most preferred by peasant-immigrants, purchased from a "Hunky" butcher in Cambria City, cost about $.08 to $.10. Counting 1 pound of meat per adult daily (except for Fridays, fast days), the monthly meat expenditure for 5 boarders was $9.60 to $12.00 (calculated from Commonwealth of Pennsylvania Bureau of Industrial Statistics, "Johnstown, Pennsylvania," in *Annual Report: 1909*, pt. 3,37:152–3. Byington gives the sum of $25.00 as the monthly butcher bill of an immigrant family; apparently, her calculation was made for the whole household: adult and minor family members and boarders. Her figure of $18.00 a month for groceries (for the whole household) would have seemed greatly inflated for the Johnstowners, who in a great majority kept gardens and poultry, thus keeping their grocery purchases down to about $10.00 a month. Except for meat, the only other food articles bought regularly from the store by the immigrant "budget" families were coffee, tea, salt, sugar, flour, potatoes and lard.

74 Molek, "First Work with the Steam Boilers," 28.

75 Interview #10, with Anthony C. (February 23, 1981); #8, with Frank S. (May 6, 1981). At the beginning of this century, the daily earnings of an unskilled industrial worker in Austria sufficed for a purchase of 4.5 pounds of meat; in Galicia, 2.0 pounds, in America, 10.0 pounds; see Zanna Kormanowa and Irena Pietrzak-Pawłowska, eds., *Historia Polski* (Warsaw, 1978), vol. 3: *1864–1918*, pt. 1, p. 644.

76 On the criteria of achievement and success as experienced by peasant-emigrants, see the excellent introduction by Witold Kula, Nina Assorodobraj-Kula, and Marcin Kula, eds., to *Listy Emigrantów z Brazylii i Stanów Zjednoczonych* (Warsaw, 1973), 85–94.

77 Kula et al., *Listy Emigrantów*, 92.

78 Drozdowski, *Pamiętniki Emigrantów*, 2:259, 302.

79 Kula et al., *Listy Emigrantów*, 85–7, 90–1; also Lengyel, *Americans from Hungary*, 137, Molek, *Slovene Immigrant History, 1900–1950*, 28.

80 Kula et al., *Listy Emigrantów*, 339.
81 Compiled from the *Reports of the Immigration Commission*, "Community A," 366–9. Peter Hill calculated that the *total* family income of the foreign-born workers in the United States in 1903 amounted to 91 percent of the income of the native-born families; see "Relative Skill and Income Levels of Native and Foreign-born Workers in the U.S.," *Explorations in Economic History* (January 1975), 53.
82 *Reports of the Immigration Commission*, "Community A," 463.
83 East Central European male immigrant population from manuscript schedules of 1900 census, traced in the 1915 Johnstown city directory.
84 Compiled from U.S. Congress, *Reports of the Immigration Commission, Immigrants in Industries*, pt. 1: *Bituminous Coal Mining*, 61st Cong., 2nd sess., Sen. Doc. 633 (Washington, D.C.: 1911), 1:354–5, 317–20. Peter Roberts reported similar differences based on the data representative for Slavic immigrant bank depositors in Pittsburgh during the period 1906–7: The average monthly savings of the married men ranged between $23.80 and $46.30. ("New Pittsburghers," 547).
85 *Johnstown Tribune*, October 8, 1913, 18; October 9, 1913, 18.
86 For instance, Stephan Thernstrom, *Poverty and Progress. Social Mobility in a Nineteenth Century City* (Cambridge, Mass.: 1964), 161; Hogan, "Education and the Making of the Chicago Working Class, 1880–1930," 242–9; Bodnar, Simon, and Weber, *Lives of Their Own*, Chap. 6.
87 Luria, "Wealth, Capital and Power: The Social Meaning of Home Ownership," 268–9.
88 Bell, *Out of This Furnace*, 56.
89 Estimate based on inspection of real estate transfers by East Central European residents of Johnstown as recorded in Grantee and Grantor Books, 1804–23, Registrar's Office, Cambria County Courthouse, Ebensburg, Pa. Similar estimate made by Duke, "Infant Mortality," 30.
90 Interview #75, with Frank G. (October 2, 1980); #27, with Helen L. (June 13, 1981). Father K., the pastor of St. Rochus Croatian Catholic Church, also loaned money to his parishioners for the purchase of homes (St. Rochus Church, "1900–75, Jubilee Album").
91 Polish Roman Catholic Union Lodge #503, Johnstown, minute books 1892–1937, entry January 1, 1911; Polish National Alliance, Lodge #1569, Johnstown, minute book, assorted entries 1914–15; interview #42, with Walter W. (February 25, 1981); "Slovenian Savings and Loans, East Conemaugh, Penna.," handwritten notes of the founder, Frank Gabrenya, May–July 1915 in the possession of his son, Robert Gabrenya.
92 Mortgagor Books, Registrar's Office, Cambria County Courthouse, Ebensburg, Pa., vol. 1, 1803–1920.
93 Ibid.
94 The figure for 1900 is for all (2,399) male East Central European im-

migrants present in Johnstown at the time of the census: single boarders and family heads. Among the household heads, the proportion
of homeowners was 16.6 percent (East Central European male immigrant population from manuscript schedules of 1900 census); Cambria County Commissioner's Office, Ebensburg, Pa., "Precepts of the
Assessors: Annual Enumeration of All Persons, Properties and Things
Subject to Taxation: 1905, 1910, 1915." Unfortunately – an error impossible to avoid without spending countless hours on random searching – those who possessed two or more houses located in different
city wards were counted each time as separate homeowners. On the
other hand, immigrants whose names I did not recognize as Slavic or
Magyar were excluded.

95 East Central European male immigrant population from manuscript
    schedules of 1900 census.

96 Cambria County Commissioner's Office, Ebensburg, Pa.: "Precepts of
    the Assessors . . . 1905, 1910," checked against East Central European
    male immigrant population from manuscript schedules of 1900 census.

97 Cambria County Commissioner's Office, Ebensburg, Pa.: "Precepts of
    the Assessors . . . 1900–1915." For comparison, in city wards 5–7,
    inhabited mostly by native-born Americans, Welsh and Germans, the
    average value of homes in 1900 was $1,127. See Johnstown City Con-
    troller, *Annual Report of the City Controller of the City of Johnstown, Penn-
    sylvania*: "Assessed Valuations of Taxable Property by Wards," (Johns-
    town, 1900). The average value of $1,450 for East Central European
    homes in 1915 was calculated excluding a group of the 40 richest im-
    migrants whose property was valued by the tax assessors at over
    $4,000 each; their inclusion would increase the average value of East
    Central European property to $3,300.

98 Stephan Thernstrom, *The Other Bostonians: Poverty and Progress in the
    American Metropolis, 1880–1970* (Cambridge, Mass.: 1973), 41–2. Also
    Lawrence Glasco, "Migration and Adjustment in the Nineteenth Cen-
    tury City: Occupation, Property and Household Structure of Native-
    born Whites, Buffalo, N.Y., 1855," in *Family and Population in Nine-
    teenth Century America*, ed. Tamara K. Hareven and Maris A. Vinovskis
    (Princeton, 1978), 155; Gordon W. Kirk and Carolyn Tyirin Kirk, "Mi-
    gration, Mobility and the Transformation of the Occupational Struc-
    ture in an Immigrant Community: Holland, Michigan, 1850–1880,"
    Journal of Social History (Winter 1974), 142–65. For a general summary
    of the mobility dispute, see Donald H. Parkerson, "How Mobile Were
    Nineteenth-century Americans?" *Historical Methods Newsletter* (Sum-
    mer, 1982), 99–111.

99 Alan Armstrong, "The Use of Information about Occupation," in *Nine-
    teenth-century Society*, ed. E. A. Wrigley (Cambridge, Mass.: 1972), 191–
    310; Roberta B. Miller, "The Historical Study of Social Mobility: A New
    Perspective," *Historical Methods Newsletter*, (June 1975), 92–7; Bruce
    Laurie, Theodore Hershberg, and George Alter, "Immigrants and In-

dustry: The Philadelphia Experience, 1850–1880," *Journal of Social History* (Winter 1975), 219–42; Theodore Hershberg, Michael Katz, Stuart Blumin, et al., "Occupation and Ethnicity in Five Nineteenth-century Cities: A Collaborative Inquiry," *Historical Methods Newsletter* (June 1974), 174–216; Michael Katz, *The People of Hamilton, Canada-West: Family and Class in a Mid-Nineteenth-century City* (Cambridge, Mass.: 1976), Chap. 4, and "Occupational Classification in History," *Journal of Interdisciplinary History* (Summer 1972), 63–88; Edward Greer, "Social Mobility in the U.S. Working Class," *Monthly Review* (February 1975), 162–71; Clyde Griffen, "Occupational Mobility in Nineteenth-century America: Problems and Possibilities," *Journal of Social History* (Spring 1972), 310–30; Clyde Griffen and Sally Griffen, *Natives and Newcomers: The Ordering of Opportunity in Mid-Nineteenth Century Poughkeepsie* (Cambridge, Mass.: 1978); James Henretta, "The Study of Mobility: Ideological Assumptions and Conceptual Bias," *Labor History* (Spring 1977), 165–78; Ewa Morawska, "The Internal Status Hierarchy in the East European Immigrant Communities in Johnstown, Pennsylvania, 1890–1930," *Journal of Social History* (Fall 1982), 75–107; Alan Sharlin, "From the Study of Social Mobility to the Study of Society," *American Journal of Sociology* (September 1979), 338–61; Thernstrom, *The Other Bostonians*, 289–302; Thomas Kessner, *The Golden Door, Italian and Jewish Immigrant Mobility in New York City, 1880–1915* (New York, 1977), introduction and chap. 3.

As to the applicability of present-day occupational hierarchies to the historical data, the sociologists seem more optimistic than are the historians. Robert Hauser demonstrated a close fit between the 1950–60 U.S. ratings and those assigned by Hershberg et al. in their study of occupations in five nineteenth-century American cities. See Robert M. Hauser, "Occupational Status in the Nineteenth and Twentieth Centuries," *Historical Methods Newsletter* (Summer 1982), 111–27; see also his article with David L. Featherman, "On the Measurement of Occupation in Social Surveys," *Sociological Methods and Research* (November 1973), 241. Donald Treiman argues for the applicability of contemporary occupational scaling to historical data in his paper "The Validity of the 'Standard International Occupational Prestige Scale' for Historical Data," delivered at the Conference on International Comparisons of Social Mobility in Past Societies, Princeton, June 1972 (as quoted in Kessner, *Golden Door*, 196). But what troubles historians is not that such backward-projected ratings as construed by present-day researchers diverge from contemporary occupational scales but rather that they may differ significantly from the evaluations ascribed to particular occupations and their hierarchies by the past actors themselves.

100 Interview #57, with Anthony C. (September 18, 1980).
101 Dun & Bradstreet, *Reference Books Containing Ratings of Merchants, Manufacturers and Traders Generally throughout the U.S. and Canada*, vol. 127 (January 1900); vol. 199 (January 1918).

102 Interview #75, with Frank G. (October 2, 1980).
103 This and related problems involved in historical mobility studies are discussed by Michael Katz in "Occupational Classification in History," 63–88, and by Clyde Griffen, "Occupational Mobility in Nineteenth-century America," 310–30, and by Clyde Griffen and Sally Griffen, *Natives and Newcomers*, Preface, 50–8, 103–13, 209.
104 Interview #94, with Mary O. (July 16, 1981).
105 Interviews #42 (February 25, 1981) and #66 (June 11, 1980), with Walter W.
106 Interview #86, with Michael M. (November 8, 1980).
107 *Johnstown Tribune*, January 1, 1908, 6; June 5, 1908, 11; June 6, 1908, 8; October 21, 1980, 10.
108 *Zgoda* (Chicago), June 30, 1910.
109 Interview #7, with John J. (June 17, 1981).
110 Kula, *Listy Emigrantów*, 254.
111 Bell, *Out of This Furnace*, 59.

Chapter 5: Johnstown and the immigrant communities between the wars

1 Data compiled from *Fourteenth Census of the United States: 1920, Occupations*, 276–81; ibid., *Abstract of the 14th Census of the United States: 1920*, 261; *Fifteenth Census of the United States: 1930, Population*, vol. 4: *Occupations by States*, 1395–7; Commonwealth of Pennsylvania, Department of Internal Affairs, Bureau of Statistics and Information, *Report on Productive Industries, Railways, Taxes and Assessments, Waterways and Miscellaneous Statistics: 1920 and 1921*, 40; *1922–1923*, 274; *1924*, 110; *1925–1926*, 273; *1927*, 268; *1928*, 272; Commonwealth of Pennsylvania, Department of Labor and Industry, *Employment Fluctuations in Pennsylvania, 1921–27*, Special Bulletin no. 24, p. 185. William T. Hogan, *Economic History of the Iron and Steel Industry in the United States* (Lexington, Mass.: 1973) vol. 2, pt. 3, pp. 899–900; *Johnstown Tribune*, 9/20/1922, 18; 10/26/1922, 3; 4/7/1926, 27; 7/1/1926, 11; 7/24/1926, 11; May–July 1927, "Industrial Reports"; 1/5/1928, 14; 1/7/1928, 13; 7/27/1928, 14–15; 11/1/1928, 15.

2 U.S. Department of Labor and Industry, "How Many Are Jobless in Pennsylvania?", *Special Bulletin* (July, 1931), 7, 13; William J. Maguire, "Review of Industrial Statistics," *Labor and Industry* (February 1932), 45–52; Pennsylvania State Emergency Relief Board, Social Surveys Section, "Unemployment in Cambria County," *Bulletin 50-A* (April 1934), MS, National Archives, Industrial-Social Branch, RG 207, pp. 1, 9–10; *Johnstown Tribune*, January 27, 1933, *Seventh Industrial Directory of the Commonwealth of Pennsylvania*, (1931), 158–9; U.S. Department of Labor, Division of Research and Statistics, "HOLC Survey File: Johnstown, Pennsylvania," 1937, MS, National Archives, Industrial-Social Branch, RG 207, p. 4.

3 George Soule, "History of the Strike in Johnstown," in *Commission of Inquiry into the 1919 Steel Strike*, Interchurch World Movement (New York, 1920), 38–42, 190–3; Bruce T. Williams and Michael D. Yates, "Upward Struggle: A Bicentennial Tribute to Labor in Cambria and Somerset Counties" (Johnstown, 1976), 10; Robert Peles, "Labor Interlude – Johnstown 1919," seminar paper, University of Pittsburgh at Johnstown, 1974; *Johnstown Tribune*, September 8, 1919, 23; September 23, 1919, 18; David Brody, *Steelworkers in America: The Non-Union Era* (New York, 1960), 233–6.

4 *Johnstown Tribune*, 6/14/1918, 12; 5/11/1921, 9; 10/19/1921, 8; 1/4/1923, 7; 3/30/1924, 16; 2/6/1930, 18; 2/28/1930, 16; Raymond E. Murphy, "The Geography of Johnstown, Pennsylvania: An Industrial Center," *Pennsylvania State College Bulletin* 13 (1934), 42–3; U.S. Federal Housing Administration, Division of Research and Statistics, Housing and Finance Agency, City Data, "Housing Market Analysis; Johnstown, Pennsylvania, November, 1941," manuscript, National Archives, Industrial-Social Branch, RG 207.

5 Williams and Yates, "Upward Struggle," 20; Peles, "Crisis in Johnstown: The 'Little Steel' Strike, 1937," seminar paper, University of Pittsburgh at Johnstown, 1975; Donald G. Sofchalk, "Steelworkers of America, United (U.S.W.A.)," in *Labor Unions*, ed. Gary Fink (Westport, Conn.: 1977), 357–9; Thomas Brooks, *The History of American Labor* (New York, 1971), 2nd ed.; Walter Galenson, *The CIO Challenge to the AFL* (Boston, 1960); Vincent D. Sweeney, *The United Steel Workers of America: Twenty Years Later (1936–1956)* (Pittsburgh, 1958).

6 Peles, "Crisis in Johnstown," 47–8.

7 Ibid., 14, 38.

8 Interview with Louis M. (October 31, 1980).

9 Interview with Charles H. (November 7, 1980).

10 Estimates based on data compiled from Commonwealth of Pennsylvania Department of Internal Affairs, *Report on the Productive Industries for 1916, -17, -18, -19*, 636–41; *Report on the Productive Industries, Taxes and Assessments, Waterways and Miscellaneous Statistics for the Year 1924*, 110–11; U.S. Department of Commerce, Bureau of the Census, *Fifteenth Census of Manufactures: 1929*, 3:461; Commonwealth of Pennsylvania, Department of Internal Affairs, *Report on the Productive Industries, Public Utilities and Miscellaneous Statistics for the Year 1930*, 266–9. The number of American, western European and eastern European workers is estimated from Table 3.6 in Chap. 3 of this book.

11 Estimated from *Fourteenth Census of the United States: 1920, Population*, vol. 4: *Occupations*, 276–80, and Table 3.6 in Chap. 3.

12 Johnstown city directories, 1920–1940 (public officials); Johnstown Police Department, permanent roll; Johnstown Fire Company, permanent roll.

13 "Conemaugh and Franklin Boroughs History, 1868–1969," Conemaugh-Franklin Centennial (1968); East Conemaugh Fire Company,

roster; Franklin Fire Company, roster; interview with Captain George F. (April 12, 1981).

14 YMCA, Johnstown, "Scrapbook," 1919, 1922; *Johnstown Tribune*, January 5, 1919, 11; February 6, 1922, 1.

15 *Johnstown Tribune*, February 2, 1917, 6. Similar formulations also in "The Evening School News Bulletin," Johnstown, November 20, 1923; "Americanization Program – Johnstown," National Archives, Judicial-Fiscal Branch, E 587, Box 92.

16 Compiled from *Abstract of the Fourteenth Census of the United States: 1920*, 360; *Fourteenth Census of the United States: 1920, Population*, 3:875; *Fourteenth Census of the United States: 1920, Compendium: Pennsylvania*, 83–4; *Fifteenth Census of the United States: 1930, Population*, 2:490; vol. 3, pt. 2, p. 688. East Central Europeans from different nationality groups had different proportions of naturalized citizens. I took a sample of 497 Slavic- and Magyar-sounding names from the Cambria County naturalization dockets for the period 1899–1912. It appears that the Slovenes and Magyars led the way in naturalization of the whole East Central European group: They constituted about 60 percent of the whole sample, a proportion much larger than their combined numerical share among the East Central Europeans in the county (Naturalization Dockets, Prothonotary's Office, Cambria County Courthouse, Ebensburg, Pa.). After World War I, the differences among groups visibly diminished. In 1930 the proportion of American citizens in particular nationality groups in Johnstown for both men and women was the following: Poles, 34 percent; Slovaks, 42 percent; Hungarians, 48 percent; Yugoslavs, 35 percent (*Fifteenth Census of the United States: 1930, Population*, 2:490).

17 Of the total of 23 East Central European churches in Johnstown before World War II, 2 were founded in the late 1930s, and their records were insufficient for my analysis; 1 did not maintain books; 1 lost its records in the floods; and in 4 parishes the books were unavailable for other reasons. The estimate of the rate of intermarriage is based on data collected from 9 Slavic parishes and does not cover marriages registered in nonimmigrant churches.

18 "Johnstown: Survey of Churches and Organizations," Pennsylvania Ethnic Heritage Studies Center, Southwestern Pennsylvania Ethnic Resources Project, 2 (1980), Archives of the Industrial Society, University of Pittsburgh (hereafter referred to as *AIS Survey, Johnstown*); *Ethnic Newspapers' Catalogue*.

19 Estimate based on sample analysis of the names of members of ethnic sports teams as printed in *Johnstown Tribune*, 1920–1940. Also interviews #29 and #50, with Michael N. (May 8, 1981, and June 3, 1981), #30 and #56, with Frank S. (September 25, 1980, and March 26, 1981), #66, with Walter W. (June 11, 1980).

20 Conclusion based on wedding, funeral, birthday, and other party an-

nouncements by East Central Europeans in *Johnstown Tribune* during the 1930s.

21　See Chap. 4 n.56 on parishes checked. One possible reason for a high rate of ethnic endogamy among the second generation East Central Europeans could have been an ample "supply" throughout the 1930s of marriageable foreign-born men. In the Slavic and Magyar parishes before World War II, I found a consistently high number of marriages recorded between American-born women and immigrant men.

　　The intermarriage rate between Rusyns from the Greek Catholic parish and Roman Catholic Slovaks in Cambria City who came from the same region in Europe, was from the beginning of the century consistently higher than among other East Central European groups. In the interwar period they intermarried at the rate of 21 percent (of all marriages recorded in the parochial records). Practically impossible to detect was "intermarriage" between the Rusyns and the Ukrainians (Lemkians) who came from the same region in Galicia and later split into two separate parishes, often repeatedly switching allegiance.

22　*AIS Survey*, Johnstown: American Carpatho-Citizens' Club of Conemaugh (1935); West End Citizens' Club (1930); Hungarian Citizens' Club (1935); Federation of Polish Citizens' Clubs (1937); Osada Polish Roman Catholic Union, Lodge #87, an association of 10 Polish Roman Catholic Union lodges (1928); Centrala Polskich Towarzystw, an association of 12 Polish societies (1937); Central Committee of the League of the Ukrainian Catholics (1936); Conemaugh Valley Federation of the Slovenska Narodna Podporna Jednota Lodges, an association of 10 Slovenian societies (1934); Slovenian Workers' Home Association (1919).

23　*AIS Survey*, Johnstown: Polish National Church, interview #103, with Michael J. (July 14, 1981); Ukrainian St. Peter and Paul Orthodox Church, interview #25, with Mary K. (June 14, 1981), #71 and #71a, with Mr. and Mrs. Peter H. (December 18, 1980); Carpatho-Russian Orthodox Church, interviews #2, with Michael P. (March 9, 1981); #3, with Mary P. (March 9, 1981), #95, with Andy A. (July 17, 1981), and also Jaroslav Roman, "The Establishment of the American Carpatho-Russian Orthodox Greek Catholic Diocese in 1938: A Major Carpatho-Russian Uniate Return to Orthodoxy," unpublished paper in author's possession; Serbian St. Petka Orthodox Church, interviews #1, with Mary B. (June 5, 1981); #4, with Nikola B. (July 14, 1981); #51, with Mike T. (June 5, 1981); #88, with Anne H. (January 21, 1981). However, the formation of a new parish did not always result in internal group strife. The cooperation between the Croatian St. Rochus and its "splinter," Slovenian St. Therese, was smooth from the very beginning (St. Therese Church, Johnstown, Pennsylvania, 1929–1979, "Golden Anniversary Book," 11). After some amount of initial friction with the older St. Stephen's Slovak Catholic parish, a new St. Francis Slovak Catholic

Church maintained good relations with it (interview #24, with Ann B., June 12, 1981).

24 *Dziennik dla Wszystkich* (Buffalo, N.Y., 1922–34), correspondence of "Bajdula from Johnstown"; interviews #57, with Anthony C. (September 18, 1980); #37, with Pete K. (March 11, 1981).

25 Interview #40, with John L. (February 26, 1981). On the conflict in the Slovenian-American communities between the "progressive" (democratic-socialist) and the "Catholic" (clerical) factions, see Mary Molek, ed., *Slovene Immigrant History, 1900–1950. Autobiographical Sketches by Ivan Molek* (Dover, Del.: 1979), 16–17:88–92, also Chapt. 9 in pt. 2.

26 From this author's correspondence concerning Verhovay Lodge #15 with P. Stelkovic, retired secretary of the Hungarian Verhovay (1981); interview #100 with Pete P. (June 12, 1981).

27 Interviews #65, with Michael N. (October 17, 1980); #35, with Charles G. (March 12, 1981); #36, with Henry S. (March 12, 1981); with Mrs. George D., a widow of one of the founders of the Slavonic League (May 20, 1981); *Johnstown Tribune*, 1/19/1933, 18; 5/10/1935, 24; 5/22/1935, 13; 11/30/1936, 10.

28 On the proliferation of women's immigrant associations, see Maxine S. Seller, "Beyond the Stereotype: A New Look at the Immigrant Woman, 1880–1980," *Journal of Ethnic Studies* (Spring 1975), 59–72.

29 On the participation of Polish women in immigrant national-patriotic organizations in America, see Thaddeus Radzialowski, "Immigrant Nationalism and Feminism: Głos Polek and the Polish Women's Alliance in America, 1898–1917," *Review Journal of Philosophy and Social Science*, 2 (1972), 183–203.

30 Interview #19, with Mary U. (June 18, 1981): "Men fussed about it [women organizing] at the beginning: 'Bunch of old hens,' they said, 'Who will take care of the children?,' but later slowly they accepted the fact." Also interview #7, with John J. (June 17, 1981). The women's branch Bialy Orzeł of the Polish National Alliance in Johnstown was formed as "the result of [women's] rebellion against men" (interview #26, with Casimira G., June 13, 1981).

31 Interview #1, with Mary B. (June 5, 1981); #11 and #27, with Helen V. (June 18, 1981); #18, with Ann H. (June 19, 1981); #22, with Mary K. (June 19, 1981); #24, with Ann B. (June 12, 1981); #26, with Casimira C. (June 13, 1981); #94, with Mary O. (July 16, 1981).

32 *AIS Survey*, Johnstown.

33 Peles, "Labor Interlude," *Johnstown Tribune*, 11/11/1919, 1; 11/12/1919, 20; 11/13/1919, 20; 11/14/1919, 9; 11/25/1919, 20; 11/17/1919, 1; 12/1/1919, 20; *Johnstown Democrat*, 11/14/1919, 16.

34 Peles, "Crisis in Johnstown," 14, 22, 38, 49, 50–1, 68.

Chapter 6: For bread with butter

1 Whiting Williams, *What's on the Worker's Mind* (New York, 1921), 297.
2 A theoretical discussion of the role of consumption and consumption patterns in integrating particular segments of the population into the larger society can be found in Talcott Parsons, "Equality and Inequality in Modern Society or Social Stratification Revisited," in *Social Stratification: Research and Theory for the 1970s*, ed. Edward O. Laumann (Indianapolis, 1970), 13–73, especially comments on pp. 29–30. On the role of the expanding technological-material environment in altering expectations and raising consumer aspirations of the lower classes, see Nathan Rosenberg, "Neglected Dimensions in the Analysis of Economic Change," *Bulletin of the Oxford Institute of Economics and Statistics* 26 (1964), 57–77; Wilbert Moore, *Industrialization and Labor: Social Aspects of Economic Development* (Ithaca, N.Y.: 1951), Chap. 5. On the lower classes imitating and emulating consumer patterns and lifestyles of the upper strata, see Thorstein Veblen, *The Theory of the Leisure Class* (New York, 1931); John H. Goldthorpe and David Lockwood, "Affluence and the British Class Structure," *Sociological Review* (July 1963), 133–63; On the "trickle effect" in the transmission of consumer goods from the elite down the stratification hierarchy, see Lloyd A. Fallers, "A Note on the 'Trickle Effect'," *Public Opinion Quarterly* (Fall 1954), 314–21; Ernestine Friedl, "Lagging Emulation in Post-peasant Society," *American Anthropologist* (June 1964), 569–87. On the role of material consumption as the working-class way to "community participation," see Robert S. Lynd and Helen Merrell Lynd, *Middletown: A Study in American Culture* (New York, 1929), and *Middletown in Transition: A Study in Cultural Conflicts* (New York, 1937).
3 Daniel Rodgers, *The Work Ethic in Industrial America, 1850–1920* (Chicago, 1978), 171–3; Williams, *What's on the Worker's Mind*, 51, 255. Letters and memoirs of peasant-immigrants often expressed a desire that "work be heavy and last without interruption," meaning it would then bring good rewards.
4 Stanley B. Mathewson, in his *Restriction of Output among Unorganized Workers* (New York, 1931), 167–71, 185, points to the rationality of such behavior of workers who by means of slowdowns and restriction of output defend themselves against layoffs and wagecuts, just as businessmen cut down the supply when the market is full and raise prices when demand is growing. See also William M. Leiserson, "The Economics of Restriction of Output," in *Restriction of Output*; Herman Feldman, *The Regularization of Employment: A Study in the Prevention of Unemployment* (New York, 1925), 278ff; David Montgomery, *Workers' Control in America* (Cambridge, 1979), 42–3, 102; David M. Gordon, Richard Edwards, and Michael Reich, *Segmented Work, Divided Workers: The Historical Transformation of Labor in the United States* (New York, 1982), 163–4, 171–2.

5 In this behavior the immigrants differed from native-born American and western European laborers with the developed class ethos of work, who ostentatiously slowed down when a boss was in sight (Montgomery, *Workers' Control in America*, 42–3).

6 Clifford Geertz, *Islam Observed: Religious Development in Morocco and Indonesia* (New Haven, 1968), 17. I am grateful to Frank Lechner of the Sociology Department at the University of Pittsburgh for pointing out to me the applicability of this metaphor to my discussion.

7 Interviews #62 and #62a, with Mr. and Mrs. Thomas B. (June 11, 1980).

8 Interview #73, with Peter F. (October 2, 1980).

9 Interview #10, with Anthony C. (February 23, 1981).

10 Marek M. Drozdowski, ed., *Pamiętniki Emigrantów.Stany Zjednoczone* (Warsaw, 1977), 1:210.

11 Ibid. 1:350–1.

12 Ibid., 2:466.

13 Estimates on the basis of information gathered in interviews #66, 70, and 102, with Walter W. (June 11, 1981); September 6, 1980; April 9, 1983); #78, with Theresa S. (October 2, 1980); #106, with Mary L. (April, 1983); #13, with Katrzyna C. (June 23, 1981); #26, with Casimira G. (June 13, 1981); #3, with Mary P. (March 1981); #87, with John B. (November 7, 1980).

14 Drozdowski, *Pamiętniki Emigrantów*, 1:210.

15 Estimates of house payments derived from calculations made by the U.S. Bureau of Labor Statistics in 1928, based on a survey of 500 families in Boston, New York, Baltimore, and Chicago: "Cost of Home Ownership and the Family Budget," *Monthly Labor Review* (May 1929) 243–4. Adjustments for Johnstown compiled from Tax Assessments, Cambria County, 1925–9, Tax Claim Bureau, Cambria County Courthouse, Ebensburg, Pa.; Book of Ordinances, City of Johnstown, 1925–9 (Taxes, Licenses); Greater Johnstown School District, Meadowvale School, Johnstown, Pa. (Delinquent Tax Office). The average time for repayment of house loans was calculated from a sample of 52 mortgage entries by Johnstown residents of Slavic and Magyar background as recorded during the 1920s in the Mortgagor Books, Registrar of Deeds, Cambria County Courthouse, Ebensburg, Pa. The average amount of mortgage taken by East Central Europeans was $2,700, ranging from $700 to $6,000, and the average length of the mortgage was about nine to ten years, ranging from two to twenty-five years. The amount of home (fire) insurance is from interview with Harry Rabinowitz, Interstate Insurance Agency, Johnstown, Pa. (August 16, 1983).

16 Interview #10, with Anthony C. (February 23, 1981). The importance attached to food by the Slavic families was observed by the Commission of Inquiry of the Interchurch World Movement investigating the 1919 steel strike in Pittsburgh and Johnstown. Marian D. Savage,

"Family Budgets and Living Conditions," unpublished report in Interchurch World Movement, *Commission of Inquiry into the 1919 Steel Strike*, Blankenhorn Papers Collection, Archives of the Industrial Society, University of Pittsburgh, Pittsburgh, Pa., 3–6.

17 Drozdowski, *Pamiętniki Emigrantów*, 2:390.

18 From interviews #106 and 106a, with Mary and John L. (April 9, 1983); #112, with Harold R. (August 16, 1983); and #87, with John B. (November 7, 1980). See also "Average Expenditure per Family and Income Groups," *Monthly Labor Review* (January–June 1920), 32–4. In her 1925 study of the family budgets of the Chicago working class, Leila Houghteling reported that 40 percent of the families owned a victrola, 20 percent a piano, 20 percent had a telephone, 7 percent a radio, and 3 percent an automobile. See *The Income and Standard of Living of Unskilled Laborers in Chicago* (Chicago, 1927), 120.

19 This observation of Julianna Puskás about the Hungarian immigrants, which she makes in her book *From Hungary to the United States, 1880–1914* (Budapest 1982, 177) applies also to other East Central European groups, particularly the Poles, but also to Croatians, and even to Slovaks and Rusyns in whose national traditions a native gentry did not play an important role. The progressivist Slovenian publicists in America seem to have been the only ones among the eight groups included in my Johnstown study who systematically denounced this "unproletarian tendency" among the immigrants. See Joseph Drasler, "Second Generation Slovenes: A Comparison between Parents and Children," *Ameriški Družinski Koledar* (Leto, 1940), 168–74.

20 *Jednota Katolicky Kalendár na Priestupny Rok 1920:* Hyjo, "Dve Zeny-Manželky," 79–82; Drozdowski, *Pamiętniki Emigrantów*, 1:144, 184, 200, 223, 470; 2:464–73.

21 East Central European male immigrant population from manuscript schedules of 1900 census, traced in Johnstown city directories for 1920, 1925.

22 U.S. Bureau of Labor Statistics, *Monthly Labor Review* (October 1929), 172–3.

23 Compiled from Commonwealth of Pennsylvania, Department of Labor and Industry, "Union Scale of Wages and Hours of Labor, 1919–1924," *Special Bulletin*, no. 18, 1934, 8–9, 11–12, 16–20, 27–34; "Union Scale of Wages and Hours of Labor, 1926," *Special Bulletin*, no. 20, 1926, 8–9, 21–83; "Union Scale of Wages and Hours of Labor, 1927," *Special Bulletin*, no. 22, 1927; 12–24. (For nonunion Johnstown manufacturers, customary wages and hours of labor were given.)

24 Data compiled from Paul Brissenden, "Earnings of Factory Workers 1899 to 1927: An Analysis of Pay-Roll Statistics," U.S. Department of Commerce, *Census Monographs*, 10 (1929), 97; "Wages and Hours of Labor," *Monthly Labor Review* (September 1929), 135. Work fluctuations in the coal mines were more pronounced, and they varied a great deal

locally. On the variations in operating time of bituminous coal mines, see "Irregularity of Employment in the Bituminous Coal Industry," *Monthly Labor Review* (January 1924), 123–5.

25 Calculated from the minute book of St. Joseph's Lodge #23 of the Slovak Jednota, 1919–30, "Potpori Horim" (sick benefits).

26 Compiled from Commonwealth of Pennsylvania, Department of Labor and Industry, "Union Scale of Wages and Hours of Labor, 1919–1924," 8–66; "Union Scale of Wages and Hours of Labor, 1926," 21–83; "Union Scale of Wages and Hours of Labor, 1927," 12–89. (For nonunionized Johnstown manufactures, customary rates were reported).

27 Compiled from Harve-Mack Coal Company's payroll records for January–March 1925 (Office of UMWA Health and Retirement Funds, Richland, Pa.). "Overtime" for an ordinary coalminer – i.e, one whose job was not mechanized and who did hand labor – also involved the time in which he worked without payment, from 4:30 A.M. to 6:30 A.M., preparing, e.g., the coal to be loaded on cars that started arriving around 7 A.M., or cleaning the area. How much he eventually made during the day depended not only on the hours put in but also on the "place" itself assigned him by the boss. Information on the earnings and conditions of work in the Johnstown mines during the 1920s is from interviews #39 (UPJ), with Joe K.; #14 (UPJ), with John S.; #15 (UPJ), with John K.; #29 (UPJ), with Frank H.; #43 (UPJ), with Joe N.; #47 (UPJ), with Gus M.; #51 (UPJ), with Martin S.; #64 (UPJ), with Pete M.

28 Commonwealth of Pennsylvania, Department of Labor and Industry, "Union Scale of Wages and Hours of Labor, 1925," *Special Bulletin* no. 9, 1926, 24. Information on supplementary sources of earnings by Johnstown's East Central Europeans during the 1920s from interview #39, with Frank B. (February 26, 1981); #66 (UPJ), with Joe B.

29 Compiled from Commonwealth of Pennsylvania, Department of Labor and Industry, "Employment Fluctuations in Pennsylvania, 1921–1927," *Special Bulletin*, no. 24, 1928, Table 18, "Seasonal Variations in Employment in the Iron and Steel Industry."

30 Interviews #13 (UPJ), with Louis P.; #30 (UPJ), with John R.; #39 (UPJ), with Joe K.; #40 (UPJ), with Jay S.; #10, with Anthony C. (February 23, 1981); #25, with Mary K. (June 14, 1981); #4, with Nikola B. (July 14, 1981); #8, with Frank S. (May 6, 1981); #39, with Frank B. (February 26, 1980).

31 Calculated from "Factory Labor Turnover," *Monthly Labor Review* (March 1927), 12–13; "Labor Turnover in American Factories during 1926–27," *Monthly Labor Review* (January 1928), 42; "Labor Turnover and Length of Service in American Factories," *Monthly Labor Review* (October 1928), 54–5; "Do Workers Gain by Labor Turnover?", *Monthly Labor Review* (June 1929), 118–19; "Labor Turnover in Amer-

ican Factories," *Monthly Labor Review* (January 1929), 41; "Labor Turn-
over in American Factories," *Monthly Labor Review* (April 1929), 766;
Eugene J. Benge, "Comparison of Labor Turnover and the Business
Cycle," *Manufacturing Industries* (October 1926), 267–8. Also Feldman,
Regularization of Employment, 5ff., 27ff., 62; Sumner H. Slichter, *The
Turnover of Factory Labor* (New York, 1919), 337–43.

32   Employment Records (permanent roll), Johnstown Coal and Coke
     Company; Office of UMWA Welfare and Retirement Funds, Wash-
     ington, D.C.: microfilm reels #879–91; Employment Records (per-
     manent roll), Berwind White Coal Company, Windber, Pa., on file at
     the company's administrative offices in Windber.
33   Interview with P. Pebley, personnel officer at Bethlehem Steel Com-
     pany in Johnstown (May 7, 1980). According to him, workers who
     voluntarily transferred from one department to another often regis-
     tered at the employment office under a different name in order to avoid
     inquiries. This practice, if indeed widespread, must have inflated the
     turnover rates recorded by the company.
34   Ibid.; Employment Records (permanent roll), Johnstown Coal and
     Coke Company; office of UMWA Welfare and Retirement Fund,
     Washington, D.C.: microfilm reels·#879–91; Employment Records
     (permanent roll), Berwind White Coal Company, Windber, Pa., on
     file at the company's administrative offices in Windber.
35   Interview #45, with George P. (January 22, 1981).
36   Interviews #51, with Mike T. (June 5, 1981); also #4, with Nikola B.
     (July 14, 1981); #52, with Yanko L. (June 5, 1981); #30 (UPJ), with
     John R.; and #40 (UPJ), with Jay S.
37   Interview #101, with Paul P. (February 23, 1981).
38   Interview #30 (UPJ), with John R.
39   Interview #39, with Frank B. (February 26, 1981).
40   East Central European population from manuscript schedules of 1900
     census, traced in the 1925 Johnstown city directory.
41   Interview #57, with Anthony C. (September 18, 1980); #51, with Mike
     T. (June 5, 1981); #81, with John M. (October 9, 1980).
42   See also "Women in Industry," *Monthly Labor Review* (June 1929), 121–
     3; "Domestic Work," *Monthly Labor Review* (February 1925), 7–9. The
     rates given in these studies are for native-born American women; "for-
     eign girls" were paid significantly less: interview #46 (UPJ), with Mrs.
     Geo. K.
43   Commonwealth of Pennsylvania, Department of Labor and Industry,
     Bureau of Women and Children, "Fourteen and Fifteen Year Old Chil-
     dren in Industry," *Special Bulletin* no. 21, 1926–7, 7, 22.
44   Interviews #63, with Emil S. (November 6, 1980); #30a, with Andy
     M. (April 3, 1981).
45   Pennsylvania Department of Labor and Industry, Bureau of Women
     and Children, "Fourteen and Fifteen Year Old Children in Industry,"

17–19. Also interviews #30a, with Andy M. (April 3, 1981); #63, with Emil S. (November 6, 1980); #76, with Mary H. (October 2, 1980); #62 (UPJ), with Charles Y.

46 Interview #87, with John B. (November 7, 1980). It was impossible to gather accurate data as to the proportion of boarder-keeping East Central European households in Johnstown during the 1920s. Houghteling's study of family budgets of working-class households in Chicago reported 21 percent boarder-keeping families in the total sample of 464. Interestingly, the difference in proportion of boarder-keeping households in the income groups below and over the $1,500 annual income bracket was only 7 percent (24 and 17 percent, respectively). See Houghteling, *Income and Standard of Living of Unskilled Laborers in Chicago*, 48–51.

47 Interview #102, with Walter W. (April 9, 1983). Similar estimates are also given in memoirs of immigrants from other small towns: Drozdowski, *Pamiętniki Emigrantów*, 1:201, 211.

48 Interview #21, with Mrs. Coleman N. (June 18, 1981); #23, with Frank B. (June 14, 1981); #27, with Helen L. (June 13, 1981); #106, with Mary L. (April 9, 1983, and March 25, 1984).

49 Raymond Murphy, "The Geography of Johnstown – An Industrial Center," *Pennsylvania State College Bulletin* 13 (1934), 36, 42.

50 Interview #87, with John B. (November 7, 1980).

51 Interviews #25, with Mary K. (June 14, 1981); #43, with Margaret G. (January 22, 1981); #80, with Steven Ch. (October 3, 1980); #89, with Pauline H. (June 11, 1980).

52 Interview #3, with Mary P. (March 9, 1981). Also, five interviews with retired Johnstown policemen (UPJ: with C.J.B., Pete Ch., Nick V., Thomas S., and S.C.H.).

53 Interview #3, with Mary P. (March 9, 1981); #30, with Frank S. (March 26, 1981); letter from Anthony C. to author (April 14, 1983).

54 Interview #102, with Walter W. (April 9, 1983).

55 In calculating the average annual expenditures on food by the lowest-income immigrant households during the 1920s, I replicated the items as specified in a report by the U.S. Bureau of Labor Statistics investigating budgets of wage-earning families in Johnstown in 1934–5. (See U.S. Department of Labor, Bureau of Labor Statistics, "Manuscript Schedules of Family Reimbursements of Wage Earners and Salaried Workers: Johnstown, Pennsylvania" National Archives, Industrial Branch). As reported in the survey, East Central European families with seven to eight members and an annual income of less than $900 were able to survive on food expenditures of $350 a year. The expenditures, adjusted for a 20 to 25 percent price decrease between mid-1920s and mid-1930s are calculated from "Average Amount and Per Cent Expenditures per Annum for the Principal Groups of Items of Cost of Living of Families in Specified Industrial Centers by Cities

and by Income Groups," *Monthly Labor Review* (May 1919), 158–9; "Changes in Cost of Living," *Monthly Labor Review* (August 1926), 200–9; Commonwealth of Pennsylvania, Department of Labor and Industry, "The Keystone Labor and Industry," (March 1938), 40–1.

I gathered the information about rent costs from interviews #66, #70, and #102, with Walter W. (June 11, 1981; September 6, 1980; April 9, 1983); on the minimum expenditures on clothing, household operation, and home furnishings from interviews #66, with Walter W. (June 11, 1980); #78, with Theresa S. (October 2, 1980); #106, with Mary L. (April 9, 1983); #13, with Katarzyna C. (June 23, 1981); #26, with Casimira G. (June 13, 1981). The average cost of light and fuel in Johnstown was estimated from data provided by M. Ada Beney, *Cost of Living in the United States, 1914–36*, National Industrial Conference Board Studies, no. 228 (1936), 80–1. For comparison, according to a calculation of the National Industrial Conference Board, the average minimum annual cost of light and fuel needed to maintain a "fair American standard of living" for the family of an industrial worker in the town of Butler, Pa., about 70 miles northwest of Johnstown, was, by the mid-1920s, $54. (Beney, *Cost of Living in the United States*, 51).

The cost of insurance and recreation was estimated from interviews #70, with Walter W. (September 6, 1980); #64 (UPJ), with Pete M. Also Slovenian Workers' Home, minute book (monthly reports on "Dohotki"), 1919–36; St. Mary Greek Catholic *Chranitel*, Johnstown, July 1920, 9–12; St. Rochus Croatian parish, church dues and donations, 1925–37. Similar information as to the range of expenditures on church, insurance and recreation by immigrant families in other American towns in Drozdowski, *Pamiętniki Emigrantów*, 1:119–23, 150–7, 174–93, 210–11; 2:389–91.

56 Interview #50 (UPJ) with Petro S.; #78, with Theresa S. (October 2, 1980); #106, with Mary L. (April 9, 1983).

57 Recalculated for a 2 + 5-member family (2 parents, 2 adult and 3 minor children) from "What Is the American Standard of Living?", *Monthly Labor Review*, (July 1919), 5–7, food expenditures adjusted to "Changes in Cost of Living," 203–10.

58 Houghteling, *Income and Standard of Living of Unskilled Laborers in Chicago*, 75–7, 88. The study reported 70 percent of the surveyed families to have declared earnings below the amount required by the "standard American budget." Among 54 selected households whose budgets were calculated in detail, over 40 percent reported spending less than $.33 per adult male per day (ibid., 80, 154).

59 National Industrial Conference Board, *The Cost of Living in Twelve Industrial Cities* (New York, 1928), 16–19.

60 St. John the Baptist Ukrainian Catholic Church in Johnstown, "Golden Jubilee Album, 1910–1960." In their memoirs, immigrants from other

American cities explicitly point out the existence of these tensions. See Drozdowski, *Pamiętniki Emigrantów*, 1:119–21, 186–90, 302, 501–2; 554–5; 2:371–2, 389–90, 436–7; 468–70.

61 Interview #41, with Mary O. (February 25, 1981); St. Mary's Greek Catholic *Chranitel*, Johnstown, February 1921, 8–9: "Tablica Ukazu-jušča Rozličny Dochodky i Vydatky Grecko-Cath. Ohro-Russkoj Cerkvy vo Johnstown, Penna. iz 1920 Roka"; *Jednota Kalendár*, 1928 (the budget of St. Stephen's Slovak parochial school in Johnstown), 66. The average mortgage indebtedness of the immigrant churches erected during the 1920s was $7,500, ranging from $3,000 (a wooden building, St. Petka's Serbian Orthodox church in Woodvale, one of the old "foreign colonies") to nearly $20,000 (Slovak St. Francis in the "better" neighborhood of Morrellville); Mortgage Books, Cambria County Courthouse, Registrar's Office, 70:330; 111:363; 161:25; 182:554; 190:822.

62 See n. 15. In 1929, the average rent in the sections of Johnstown inhabited by East Central Europeans ranged from $15 to $30 a month (U.S. Department of Labor, Division of Research and Statistics, "HOLC Survey File – Johnstown, Pa., 1937), National Archives. According to the 1930 census, about 40 percent of the total number of families renting in Johnstown paid monthly rent of $15 to $25; we can assume that most of the East Central European families were in this bracket (*Fifteenth Census of the United States: 1930, Population*, 6:75).

63 Marian Tarkowski, "Położenie Robtników Polskich w Okresie Kryzysu," *Ameryka Północna* (Warsaw, 1975), 1:307.

64 Interview #66, with Walter W. (June 11, 1980).

65 In comparison with the subsistence-level income group, the budgets of less hard-pressed households could cover, alternately or in some combination, an increase in expenditures by as much as 100 percent for food, 150 percent in rental costs and clothing, over 200 percent in church dues and collections, and a seven- to nine-fold increase in spending on home furnishings (the disproportionate expansion of the latter expenditure category was due mainly to a very low base in the minimum group). With the exception of food, on which even the slightly better-off immigrant families spent substantially more than the poorest ones, this range of increase corresponded approximately to the figures reported in the itemized yearly expenditures of average Pittsburgh families by income groups: "Average Amount and Per Cent Expenditures . . . for the Principal Groups of Items of Cost of Living of Families in Specified Industrial Centers by Cities and by Income Groups," 159. In Johnstown, during the Depression, two seven-member East Central European families randomly selected from the sample surveyed by the Department of Labor declared annual food expenditures ranging from $331 (with a total family income of $956) to $633 (with an income of $1,643). See U.S. Department of Labor, Bureau of Labor Statistics,

"Manuscript Schedules of Family Reimbursements of Wage Earners and Salaried Workers: Johnstown, Pennsylvania," schedule 11, p. 22.

66 A sample of 145 Slavic- and Magyar-sounding names was taken from two sources: (1) the Grantee and Grantor Index Books in the Recorder's Office at the Cambria County Courthouse; (2) the transcripts of real estate transfers published regularly in the *Johnstown Tribune* during the 1920s. The names were subsequently checked in the deed records. The average price paid by the immigrants for their homes was $3,250, but the actual range in my sample was a wide $1,000–6,000.

67 Calculated from Johnstown city directory, "Street and Avenue Guide and Directory of Households," a new section included for the first time in 1929. In each area – Cambria City, Moxham, Morrellville – I checked fifteen streets on which, as I knew from other sources, there was the greatest concentration of East Central Europeans. The total number of families with Slavic- and Magyar-sounding names checked for was 1,241.

68 "Vykaz Ukazujušči Imena Farnikov i Kollektu in Fundacii iz 1920r," St. Mary's Greek Catholic *Chranitel*, Johnstown, July 1920, 9–12.

69 The data presented here on immigrant homeownership and church contributions suggests a need for further verification of an assumption current among some labor and ethnic historians that purchase of a home by an immigrant family forced its members to reduce practically all other expenditures to the bare subsistence level. Although for a large number of struggling households this was indeed the case, there were also others for whom the purchase of a home – a symbol of elevated status in the immigrant communities – was accompanied by increased contributions to the church, also an important component of social prestige among East Central Europeans.

70 *Men*: ordinary laborers, $700 to $900; better-skilled workers, $1,300; clerks, cashiers, salesmen, $1,000. *Women*: maids, servants, cooks, $250; factory laborers, $400; clerks, salesgirls, cashiers, $400; teachers, nurses, $1,000.

71 Estimated from *Fourteenth Census of the United States: 1920, Population*, 2:794, 954–7, 1152; *Fifteenth Census of the United States: 1930, Population*, "Special Report on Foreign-born Families by Country of Birth of Head," 4:151, 193–4, *Population*, vol. 6, "Families," 1152.

72 St. Mary's Greek Catholic *Chranitel*, Johnstown, February 1921, 4.

73 East Central European male immigrant population from manuscript schedules of 1900 census, traced in Johnstown city directories for 1915, 1920, 1925 and 1930.

74 Interview #95, with Andy A. (July 17, 1981).

75 Interview #85, with Cecelia M. (November 8, 1980).

76 William Maguire, "Review of Industrial Statistics," *Labor and Industry* (February 1930), 38; and "Review of Industrial Statistics," *Labor and Industry* (February 1932), 45, 52.

77 Data for 1934 from Pennsylvania State Emergency Relief Board, Department of Research and Statistics, *Social Survey Section*, "Unemployment in Cambria County," bulletin no. 50-A, (1934), MS, National Archives, 3–12.

78 Compiled from "Wages and Hours of Labor," *Monthly Labor Review* (December 1933), 1466–71.

79 Compiled from Commonwealth of Pennsylvania, Department of Labor and Industry, "Keystone Labor and Industry," 1:38–9, 56; interviews #22 (UPJ) with Geo. L.; #32 (UPJ), with Edward N.; #46 (UPJ), with Geo. K.

80 Interview #69, with John B. (December 18, 1980).

81 Interviews #50, with Michael N. (June 3, 1981); #66 and #70 with Walter W. (June 6, 1980, and September 6, 1980).

82 Pennsylvania State Emergency Relief Board, "Unemployment in Cambria County," 11.

83 Interviews #26 and #91, with Casimira G. (November 20, 1980, and June 13, 1981); #72, with Anne Z. (October 2, 1980).

84 Pennsylvania State Emergency Relief Board, "Unemployment in Cambria County," 1.

85 Interview #72, with Anne Z. (October 2, 1980); #73, with Peter F. (October 2, 1980); #80, with Pauline H. (June 11, 1980).

86 Interviews #26 and #91, with Casimira G. (November 20, 1980, and June 13, 1981); #60, with Julia R. (June 11, 1980); #72, with Anne Z. (October 2, 1980); #76, with Mary H. (October 2, 1980); #89, with Pauline H. (June 11, 1980); #92, with Marianna P. (November 21, 1980).

87 Interviews #50, with Michael N. (June 3, 1981); #73, with Peter H. (October 2, 1980); #70, with Walter W. (October 2, 1980); #76, with Mary H. (October 2, 1980).

88 Interview #66, with Walter W. (June 11, 1980).

89 Compiled from Commonwealth of Pennsylvania, Department of Labor and Industry, "Keystone Labor and Industry," 39–41, 56.

90 Naturally, these adjustment devices were also widely used by native American families in middle- and lower-income groups. See Winnifred D. Wanderee Bolin, "The Economics of Middle-income Family Life: Working Women during the Great Depression," *Journal of American History* (June 1978), esp. 67.

91 Interview #69, with John B. (December 18, 1980). For instance, the Slovak *Jednota Kalendár*, which had many subscribers in Johnstown, regularly printed advertisements by the Penn Traffic Department Store, the old company store in Johnstown: "Vlastne jatky . . . a preto kupite u nich lacnejsie nez kdekol'vek": (It has its own butcher, so you will buy there cheaper than elsewhere").

92 Interview #54, with Joseph R. (May 7, 1981). According to a study of working-class budgets in Washington County in western Pennsylvania conducted in 1931, for over one-third of unemployed families

store credit was the chief means of support and for an additional 40 percent a partial one. See Elisabeth S. Johnson, "The Coal Miner and His Family in Strike Times of 1931," *Labor and Industry* (November 1931), 7.

93   Interview #25, with Mary K. (June 14, 1981).

94   Interview #69, with John B. (December 18, 1980).

95   U.S. Department of Labor, Division of Research and Statistics, "HOLC Survey File – Johnstown, Pennsylvania, 1937," 4; John Sperling, *Great Depressions: 1837–1844, 1893–1898, 1929–1939* (Chicago, 1966), 136–8.

96   Interview #66, with Walter W. (June 11, 1980).

97   U.S. Department of Labor, Division of Research and Statistics, "HOLC Survey File – Johnstown, Pennsylvania, 1937," Area Description C1, C2, C3, C10, C11, D1, D2, D4, D7, D8, D9, D10.

98   Ibid.

99   U.S. Department of Labor, Bureau of the Labor Statistics, "Manuscript Schedules of Family Disimbursements of Wage Earners and Salaried Workers, Johnstown, Pennsylvania, 1934/5." The annual average expenditures on food of the East Central European families consisting of six to eight members were about $350 to $400; the average number of gainfully employed persons per household was two to three.

100 Ibid.

101 Interview #5, with John B. (May 10, 1980). The increase in family expenditures on recreation during the Depression was reported in a 1936 study by Roland S. Vaile, *Research Memorandum on Social Aspects of Consumption in the Depression* (New York, 1972), 24–35.

102 Interview #66, with Walter W. (June 11, 1980).

103 Compiled from the minute books of the Slovenian Workers' Home in Moxham, Pa., 1930–40.

104 East Central European immigrant population from manuscript schedules of 1900 census, traced in Johnstown city directories for 1930 and 1940.

105 Notations in Cambria County Commissioner's Office, "Precepts of the Assessors: Annual Enumeration of All Persons, Properties and Things Subject to Taxation, 1940," Ebensburg, Pa. I checked the City of Johnstown, the boroughs of Westmont, Southmont, Brownstown, Lower Yoder, Coopersdale, Fernsdale, Lorain, Franklin, and East Conemaugh.

106 Ibid.

Chapter 7: Internal social stratification in the immigrant communities

1   "Many Irish laborers," states James Henretta, in a comment that applies equally to East Central European workers, "did not 'want' to invest their hard-earned dollars . . . in the expensive education of their children, or the acquisition of new occupational skills. They 'preferred' to

support the Roman Catholic church and to achieve the security of home ownership. A mere statistical comparison of their occupational and economic success with that of the members of other ethnic groups [with different priorities] distorts the significance of their lives. The very features that make the quantitative mode of understanding such a powerful analytic tool – its empiricism, narrow focus and statistical precision – serve to conceal the phenomenological essence of the life-worlds [of immigrants] in the industrial cities of the United States." See "Social History as Lived and Written," *American Historical Review* (December, 1979), 1316.

The increased interest among historians in the study of social stratification has thus far produced more applied research than theoretical discussion and refinement of concepts. With the exception of a discussion by Michael Katz, "Social Class in North American Urban History," *Journal of Interdisciplinary History* (Spring 1981), 579–607, which addresses the theoretical issues, the debate among social historians interested in stratification and mobility has for the most part focused on problems of application of occupational ranking to historical data (see Chap. 4, n. 99, this volume).

2   There is no need to enter here into the long-standing controversy between the advocates of two master sociological theories of social stratification: the functionalist or integration theory, and the class or conflict theory. Some theorists of social stratification view these two perspectives as irreconcilable, and see no possibility for the development of one integrated macrosociological theory. Others attempt to combine them into a unified theory of conflict and integration. On these two theories, see Seymour M. Lipset, *International Encyclopaedia of Social Sciences* s.v. "Social Stratification, Social Class," 296–316; Ralf Dahrendorf, *Class and Class Conflict in Industrial Society* (Stanford, 1959); Stanislaw Ossowski, *Class Structure in the Social Consciousness* (London, 1963); Peter van Berghe, "Dialectic and Functionalism: Toward a Theoretical Synthesis," *American Sociological Review* (October 1963), 695–705; Gerhard Lenski, *Power and Privilege: A Theory of Social Stratification* (New York, 1966); Erik Allardt, "Theories about Social Stratification," in John A. Jackson, ed., *Social Stratification* (Cambridge, 1968), 14–25; Runciman, "Class, Status and Power?", in Jackson, *Social Stratification*, 26–52.

For the purposes of the reconstruction of the *internal* group differentiation of one "class subsegment" of American society – the ethnic community – the functionalist perspective appears more useful; for the interpretation of the immigrant's structural position in the larger dominant society, the class approach seems more suitable.

3   This interpretation is my own modified version of the proposition offered by Richard P. Coleman, Lee Rainwater, and Kent A. McClelland in *Social Standing in America: New Dimensions of Class* (New York, 1978), 3–13.

4   After ibid., Introduction and pt. 1.

5   Among community studies of social stratification and social perceptions
    of group hierarchy, I found the following classic ones particularly ap-
    plicable to the situation in Johnstown: Allison Davis, Burleigh B. Gard-
    ner, and Mary R. Gardner, in *Deep South: A Social Anthropological Study
    of Caste and Class* (Chicago, 1941); Sydel F. Silverman, "An Ethnographic
    Approach to Social Stratification: Prestige in a Central Italian Com-
    munity," *American Anthropologist* (August 1966), 899–922; Joseph Lo-
    preato, "Social Stratification in an Italian Town," *American Sociological
    Review* (August 1961), 585–96; Judith R. Kramer and Seymour Levent-
    man, *Children of the Gilded Ghetto* (New Haven, 1961); Leonard W. Moss
    and Stephen C. Cappanari, "Estate and Class in a South Italian Hill
    Village," *American Anthropologist* (April 1962), 287–301; Robert T. An-
    derson and Gallatin Anderson, "Changing Social Stratification in a Dan-
    ish Village," *Anthropological Quarterly*, 32 (1960), 98–105; Robert T. An-
    derson and Gallatin Anderson, "The Indirect Social Stratification of
    European Village Communities," *American Anthropologist* (October
    1962), 1016–25; August B. Hollingshead, *Elmstown's Youth* (New York,
    1949), and "Trends in Social Stratification," *American Sociological Review*
    (December, 1952), 679–86; Harold F. Kaufman, "Defining Prestige Rank
    in a Rural Community," *Sociometry* (May 1945), 199–207. Also Melvin
    Tumin and Arnold Feldman, "Reference Groups and Class Orienta-
    tions," in *Social Class and Social Change in Puerto Rico*, ed., Melvin Tumin
    (Princeton, 1961); F. M. Martin, "Some Subjective Aspects of Social
    Stratification," in *Social Mobility in Britain*, ed. David V. Glass (London,
    1965), 51–75.
       The so-called community or anthropological treatment of social strat-
    ification has been the object of critical barrages from the field of soci-
    ology for a long time. The criticisms most often raised concern the sub-
    jectivity of interpretations "imposed" by the researcher on the studied
    reality, and the incomparability and lack of representativity of findings.
    (For an assessment of these problems, see the debate that ensued in
    the major American sociological journals in the years 1942–52 after the
    publication of Lloyld Warner's *Yankee City* series; cf. also Colin Bell and
    Howard Newby, *Community Studies: An Introduction to the Sociology of
    the Local Community* [New York, 1973]; Chaps. 3, 4, and 6; Maurice R.
    Stein, *The Eclipse of Community: An Interpretation of American Studies*
    [Princeton, 1960], pts. 1 and 2).
       Obviously these same strictures might be applied to this study. Al-
    though I do not think I "imposed" the status divisions on the "studied
    reality" (see the discussion of the methods used to reconstruct social
    hierarchy in the immigrant communities), my interpretations are un-
    avoidably "subjective," and my informants – old people, survivors of
    the past generation, were not a "representative sample." In addition,
    since this type of social-historical investigation of the internal social
    stratification of the immigrant communities has not been attempted
    before, there are no other results with which to compare my findings.

But this situation, precisely, fully justifies, I believe, the approach taken here. There is a gap in ethnic historiography that must be filled by collecting more "inside" data on the social and cultural functioning of the immigrant communities. This analysis of the internal group social hierarchy, using the "lightest touch" possible in trying to avoid the recognized traps of local community studies, is meant as a contribution toward this goal.

6   An interesting critique of formalized and highly structured interviews in the study of social perceptions of stratification can be found in Peter Hiller, "Nature and Social Location of Everyday Conceptions of Class," *Sociology* (January 1975), pp. 5–7.

7   One of the criticisms directed against the community studies of social stratification has concerned their upper-class bias in the presentation of status dimensions. My 35 respondents who furnished information on the basic status dimensions in the immigrant communities were also asked to describe the economic position – income, occupation, home-ownership status, and place of residence in the city – of their own families prior to and following World War I. They represented lower, middle and upper levels of the immigrant socioeconomic ladder as reconstructed in this chapter. I placed approximately 25 percent of my informants in or around the top of the East Central European interwar hierarchy, about 30 percent in the middle, and 25 percent in the lower status group. The remaining 20 percent seem to have "fluctuated" between the lower and middle categories. Despite the differences in their family's socioeconomic standing, informants in all three social groups tended to point out similar stratification factors in their communities. There appeared, however, to be some status-based differences in their evaluations of the immigrant stratification system that I will discuss.

8   On "classless but nonegalitarian" social systems, see Ossowski, *Class Structure in the Social Consciousness*, esp. 94–9, 149. The immigrant social stratification also contained a small stratum of small family business-men, entrepreneurs, and craftsmen, who, although they possessed control over their enterprises, had no or minimal control over labor. Moreover, with the exception of the thin top layer of this group, its "contents" were fluctuating as immigrants shifted between blue-collar work and small business occupations. From the perspective of class analysis, these considerations justify the treatment of the immigrant communities as fundamentally working-class units. On the class position of the "petty bourgeoisie," see Erik Olin Wright, "Class Boundaries and Contradictory Class Locations," in *Classes, Power and Conflict: Classical and Contemporary Debates*, ed. Anthony Giddens and David Held (Berkeley, 1982), 112–30. John Bukowczyk makes interesting observations on the shifting class attitudes and behavior of the Polish immigrant middle class in Bayonne, N.J., in the first decades of this century: "The Transformation of Working-Class Ethnicity: Corporate

Control, Americanization and the Polish Immigrant Middle-Class in Bayonne, New Jersey, 1915–1925," *Labor History* (Winter 1984), 53–82, and "Polish Factionalism and the Formation of the Immigrant Middle Class in Brooklyn, 1880–1929," in *Immigrant Communities in America*, ed. John Bodnar, forthcoming.

9 On the role of "seniority" in the emergence of social stratification from the originally undifferentiated group, see the discussion by Eva Rosenfeld, "Social Stratification in a 'Classless' Society," *American Sociological Review* (December, 1951), 766–75.

10 Mary Molek, ed., *Slovene Immigrant History, 1900–1950: Autobiographical Sketches by Ivan Molek* (Dover, Del.: 1970), 24–5.

11 Some sociologists see the transmission of resources and access to desired positions to others who share the same primordial identity as one of the crucial aspects of strata formation. See, for instance, S. N. Eisenstadt, "Prestige, Participation and Strata Formation," in Jackson, *Social Stratification*, 73–5. On "social closure" – the process by which resources and rewards are appropriated by particular groups in society – see Frank Parkin, "Social Closure and Class Formation," in *Classes, Power and Conflict, Classical and Contemporary Debates*, ed., Anthony Giddens and David Held (Berkeley, 1982), 175–85.

12 Letter from Albert Stelkovics, acting secretary of William Penn (Verhovay) Association, to author (June 30, 1981). Interview #100, with Stephen P. (June 12, 1981). Also #92, with Marianna P. (November 21, 1980); #29, with Michael N. (May 8, 1981).

13 Interview #30a, with Andy M. (April 3, 1981). Also #9 and #10, with Anthony C. (October 10, 1980, and February 23, 1981); #30, with Frank S. (March 26, 1981); #34, with John B. (February 24, 1981); #37, with Pete K. (March 11, 1981); #38, with Andy A. (February 25, 1981); #40, with John L. (February 26, 1981); #93, with Edward Y. (December 5, 1980).

14 Interview #21, with Coleman N. (June 18, 1981).

15 Unfortunately, because of the floods, most of the organizational records of the East Central European societies in Johnstown are incomplete, and so the figures given here are merely estimates. The proportion of "over 70 percent" was calculated on the basis of organizational records of 10 among the largest Slavic and Magyar societies in the city.

16 Calculated on the basis of organizational records of 20 East Central European societies in Johnstown (names traced in city directories). This pattern conforms to that found by Josef Barton among the Slovenes and Croatians in Cleveland, but not among the Slovaks, whose leadership, as Barton reports, after 1900 moved into the hands of the workers; see "Eastern and Southern Europeans," in John Higham, ed., *Ethnic Leadership in America* (Baltimore, 1978), 150–75. Information on the participation of immigrant businessmen in ethnic societies in Johnstown is from interview #27, with Helen L. (June 13, 1981); #30, with

Frank S. (March 26, 1981); #37, with Pete K. (March 11, 1981); #38, with Andy A. (February 25, 1981); and #42, with Walter W. (February 25, 1981).

17 Interview #6, with John L. (May 15, 1981).

18 St. Peter and Paul Ukrainian Orthodox Church, list of officers, 1920s and 1930s; Polish National Alliance, Lodge #1327, list of officers, 1920 and 1930s; Slovak Evangelical Union, Lodge #239 and #197, list of officers, 1920s and 1930s.

19 Interview #30, with Frank S. (March 26, 1981). Apparently the proportion of skilled workers among the leaders of immigrant societies was higher before 1900–5. This tendency was most pronounced in the Hungarian group and also, to a lesser extent, among the Poles (from the "Prussian" partition).

20 Interview #40, with John L. (February 26, 1980). Interestingly, the Slovak Lutheran group had during the 1920s and 1930s an overrepresentation (19 percent) of skilled workers on the church board. The majority of them – but no more than a handful of people altogether – brought their skills from the old country rather than having acquired them in Johnstown. Maybe, then, it was the American apprenticeship in skilled jobs in the mills that set the immigrant workers apart from their communities, whereas those who had learned their crafts in Europe and then managed to find good jobs in Johnstown remained active in their ethnic groups (interview #109, with Paul P., July 21, 1983).

21 Interview #37, with Pete K. (March 11, 1981).

22 Interview #17, with Helen V. (June 18, 1981); #22, With Mary K. (June, 1981).

23 Names from organizational records of 20 East Central European societies were subsequently checked for homeownership in the 1929 Johnstown city directory, Street Guide Addendum.

24 Interview #3, with Mary P. (March 9, 1981). Unfortunately, the records are incomplete and no firmer conclusions can be formulated. The problem of women's ethnic organizational participation in enhancing the family status very much deserves closer research attention.

25 Interview #1, with Mary B. (June 5, 1981); #3, with Mary P. (March 9, 1981); #13, with Katarzyna C. (June 23, 1981); #19, with Mary U. (June 18, 1981); #20, with Mary K. (June 18, 1981); #43, with Margaret G. (January 22, 1981); Greek Catholic Union of the U.S.A., "Golden Jubilee Book, 1892–1942," 403; "Dedication and Conservation of St. Nicholas Serbian Orthodox Church, Johnstown, Pennsylvania, October 18, 1964," 13; Antoni Cyburt, "Historia Polonii w Johnstown," unpublished paper.

26 Interview #37, with Pete K. (March 11, 1981); #87, with John B. (November 7, 1980).

27 Theodore Hershberg, Michael Katz, Stuart Blumin, et al., "Occupations and Ethnicity in Five Nineteenth-century Cities: A Collaborative Inquiry," Historical Methods Newsletter (June 1974), 174–216. On the dis-

cussion on the applicability of contemporary occupational classifications to historical data, see Chap. 4, n. 99, this volume.

28   The list of 48 occupations probably does not cover the total range of
occupations actually performed by East Central Europeans in Johnstown. The 1920 census listed in the city over 200 different occupations:
From this number a dozen or so jobs performed by the immigrants
could be added to my list. I did not seek to supplement it, however,
since it clearly exhausts the most common immigrant occupations and
permits the reconstruction of the basic occupational classes – the major
purpose of the operation.

29   If one were to describe specific jobs in the mills with concrete work
characteristics – cleaner or dirtier, lighter or heavier, more or less independent, mechanized or not – probably much more refinement and
status differentiation would have emerged in the immigrant occupational ranking. As it is, unspecified semiskilled occupations are classified together with common labor in the fifth category.

30   Status as a reputational attribute is allocated around a complex, mul-
tidimensional set of characteristics of an *individual* as they are perceived
and evaluated by others in the course of personal contact. Status as an
attribute of *position*, on the other hand, otherwise referred to as "at-
tributional" or class status, is assigned on the basis of one or more
clearly defined, replicable, and "depersonalized" traits. See Frank Parkin, *Class Inequality and Political Order* (London, 1971), 34–5; also Bell
and Newby, *Community Studies*, Chap. 6.

31   Paul M. Siegel, "Occupational Prestige in the Negro Subculture," in
Social Stratification: Research and Theory for the 1970s, ed. Edward O. Laumann (New York, 1970), 156–72.

32   On the permeability of occupational boundaries and the fluidity of the
occupational structure in nineteenth-century American cities, see Clyde
Griffen, "Occupational Mobility in Nineteenth-century America: Problems and Possibilities," *Journal of Social History* (Spring 1972), 310–31;
Clyde Griffen and Sally Griffen, *Natives and Newcomers: The Ordering of
Opportunity in Mid-Nineteenth-Century Poughkeepsie* (Cambridge, Mass.:
1978).

33   In order to compare the occupational distribution of 485 persisters since
the 1900 census – the "old-timers" well-established in Johnstown – with
that of the whole East Central European immigrant population in the
city in 1925, I counted the number of Slavic and Magyar-sounding
names in the Johnstown business directory for that year. It is admittedly
a rather gross method of verification. First, the data for better-skilled
mill workers are missing. Second, some immigrant entrepreneurs may
have anglicized their names. Third, the business guide also covers representatives of the second generation. By 1925, however, the number
of adult second generation East Central Europeans sufficiently independent to carry on their own businesses was still rather limited (my
1900 sample of second generation adults included in 1925 20 such cases,

and they were subtracted). Among the total number of about 3,000 adult East Central European immigrant men in Johnstown in the mid-1920s those employed in business and services constituted approximately 8 percent (as opposed to about 12 percent in the 1900 sample).

34   St. Emerich Hungarian Catholic Church, "Twenty-Fifth Anniversary Album, 1930."

35   Interview #21, with Coleman N. (June 18, 1981).

36   The situation of the Jewish population in Hungary at the turn of the century was more favorable than elsewhere in eastern Europe. The Hungarian Jews enjoyed legal equality, and in the last third of the nineteenth century their social and economic assimilation had been advanced quite rapidly, particularly in the cities, where they were becoming Magyarized in increasing numbers. See Randolph L. Braham, "Hungarian Jewry," *Journal of Central European Affairs* (1960), 90–112; Erno Laszlo, "Hungarian Jewry: Settlement and Demography, 1735 to 1910," in *Hungarian-Jewish Studies*, ed., Randolph L. Braham (New York, 1966), 61–117; Aron Moskovitz, *Jewish Education in Hungary* (New York, 1964).

37   Interview #3, with Mary P. (March 9, 1981).

38   Interviews #9 and #10, with Anthony C. (October 10, 1980, and February 23, 1981); #87, with John B. (November 7, 1980); #8, with Frank S. (May 6, 1981).

39   Interview #42, with Walter W. (February 25, 1981); also #4, with Nikola B. (July 14, 1981); #25, with Mary K. (June 14, 1981); #27, with Helen L. (June 13, 1981); #30, with Frank S. (March 26, 1981); #85, with Cecilia M. (November 8, 1980); #87, with John B. (November 17, 1980). On the role of material artifacts as attributes of social standing, see Edward O. Laumann and James S. House, "Living Room Styles and Social Attributes: The Patterning of Material Artifacts in a Modern Urban Community," *Sociology and Social Research* (April, 1970), 321–43.

40   Holy Cross Slovak Lutheran Church, "Golden Jubilee Album, 1914–1964"; St. Mary's Greek Catholic Church, *Chranitel*, Johnstown, December 1920, 10–11.

41   Interview #10, with Anthony C. (February 23, 1981). There had in fact been a number of immigrants in Johnstown who were known in their communities as "moneyed" but who never publicly displayed their wealth and led the most modest lives, kept saving, and did not invest. If not "externalized" in some fashion through business or real estate investment, home purchases, dress, treating others, or ethnic communal sponsorship, wealth itself did not seem to have significantly contributed to the social status of an individual family in the immigrant community.

42   It is extremely difficult to estimate the actual incomes of immigrant businessmen because these incomes fluctuated so much and so widely. Even a temporary slowdown at Bethlehem, to which East European families reacted immediately by eliminating a number of purchases,

was sufficient to reduce the weekly profits of immigrant stores by 50 to 70 percent. During a season their sales varied widely from a few dollars a day, in "quiet times," to $150 and more in busy periods. As bankruptcy records indicate, in good times gross income of a prosperous and established entrepreneur in Johnstown ranged between $25,000 and $30,000 a year. Of this sum, he would usually spend approximately $7,000 to $8,000 in overhead expenses and $15,000 or more for new merchandise. A smaller enterprise, averaging a gross income of $8000 to $10,000 annually, expended about $4,000 to $5,000 to restock and $3,000 to $3,500 for overhead. Information compiled from Cambria County Commissioner's Office, Ebenburg, Pa., "Precepts of the Assessors: *Annual Ennumeration of All Persons, Properties and Things Subject to Taxation,*" 1920, 1925, 1930, for Slavic- and Magyar-sounding names of persons engaged in business; Office of the Clerk, U.S. Bankruptcy Court, Western District of Pennsylvania, Pittsburgh; bankruptcy files of 30 East Central European businessmen with businesses in Johnstown's "foreign colonies," 1918–40, Federal Archives and Records Center, Philadelphia; interview #74, with Frances K. (October 2, 1980); #102, with Walter W. (April 9, 1983); #104, with Mary B. (April 9, 1983); #47, with Mary D. (July 1, 1981); #35, with Charles G. (March 12, 1981).

43 Dun & Bradstreet, "Johnstown, Pennsylvania," in *Reference Books Containing Ratings of Merchants, Manufactures and Traders Generally throughout the United States and Canada,* vol. 227, *1925*; vol. 243, *1929.*

44 Figures derived from Grantee and Grantor Index, Cambria County Courthouse, Ebensburg, Pa. Grantee Index: 14/212; 316/205; 145/269; 103/300; 286/391; 197/255, 451; Grantor Index: 63/235; 7/300; 156/451; 309/214; 288/229; 147/245; 519/253; 217/280; 50/279; 20/300; 11/333; 39; 214; 50/240; 350, 248, 278/364; 191/376; 169/388.

45 The estimate of 20 percent was calculated in the following way: During the 1920s approximately 250 East Central European businesses of various kinds were being operated in Greater Johnstown. Of this, as we have seen, about 30 to 40 owners were "rich" entrepreneurs. On the basis of mercantile taxes paid and Dun & Bradstreet's credit ratings, I estimated that another 50 to 60 immigrant businessmen could have received an annual income of over $2,000: They were included in the second economic stratum. In the preceding chapter (Table 6.6), we saw that between one-fifth and one-fourth of the immigrant working-class families received a total annual income of over $2,000. Since there were in Johnstown and the boroughs about 3,000 East Central European households, the size of the second-from-top stratum hovered, then, around 650, that is about 20 percent of the total. (The number of households estimated from the ethnic parochial records and from the *Fifteenth Census of the United States: 1930,* vol. 4: *Population:* "Special Reports on Foreign-born Families by Country of Birth of Head," 151).

46 Interview #82, with Anna C. (October 9, 1980). The evidence from my

Johnstown study, although it indicates that immigrants did place considerable value on informal basic learning, does not support Timothy Smith's thesis about their supposedly high aspirations for formal schooling ("New Approaches to the History of Immigration in Twentieth-century America," *American Historical Review* (July 1966), 1273–5, and "Immigrant Social Aspirations and American Education, 1880–1930," *American Quarterly* (Fall 1969), 523–44.

47   In his discussion of the role of education in the formation of the Chicago working class, David Hogan observes that even in the 1920s, "Compared to the economic value of their children's education, schooling [beyond the age of 14 still] did not appear to the immigrants as an economically rational course of action." See "Education and the Making of the Chicago Working Class, 1880–1930," *History of Education Quarterly* (Fall 1978), 233.

48   East Central European names from Johnstown High School and Catholic High School graduation books, 1918–28, traced in city directories for fathers' occupations.

49   Interview #17, with Helen V. (June 18, 1981).

50   Interview #65, with Michael N. (October 17, 1980); #70, with Walter W. (October 2, 1980); #97, with Pete K. (July 14, 1981); #35, with Charles G. (March 12, 1981); #36, with Henry S. (March 12, 1981). On the role of immigrant middle-class leaders in Bayonne, N.J., in Americanization programs and corporate control of workers, see Bukowczyk, "Transformation of Working-class Ethnicity"; on the mediating role or the ethnic elites in linking the immigrant communities and the dominant American society, see Smith, "New Approaches to the History of Immigration in Twentieth-century America," 1265–80.

51   I detected this attitude in several conversations with East Central Europeans in Johnstown: interview #3, with Mary P. (March 9, 1981); #4, with Nikola B. (July 14, 1981); #8, with Frank S. (May 6, 1981); #10 and #57, with Anthony C. (February 23, 1981, and September 18, 1980); #33, with Michael O'K. (March 28, 1981); #34, with John B. (February 24, 1981); #36, with Henry S. (May 5, 1981); #37, with Pete K. (March 11, 1981); #38, with Andy A. (February 25, 1981); #40, with John L. (February 26, 1981); #52, with Yanko L. (June 5, 1981); #62, with Thomas B. (June 11, 1980); #63, with Emil S. (November 6, 1980); #86, with Michael M. (November 8, 1980).

52   On the role of "family reputation" in the Polish immigrant communities, see Paul Wrobel, *An Ethnographic Study of Polish American Family, Parish and Neighborhood* (Baltimore, 1975); also Helena Znaniecki-Lopata, *Polish Americans: Status Competition in an Ethnic Community* (Englewood Cliffs, N.J.: 1976).

53   Interview #16, with Mary D. (June 19, 1981); #30, with Frank S. (March 26, 1981).

54   Compiled from organizational records of St. John Slovak Evangelical Church 1920–40; Slovak Evangelical Union, Lodges #239 and #197,

records of officers; St. Casimir Polish Roman Catholic Church, church board; Polish Roman Catholic Union, Lodge #503, records of officers; Polish National Alliance, Lodges #832 and #1569, records of officers; Slovak Jednota, Lodge #23, records of officers; Slovenian Workers' Home, records of officers; St. Rochus Croatian Catholic Church, parochial board; Croatian Fraternal Union, Lodge #8, records of officers; St. John the Baptist Russian Orthodox Church, parochial board; Russian Orthodox Brotherhood, records of officers.

55 The size of particular nationality groups among immigrant persisters since 1900 was much too small for comparative generalizations. We may, however, note that the Magyars, Slovaks, and Poles from the "Prussian" partition – the older settlers and the ones with established "German connections" at Bethlehem – comprised a greater proportion of the recorded "multiple achievers" than did the remaining immigrant groups.

56 Dun & Bradstreet, *Ratings*, "Johnstown, Pennsylvania," vol. 187, January 1915; vol. 199, January 1918; vol. 209, January 1920; vol. 227, January 1925; vol. 243, January 1929; vol. 258, January 1932.

57 The list is not exhaustive, since the restaurants, cafés, inns, and hotels were usually listed by their own names rather than by the names of the proprietors. On the other hand, my list also includes second generation East Central European entrepreneurs. The population of East Central European entrepreneurs in the city grew during the decade following World War I by about 20 percent; in the same period, the overall numerical growth of Johnstown's employment in business and services of the type represented in the East Central European communities was 18 percent. (*Fourteenth Census of the United States: 1920*, vol. 4: *Population: Occupations*, 276–81; *Fifteenth Census of the United States: 1930, Population*, "Occupations by States," 1395–7).

58 For comparison, I compiled a "control" list of 371 groceries owned by persons with American-sounding names (I selected the grocery business because it was the most popular type of business among East Central Europeans in Johnstown). The patterns of business turnover in both groups were quite similar. Thus, the average gross rate of business turnover among the "American" grocers was 45 percent for the whole period 1915–29; the proportion of new entries between 1915 and 1925 was 50 percent; between 1925 and 1929, 35 percent. Between 1929 and 1937 the number of "American" grocers decreased by 33 percent.

59 Norbert Wiley, "The Ethnic Mobility Trap and Stratification Theory," *Social Problems* (Fall 1967), 148. On the ethnic occupational niches or enclaves and intragroup status mobility, see Stanley Lieberson, "Ethnic Groups and the Practice of Medicine," *American Sociological Review* (October 1958), 542–49; Ivan Light, *Ethnic Enterprise in America: Business and Welfare among Chinese, Japanese, and Blacks* (Berkeley, 1972); Edna Bonacic, "A Theory of Middleman Minorities," *American Sociological Review* (October 1973), 583–94; Edna Bonacic, Ivan Light, and Charles Choy

Wong, "Small Business among Koreans in Los Angeles", in *Counter-point: Perspectives on Asian America*, Emma Gee (Los Angeles, 1976), 436–9; Lawrence A. Lovell-Troy, "Clan Structure and Economic Activity: The Case of Greeks in Small Business Enterprise," in *Self-help in Urban America: Patterns of Minority Business Enterprise*, ed. Scott Cummings (Port Washington, N.Y.: 1980), 58–89; Edna Bonacic and John Modell, *The Economic Basis of Ethnic Solidarity: Small Business in the Japanese-American Community*. (Berkeley, 1980); Kenneth L. Wilson and Alejandro Portes, "Immigrant Enclaves: An Analysis of the Labor Market Experiences of Cubans in Miami," *American Journal of Sociology* (September 1980), 295–319; Illsoo Kim, *New Urban Immigrants: The Korean Community in New York* (Princeton, 1981).

60 Interview #32, with George M. (March 28, 1981). Even the wealthiest and best-established East Central European leaders and businessmen remained outside the social networks of the local American community. By the end of the 1930s, of 474 members of the respected Johnstown Chamber of Commerce, only 8 (1.7 percent) were of East Central European origin, despite the fact that there were in town well over 200 Slavic and Magyar businessmen. Neither of the two country clubs, the Sunnehanna and the Elks, nor the prestigious executive Bachelor's Club admitted East Central European members. Actually, the only one from among the most successful and best-known Slavic merchants and local ethnic leaders who ever attempted to join the Sunnehanna Club before World War II was twice refused. It was only in 1952 that his reapplication was eventually accepted. (Johnstown Chamber of Commerce, permanent roll; Sunnehanna Country Club, membership file.)

61 Interview #103, with Michael J. (July 14, 1981).

62 Interview #37, with Pete K. (March 11, 1981); #1, with Mary B. (June 5, 1981).

63 Interview #27, with Helen L. (June 13, 1983); #30, with Frank S. (March 26, 1981).

64 The Slovenes appear to have been the only group among the eight that I studied in Johnstown who more systematically projected class resentment on the outside. Earlier in this chapter I showed an interesting form of "class solidarity" in this group, with the local Socialist lodge, composed of immigrant businessmen and laborers, together protesting "the capitalist exploitation by the American company owners." The American Slovenes have had the tradition of the social-democratic progressive movement that started in Europe and flourished in the immigrant communities in this country as a successful competitor of the "clerical" orientation (see Joseph Stipanovich, "'In Unity Strength': Immigrant Workers and Immigrant Intellectuals in Progressive America: A History of the South Slav Democratic Movement, 1900–1918," Ph.D. thesis, University of Minnesota, 1978). This could be one explanation of the more developed "proletarian consciousness" among the Slovenes in Johnstown. Also, many of them were coal miners and moved in-

tensely between mines in the area. My interviews suggest that in this nonunion company town, the immigrant coal miners were apparently more strongly class-resentful and conflict-conscious than were the steel-workers. One possible explanation is that before the 1922 coal strike, a good number of coal-mining towns in the area were already union-ized, and the immigrant miners moving to Johnstown brought with them sharpened feelings of class oppression. Another factor could have been a stronger sense of occupational identity among the miners, par-ticularly those from isolated coal-mining towns around Johnstown, re-sulting from unusually hard and hazardous conditions of work that led to a stronger sense of class exploitation. See John Brophy, *A Miner's Life* (Boston, 1964); David A. Corbin, *Life, Work and Rebellion in Coal Fields* (Urbana, Ill.: 1981); C. Kerr and A. Siegel, "The Inter-industry Propensity to Strike: An International Comparison," in *Industrial Con-flict*, ed. A. Kornhauser, R. Dubin, and A. M. Ross (London, 1954); N. Dennis, F. Henriques, and C. Slaughter, *Coal Is Our Life* (London, 1956).

65 Interview #10, with Anthony C. (February 23, 1981).

66 On the sense of economic "movement" among the nonmobile who experience improvement in the material conditions of life, see Coleman, Rainwater, and McClelland, *Social Standing in America*, 226–31; Peter M. Blau and Otis Dudley Duncan, *The American Occupational Structure* (New York, 1967), 436–41.

67 David Lockwood, "Sources of Variation in Working-class Images of Society," *Sociological Review* (November 1966), 249–67. In a series of theoretical debates and empirical research that followed the publication of Lockwood's essay, his typology was subjected to critical reassess-ment. See, in particular, Martin Bulmer, ed., *Working-class Images of Society* (London, 1975), which contains sixteen papers presented at a conference held in September 1972 in Durham, England, devoted spe-cifically to the debate on Lockwood's typology. Also, from among the most renowned studies on the topic: Parkin, *Class Inequality and Political Order* (London, 1971), Chap. 3; D. Kavanagh, "The Deferential English: A Comparative Critique," *Government and Opposition* (May 1971), 333–60; Colin Bell and Howard Newby, "The Sources of Variation in Ag-ricultural Workers' Images of Society," *Sociological Review* (May 1973), 229–53; Newby, *The Deferential Worker: A Study of Farm Workers in East Anglia* (London, 1977); Peter Hiller, "Continuities and Variations in Everyday Conceptual Components of Class," *Sociology* (April 1975), 255–89, and "Nature and Social Location of Everyday Conceptions of Class"; Howard H. Davis, *Beyond Class Images* (London, 1979); Kenneth Roberts, F. G. Cook, S. C. Clark, et al., *Fragmentary Class Structure* (London, 1977). An interesting alternative model of class-based per-ceptions of the normative order related to social inequality has been proposed by Parkin, who distinguishes between "dominant," "sub-ordinate," and "radical" meaning systems (*Class Inequality and Political Order*, Chap. 3). For the purposes of this analysis, however, concerned

with the social consciousness of East European peasants who became industrial workers in a small autocratic town in America at the beginning of the century, I find Lockwood's concepts more useful.

68 A number of sociological studies that derived from Lockwood's essay have demonstrated that the social consciousness of workers is not composed of distinct, coherent, and internally consistent types but, rather, of confused and fragmented images, situationally activated. See Jim Cousins and Richard Brown, "Patterns of Paradox: Shipbuilding Workers' Images of Society," in *Working-class Images of Society*, 55–83 and, in the same volume, Roderick Martin and R. H. Fryer, "The Deferential Worker?", 98–116; Eric Batstone, "Deference and the Ethos of Small-Town," 116–31; R. M. Blackburn and Michael Mann, "Ideology in the Non-skilled Working-class," 131–63; Mann, *Consciousness and Action in the Western Working Class* (London, 1973); Newby, *Deferential Worker*; Roberts et al., *Fragmentary Class Structure*; Davis, *Beyond Class Images*.

69 Thomas Bell, *Out of This Furnace* (Pittsburgh, 1976), 123.

70 Interview #13, with Katarzyna C. (June 23, 1981); #52, with Yanko U. (June 5, 1981); #3, with Mary P. (March 9, 1981).

71 St. Mary's Greek Catholic *Chranitel*, Johnstown, May 1921, 8.

72 Lockwood, "Sources of Variation in Working-Class Images of Society," *Sociological Review* (November 1966), 249–67.

73 James Curran, "Class Imagery, Work Environment and Community: Some Further Findings and a Brief Comment," *British Journal of Sociology* (March 1981), 111–26.

74 The attitudes of immigrant workers at Bethlehem Steel were similar to those observed in other American factories at the beginning of the century: "First generation newcomers from rural backgrounds," noted Tamara Hareven about the textile mill workers in Manchester, N.H., "were in awe of the bosses and the [industrial] system and tended to act more submissively than experienced workers. They were more inclined to individual interaction with bosses, either directly or through relatives, than toward group action." *Family Time and Industrial Time* (New York, 1982), 150. Similar observations also in David Montgomery, *Workers Control in America* (Cambridge, 1979).

75 Newby, *Deferential Worker*, 417.

76 Wincenty Witos, *Moje Wspomnienia* (Paris 1964), 1:85.

77 Bell, *Out of This Furnace*, 66.

78 John H. Goldthorpe and David Lockwood use the term *instrumental collectivism*, denoting a predominantly utilitarian, nonaffective reliance on communal solidarities and collective action to foster individual economic goals, to describe the convergent attitudes of the "new" working and the "new" middle classes in postwar British society ("Affluence and the British Class Structure," *Sociological Review* [July 1963], 133–62). Peasant-immigrants in America in the first half of this century for whom ethnic communal attachments and membership were at the same time an end and a means seem more appropriately described as "instru-

mentalists-participators." On "particularism" and "communal privatism" as characteristic of American working-class culture, see Gabriel Kolko, *Main Currents in Modern American History* (New York, 1976), Chap. 3: "The American Working Class – Immigrant Foundations"; Ira Katznelson, *City Trenches: Urban Politics and the Patterning of Class in the United States* (New York, 1981); David M. Gordon, Richard Edwards, and Michael Reich, *Segmented Work, Divided Workers: The Historical Transformation of Labor in the United States* (New York, 1982); William Kornblum, *Blue Collar Community* (Chicago, 1974). See also John Bodnar, *Workers' World Kinship, Community and Protest in an Industrial Society, 1900–1940* (Baltimore, 1982), particularly his notion of ethnic "enclave," designating the segmented, circumscribed world of family, kin, and local community.

79   Among the most prominent adherents of the "unitary" vision of the societal value system are Talcott Parsons, *The Social System* (London, 1951); Eli Chinoy, *Automobile Workers and the American Dream* (Boston, 1955); Gabriel A. Almond and Sidney Verba, *The Civic Culture* (Princeton, 1963); Seymour M. Lipset, *The First New Nation* (London, 1964); Robert A. Dahl, *Pluralist Democracy in the United States: Conflict and Consent* (Chicago, 1967); David Easton and Jack Dennis, "The Child's Acquisition of Regime's Norms: Political Efficacy," *American Political Science Review* (March 1967), 25–38. The "pragmatic" interpretation has been most fully developed by Parkin, *Class Inequality and Political Order*; Mann, "The Social Cohesion of Liberal Democracy," *American Sociological Review* (June 1970) 423–39; and *Consciousness and Action in the Western Working Class*; Nicholas Abercombie and Bryan S. Turner, "The Dominant Ideology Thesis," *British Journal of Sociology* (June 1978), 149–70. See also an interesting analysis of "quiescence" among Appalachian workers by John Gaventa, *Power and Powerlessness: Quiescence and Rebellion in an Appalachian Valley*, (Oxford, 1980). Even the most committed partisans of the "pragmatism" thesis admit, however, that empirical verification of the controversy concerning "false consciousness" versus "authenticity" of working-class worldviews remains "a formidable task, barely begun" (Mann, "Social Cohesion of Liberal Democracy," 425).

80   Edward Shils, *Political Development in the New States* (Gravehage, Netherlands, 1962), 14, 64–70.

Chapter 8: The second generation

1   The immigrant children who were traced in city directories were born in 1900 or earlier. With few exceptions, the second generation I interviewed in Johnstown were born between 1900 and 1912.

2   East Central European population, from manuscript schedules of 1900 census, traced in Johnstown city directories for 1920 and 1930.

3   Johnstown city directories, 1937, 1940, *Street and Avenue Guide and Di-*

rectory of Households. I sample-checked the areas with the greatest concentration of East Central Europeans: 10 streets in Moxham, 11 in Oakhurst, 11 in Brownstown, 15 in Cambria City, and 13 in Woodvale. The figures on "residential proximity" are calculated from the 1900 sample, traced in city directories.

4   On the counterbalance between citizenship (the "equalizer") and class (the "disequalizer") in American society, see Thomas H. Marshall, *Class, Citizenship and Social Development* (Westport, Conn.: 1973); also an essay on this topic by Anthony Giddens, "Class Division, Class Conflict and Citizenship Rights," in his *Profiles and Critiques in Social Theory* (Berkeley, 1982), 164–81. To use an unqualified term, (class/ethnic) *ascription* in relation to the situation of the second generation East Central Europeans in Johnstown would seem to me an exaggeration, since there did exist for them some, albeit limited, channels to use in moving further into the American world. I am therefore using a somewhat awkward term, *near-ascription*, to indicate the existence of this opening.

5   Quoted after William Issel, "Americanization, Acculturation and Social Control: School Reform Ideology in Industrial Pennsylvania, 1880–1910," *Journal of Social History* (Summer 1979), 576.

6   On the "ideological" content of American school textbooks in the late nineteenth and early twentieth centuries, see the discussion by Daniel Rodgers in *The Work Ethic in Industrial America, 1850–1920* (Chicago, 1978), particularly Chap. 5: "Splinterings: Fables for Boys." For general treatment of the social control functions of the American educational system, see Colin Greer, *The Great School Legend: A Revisionist Interpretation of American Public Education* (New York, 1972); Michael Katz, *Class, Bureaucracy and Schools: The Illusion of Educational Change in America* (New York, 1971), and Katz, ed., *Education in American History: Readings on the Social Issues* (New York, 1973); David B. Tyack, "City Schools at the Turn of the Century: Centralization and Social Control," Stanford University, School of Education, 1969 (mimeographed); Samuel Bowles, "Unequal Education and the Reproduction of the Hierarchical Division of Labor," in *The Worker in "Post-Industrial" Capitalism: Liberal and Radical Responses*, ed. Bertram Silverman and Murray Yanowitch (New York, 1974), 225–36; Samuel Bowles and Herbert Gintis, *Schooling in Capitalist America: Educational Reform and the Contradictions of Economic Life* (New York, 1976); also Martin Carnoy, *Education as Cultural Imperialism* (New York, 1974).

7   Interview #54 (UPJ), with Andrew B.; similar recollections also from interview #26, with Casimira G. (June 13, 1981); #51, with Michael T. (June 5, 1981); #65, with Michael N. (October 17, 1980); #93, with Edward Y. (December 5, 1980); #46, with William K. (January 22, 1981).

8   Garfield Junior High School, "Chronology and Family History of Pupils," permanent roll cards, 1925–38.

9   Interview #51 and #51a, with Mike and Mary T. (June 5, 1981).

10   Interview #26, with Casimira G. (June 13, 1981).
11   Interview #61, with Joseph H. (January 6, 1980).
12   I wish to thank Stephan Thernstrom for pointing out some other pos-
     sible explanations for the higher proportion of parochial school children
     going on past the sixth grade: At the beginning of the century the public
     school may have been more demanding academically than parochial
     schools; or, given the tuition, parochial school students perhaps came
     from better-off families and for that reason were more likely to continue
     their education longer. On the other hand, as reported by the Immi-
     gration Commission, the majority (75 percent) of the East Central Eu-
     ropean children enrolled in Johnstown's public schools came from well-
     established immigrant families who at the time of the investigation had
     already been in America for over ten years, and could be expected to
     let their children attend school longer. See U.S. Congress, "Johns-
     town," in *Reports of the Immigration Commission, The Children of Immi-
     grants in Schools*, 61st Cong., 3rd sess., Sen. Doc. 749 (Washington,
     D.C.: 1911), 3:386, 404–19, 450; St. Stephen's Slovak Catholic parochial
     school records, permanent roll, 1902–8.
13   Garfield Junior High School, permanent roll, 1932–8.
14   Interview #65, with Mike N. (October 17, 1980).
15   Interview #93, with Edward Y. (December 5, 1980); similar information
     from interview #43, with William K. (January 22, 1981). This openly
     differential treatment in Johnstown public schools of lower-class "for-
     eign" children stands in sharp contrast to the "egalitarian model of the
     American school system" postulated by Ralph Turner in opposition to
     the British one, in "Modes of Social Ascent through Education: Spon-
     sored and Contest Mobility and the School System," *American Socio-
     logical Review* (December 1960), 855–67. On the "tracking" system in
     American education, see Bowles and Gintis, *Schooling in Capitalist Amer-
     ica*; James E. Rosenbaum, *Making Inequality: The Hidden Curriculum of
     High School Tracking* (New York, 1976); Greer, *Great School Legend*; Ran-
     dall Collins, *The Credential Society: An Historical Sociology of Education and
     Stratification* (New York, 1979).
16   Interview #51, with Mike T. (June 5, 1981). On the anticipatory so-
     cialization of class roles and realities, see Robert K. Merton, "Social
     Structure and Anomie," in *Social Theory and Social Structure* (New York,
     1962); Herbert H. Hyman, "The Value-Systems of Different Classes: A
     Social Psychological Contribution to the Analysis of Stratification," in
     Class, Status and Power; A Reader in Social Stratification, ed. Reinhard
     Bendix and Seymour Martin Lipset (New York, 1966), 488–99; Ephraim
     H. Mizruchi, *Success and Opportunity: A Study of Anomie* (London, 1964),
     Chap. 4; Urie Bronfenbrenner, "Socialization and Social Class through
     Time and Space," in *Readings on Social Stratification*, ed. Melvin Tumin
     (Prentice-Hall, 1970), 204–27; Melvin Tumin and Arnold Feldman, "Ref-
     erence Groups and Class Orientations," in Tumin, *Readings on Social
     Stratification*, 280–94; Dorothy L. Meier and Wendall Bell, "Anomia and

Differential Access to the Achievement of Life," in Tumin, *Readings on Social Stratification*, 340–56; Herbert J. Gans, "The Subcultures of the Working Class, Lower Class and Middle Class," in *The Logic of Social Hierarchies*, ed. Edward O. Laumann, Paul M. Siegel, and Robert W. Hodge (Chicago, 1970), 575–89; Peter M. Blau and Otis Dudley Duncan, *The American Occupational Structure* (New York, 1967), Chap. 9; Francis G. Caro and C. Terence Pihlblad, "Aspirations and Expectations," *Sociology and Social Research* (July 1965), 465–75; Michael P. Carter, *Home, School and Work: A Study of the Education and Employment of Young People in Britain* (Oxford, 1962); Jules Henry, "Attitude Organization in Elementary School Classrooms," in *Education and Culture*, ed. G. D. Spindler, (New York, 1965); Lillian B. Rubin, *Worlds of Pain: Life in the Working-class Family* (New York, 1976). For a cogent review of sociological literature on the anticipatory lowering of aspirations among members of the lower classes, see Michael Mann, "The Social Cohesion of Liberal Democracy," *American Sociological Review* (June 1970), 426–32.

17 Interview #63, with Emil S. (November 6, 1980); the same in #87, with John B. (November 7, 1980).

18 Interview with Charles H., who was general foreman of Bethlehem Steel's mechanical department in the 1920s and 1930s (November 7, 1980).

19 Interviews #42 and #66, with Walter W. (June 11, 1980, and February 25, 1981); #51, with Mike T. (June 5, 1981); #75, with Frank G. (October 2, 1980); #87, with John B. (November 7, 1980); #45 with Geo. P. (January 22, 1981); #109, with Paul P. (July 21, 1983); #40 (UPJ), with Jan S.; #13 (UPJ) with Louis P.; #28 (UPJ), with Michael Ch.

20 This appears to contradict the findings (n. 12, this chapter) that a greater proportion of immigrant children enrolled in parochial schools than those attending public ones continued their education beyond the sixth grade. If the public school data reported by the Immigration Commission are indeed correct, it could mean that the alienation of second generation East Central European children in American schools was a stronger agent in disrupting their education than were the admonitions of the priests in parochial schools.

21 Joseph Drasler, "Second-generation Slovenes: A Comparison between Parents and Children," *Ameriški Družinski Koledar* (Leto, 1940), 169–71.

22 Garfield Junior High School, assorted records, 1927–38.

23 Interviews #22 (UPJ), with Geo. L.; #28 (UPJ), with Michael Ch.; #32 (UPJ), with Edward N.; #54 (UPJ), with Andrew B.

24 Interview #50, with Mike N. (June 3, 1981).

25 Interview #97, with Pete K. (July 14, 1981); also #7, with John J. (June 17, 1981); #96, with Mike T. (July 14, 1981).

26 This was the advice Thomas Bell's Slovak hero, Kracha, gave young Mike Doberjack when he appeared to become too politically excited during Bryan's first campaign. See *Out of This Furnace* (Pittsburgh, 1976), 124.

27 Interview #29, with Mike N. (May 8, 1981).
28 Interview #50, with Mike N. (June 3, 1981).
29 Interview #73, with Peter S. (October 2, 1980).
30 Interview #87, with John B. (November 7, 1980).
31 Interview #61, with Joseph H. (November 6, 1980).
32 Interview with Louis M., who was superintendent at Bethlehem Steel during the 1920s and 1930s (October 31, 1980).
33 Interviews #61, with Joseph H. (November 6, 1980); #40, with John L. (February 26, 1981); #34 and #87, with John B. (February 24, 1981, and November 7, 1980); #42, with Walter W. (February 25, 1981); #23 and # 39, with Frank B. (June 13, 1981, and February 26, 1981); #93, with Edward Y. (December 5, 1980); #63, with Emil S. (November 6, 1980); #75, with Frank G. (October 2, 1980); #37, with Pete K. (March 11, 1981).
34 Like the immigrants, the second generation tended to evaluate the prestige of particular businesses in their communities on the basis of their size and prosperity, adjusting the "status ranking" in each individual case. Generally, however, they ranked running a small retail business lower than having steady industrial employment.
35 Interviews #73, with Peter H. (October 2, 1980); #86, with Michael N. (November 8, 1980); also #61, with Joseph H. (November 6, 1980); #81, with John M. (October 9, 1980); #23, with Frank B. (June 14, 1981); #37, with Pete K. (March 11, 1980); #50, with Mike N. (June 3, 1981); #41 (UPJ), with Rudy K.
36 Bell, *Out of This Furnace*, 337.
37 Interview #19, with Mary U. (June 18, 1981).
38 Interviews #19, with Mary U. (June 18, 1981); #15, with Julia K. (June 19, 1981); #88, with Anne H. (January 21, 1981); #94, with Anne O. (July 7, 1981); #92, with Marianna P. (November 21, 1980).
39 This is a tentative estimate, the best I could arrive at given the incomplete sources. It is based on the baptismal records of 10 East Central European parishes in Johnstown and calculated for women born between 1900 and 1910. Out of the total number of 317 second generation women whose marriages were recorded in the parochial books, only 110 were "stable," i.e., had apparently stayed in the parish through the end of World War II, so that I could trace their children through the baptismal records. Even for this reduced number, however, the count is only approximate, since some families could have left Johnstown for a period of time and had their children baptized elsewhere. The parishes whose records I checked and the numbers recorded were as follows: St. Francis Slovak Catholic (47), St. Stephen Slovak Catholic (60), St. Mary Greek Catholic (72), Polish National Catholic (17), St. John Slovak Lutheran (24), St. Emerich Hungarian Catholic (16), St. John the Baptist Russian Orthodox (14), St. John Ukrainian Byzantine Catholic (21), St. Therese Slovenian Catholic (28), St. Rochus Croatian Catholic (18). Somewhat reassuringly, the calculation of the number of

children reported in thirty of my personal interviews conducted with second generation East Central Europeans in Johnstown that specifically dealt with the problems of the family rendered the same average figure. In Pittsburgh, Corinne Krauze reported a higher average number of children (4.8) born to 25 older-cohort American-born Slavic women ("Age at Marriage, Fertility and Family Roles among Two Generations of Italian, Jewish and Slavic American Women in Twentieth-century Pittsburgh," unpublished essay, 20).

40   Interview #95, with Andy A. (July 17, 1981).
41   Interview #82, with Anna C. (October 9, 1980).
42   Interview #64, with Charles M. (October 31, 1980).
43   Interview #29, with Mike N. (May 8, 1981).
44   Interview #87, with John B. (November 7, 1980).
45   Ibid.
46   No more than 25 percent of the total number of persister "achievers" were found to have held their elevated positions only once, whereas 43 percent of the returnees were so recorded. But the proportion of more solid achievers – men holding better jobs twice – was similar in both groups (22 and 19 percent, respectively), and 24 percent of the returnees, as opposed to only 12 percent of the persisters, were three-time achievers.
47   The increased occupational "shifting" among immigrants in the 1920s and 1930s was also reported by Stephan Thernstrom in Boston ("Immigrants and WASPs: Ethnic Differences in Occupational Mobility in Boston, 1890–1940," in *Nineteenth-century Cities: Essays in New Urban History*, ed. Stephan Thernstrom and Richard Sennett (New Haven, 1969); by Josef Barton in Cleveland (*Peasants and Strangers: Italians, Rumanians and Slovaks in an American City, 1890–1950* [Cambridge, Mass.: 1975], and by Bodnar, Simon, and Weber, *Lives of Their Own*).
48   By the 1930s, the numerical size of the eight nationality groups involved in the study was much too small to warrant more than a comment. Of all groups in the study, the American-born Poles and Hungarians had the largest proportion of occupational "achievers" (over one-half of all Polish "achievers" were sons of immigrants from the "Prussian" partition). Both immigrant groups, Hungarians and "Prussian" Poles, were early settlers in Johnstown, and both had developed and maintained helpful connections with Germans in the mills. The second generation's occupational "success" – that is, a greater proportion having achieved occupational positions above the unskilled and unspecified semiskilled level, could have been due to the "halo effect" of the working connections established by the immigrants and transmitted to their sons (the numbers in each group were too small to permit me to examine the rate of retention of elevated positions).
49   For dichotomized comparisons, for instance, comparing blue- versus white-collar fathers and blue- versus white-collar sons, the model spec-

ifying the odds-ratio is as follows:

$$\frac{f_{11}/f_{12}}{f_{21}/f_{22}} = \frac{f_{11}f_{22}}{f_{12}f_{21}}$$

It indicates the probability or chance that a son of a blue-collar father would hold a white-collar position rather than work as a manual laborer, relative to the chance that a son of a father holding a white-collar job would be found in a white-collar occupation rather than a manual one. A result of 1 indicates a random distribution of positions – i.e., no correlation between the fathers' and sons' statuses; a result larger than 1 means the unequal distribution of occupational chances among sons, contingent upon fathers' position. See Robert M. Hauser, John N. Koffel, Harry P. Travis, et al., "Temporal Change in Occupational Mobility: Evidence for Men in the United States," *American Sociological Review* (June 1975), 259–79.

50 In Table A. 19 (men), samples comprising three "vertical" sets, comparing fathers and sons at time points fifteen and more years apart, five years apart, and concurrently, were not independent, and I did not test for significance. As for "horizontal" comparisons (blue-/white-collar versus unskilled/skilled), I tested assuming simple random sampling and found that in panels 2 and 3 the null hypothesis can be rejected. Some cell frequencies are very small, however; we would need sample sizes several times larger, to obtain statistical significance. The result obtained in Table A. 20 (women) was significant at a .01 level.

51 To get a second look at the businessmen-fathers' capacity to transfer their elevated occupational status to their children, I took from the Johnstown business guides an additional sample of 47 East Central European immigrant entrepreneurs successfully established in business. As a measure of their success in maintaining elevated occupational status, I took their appearance in business guides at at least three of my five-year checkpoints between 1915 and 1930. I then identified their sons and traced their careers through 1949–50 in Johnstown city directories. Of the total number of 81 sons of immigrant businessmen, 48 percent, "ended" their careers, by 1949 or 1950, as ordinary laborers. Of the remainder, 15 percent held skilled manual positions; 33 percent were in business and clerical occupations (about 50 percent of them worked for their fathers); and 4 percent were professionals. The overall proportion of sons of immigrant businessmen among white-collar workers was over twice as large as that found in 1949 among the second generation males from my 1900 sample (Johnstown business guides, 1915, 1920, 1930, 1940, 1949–50).

52 Johnstown Public School Directory, 1915–41; Johnstown Business Guides, 1914–41; Johnstown High School and Catholic High School Graduation Books, 1915–30; Department of Public Instruction, State

Board of Examiners for Registration of Nurses, Register Books, 1915–35, Pennsylvania State Archives, Harrisburg, Pa.

53 Interviews #51a, with Mary T. (June 15, 1981); #1 and #53, with Mary B. (June 6, 1981); #18 and #88, with Anne H. (June 19, 1981, and January 21, 1981). I tried unsuccessfully to find out if there might have been something in the Serbian cultural tradition that could possibly make Serbian immigrant women more supportive of their daughters' education than immigrant women from other Slavic groups. My second generation Serbian informants in Johnstown told me that their mothers often "stood up to [their fathers]" and stuck by their opinions, which generated a considerable amount of marital conflict. It was also the Serbian women who, in the 1930s, initiated and carried through in Johnstown the secession from St. Nicholas Church and who were the prime agents in establishing the new parish (see Chap. 5). Interethnic differences in the family patterns among Slavic groups require further exploration.

54 Interview #53, with Mary B. (June 5, 1981).

55 Interview #23, with Frank B. (June 14, 1981).

56 East Central European second generation male population from manuscript schedules of 1900 census, traced in Johnstown city directories for 1920, 1930, 1940 and 1949.

57 A precursor of these was a project conducted in Johnstown in the late 1930s that specified the housing needs in particular neighborhoods. See U.S. Federal Housing Administration, Division of Research and Statistics, Housing and Finance Agency, "City Data," in *Housing Market Analysis: Johnstown, Pennsylvania* (November 1941), Industrial-Social Branch, RG 207, National Archives. At that time a home buyer in one of Johnstown's immigrant sections could easily obtain a $3,000 to $4,000 mortgage at 4.5 percent annual interest, payable in monthly installments of $20 to $23.

58 East Central European second generation male population from manuscript schedules of 1900 census, traced in Johnstown city directories for 1930, 1940, and 1949; *Seventeenth Census of the United States: 1950, Housing,* vol. 1; *General Characteristics,* pt. 5, pp. 38–22. As late as 1930, there was no difference in the proportion of homeowners among the persisters and those who were not present in Johnstown at my checkpoint ten years earlier; both groups had a rate of 14 percent. By 1940, the rate of homeownership among the returnees – men who were absent in 1930 – had remained unchanged (15 percent), whereas among the persisters it rose to 22 percent, not very much of a difference but suggesting that although moving around after jobs could have helped to counteract the adversities of the Depression, it did not, predictably, speed up home purchasing.

59 Interviews #42, with Walter W. (February 25, 1981); #67, with Andy M. (September 13, 1980); also #37 and #97 with Pete K. (March 11,

1981, and July 14, 1981); #30, with Frank S. (March 26, 1981); #96, with Mike T. (July 14, 1981); #109, with Paul P. (July 7, 1983).

60 Interview #42, with Walter W. (February 25, 1981).

61 Interview #50, with Mike N. (June 3, 1981).

62 Eli Chinoy, *Automobile Workers and the American Dream* (Boston, 1955), 124, 130. A similar interpretation is found in Ephraim H. Mizruchi, *Success and Opportunity: A Study of Anomie* (New York, 1964), esp. Chap. 4, "Social Class and Success."

63 Mann, "Social Cohesion of Liberal Democracy," 425.

64 Interview #80, with Stephen Ch. (October 3, 1980).

65 Interview #34, with John B. (February 25, 1981).

Appendix

Table A.1. *Persistence of East Central European male immigrants in Johnstown, 1900–1940 (persisters and returnees), corrected for mortality*

Age in 1900	Present in 1900 (N)	Survival Rate, 1900–5	Est. Survivors to 1905 (N)	Present in 1905 (N)	Persistence Rate, to 1905 (%)	Est. Survivors to 1910[b] (N)	Present in 1910 (N)	Persistence Rate to 1910 (%)
1–14[a]	43	.983	42	6	.14	41	6	.15
15–29	1,137	.969	1,102	588	.52	1,088	412	.38
30–44	1,026	.943	967	621	.64	903	401	.44
45–59	149	.878	131	78	.60	110	27	.25
60+	8	.712	6	1	.16	4	—	—
Total	2,363		2,248	1,294	.57	2,146	846	.39

[a] The Glover life tables for foreign-born males on which I based part of my calculations start from age 1. Fortunately, my 1900 sample included only a few immigrants who were less than one year old at that time.

[b] Estimated survivors for each decade through 1940 are calculated in the same fashion as for 1900–5, using the appropriately updated life table survival rates.

Source: East Central European immigrant male population from manuscript schedules of 1900 census, traced in Johnstown city directories for 1905, 1910, 1920, 1930, and 1940; James W. Glover, *United States Life Tables, 1890, 1901, 1910, and 1901–1910* (Washington, D.C.: 1921), 96–8, 104–6; Elbertie Foundray, *United States Abridged Life Tables, 1910–1920* (Washington, D.C.: 1923), 12–13; Joseph A. Hill, *United States Life Tables, 1929 to 1931, 1920 to 1929, 1919 to 1921, 1909 to 1911, 1901 to 1910, 1900 to 1902* (Washington D.C.: 1963), 20–1, 44–5; *Sixteenth Census of the United States: 1940, Vital Statistics Rates in the United States, 1900–1940* (Washington, D.C.: 1943), 166–7, 188–9. The survival rate $_np_x$ was calculated from the formula $l_x + n/l_x$ from G. W. Barclay, *Techniques of Population Analysis* (New York, 1958).

Est. Survivors to 1920 (N)	Present in 1920 (N)	Persistence Rate to 1920 (%)	Est. Survivors to 1930 (N)	Present in 1930 (N)	Persistence Rate to 1930 (%)	Est. Survivors to 1940 (N)	Present in 1940 (N)	Persistence Rate to 1940 (%)
39	15	.38	35	20	.57	31	18	.58
990	324	.33	859	259	.30	656	141	.21
716	215	.30	503	106	.21	227	24	.11
59	6	.10	22	—	—	4	—	—
1	—	—	—	—	—	—	—	—
1,805	560	.31	1,419	385	.27	918	183	.20

Table A.2. *Persistence in Johnstown of male immigrants in eight nationality groups, 1900–1940 (uncorrected for mortality)*

Year	Poles				Hungarians	Croatians	Serbs	Slovaks	Slovenes	Ukrainians	Rusyns
	Austrian	German	Russian	Unknown							
1900 (N = 2,399)											
N	107	34	41	71	158	84	104	1,406	85	93	216
1915 (N = 753)											
N	29	13	9	16	52	34	32	444	27	25	72
% of 1900	27	38	22	23	33	40	31	32	32	27	33
1925 (N = 499)											
N	14	10	4	13	35	18	24	295	20	20	46
% of 1915	48	77	44	81	67	53	75	66	74	80	64
1930 (N = 385)											
N	11	5	4	10	26	14	22	231	15	12	35
% of 1925	79	50	100	77	74	78	92	78	75	60	76
1940 (N = 183)											
N	6	3	2	7	9	8	12	108	5	8	15
% of 1930	55	60	50	70	35	57	55	47	33	67	43

Note: The data include both persisters and returnees (percentages in rounded figures).
Source: East Central European male immigrant population from manuscript schedules of 1900 census, traced in Johnstown city directory for 1915, checked in immigrant parochial and organizational records, 1890–1915, and followed in city directories for 1925, 1930, and 1940. On verification of the ethnic backgrounds of the immigrants see also p. 311 n.31.

Table A.3. Homeownership among male immigrants in eight nationality groups, 1900–1940

Year	Poles				Hungarians	Croatians	Serbs	Slovaks	Slovenes	Ukrainians	Rusyns
	Austrian	German	Russian	Unknown							
1900											
No. of homeowners (N = 108)	0	6	2	2	8	7	4	67	3	3	6
% of all present[a]		18	5	3	5	8	4	5	4	3	3
1910											
No. of homeowners (N = 119)	0	5	1	5	7	4	1	81	3	7	5
% of all present		29	13	24	9	12	3	6	9	23	7
1920											
No. of homeowners (N = 133)	3	3	4	2	11	7	3	74	6	10	10
% of all present	16	33	50	20	28	33	15	23	27	40	20
1930											
No. of homeowners (N = 118)	5	3	2	2	8	4	2	70	5	8	9
% of all present	45	60	50	20	31	29	9	30	33	67	26
1940											
No. of homeowners (N = 50)	3	1	1	2	1	3	0	32	1	4	2
% of all present	50	33	50	29	11	38		30	20	50	13

Note: The data include both persisters and returnees (percentages in rounded figures).

[a] The proportion of homeowners among *household heads* were as follows: Poles (German) 27 percent; Poles (Russian), 13 percent; Hungarians, 16 percent; Croatians, 25 percent; Serbs, 22 percent; Slovenes, 10 percent; Slovaks, 18 percent; Ukranians, 8 percent; Rusyns, 9 percent.

Source: East Central European male immigrant population from manuscript schedules of 1900 census, traced in the 1910, 1920, 1930, and 1940 Johnstown city directories.

Table A.4. *Tax valuations of immigrant homes, 1910, 1915*

Value of Home	1910		1915	
	$(N)^a$	(%)	(N)	(%)
Less than $500	122	38.2	67	11.2
$500–999	136	42.5	150	25.0
$1,000–1,999	51	15.9	223	37.1
$2,000–4,000	11	3.4	114	19.0
Over $4,000			46	7.7
Total	320	100	600	100

Note: At the beginning of the century and until World War II, real estate taxes in Johnstown were assessed "at the discretion of city assessors" who each "had their own system and assigned [taxes] on the block basis at different ratios." The values assessed differed widely–from 50 to 80 percent of the market value of the property, with the poorer sections of town usually assigned lower rates (interview with Michael Jerome, Tax Assessor, Tax Assessment Office, Cambria County Courthouse, July 17, 1983).

[a] The numbers in the table are smaller than the actual numbers of East Central European homeowners, since the value of the house was not noted for all of them.

Source: Cambria County Commissioner's Office, Ebensburg, Pa., "Precepts of the Assessors: Annual Enumeration of All Persons, Properties and Things Subject to Taxation," 1910, 1915.

Table A.5. *Shifts in immigrant homeownership between 1905, 1910, 1915 (in %)*

Homeownership Status in 1905	1915 Owners, status in 1910				1915 Renters, status in 1910[a]			
	Absent	Owns	Rents	Total	Absent	Owns	Rents	Total
Absent	5.8 (8)	1.5 (2)	5.1 (7)	12.4 (17)	21.2 (125)	0.2 (1)	10.7 (63)	32.0 (189)
Owns	2.2 (3)	24.8 (34)	4.4 (6)	31.4 (43)	0.7 (4)	1.7 (10)	0.8 (5)	3.2 (19)
Rents	8.8 (12)	14.6 (20)	32.8 (45)	56.2 (77)	20.5 (121)	2.7 (16)	41.5 (245)	64.8 (382)
Total	16.8 (23)	40.9 (56)	42.3 (58)	100.0 (137)	42.4 (250)	4.6 (27)	53.0 (313)	100.0 (590)

Note: Numbers in parentheses represent *N*. Cell percentages are calculated from totals in the respective general categories of "owners" and "renters" in 1915; marginal row and column percentages add up to 100 percent.
[a] The category of "renters" includes those who rented and boarded, as opposed to owners.
Source: East Central European immigrant population from manuscript schedules of 1900 census, traced in Johnstown city directories for 1905, 1910, 1915.

Table A.6. *Occupational shifting of male immigrants, 1900–1915 (N)*

Achievement Category	Transfers between Ordinary Labor and Specified Semiskilled Jobs			Transfers between Ordinary Labor and Skilled Jobs			Transfers between Ordinary Labor and Business Jobs			Elevated Positions Held at All Four Checkpoints, 1900–15
	Total N	Direct	Mediated	Total N	Direct	Mediated	Total N	Direct	Mediated	
One-time achievers	41			48			58			
Persisters	22			23			30			
Returnees	19			25			28			
Two-time achievers	10			9			21			
Persisters	8	6	2 (B,[a] 1; S, 1)	9	7	2 (B, 1; SS, 1)	16	15	1 (SS)	
Returnees	2	1	1 (B)	0			5	3	2 (SS, 1; S, 1)	
Three-time achievers				3			18			
Persisters				2	2		17	15	2 (SS)	
Returnees				1	1		1	1		
Four-time achievers										*Total N*, 11: 3 at the skilled level, 8 in business occupations
Total N	51			60			97			11

Note: This table accounts for all recorded occupational shifts, direct as well as mediated, accomplished by immigrants between 1900 and 1915. "Returnees" are immigrants who were absent in 1905 and/or 1910 but were recorded as present in 1915.
a B = "mediated by business"; S = "mediated by skilled"; SS = "mediated by semiskilled."
Source: East Central European male immigrant population from manuscript schedules of 1900 census, traced in Johnstown city directories for 1905, 1910, and 1915.

Table A.7. Turnover of East Central European businesses in Johnstown, 1900–1915

No. of Businesses	1900	1905	1907	1908	1912	1914	1915
Present since preceding checkpoint[a]		6 (54.5%)	25 (55.6%)	35 (60.3%)	31 (56.4%)	42 (56.8%)	43 (51.8%)
New		39	33	20	43	41	47
Total	11[b]	45	58	55	74	83	90

a For example, in 1905, 54.5% or 6 of the 11 businesses recorded in 1900 were still present. "Checkpoint," in each case, is the preceding date on the table.
b According to the census for 1900, there were 18 Slavic and Magyar entrepreneurs in Johnstown. My figure of 11 is derived from the "Mercantile Appraiser's" lists in the Johnstown Tribune. Since these lists omitted certain areas of the city, it is possible that the additional 7 came from those areas. It is also possible, however, that within the time that elapsed between the taking of the census and the mercantile appraisal, 7 of the store owners went out of business.
Source: Mercantile appraiser's lists, Johnstown Tribune, May 24, 1900, p. 7; May 13, 1905, p. 6; June 7, 1907, pp. 12–13; May 22, 1908, p. 8; May 20, 1912, pp. 12–13; June 18, 1914, pp. 14–15; June 14, 1915, pp. 14–15.

Table A.8. *Intracity residential mobility of male immigrants (persisters) 1910–1940 (in %)*

Period	Remained at Same Address	Moved within Same Ward	Moved to Different Ward	Total N
1910–20	19.2 (68)	23.7 (84)	57.1 (203)	355
1920–30	37.2 (99)	18.4 (49)	44.4 (118)	266
1930–40	64.2 (113)	17.6 (31)	18.2 (32)	176

Note: Numbers in parentheses represent N.
Source: East Central European male immigrant population, from manuscript schedules of 1900 census, traced in Johnstown city directories for 1910, 1920, 1930, and 1940.

Table A.9. *Residential movements of male immigrants (persisters) between foreign colonies and secondary settlements, 1910–1940 (in %)*

Period	Remained within Primary Foreign Colonies	Remained within Secondary Colonies	Moved from Primary to Secondary Colonies	Moved from Secondary to Primary Colonies	Moved to and within Mixed Neighbor-hoods	Total N
1910–20	50.0 (177)	17.8 (63)	24.3 (86)	5.6 (20)	2.3 (8)	354
1920–30	39.8 (106)	39.8 (106)	14.0 (37)	3.0 (8)	3.4 (9)	266
1930–40	40.6 (71)	48.6 (85)	4.0 (7)	1.7 (3)	5.1 (9)	175

Note: Numbers in parentheses represent N.
Source: East Central European male immigrant population from manuscript schedules of 1900 census, traced in Johnstown city directories for 1910, 1920, 1930, and 1940.

Table A.10 *Average prices of homes purchased by East Central Europeans in foreign colonies and secondary immigrant settlements, 1920s*

Average Prices of Homes	1919–22	1924–6	1928–30
Foreign colonies	$2,700	$2,770	$2,840
Secondary immigrant settlements	3,000	3,650	3,850

Source: A sample of 145 Slavic- and Magyar-sounding names (both immigrant and second generation) of home sellers and purchasers was taken from the Grantee and Grantor Index Books and subsequently traced in the Deed Books, Recorder's Office, Cambria County Courthouse, Ebensburg, Pa., and in the transcripts of "Real Estate Transfers" published by the *Johnstown Tribune* between January 8, 1919, and July 3, 1930.

Table A.11. *Tax valuations of homes owned by East Central European ordinary laborers, 1920, 1925, 1930–1931 (in %)*

Tax Value of Home	Less than $1,000	$1,000– 1,999	$2,000– 2,999	$3,000– 3,999	$4,000 and over
1920 (N = 391)	23.3 (91)	53.2 (208)	19.7 (77)	3.1 (12)	0.7 (3)
1925 (N = 535)	12.0 (64)	49.5 (265)	26.0 (139)	9.5 (51)	3.0 (16)
1930–1 (N = 559)	11.1 (62)	47.4 (265)	28.8 (161)	8.2 (46)	4.5 (25)

Note: Figures in parentheses in the table represent N. See also the note in Table A.4 concerning real estate tax assessment in Johnstown and the comment in note to Table 6.4 concerning 1930 tax records.
Source: Slavic- and Magyar-sounding names (both immigrant and second generation) from Cambria County Commissioner's Office, Ebensburg, Pa., "Precepts of the Assessors: Annual Enumeration of All Persons, Properties and Things Subject to Taxation," 1920, 1925, 1930, traced in "County Assessment for the Year of 1931," *Johnstown Tribune*, January 27–December 1, 1932.

Table A.12. *Tax valuations of homes owned by East Central European ordinary laborers in foreign colonies and secondary immigrant settlements, 1920, 1925, 1930–1931 (in %)*

Locality	Average Tax Valuations	Valuations of East Central European Homes				
		Less than $1,000	$1,000– 1,999	$2,000– 2,999	$3,000– 3,999	$4,000 and over
Foreign colonies						
1920 (N = 232)	$1,620	30.1 (70)	53.4 (124)	13.5 (31)	1.7 (4)	1.3 (3)
1925 (N = 267)	1,640	16.5 (44)	56.1 (150)	18.4 (49)	5.6 (15)	3.4 (9)
1930–1 (N = 444)	1,690	13.5 (60)	50.7 (225)	26.6 (118)	7.7 (34)	1.5 (7)
Secondary settlements						
1920 (N = 159)	$2,000	13.2 (21)	52.8 (84)	28.9 (46)	5.1 (8)	(0)
1925 (N = 266)	2,420	7.1 (19)	43.2 (115)	33.5 (89)	13.6 (36)	2.6 (7)
1930–1 (N = 107)	2,800	1.9 (2)	37.4 (40)	42.0 (45)	11.2 (12)	7.5 (8)

Note: Figures in parentheses represent N. On real estate tax assessment in Johnstown, see general note in Table A.4 and note to Table 6.4 concerning 1930 tax records.
Source: Cambria County Commissioner's office, Ebensburg, Pa., "Precepts of the Assessors: Annual Enumeration of All Persons, Properties and Things Subject to Taxation," 1920, 1925, 1930, traced in "County Assessment for the Year of 1931," *Johnstown Tribune*, January 27–December 1, 1932.

Table A.13. *Occupatinal shifting of male immigrants, 1915–1930 (N)*

Achievement Category	Transfers between Ordinary Labor and Specified Semiskilled Jobs			Transfers between Ordinary Labor and Skilled Jobs			Transfers between Ordinary Labor and Business Jobs			Elevated Positions Held at All Four Checkpoints, 1915–30
	Total N	Direct	Mediated	Total N	Direct	Mediated	Total N	Direct	Mediated	
One-time achievers	19			14			20			
Persisters	10			7			14			
Returnees	9			7			6			
Two-time achievers	7			8			22			
Persisters	5	2	3 (S, 1; B, 2)[a]	7	5	2 (SS, 1; B, 1)	15	12	3 (SS, 2; S 1)	
Returnees	2	1	1 (B)	1	1		7	6	1 (S 1)	
Three-time achievers	9			7			12			
Persisters	9	3	6 (B, 4; S, 1, S & B 1)	6	4	2 (B, 1; SS, 1)	12	6	6 (SS, 4; SS & S, 1; S & B, 1)	
Returnees	0			1			0			
Four-time achievers										Total N, 19: 3 at skilled level, 16 in business occupations
Total N	25			29			54			19

Note: Total N of immigrants traced = 304. This table accounts for all recorded occupational shifts, direct as well as mediated, accomplished by immigrants between 1915 and 1930. "Returnees" are immigrants who were absent in 1920 and/or 1925 but were recorded as present in 1930.

a S = "mediated through skilled"; B = "mediated through business"; SS = "mediated through specified semiskilled."

Source: East Central European male immigrant population from manuscript schedules of 1900 census, traced in Johnstown city directories for 1915, 1920, 1925, and 1930.

Table A.14. Shifts in immigrant homeownership between 1915, 1920, and 1925 (in %)

Homeownership Status in 1915	1925 Owners, Status in 1920				1925 Renters, Status in 1920			
	Absent	Own	Rent	Total	Absent	Own	Rent	Total
Own	2.7 (3)	45.5 (51)	1.8 (2)	50.0 (56)	3.2 (8)	1.6 (4)	3.2 (8)	8.0 (20)
Rent	7.1 (8)	20.6 (23)	22.3 (25)	50.0 (56)	22.7 (56)	2.0 (5)	67.3 (166)	92.0 (227)
Total	9.8 (11)	66.1 (74)	24.1 (27)	100.0 (112)	25.9 (64)	3.6 (9)	70.5 (174)	100.0 (247)

Note: The category of "renters" also includes boarders. "Unknown," in all categories, are excluded from the calculations. Cell percentages are calculated from totals in the respective general categories of "owners" and "renters" in 1925; marginal row and column percentages add up to 100 percent. Figures in parentheses represent N.

Source: East Central European immigrant population from manuscript schedules of 1900 census, traced in Johnstown city directories for 1915, 1920, and 1925.

Table A.15. *Shifts in immigrant homeownership between 1920, 1925, and 1930 (in %)*

Homeownership Status in 1920	1930 Owners, Status in 1925			1930 Renters, Status in 1925		
	Own	Rent	Total	Own	Rent	Total
Absent	7.5 (8)	8.4 (9)	15.9 (17)	1.0 (2)	28.8 (57)	29.8 (59
Own	49.5 (53)	1.9 (2)	51.4 (55)	3.0 (6)	2.0 (4)	5.0 (10
Rent	23.4 (25)	9.3 (10)	32.7 (35)	3.0 (6)	62.2 (123)	65.2 (129
Total	80.4 (86)	19.6 (21)	100.0 (107)	7.0 (14)	93.0 (184)	100.0 (198

Note: The category of "renters" also includes boarders. "Unknown," in all cate gories, are excluded from the calculations. Cell percentages are calculated from totals in the respective general categories of "owners" and "renters" in 1930 marginal row and column percentages add up to 100 percent. Figures in paren theses represent *N*.

Source: East Central European immigrant population from manuscript schedule of 1900 census, traced in Johnstown city directories for 1920, 1925, and 1930.

Table A.16. *Occupational shifting of second generation men, 1915–1920 to 1949 (N)*

Achievement Category	Direct Transfers				Mediated Transfers between Occupational Levels
	Between Ordinary Labor and Specified Semiskilled Jobs	Between Ordinary Labor and Skilled Jobs	Between Ordinary Labor and Clerical Jobs	Between Ordinary Labor and Business Jobs	
One-time achievers	18	21	7	3	0
Persisters	10	8	2	0	
Returnees	8	13	5	3	
Two-time achievers	5	7	2	1	15
Persisters	3	4	2	1	7
Returnees	2	3	0	0	8
Three-time achievers	2	4	0	0	19
Persisters	1	2			6
Returnees	1	2			13
Four + -time achievers[a]	1	3	1	3	20
Persisters	0	1	1	3	14
Returnees	1	2	0	0	6
Solid achievers[b]	0	2	0	4	7
Total N	26	37	10	11	61

Note: N = 145 in this table and consists of two groups: men who had been present in Johnstown at least two times between 1915 and 1949, and those present at least two times between 1920 and 1949.

[a] "Four+/Time Achievers" cover those who held elevated occupational positions at 4 checkpoints for the group traced between 1920 and 1949, and at 5 checkpoints for the group traced between 1915 and 1949.

[b] "Solid achievers" includes those occupying elevated positions at 5 checkpoints for the group traced between 1920 and 1949, and at 6 checkpoints for the group traced between 1915 and 1949.

Source: East Central European American-born male population from manuscript schedules of 1900 census, traced in Johnstown city directories for 1915, 1920, 1925, 1930, 1940, and 1949.

Table A.17. *Occupational distribution of immigrant and second generation East Central European men (persisters and returnees) in Johnstown, 1915– 1949 (in %)*

Occupational Category	1915 I	1915 SG	1920 I	1920 SG	1925 I	1925 SG	1930 I	1930 SG	1940 I	1940 SG	1949 I	1949 SG
Ordinary labor												
%	83.0	67.1	84.3	69.4	75.5	61.7	75.9	73.0	81.5	74.3	—	60.2
N	(624)	(259)	(468)	(281)	(369)	(214)	(189)	(224)	(75)	(229)		(157
Specified semiskilled												
%	3.1	7.8	1.6	7.2	4.3	12.7	5.2	5.2	—	5.2	—	10.7
N	(23)	(30)	(9)	(29)	(21)	(44)	(13)	(16)		(16)		(28
Skilled												
%	4.4	9.3	5.2	10.6	7.8	9.8	5.2	7.5	4.3	7.5	—	13.4
N	(33)	(36)	(29)	(43)	(38)	(34)	(13)	(23)	(4)	(23)		(35
Business and clerical												
%	9.5	15.8	8.9	12.8	12.4	15.8	13.7	14.3	14.2	13.0	—	15.7
N	(71)	(61)	(49)	(52)	(61)	(55)	(34)	(44)	(13)	(40)		(41

Note: Total N for immigrants was 751 (1915); 555 (1920); 489 (1925); 249 (1930) and 92 (1940); by 1949, only a handful of immigrants was left from the 1900 census who were still gainfully employed. Total N for second generation was 386 (1915) 405 (1920); 347 (1925); 307 (1930); 308 (1940); 261 (1949). In headings, *I* = immigrants, *SG* = second generation.
Source: East Central European male population from manuscript schedules of 1900 census, traced in Johnstown city directories for 1915, 1920, 1925, 1930, 1940.

413

Table A.18. *Occupational distribution of the second generation East Central European women in Johnstown, 1915–1949 (in %)*

Occupational Category	1915 (N = 53)	1920 (N = 62)	1925 (N = 36)	1930 (N = 16)	1940 (N = 7)	1949 (N = 4)
Domestic service	32.0 (17)	4.8 (3)	8.3 (3)	18.7 (3)	28.6 (2)	0
Factory work	17.0 (9)	27.4 (17)	16.7 (6)	0	0	0
Clerical and sales	51.0 (27)	59.7 (37)	63.9 (23)	56.3 (9)	42.8 (3)	50.0 (2)
Professions (teaching, nursing)	0	8.1 (5)	11.1 (4)	25.0 (4)	28.6 (2)	50.0 (2)

Note: For each year, the figures refer to the total number recorded for occupations in particular categories (occupations of women recorded as gainfully employed more than once are counter separately for each year). The figures at the final three checkpoints (1930, 1940, and 1949) are based on minuscule numbers and reflect the personal commitment of a handful of women who kept on working at their occupations through the whole period under study. Figures in parentheses represent *N*.
Source: Native-born East Central European female population from manuscript schedules of 1900 census, traced in the 1915, 1920, 1925, 1930, 1940, 1949 Johnstown city directories.

Table A.19. Intergenerational occupational mobility: comparison of fathers and sons, 1915–1949 (odds-ratios)

Blue- vs. White-Collar Occupations — Son's Occupation

Father's Occupation	Blue-collar (%)	(N)	White-collar (%)	(N)	Odds-ratio
At time points 15 or more years apart[b]					
Blue-collar	90	(127)	10	(14)	3.3
White-collar	73	(22)	27	(8)	
At time points 5 years apart[d]					
Blue-collar	89	(164)	11	(20)	4.6
White-collar	64	(16)	36	(9)	
At concurrent time points[e]					
Blue-collar	90	(148)	10	(17)	7.4
White-collar	54	(13)	46	(11)	

Within Blue-Collar: Unskilled and Unspecified Semiskilled vs. Specified Semiskilled and Skilled Occupations — Son's Occupation

Father's Occupation	U and USS[a] (%)	(N)	SS and S (%)	(N)	Odds-ratio
At time points 15 or more years apart[b]					
U and USS	84	(99)	16	(19)	1.6[c]
SS and S	77	(10)	23	(3)	
At time points 5 years apart					
U and USS	81	(121)	19	(28)	1.2
SS and S	79	(11)	21	(3)	
At concurrent time points					
U and USS	83	(111)	17	(22)	3.4
SS and S	60	(9)	40	(6)	

[a] U = unskilled; USS = unspecified semiskilled; SS = specified semiskilled; S = skilled.
[b] Pairs were 1915 (father) and 1930 (son); similarly, 1925 and 1940; 1925 and 1949.
[c] Moving 1 case between the bottom cells depressed the odds-ratio to 1.
[d] Pairs were 1915 (father) and 1920 (son); similarly, 1920 and 1925; 1925 and 1930.
[e] Pairs were concurrent, for 1915, 1920, 1925, and 1930. The odds-ratios for 1940 could not be calculated because of empty cells.

Source: East Central European male population from manuscript schedules of 1900 census, traced in Johnstown city directories for 1915, 1920, 1925, 1930, and 1949.

Table A.20. *Intergenerational occupational mobility: comparison of fathers and daughters, 1915–1949 (odds-ratio)*

Father's Occupation	Daughter's Occupation				Odds-ratio
	Blue-collar (N)	(%)	White-collar (N)	(%)	
Blue-collar	41	50	41	50	4.8
White-collar	5	17	24	83	

Note: Concurrent checkpoints (years when both daughter and father were listed in Johnstown city directories as gainfully employed) were used. Total N for daughters does not add up to the total number of second generation women recorded as gainfully employed between 1915 and 1949: Some had to be excluded, since their fathers' were not listed in those years.
Source: East Central European population from 1900 census, traced in Johnstown city directories for 1915, 1920, 1925, 1930, 1940, and 1949.

Table A.21. *Shifts in homeownership of the second generation males in Johnstown, 1930, 1940, and 1949 (in %)*

Homeownership Status in 1930	1949 Owners, Status in 1940			1949 Renters, Status in 1940		
	Own	Rent	Total	Own	Rent	Total
Own	20.0 (14)	2.9 (2)	22.9 (16)	4.6 (4)	3.5 (3)	8.1 (7)
Rent	20.0 (14)	57.1 (40)	77.1 (54)	7.0 (6)	84.9 (73)	91.9 (79)
Total	40.0 (28)	60.0 (42)	100.0 (70)	11.6 (10)	88.4 (76)	100.0 (86)

Note: Cell percentages are calculated from totals in the respective general categories of "owners" and "renters" in 1949; marginal row and column percentages add up to 100. Figures in parentheses represent *N*.
Source: Native-born East Central European male population from manuscript schedules of 1900 census, traced in Johnstown city directories for 1930, 1940, and 1949.

Index

Note: Most of the topics listed in the index are grouped alphabetically (and repeated when applicable) under general headings that correspond to the subject matters dealt with in the book (e.g., rural societies, in East Central Europe; peasants, in East Central Europe; immigrants, in Johnstown; second generation, in Johnstown). To facilitate intergroup comparisons, separate headings are also included for particular countries in Europe (e.g., Hungary, Poland, Slovenia) and for particular ethnic groups in Johnstown (e.g., Magyars, Poles, Slovenes).

417

DA